PROLEGOMENA TO ETHICS

PROLEGOMENA

TO

ETHICS

WITH *A Digest of Ethics*

TIMOTHY J. BROSNAHAN, S.J.
Formerly Professor of Ethics
Woodstock College

EDITED BY
FRANCIS P. LeBUFFE, S.J., PH.D.
Formerly Professor of Jurisprudence
Fordham University School of Law

FORDHAM UNIVERSITY PRESS

NEW YORK   1941

IMPRIMI POTEST
JAMES J. SWEENEY, S.J.
Praep. Prov. Marylandiae-Neo-Ebor.

NIHIL OBSTAT
ARTHUR J. SCANLAN, S.T.D.
Censor Librorum

IMPRIMATUR
✠ FRANCIS J. SPELLMAN, D.D.
Archbishop of New York

February 21, 1941

CONTENTS

v

PART III—*Appendices*

FOREWORD

THE AUTHOR of the present work, the Rev. Timothy Brosnahan, S.J., was an outstanding figure in the world of education and philosophy during the two decades that preceded his death in 1915. He was one of the pioneers of the Catholic Educational Association and the papers he read at its Annual Conventions were marked by their scope, depth, and timeliness. To the world at large he was best known because of his rebuttal (1900) of the attack on Jesuit Education by Dr. Charles W. Eliot, then President of Harvard University. His demolition of Dr. Eliot was so complete that even the secular press took note of the discomfiture of the President of Harvard.*

When Father Brosnahan died twenty-six years ago, he was at work writing an Ethics which was to have been a complete exposition of that subject. It was the mature work of a great scholar in Ethics; but death found it incomplete. It was not intended to be a textbook, but rather a source book, and that, too, for mature thinkers. What the size of the completed work would have been may be gathered from what is published now.

Father Brosnahan was a slow, careful writer, and wrote and rewrote, weighing words exactly. He did not pass on to the second chapter until he was satisfied with his exposition of the matter contained in the first chapter. It is to this trait that we owe the fact that what he left was a finished product so far as it went. What we have, therefore, is incomplete, but not unfinished.

This method of writing his Ethics in English was not difficult, as he had already published for Jesuit seminary classroom-use a rather exhaustive *Adversaria Ethica*. Moreover, he had issued, in 1913, a small book entitled *Digests of Lectures on Ethics*, which was, in reality, a concentrated summary-analysis of what he hoped to enlarge into his definitive larger work. These *Digests* proved of distinct help to teachers of Ethics, and hence are reprinted in this volume, since they have been long out of print.

---

*This rebuttal was frequently republished and may be procured from the America Press, New York.

Thus with his *Adversaria Ethica* and his *Digests* before him, he had a well-formed plan of the work, and was able to finish off each chapter. Not that he wrote a chapter once only and considered it finished. His manuscript shows a wording and re-wording, a weighing of noun and adjective and verb which is evidence of his high scholarship and painstaking authorship.

To the volume have been added the Essay on "The Kantian Ought," and a few ethical notanda left by Father Brosnahan. These have been included because they seemed to have something of enduring value.

Those who knew Father Brosnahan, recognized in him a real thinker. He had a passion for logical thinking and insisted on the "privilege of thinking" as the distinctive human trait. One of his oft-repeated challenges was: "Don't dignify that process you went through by the good name of thought." It was the recognition of the value of "thought" that he tried hardest to instill into his pupils.

This book is presented to the public just as Father Brosnahan left it. Most of the matter is timeless; some of it however is topical, dealing with subjects of passing interest, or with now outmoded aspects of still vital subjects. However, it was judged best to issue the book as the author left it, without addition or curtailment. Certainly those who knew Father Brosnahan would prefer it so.

Because of the incompleteness of the work, it was impossible during all these years for the present editor to secure a publisher. However, in the interest of Catholic scholarship, Rev. Robert E. Holland, S.J., Director of Fordham University Press, has consented to make the necessary outlay. To him a debt of gratitude is owed. The present editor wishes to thank Mrs. Josephine Stewart Agolia, who did a fine job of typing Father Brosnahan's handwritten manuscript, and assisted with proofreading. Rev. James J. Lynch, S.J. and Rev. Aloysius M. Torre, S.J. were also generous in criticizing the typed manuscript before it went to the printer.

F. P. LeBuffe, S.J.

St. Ignatius, New York
Sexagesima Sunday, 1941

Part I

PROLEGOMENA TO ETHICS

Introductory

Ethics is universally conceded to be a department of knowledge dealing with, and viewing under a definite and special aspect, human conduct and character. If it is a science, it will necessarily presuppose some paramount and distinctive fact. It cannot be concerned with a mere aggregate of unrelated facts; nor with an aggregate of facts bearing some relation to one another, but irreducible to a common predicament; nor with a mental figment. Even if it were concerned with a delusion, the delusion is a fact.

Now since man in his higher nature is a cognitive and volitional being, this fact may be a judgment of the intellect regarding conduct, a radical impulse of the will towards good, or a synthesis of both. Insofar as it is a moral judgment, it declares what forms and modes of conduct are befitting man's nature; insofar as it is an impulse of the will, it impels him in all his activities to seek the good of his nature; and insofar as it is a synthesis of both, he is conscious of an obligation to seek the good of his nature through what is becoming to that nature. This consciousness is expressed in the word, *ought.* The fact of which the word, *ought,* is an expression, will involve certain postulates which are immediately connected with it either as logical antecedents or consequences, and which, though not belonging to the subject-matter of Ethics, must necessarily be assumed as presuppositions of it.

WHAT IS THE FACT? The paramount fact of Ethics must be a fact of our moral experience that is: *primary,* i.e., ultimate, not resolvable into an ulterior fact; *universal,* underlying or implicated in all other moral facts; *specific,* peculiar to this special science, and discernible from facts of a non-moral character. Now in our moral experience one fact stands out pre-eminently, primary, universal, and specific. Every man who has attained the use of reason is aware of a magisterial power incorporated in his being, that watches over his conduct, hales him before its tribunal, and judges him impartially and without appeal.

He finds himself warned, threatened, or condemned by an

3

authority identified with his reason, and apparently independent of and superior to him; and though he is accused and accuser, defendant and judge, he is conscious of a reverential fear of this mysterious tribunal that precludes hope of acquittal on other than equitable grounds. Its accusations cause a distress that cannot be alleviated; its approbation affords one of the most agreeable of spiritual pleasures. When it approves or excuses we experience a glow of comfort that is undiminished in the face of external condemnation; when it reproaches, the approbation or flattery of others brings no surcease of inward pain. Its decisions are not only imperative on us, they are unconstrained by others. Its dictates are those of a sovereign magistrate to whom we are subject, and whose sentence is authoritative and final.

THE FACT IS PRIMARY. This indwelling power has been variously designated. For the present we shall call it conscience. The functions of conscience are threefold: it judges, condemning, commending or exculpating the past act; it witnesses, accusing, justifying or defending the present act; it dictates, commanding, permitting or forbidding the future act. Although that function of conscience is more prominent and falls more readily under observation which is concerned with past acts, it is not the primary function. The judge who pronounces sentence on the past, and the accuser who witnesses to the present necessarily presuppose the monitor that categorically dictates regarding the moral quality of the act before it is placed. The existence therefore of an inward monitor that categorically dictates what we must do, what we must not do, or what we may do or leave undone, is the primary fact of our moral experience, the rational ground of the accuser and judge.

The pain, the pleasure, or neutral comfort consequent on the judicial activity of conscience are more noticeable than its admonitory voices. The self-approval and remorse that abide with us after the commission of wrong is more acutely conspicuous than the remembrance of the still small voice that distinctly forbade the deed; and the peace that dwells in the soul after triumph over temptation is more palpably felt than the warning prohibitions that are only a recollection. Yet the instigating and prohibitive mandate of conscience necessarily antecedes its other acts, and is the source, the reason and principle of them.

THE FACT IS UNIVERSAL. Whatever be the nature of this fact, howsoever it may be accounted for by theories, or analyzed psychologically, it is as patent and universal a fact as any that ever formed the subject-matter of a science. It is involved in all our moral experience, our moral conduct and character. Every man as soon as reason is sufficiently developed, experiences a keen sense of remorse or approbation, or at least a neutral sense of immunity from fault, which he traces finally to the fact that he has disobeyed or obeyed the dictates of his conscience.

(a) It is true that this painful or pleasant sensibility may vary in intensity for different individuals, or for different moods of the same individual; may be more readily excited in some than in others, and may be at one time more insistent than at others. But this only proves that there are grades in moral development or variations in moral alertness, as there are, for instance, in intellectual development or attention.

(b) It is also true that the keenness of conscience may be blunted by habitual disregard, that a man may come in time to have a coarse conscience, to be less sensitive regarding the moral quality of his conduct than he was formerly. But the same may be said of his intellectual powers without calling their existence into question.

(c) It may be objected that there are men who have never had, or at least have lost consciousness of an internal tribunal of conduct. History would seem to afford us examples of such men. Our reply is that we admit the possibility and the fact of men being so swayed by passion, self-love, greed, hate or ambition as ruthlessly to override all the accepted restraints of conduct. The laws of morality, whatever they be, impose no physical necessity; they are not like the laws of gravitation that execute their own decrees. Men may condemn them in outward action, may so behave before the eyes of the world as to leave the impression of being unconscious of their imperious pleadings, may so engage themselves in an uninterrupted round of strident activities as to keep themselves almost continuously distracted from the admonitions of an interior voice. But we may seriously doubt whether anyone possessing in common with us the use of reason ever wholly extinguished the promptings and pleadings of conscience. We cannot of course investigate the innermost recesses of any human heart but our own, and therefore we cannot refute experimentally the assertion that there have been men who on the commission of crime experienced no qualms of conscience. Nevertheless the fact we deal with may be individually verified and may be inferred in others from manifestations in ourselves, and is testified to by the literature and laws of all ages. We have therefore such verification of its universality as we have of any other mental quality. We know other men perceive colors, possess reason, dislike pain and reverence uprightness only from the similarity of their judgments and actions with ours. Finally we may concede that habitual violence done to conscience may result in various grades of moral hebetude or insanity. If such men are or have been, they are not subjects of Ethics; but at the same time we may observe that they would be universally regarded as abnormal and unfit for human society.

THE FACT IS SPECIFIC. The primary act of conscience has a twofold aspect: it is a judgment discriminating between right and wrong; and it is a categorical imperative commanding or permitting the right and prohibiting the wrong. In its first aspect conscience is a *moral sense,* perceiving and necessitating judgments of the intellect; in its second aspect it is a *sense* of duty, binding the will.[1] Although these two aspects are clearly distinguishable in thought,[2] they are but two phases of the same indivisible act. Cardinal Newman says:[3]

Though I lost my sense of the obligation which I lie under to abstain from dishonesty, I should not in consequence lose my sense that such actions were an outrage offered to my moral nature. Again, though I lost my sense of moral deformity, I should not therefore lose my sense that they were forbidden me.

Insofar as Cardinal Newman wishes to emphasize the possibility of distinctly considering two phases of an act that are never separable in fact, his remark can be verified by personal introspection. Without entering into any exhaustive study of the moral sense and the sense of duty, since it is the present purpose only to define clearly a fact cognizable by every one, we may say that the moral sense enuntiates a rule of right conduct and the sense of duty proclaims a law. A rule is a standard by which things are measured, or a norm to which they are to be conformed; a law presupposes a rule and superadds the idea of necessity or compulsion. The primary act of conscience, therefore, is not only a rule that measures and determines right and wrong, but also a law that orders obedience.

Now the fact with which Ethics deals is the complete fact in its twofold aspect. Taken in its full meaning it is a specific fact, differentiated from other imperious impulses of our composite nature. We are conscious of esthetic judgments which are sometimes a sense of the beautiful in nature or in art, sometimes a vivid sense of the becoming, the graceful, and the attractive in behavior. These latter judgments, especially, must be distinguished from the judgments of conscience. With regard to the sense of the beautiful in nature or art there is no difficulty, since primarily it views things in a purely objective way and not in any special relation to the percipient; the sense of duty on the other hand contemplates the actions as of the subject, and as actually or potentially imputable to him.[4]

But the sense of social behavior, propriety or honor often bears a resemblance to the sense of duty, and is not infrequently confounded with it. Moreover the sense of social behavior is often allied to the sense of duty; social sanctions do act as direct incitements to moral conduct that comes or may come within the purview of others, and so even indirectly influences personal and private morality. It is a fact that if one is betrayed into any kind of social impropriety, or has behaved himself well in trying social circumstances, even if morally justified in acting otherwise, the resulting feelings are keenly distressing or agreeable, are self-reprobating or self-approving; and that these feelings or the apprehensions of them act as imperatives of conduct.

The difference however between the sense of social behavior and the sense of duty is well-defined. First, the pains or pleasures consequent on one's violation or observance of the social proprieties are distinct from those of conscience. They result even if he who experiences them is conscious that his failure is accidental and excusable, or that his success is not attributable to any prudence or self-control on his part. They are sometimes excited even though he is cognizant of the moral rectitude of his conduct or aware of a moral lapse. Secondly, they have special relations to the approbation or disapprobation of others, to the social advantage or disadvantage thence accruing, to respectability or disrepute. They are personal affections, it is true, but derived from the opinions or feelings of others, and regard primarily a social tribunal and the external aspects of conduct. Lastly they are not categorical, but conditional; they do not compel absolutely, but relatively, in the supposition that one values as an end, and insofar as one values as such, the approbation and esteem of his fellow man. Looked at in themselves, therefore, they will impel to one course of conduct with one's social superiors, to another with one's social equals and to another with one's social inferiors.

With the sense of duty it is otherwise. First, if one has fallen into any kind of immorality his sense of guilt is conditioned only by his consciousness of responsibility. As in the case of social improprieties, he may indeed regret the accident or feel ashamed of the inadvertence or want of foresight that led him to do a harmful or personally unbecoming action, but he clearly distinguishes these feelings from the sense of guilt. Or on the contrary, even though his action may have been highly pleasurable or of distinct personal service, he may find it morally culpable and experiences thereupon a lively sense of compunction and remorse. Secondly, though the morally culpable action be tolerated or condoned in the society of which he is a member, though it bring him social standing, prominence or influence therein, the inward accuser and judge vexes and worries him. Furthermore, even if the action which is recognized to be immoral, be performed in the utmost privacy, be witnessed by no human being, be known to himself alone, he is shamefaced in his own presence, and knows that he is a culprit standing before a tribunal. Lastly he feels himself confronted by a personal judge, magisterial in his decrees, absolute in his standards and ultimate in his decisions. He recognizes that his condemnation is not conditioned by any utility or advantage sacrificed, though this may or may not accompany his sense of guilt. He realizes that he has violated a law that is final, that is independent of his free will, superior to the enactments of society or legality, binding even at the sacrifice, it may be, of personal gratification, interest or existence.

The primary fact of conscience is, therefore, distinctive, bearing upon the details of a class of actions that are specifically diverse from those actions with which other intellectual senses are concerned; and it is this fact and the moral order objectively responding to it that determines the reason and ground of the science of Ethics.

THE CHARACTER OF THE INVESTIGATION. The existence of conscience gives rise to the science of Ethics. The precise character of the investigation that is proper to Ethics is easily recognized, if we keep in mind that conscience makes this twofold declaration: (a) that there is a distinction between right and wrong conduct; (b) that we ought to do the right and avoid the wrong. It declares in other words what *is* an ideal, and what *ought to be* a reality; that there is a norm of right and wrong, which the mind perceives, but does not create; and that there is an obligation, manifested to us by an inward monitor, of adjusting our conduct to this norm.

Ethics must therefore be an *empirical* science insofar as it is concerned with concrete facts, and not, as pure mathematics for instance, with mental abstractions; and insofar as it uses experience and observation in determining whether given actions are or are not conformed to principles, and when and how principles are applicable to conduct. It must be a *rationalistic* science insofar as its principles are not derived from experience, and insofar as it assigns reasons, known either immediately, or by purely intellectual processes, for the righteous or unrighteous character of conduct. Finally, it must be a *teleological* science insofar as it presents an ideal of conduct for attainment which, as preconceived and present in apprehension, causes action in conformity with it; and furthermore as a teleological science it must be altogether *sui generis,* in that it makes the end to be obtained unconditionally obligatory.

Two questions therefore form its starting point: (a) what is the ultimate norm of the distinction between right and wrong, and (b) what is the ultimate ground of the concept of obligation implied in the word "ought."

CONSCIENCE AND ETHICS. The existence of conscience, which not only informs us what is to be done, but also magisterially dictates that it shall be done, gives rise to the science of Ethics. Abolish this fact, and we may yet have various historical, psychological, or social sciences regarding human conduct or customs, but we shall not have a science of Ethics, in which the concepts underlying the words, "ought," "moral obligation," and "duty" find any adequate recognition. Now ethical systems may of course be classified from different viewpoints. The usual classification is derived from the ultimate norm of right and wrong which they respectively determine. But it is clear that ethical systems should primarily be classified in accordance with the way they regard moral obligation.

EMPIRICISM. First, then, we have systems of Ethics so-called in which the sense of moral obligation has no proper place, either because it is avowedly excluded from consideration or because its nature is misrepresented. An investigation of the primary and specific fact of conscience may consist in the mere analysis of its connotations and applications, the classification of these under various defined and orderly heads and their final synthesis into one comprehensive fact. The mind may contemplate the presence of certain undeniable precepts of morality, their mutual relations, the beauty, harmony, and grace their observance gives to human life, their necessity for the ennobling, the well-being, or even the peace and existence of the individual and the race. It may resolve the separate precepts into ultimate elements, compare the likeness or unlikeness of these, and distribute them into different categories relating to different conditions and states of life. It may finally by progressive and ascending combinations reduce to a common term the ordered and classified mandates of morality. But this common term, whether it be called a categorical imperative, a dictate of reason, of self-love, of moral sympathy, of social benevolence, a rational instinct or an impulse of nature, cannot be the source and explanation of itself. A writer may indeed abstain from pushing his inquiry beyond this term, may profess to confine himself to constructing a rational and ordered code of morals, and so omit deeper investigation into the grounds or force of these categorical imperatives, being satisfied with recognizing them and drawing out their implications. Or he may maintain that beyond this term lies the unknowable—dim, mysterious, and impervious to human faculties. But in either case he has not developed a philosophy of Ethics, but an experimental grammar or guidebook of morals, which in the first case is, or may present, a true system though incomplete, but in the second case is not only incomplete but false, because of the arbitrary limitation of human knowledge to that which is presented by observation and introspection.

Both classes of writers may be conveniently and justly denominated Empiricists. The empirical school of moralists began to take definite shape in England and France towards the end of the seventeenth century. It owed its origin undoubtedly to Bacon (1561-1626) and to the extension of the inductive methods following on the publication of *The Advancement of Learning,* and its philosophic standing to Locke (1632-1704) who in his *Essay Concerning Human Understanding* (1690) made experience the source of all our ideas and the barrier of all our knowledge, and in his *Two Treatises on Government* (1690) applied the principles of his philosophy to the nature, growth, and rights of civil society. Thereafter, Empiricism began to inform the speculative and practical philosophy of nearly all Europe, especially that of France under the leadership of Condillac (1715-1780).

So far, however, as the philosophy of morals is concerned, the Empiricists are divided into two separate and opposing schools: one materialistic, the other spiritualistic. The materialistic school took on many shapes. In France the Ethics of Epicurus was galvanized into new life by Montesquieu, Voltaire, Diderot, and Rousseau, and has been modified and refined since in various ways by those who make pleasure or happiness the final ground of morality. In England Materialism gave birth to the Utilitarian school of moralists, who declare self-interest or the greatest utilitarian good of the greatest number the ultimate motive of moral conduct. The doctrine of the school has changed much from Bentham who frankly proclaims that the word, "ought," should be "banished from the vocabulary of morals" and "self-interest" be substituted therefor; to John Stuart Mill, who, out of deference to the healthier and less egoistic sentiment of recent times, attempted to give to Utilitarianism a more elevated and a more benevolent character. It received its most notable modification, however, from modern Positivism and at the hand of Herbert Spencer took on some semblance of a science. Spiritualistic Empiricism begins with Shaftesbury (1691-1713) who in revolt against the English Materialism of his time betook himself to psychological experience, and was really the author of the views that were developed in the Scottish schools especially by Hutcheson (1669-1747) and Reid. They invented a "common moral sense," a rational instinct, a sense of social benevolence, and attributed to it the innate faculty of eliciting moral judgments.

All these systems have this character in common that in their last analysis they reduced the phenomena of conscience to a unitary term and explain the diverse facts of moral experience either by reiterating them under another and a more generic name, or by tracing their magisterial origin to some imperious and dominating impulse of our rational nature. We are told by the Earl of Shaftesbury that we are endowed with a "moral sense" capable of perceiving the moral quality of actions and of arousing moral likings and aversions. Bentham and his followers resolve all virtue into a principle of self-love "which approves or disapproves of every action whatsoever, according to the tendency which it appears to have to augment or diminish the happiness of the party whose interest is in question."[5] Vice is "a mistake in estimating the value of pleasures and pains. It is a false moral arithmetic."[6] The inward monitor therefore that categorically commands moral actions is self-love. This is ultimate and must be obeyed. When its dictates are erroneous our actions are morally bad; when it judges rightly our actions are

morally good. Nietzsche makes the norm of morality conformity with
an instinctive impulse of the philosophic animal "towards an opti-
mum of favorable conditions in which he can best display his
strength and attain to fullness the feeling of his power."

These three explanations—an intellectual faculty, perceiving by
reflection the objective moral value of voluntary actions; an emotional faculty, tending to the diffusion of happiness; and an emotional faculty impelling to aggression—are either singly or in combination the prominent features of most systems of Ethics that have
obtained vogue during the last three centuries.

EVOLUTIONISM. To the same class belong other writers who
admit that there is some peculiar compulsion characteristic of moral
precepts, but confine themselves to seeking its genetic origin through
evolutionary processes. The rational ground of moral obligation they
do not attempt to give, and the nature of it they degrade. They
confine themselves to seeking the genetic reason of the sense of duty.
The existence of the sense of duty they admit. What gave birth to it
they endeavor to discover. This class of Ethicists is the outcome of
the almost universal dominance exerted by the evolutionary theory
over recent philosophic thought. The methods of evolution were presumed to have a valid and exclusive application to every domain
of thought and to every problem of existence. The evolutionary
process was not only an explanation of present conditions and exist-
ences, it was the only explanation. When it has registered its decision *finita est causa;* there was no other aspect under which the
subject of investigation could be considered.

Two main currents of thought which sometimes converge, and
in a wide sense always partly commingle, contain the wisdom of this
school: the psychological and the historical. The first traces the
sense of moral obligation to a primordial biological impulse that is
at bottom an instinct of self-preservation, and identifies it with an
acquired habitual impulse, which was evolved from the primordial
instinct through hereditary transmission, but modified in the process
of transmission by experience and associations of phantasms and of
ideas, and fixed as a permanent disposition by cerebral structure.
In fact, therefore, it does not differ in kind from other imperious
impulses of our nature which are held by evolutionists to be the
result of similar antecedents.

The other school insists more on the interaction of historical
causes; the confluences of social conditions, the jostling of the races

for supremacy, the teaching of leaders who won or extorted obedience, intellectual submission, or religious reverence. Causes of this kind, acting through a long series of years, have taught men that what they look on as precepts of morality are in the long run for the best interests of the individual and produce the greatest all round well-being. They produce those stereotyped modes of conduct, which we call custom, and which are in fact only instincts of the race that have become conscious of themselves. Moral obligation is therefore an authoritative mandate of the race which seeks to preserve and elevate itself by preserving and elevating the individual. Conscience is a conscious participation, more or less idealized, of the racial instincts that have been transformed into custom.

The doctors of this school, who have modestly dubbed themselves the "leaders of advanced thought" never seemed to have realized that even though their premises were granted and the validity of their reasoning accepted, they have left us as much in the dark regarding the nature of that peculiar obedience exacted by the inward monitor as we were before. Whence springs the meaning of the word "ought"? Is it, after the deluge of words that have been poured out in tracing its antecedents, what Bentham declared it to be, "the talisman of arrogancy, indolence and ignorance," "an authoritative impostor"?[7] If in its last analysis it simply declares what *is* as the consequent of a long series of unmoral antecedents, it assuredly *ought* to be "banished from the vocabulary of morals," as the expression of a strong delusion. Either the mysterious imperative of conscience is foundationless, and evolutionary processes have engendered in our higher nature a miserable and vexatious lie, or we must seek for its source outside the domain of physical antecedent and consequent.

There are, of course, various ways in which these doctrines are presented. They all, however, agree in this, that the sense of moral obligation is nothing more than a conscious impulse to do what is for our well-being or for the well-being of the race. They may accordingly be grouped under a common name —Eudaimonism.

RATIONALISTIC DEONTOLOGISM. Secondly, we have systems of Ethics in which moral obligation is recognized as a necessity superior to that imposed by any rule of self-interest, propriety or usage; and essentially distinct from physical necessity, whether it be the physical necessity of a series of causal antecedents that inevitably produce their result, or the physical necessity of evidence to which the mind cannot refuse assent. Writers of this class realize that man, in those actions which are under his control, is the subject of some power whose mandates, known to him by reason, he ought to obey. They acknowledge that the necessity peculiar to moral obligation is imposed on the will itself, which, while physically capable of acting or of not acting, of acting in this way or in that, is constrained by some authority to whom it owes absolute obedience.

Now, dismissing errors of detail with which we are not at present concerned, the fundamental error of this school is that its expositors either assign no ultimate authority whom man ought to obey, or assign one which has not of itself the power or the right of exacting such obedience as moral obligation reveals. If we ask who it is that ultimately commands moral actions, we get various answers which all agree in idealizing some abstraction and endowing it with attributes of absolute authority and supremacy. Now, whether this supreme power be autonomous reason, or the State, as the self-conscious ethical substance, or humanity conceived as the ultimate rational being, a sort of Universal Ego, the ideals of which determine right for the individual and command attainment, no answer is given to the questions: why must I do what is right? why must I obey? We shall call this school of Ethics, Rationalistic Deontologism.

THEONOMIC DEONTOLOGISM. Thirdly, we have systems of Ethics in which moral obligation retains the significance which the introspection of consciousness tells us that it possesses. The words "ought" and "duty" are not denuded of the categorically imperative character which mankind has ever instinctively assigned them. But furthermore this school finds the ultimate source of moral obligation in a Being of whom man is the creation and image, who though distinct from, independent of, and infinitely transcending His creation, works with it always and manifests Himself through it, and in no part of it so clearly, sublimely, and holily as in the human conscience.

It declares, therefore, that the only adequate explanation of the sense of moral obligation is the existence of a Supreme Being possessing absolute right to command and all power to give His commands their proper effect; and that conscience is the impress of God in the soul and the voice of God in the heart. The school of Ethics comprised under this general description we shall designate Theonomic Deontologism.

PROVINCE OF ETHICS. Ethics not only deals with a specific fact but views it under a specific aspect. Unless this is kept in mind we may construct a practical code of morals, an experimental science of conduct, a psychology of the ethical sense, or a natural history of its growth and formation, but we have not developed a science and philosophy of Ethics; rather we have reduced a distinctive and independent science to a department of already existing sciences.

The problem of Ethics belongs neither to natural sociology or anthropology, nor to psychology. These may supply it material for its consideration, postulates for its upbuilding, rules for the exact apprehension of its facts, but in method, in scope, and outlook, and in term of attainment they are apart from it. Ethics does not profess to discover what man can and will do or what he has habitually done, what his nature by a series of antecedent causes, natural or artificial, is adjusted to do, nor merely what it would be beneficial for him or the race to do; but what he ought to do, what he is obliged to aim at doing, how he should direct his voluntary activities to attain an end that is unconditionally obligatory. Other sciences insofar as they relate to man and are confined to the region of physical causality, are propaedeutic to Ethics, but are, of their nature, outside the science of final causes. Again, sciences that establish the relations between means necessary or conducive to the attainment of ends may be subordinate to Ethics and subject to its regulative preeminence, but are not ethical unless they make the end obligatory. Many such sciences, as for instance the science of economics, or of dietetics, teach us that if we wish to attain a specific end, we must use defined and suitable means. Ethics tells us unconditionally that we ought to seek the end.

Ethics ranges midway between sciences that disclose forces blindly and of necessity impelling, and sciences that direct through prevision to an end desirable but not obligatory. It is analogous to both: to the sciences of efficient causality insofar as its laws are compelling; to sciences of final causality insofar as that compulsion is not physical causality. The problem of general or fundamental Ethics, therefore, is, accepting the existence of an internal monitor of conduct to investigate the source and validity of the authority by which it dictates: what we ought to do, even though it be disagreeable to us, dangerous, or fatal to our physical well-being; what we ought not to do, howsoever pleasurable it be, whatever measure of profit it may bring; what we may do or leave undone as we please without fear of after-compunction and self-reproach. It must therefore investigate the ultimate norm of right conduct, revealed by the moral sense, and must discover the ultimate authority with which the voice of conscience speaks. Having done this, it has laid the secure foundations on which the superstructure of special Ethics is raised, wherein the mandates of conscience as they regard man in his relation to God, to self and to his fellow man are reduced to a scientific body of truth.[8]

NOTES

1. The advice may be uncalled for, but to avoid possible misconception, the reader is advised that the word "sense," as used in these phrases, designates an intellectual faculty, which in the vividness and compelling character of its judgment, bears a resemblance to the acts of the sensitive faculties.

2. St. Ignatius, *Spiritual Exercises,* First Week, Second Exercise, Second Point: *Secundum, ponderare peccata, inspiciendo foeditatem et malitiam, quam quodvis peccatum mortale commissum habet in se, etiamsi non esset prohibitum.*

3. *Grammar of Assent,* Pt. I, Ch. V, §1.

4. When Huxley said that a sense of duty was like an ear for music, which some had, and others did not have, he was simply indulging in one of those extravagant expressions which so often disfigure his popular writings and expose his irreverence towards truth.

5. *Principles of Morals and Legislation,* Ch. I.

6. *Deontology,* ed. by Sir J. Bowring, Vol. I, p. 131.

7. *Deontology,* Vol. I, p. 31.

8. Fr. Brosnahan made a detailed and schematic classification of the systems of Ethics, a copy of which he sent to the present editor.

SYSTEMS OF ETHICS CLASSIFIED

I. In respect of the *ultimate category:*
   (a) *Eudaemonism,* if the ultimate category is "the good," "the end," e.g., Aristotle.
   (b) *Deontologism,* if the ultimate category is "the ought," e.g., Scholasticism.
II. In respect of the *ultimate good* to be sought:
   (a) The perfective good (*bonum honestum*) of man as a whole and in all his relations, entailing therefore pleasurable good, e.g., Scholasticism.
   (b) The perfective good, excluding all pleasurable aspects, e.g., Stoicism.

    (c) The pleasurable or "happiness-giving" good.

        (1) *Hedonism,* when the pleasure of the individual is sought. Epicurus, Bentham.

        (2) *Utilitarianism,* when the greatest happiness of the greatest number is sought; so called because it measures the morality of an act by its utility to increase this happiness. J. S. Mill.

        (3) *Evolutionism,* when development of personality is sought.

           (i) *Individualistic,* if "self-realization" is sought. Leibnitz.

           (ii) *Transcendental,* if the unfolding of the Absolute through the individual is sought. Hegel, T. H. Green, Bradley.

III. In respect of the *ultimate ground* of ought:

    (a) *Theonomic,* if the ultimate ground is found in God's idea or law. Plato, Scholasticism.

    (b) *Rationalism,* if the ultimate ground is found in the reason of the individual. Stoicism, Kant.

    (c) *Idealism,* if it is found in the universal reason. Hegel.

IV. In respect of the *source* of ethical first principles:

    (a) *Empiricism,* if first principles are inductively inferred from the experience of the individual or of the race, i.e., from the data of empirical psychology, history and anthropology. Positive Ethics, Pragmatism.

    (b) *Intuitional,* if first principles are immediately known from reason. Scholasticism, Kant, Cudworth.

    (c) *Moral Faculty Theory,* if immediately known by a specific faculty:

        (a) *Sensism,* if known through a special sense.

        (b) *Conscience Theory,* which makes this faculty spiritual, distinct from reason and will, and supreme over both, and calls it conscience. Reid.

        (c) *Esthetic,* if known through feeling, affection, or a taste for conduct. Shaftesbury, Hutcheson, Hume.

CHAPTER I

Ethics: A Definition

Ethics is a department of thought that investigates and determines the principles by which conduct ought to be regulated, and in accord with which character ought to be formed.

Name. The English word *Ethics* is formed from the Greek word ἠθικά. This Aristotle derives from ἔθος, to which he allies the lengthened form ἦθος.[1] The first of these terms signifies a customary way of acting, and is equivalent to the Latin word, *mos,* from which Cicero formed the adjective, *moralis,* on the analogy of the Greek ἠθικός.[2] The other term denotes a certain combination of natural dispositions fixed into habit, which become thereby a principle or faculty of repeated similarity of action. *Mos,* especially in its plural form, *mores,* has often this meaning also.

Definition. Every department of thought or organized body of knowledge presupposes as the subject of its inquiry some distinctive fact or aggregate of facts reducible to a common predicament. At the outset some definition of this body of knowledge is required, if the inquiry is to proceed methodically. The most appropriate introductory definition of Ethics is derived from the etymology and historical usage of the name by which this body of knowledge is designated.

The Fact. The fact that Ethics presupposes and which it seeks to analyze is this: by an intellectual impulse we are prompted to commend and approve certain actions of our own or of other men as having a specific and paramount worth, and to disapprove and blame others as wanting it. Now men's actions are regarded as having worth on many different grounds. They may, for instance, be judged useful economically, attractive socially, sagacious politically, or they may be judged good morally. Moreover, our reason assures us with a certainty which we cannot gainsay without logically disbelieving every deliverance of reason, that there are some

19

actions that we ought to do, and others that we ought not to do; or in other words that some have qualities that make them good and right, and others, qualities that make them evil and wrong. It is this last estimate of them, and the interpretation of it that brings them within the province of Ethics. The peculiarity of this estimate is: first, that it is *universal,* that is, applicable, and in fact applied, however erroneously at times, to all actions for which men feel they are responsible; secondly, that it is *supreme,* regulative, namely, of all other estimates; and thirdly, that it is *general,* characteristic namely of the race, and hence called by a name that signifies *customary.* The ethical fact, therefore, is that certain human actions, to which the name *conduct* has been applied, are receptive of a quality which reason dictates they *ought* to possess.

CONDUCT. Customary actions (ἔθος) are those which under similar circumstances are uniformly, consciously, and deliberately performed in the same way. They differ from instinctive or habitual actions inasmuch as they are always subsequent to prevision and accompanied by the free exercise of the will. Custom should especially be distinguished from habitual actions arising from an acquired aptitude of the will with which it may sometimes be confused; since custom imports continuous volition, or the active determination of the will to keep doing what one has done, whereas a habit of the will oftentimes produces actions which antecede volition, which, namely, though voluntary, insofar as they proceed from the will, are nevertheless not volitional but the effect of impulse. Customary actions, it is true, may be and usually are originated by adaptive instincts that subserve the well-being of the individual or the race, and by habits either of the sensuous or of the rational appetencies, but only insofar as these are under the control of the will. On the other hand, a customary mode of action may be adopted and pursued for the purpose of forming desirable habits and controlling impulsive will movements. That a course of action is said to be customary expresses nothing more than that it is continuous and uniform, and directed by the will to the realization of an apprehended purpose.

The primary element of custom, therefore, is *conduct,* which is defined as action springing from motive, and adjusted to the attainment of a desired end. Conduct when it becomes regular and constant is custom. Custom is subsequent to conduct. Its determinants are ultimately those springs of conduct which either for an individual or for the many who compose a social body are commonly and uniformly efficacious. But motives to action which uniformly, constantly, and universally affect men, necessarily respond to an inner and essential demand of his nature, and conduct resulting therefrom exhibits the activity of that nature in its specific and supreme aspect. Hence that customary conduct which arises from an innate tendency of reason to discriminate between right and wrong, and to attach the highest value to right conduct, receives by historical usage the name *Ethical* or *Moral,* in order to distinguish it from customs of an inferior kind, and to designate it as preeminently the distinctive custom of mankind.

Wundt conceives custom to be the outgrowth of evolutionary processes looking to the well-being of the individual and the race,[3] and morality a later derivative of it. He says: "The customs of primitive times is the root of morality." In exposing his views he is not as consistent as one would like a philosopher to be. He asserts, that there is no native connection between the moral and the customary; that even in Greek the connection "had no root in any ultimate tendency of the popular consciousness, but was effected by" Aristotle, to whom the close relationship of the words ἦθος and ἔθος seemed to be in itself an argument for the connection between virtue and custom; and "that in the linguistic usage of the time their significance was felt to be different." Later, however, he finds "a close connection between" and "an original unity of" custom and morality; "an unity which has left its traces in the equal dependence of Aristotle's *ethos* and Roman common law upon the idea of custom." Furthermore, he concedes that "modern philology also considers the words to have been originally identical, and this decides in favor of the etymological essay of the ancient philosopher." Lastly, we may safely assume that Aristotle was as well acquainted with the linguistic usage of his time as is Wundt.

Wundt's arguments are the usual historical assumptions of the evolutionary hypothesis as applied to sociology. His definition of custom will illustrate one of the fallacies characteristic of the school to which he belongs, the fallacy, namely, of finding in the consequent the origin of the antecedent. "Custom," he says, "in the sense in which the word is ordinarily used today, means a norm of voluntary action that is valid for a rational or tribal society." This, of course, is not true. Custom as such is a constant and uniform mode of conduct. Inferentially it implies a norm insofar as it is the outward expression in conduct of a commonly perceived and accepted rule of volitional actions, and manifests to the individual the acceptance by the community of this rule as generally binding. But to make custom itself the norm is to reverse the relation of antecedent and consequent. When a native connection, therefore, between custom and ethics is asserted, the sense is not that custom, arising from biological or psychological causes, gives rise to the ideas of right and wrong; but on the contrary that the conscious impulse to discriminate between right and wrong, which is the endowment of every one possessing the use of reason gives rise to a uniform way of thinking and acting in conformity with a commonly perceived and accepted norm.

Some modern writers[4] seem to fear that the Aristotelian and Scholastic derivation of the term *ethical* from a word signifying "customary," would "favor the conception of Ethics as a purely historical or anthropological science." This fear is groundless, if it is recognized that custom is the consequent and not the antecedent of the determining principles of conduct. Undoubtedly there may be a positive science dealing with the facts of conduct as exhibited in the history of various races and peoples; and it might be advisable to confine the designation, *Science of Morals,* to such a descriptive and explicative body of knowledge, reserving the name *Ethics* for the regulative rational science. But such a science of morals could give no ultimate account of the fundamental ethical fact. It could not assign an ultimate reason why one ought to do what one conceives to be customary. Its functions would be to observe, describe, and classify the manifestations of this fact. It could not explain the motive force behind it, except by begging its premises from another and a higher science.

CHARACTER. Not every combination of natural dispositions fixed into habit is ethical ($\check{\eta}\theta o\varsigma$). This will be made clear by defining the sense in which the terms, disposition and habit are used. In a primary sense, then, *disposition* is a native aptitude and inclination to act in a certain way, and a consequent capacity for certain forms of development. Every faculty is, of course, adapted by nature to the attainment of its proper object, otherwise it would not be a faculty. The intellect, for instance, has a fitness for and bent towards truth; but a given intellect may besides be endowed by nature with a special aptitude and inclination to acquire one class of truths more readily than another. In a secondary sense, disposition is a tendency that has been awakened by previous workings of aptitude and inclination. It is more than inclination, since it superadds to mere bent, which is passive, a relation to action. So understood it is the initial factor of habit in formation. Habit is a quality super-induced in a faculty by repeated performance of its functions, giving an impulse to, and an ease in the exercise of its proper ac-tivity. Impulse, therefore, and facility are the distinctive notes of habit.

Dispositions are congenital, habits are acquired. Dispositions are plastic, receptive of form through use, and liable to degeneracy from disuse; habits are stable, and once fixed can be thrown off only by the continued exercise of contrary acts. Dispositions are regarded by many modern psychologists as qualities of the bodily organism, af-fecting, however, and affected by, mental processes; but conceding the intrinsic union of body and soul in man, they should be at-tributed rather to the faculties of man's composite nature. Habits, strictly speaking, are qualities of a spiritual faculty, though in an appropriated sense the word is applied to those impulses to uniform activity arising from the correlation of associated sensuous images. Dispositions are co-operative factors in the acquisition and main-tenance of habits, and habits in turn react on the dispositions which they utilize, and which they endow with vigor and permanence.

Habits are of two kinds: habits that are concerned with thought and habits that are concerned with conduct. The former determine intellectual disposition in a particular direction, and give at the same time facility in the exercise of corresponding function; the latter confer impulse and ease in the active determination of the will to definite ends. Dispositions, intellectual habits, and habits of conduct are not three unrelated and disconnected qualities, but by their interaction in the same unitary nature, blend into a whole and conjointly concur to form one type of moral personality as distin-guished from another. Of these, dispositions are an original endow-ment of nature; intellectual habits, the effect partly of dispositions, partly of education; and habits of conduct are the product of will freely exercised on dispositions, emotions, thoughts and actions. The sheaf of qualities that individuate personalities coalesce in two syn-theses, namely, temperament and character which constitute the matter and form of personality.[5] The congenital and evolved dis-positions, mutually tempering one another are fused into a resultant or prevailing disposition. The mental constitution due to this fusion is called *temperament*. On temperament as a basis, character is built. What dispositions are to temperament, that habits of conduct are to character. *Character,* therefore, may be defined as an integration of habits of conduct informing temperament. The ultimate factors of it, as of custom, is conduct. Once formed, however, it becomes one of the concurrent principles of conduct, restrains or moderates the expression of temperament; and reveals personality in its highest or moral form.

Etymologically character means a significant or representative mark, cut or stamped on a hard material. Thence it came to be applied to a combination of qualities that distinguishes one individual or one group of individuals from others. The sum of properties by which individuals are known, described, and classified are evidently different for various sciences. Character, therefore, as understood in a biological, psychological, or ethical sense, connotes traits of distinct ends. The ethical traits that give to a person his moral character should not be confounded with the traits that determine his temperament. The relation of temperament and character, and the difference between them, has been involved in confusion by modern physiologists and psychologists who view every subject through an evolutionary haze.[6]

OUGHT. The difference between Ethics and other departments of knowledge is summed up in the notion which is either explicit or implied in every judgment predicating right and wrong of conduct. This notion is expressed by the word "ought." It is not the office of Ethics, therefore, to ascertain what actually is, or has been, nor the relations between them; but to determine what *ought* to be. Its inquiry does not regard conduct as a merely actual event, the modes and conditions of whose occurrence are to be studied and classified simply as facts. Its research goes higher: it asks what conduct, present or prospective, ought to be, or what past conduct ought to have been. The word "ought" consequently is either the expressed or implied copula of every ethical judgment. It is for a practical proposition regarding conduct what the substantive verb *"is"* is for a speculative proposition regarding facts.[7]

It is true that "ought" is sometimes employed in other than its ethical sense. By a loose and inexact usage it expresses a conjectured necessity, the frustration of which is not deemed impossible, as when a weatherwise farmer gazing on the sky says, "It ought to rain tomorrow." Again, it is used in a derivative sense to denote a necessity of acting conditioned on expediency, propriety, or an end which is the ideal of an avocation or profession, or of one's social condition in life. In this derivative sense we say that a politician ought to know human nature, without implying that one ought to be a politician. Furthermore it is used analogously instead of "should," to signify the ultimate reasonableness of a mode of acting. I may, for instance, say that a man of science ought not to give unwavering assent to a mere hypothesis; meaning that such assent is in opposition to the unconditioned laws of reason.

But the *Ought* of Ethics has a meaning different from any of these three. In the first place, it is *certain and objective.* It is a psychological fact that man finds within himself a faculty by which he necessarily recognizes that certain modes of action are good and others evil, and acknowledges that he ought to do the one and avoid the other. We can no more deny that practical reason declares to us a moral law than we can deny that our senses declare to us the existence of an external world. If we cannot accept as certain the clear averments of our reason, we have no grounds for believing anything whatsoever. On the other hand, these deliverances of reason declare truths that have validity independently of the perceiving mind. Their objectivity is averred equally with their certainty. The principles of conduct are not true because reason is so constituted that under given conditions it pronounces them to be true; but because they are true, reason, which has been fitted for their perception by Him who framed it, inevitably assents to them. Human reason does not make the laws of conduct any more than it makes the laws of projectiles; it simply reveals them.

In the second place, the *Ought* of Ethics is *absolute,* in the sense that its cogency is not conditioned on any further purpose one may have resolved on, or contingent on one's inclinations or desires. When I affirm that I ought to take a certain train in order to reach a certain town at a given time, or that I ought to adopt a certain code of behavior in order to succeed professionally or socially, my meaning is that if a given end is to be attained, a determined means must be used. When, however, I affirm that a reasonable man ought to worship his Creator, I assert not only the duty of worship, but also of the condition being fulfilled on which the duty is predicated. The incidence of the *Ought* is ultimate, and comprehensive of cognate and implied conditions.

In the third place, the *Ought* of Ethics is *emotive*. Its bond ultimately is on the will, not on the reason. Its cogency, though perceived by the faculty that is determined by truth, directly affects the faculty that is moved by good. It is not the cognoscitive faculty that ought or ought not to do, but the faculty that is the first efficient principle of all rational movement and action for which man is responsible.

OUGHT AND IS. Two opposite schools have attempted to explain away the *Ought* of Ethics or to identify it with *Is*. The Empiricists regard Ethics as a department of psychology or a branch of sociology, whose function is to define in the abstract what as a matter of fact man by psychological necessity seeks through his actions; or by correlating the facts of sociology to discover the moral customs and beliefs that have prevailed in the course of history. The Empiricist goes outside his province when he undertakes to say what man *ought* to do. The leaders of these schools either ignore the concept of obligation, as do the members of the historical school;[8] or contend, with Bentham, that if the use of the word "ought" "is admissible at all, it *ought* to be banished from the vocabulary of morals."[9] These theories in effect are a confession that their advocates either deny the fundamental fact of Ethics or have failed to construct a philosophy that takes cognizance of it. They deny too that there is any single ultimate end or ideal of conduct.

For opposite reasons Idealists of the Hegelian type deny a difference, philosophically speaking, between *Ought* and *Is*. If the Empiricists reduce the *Ought* to an empirical *Is;* the Hegelians insist that the *Ought* for the philosopher is an ideal *Is;* not however in the sense that it is merely an object of thought, for the Idea in Hegelian philosophy is the ultimate ground of being and thought. Hegel writes:[10]

The object of philosophy is the Idea, and the Idea is not so impotent as merely to have a right or an obligation to exist without actually existing. The object of philosophy is an actuality.

Of this "actuality," external and transitory objects, social regulations, and conditions are only the superficial outside. With this superficial outside, however important it may be relatively to certain times and special circles, Ethics, as a part of philosophy, has no concern.[11]

Now we do not deny that Ethics deals with an ideal of conduct, nor that this ideal is real in the sense that it has objective validity, nor that it rests ultimately on an absolute and infinite Actuality. *Ought,* however, is the expression not only of an ideal reality, but, since the ideal may be frustrated in actual conduct, of an obligation also to make the ideal reality an actual reality. Our moral life is a process and a struggle toward an ideal, the attainment of which depends on our free endeavor. To etherialize the philosophy of it until it loses practical reality in a metaphysics which refuses actuality to all but what it deigns to consider, is to ignore the supreme fact of life. The principles therefore which ought to regulate conduct, do affirm what *is,* namely, an ideal reality, but an ideal reality that *ought* to become actual in our volitional activity. If the possibility of defection from the ideal is denied, because of the necessary unfolding of an Absolute, or if the ideal is not ultimately grounded on an Actuality which authoritatively imposes a bond on defectible wills, then the idea of *Ought* is an unreality and a delusive figment of the human mind.

ANALYSIS OF OUGHT. Sidgwick and many modern Intuitionists maintain with some insistence that the notion underlying the word "ought", is ultimate and unanalyzable.[12] Yet *Ought* signifies an objective, absolute, and emotive necessity imposed on the will, and consequently presupposes a logical necessity imposed on the intellect. Such a necessity may be resolved into simpler notions. When I say that a man ought to show benevolence to his neighbor, three mental acts are involved: (a) a judgment which declares an objective and that is proper to actions controllable by reason; (b) a judgment that this end is an unconditioned object of will, and that consequently actions directed to its attainment are good or perfective of the nature of which will is the appetitive and conative faculty; (c) a judgment that the necessity of attaining the end and realizing the good through the free actuation of will, is preremptory, though not compelling.

The first and second of these judgments, though practical in respect of matter, are speculative in mode. They affirm an *end* as the ideal of conduct, and a *good* as the appropriate object of will. The third, which authoritatively affirms what is to be done, or what is *right,* is practical in respect of matter and in mode. These three conceptions, the *end,* the *good,* and the *right* constitute the formal principle of Ethics. In every ethical judgment there is implied the idea of something that it is reasonable to aim at doing, of something that appeals to will as being intrinsically good to do, and of something which practical reason cannot help recognizing as right to do. The end and the good differ only as an object that is perceived by the intellect to be the appropriate term of volitional activity, and as a perfection that is capable of satisfying rational appetency. The necessity that the judgments regarding them impose, may be denominated ultimate reasonableness. It is the logical necessity that the intellect is under of seeing that a given way of acting is or is not in accord with reason. The right, known by practical reason, affects the will in its capacity for choosing between alternative modes of conduct, and the necessity which it imposes is called *obligation*.[13]

We can therefore distinguish a twofold norm of morality. One incomplete, which furnishes a *rule* by which the worth of conduct is measured, and good is discerned from evil; another, complete, which conveys the idea of law prescribing right and prohibiting wrong conduct. The notion of *Ought* contains the idea of both rule and law. The ethical judgment of which it is the copula affirms either what one is morally necessitated to do, or to avoid doing, or with what quality one is morally necessitated to invest an action freely posited.

DIVISIONS OF ETHICS. We have seen: (a) that "ethical" means what is customary for the race; (b) that the customary is uniformly recurrent conduct or volitional activity; (c) that conduct uniformly recurrent, conforms to some norm; (d) that the norm to which conduct is uniformly conformed, exhibits an universally perceived and accepted rule and law; (e) that *Ought* is the expression of this norm; (f) that conduct habitually conformed to this norm, produces a type of moral personality, which is called character.

Ethics may therefore be defined as a department of thought that investigates the principles by which conduct ought to be regulated, and in accord with which character ought to be formed.

In this definition of Ethics, therefore, three notions are contained: conduct, ought, character. These notions, which are only outlined in the exposition just given, are unfolded and defined in General Ethics, which will therefore contain a treatise on Conduct, the End, the Good, the Right, and Character. Special Ethics deals with the detailed applications of the principles established in General Ethics to specific forms of conduct, whether individual or social.

NOTES

1. Ἡ δ' ἠθικὴ ἐξ ἔθους περιγίνεται, ὅθεν καὶ τοὔνομα ἔσχηκε μικρὸν παρεκκλῖνον ἀπὸ τοῦ ἔθους. *Ethica Nicom.*, Lib. II, 1103 Bekk. St. Thomas in *S. T.*, 1.2, qu. 58, a. 1, says: "Mos autem duo significat: quandoque enim significat consuetudinem . . . quandoque vero significat inclinationem quandam naturalem, vel quasi naturalem, ad aliquid faciendum. . . . Et hae quidem duae significationes in nullo distinguuntur apud Latinos quantum ad voces, in Graeco autem distinguuntur; nam *ethos* quod apud nos *morem* significat, quandoque habet primam longam, et scribitur per η . . . quandoque habet primam correptam et scribitur per ε." Cf. also, *Com. in Eth. Nic.*, Lib. II, *loc. cit.*

2. *De Fato*, init.: "Quia pertinet ad mores, quos ἤθη Graeci vocant, nos eam partem philosophiae 'de moribus' appellare solemus. Sed decet augentem linguam Latinam nominare moralem."

3. *The Facts of the Moral Life*, Chs. I, II.

4. Ladd, *Philosophy of Conduct*, p. 8.

5. I use the word *personality*, as is evident, in its psychological, not ontological, sense.

6. *Neo-Scholastique*, Mai, 1909, p. 192.

7. It is not contended, of course, that every enuntiative proposition may not be reduced to a form in which the substantive verb *"is"* is the copula, but that materially the ethical copula is peculiar.

8. Levy-Bruhl, in his book entitled *La Morale et la Science des Mœurs* is one of the ablest exponents of this school.

9. *Deontology*, Vol. I, p. 32.

10. *The Logic of Hegel*, tr. by William Wallace, Introd., sect. 6.

11. The bearing of the Hegelian metaphysics on knowledge is clearly exposed and critically examined by Leslie J. Walker, S.J., *Theories of Knowledge*, Chs. VIII-X; and its ethical value by Michael Cronin, D.D., *The Science of Ethics*, Ch. XIII.

12. Their meaning seems to be that oughtness is not determined by the external consequences of an act, nor an inference from experience, which all Intuitionists admit. But in their exclusive care to reject Empiricism or Utilitarianism they go to another extreme.

13. For Kant's analysis of *Ought*, see Appendix A.

CHAPTER II

ETHICS: A SCIENCE

Ethics is a normative science, based on the principles of reason, and distinct from all other sciences concerned with conduct.

SCIENCE. The term *science,* which etymologically signifies knowledge about a thing, is by usage applied to systematized knowledge about many things which come under a common category. Any body of truths, therefore, co-ordinated under principles from which they are deduced, and methodically formulated into a system, is a *science.* Every science deals with a generic subject-matter common to it and other sciences, which the Schoolmen called its *material object.* This it investigates in the light of principles peculiar to itself, on which it establishes its conclusions. The distinctive view of the subject-matter characteristic of a science is denominated by the Schoolmen its *formal object.*[1]

That Ethics is a science in the sense defined will fully appear from the development of this treatise. It may, however, be shown provisionally from the conclusion reached in the preceding proposition (*Chapter I*). There we saw that all man's activity insofar as it is under the control of his will, falls within the purview of Ethics. At the same time it may be the subject-matter of other sciences. There may in fact be as many sciences dealing with conduct in part or in whole as there are specific ends to which it is directed, and consequently specific aspects under which it may be viewed. Ethics, therefore, has a subject-matter common to itself and other departments of knowledge. Furthermore, it views conduct in the light afforded by the rationally known principles of right and wrong. This specific aspect of conduct is considered by Ethics alone. Lastly, it investigates the meaning, unfolds the consequences, establishes the validity of the rules and laws by which conduct is regulated and governed, and reduces these to an orderly and consistent whole in which each retains its proper relation of dependence or preeminence. Since Ethics is a body of truth of the kind described, it is, therefore, a science.

Some writers on morality describe Ethics as an Art of Conduct. But art, which is the skilled application of knowledge to work, does not determine what thing ought to be done and why, but how it should be done in order to reach a perfection that is fixed by a chosen end. Again, an artist is good when the work he produces has a given quality, whatever be his purpose in working, and consequently artistic goodness is in the thing produced—a poem, a painting, or a piece of music—rather than in the artist. On the other hand, a man is good through inner rectitude of will, and his outer action is good only because of dependence on this. Ethics is, therefore, evidently not an art. It does not tell us *how* we should set about doing, in order that our conduct be good, but what our conduct ought to be and why; nor does it directly and immediately consider the outward features of the moral act. Logically, theories which make self-interest, or common well-being the only tests of rightness, are attempts at constructing an art of conduct, or more precisely, an art of behavior, since they fix their regard exclusively on the resulting consequences of the volitional act.

The title of science is refused to Ethics by those who restrict the term to the narrow sense assigned it by the positivist and evolutionary schools of philosophy. Indeed, if only knowledge of phenomena and their relations forms the subject-matter of science, then undoubtedly Ethics is not a science. But this is an arbitrary limitation on the meaning of the word; and the controversy as to whether Ethics is a science or not becomes one of words. The real question is, whether there is a body of truths known by reason which can be studied in the light of general principles equally known by reason, and reduced to system.[2]

There are others who are at a loss how to class Ethics. Martineau says:[3]

I cannot treat Ethics as a *Science,* giving an account of what *is.* It would be nearer the truth to call it an *Art,* or System of rules directed upon an *end.* But the species of ends contemplated in the common use of the word Art differs in two respects from that which here concerns us; they are products external to the artist . . . and they are definite acts or objects. The end of the moral consciousness on the other hand is intrinsic . . . and is also indefinite in range, being nothing less than a perfection eternally in advance of the will.

The Kantian position taken in this second reason is, as we shall see, untenable. Martineau might have added that the end of an art, as commonly understood, is not absolute, while the end of the moral consciousness is.

NORMATIVE SCIENCE. Sciences have been variously classified. In respect of their attainment, however, they may be grouped under two heads: those which consider the nature of things, and explain them by principles corresponding to the grade of abstraction under which they are contemplated; and those which estimate the meaning and value of things in their bearings on action. In both cases it is the intellectual faculty alone that is engaged. But in one case the intellect, as it were, looks after its own interests, in the other it ministers to the will. These two classes of sciences are called respectively *speculative* and *practical.*[4] In the former the intellect seeks knowledge of truth and rests in its possession; in the latter it ordains knowledge it acquires to the attaining of a purpose. Thus, psychology would consider human acts speculatively, whereas political economy would consider them practically.

Practical sciences are again of two kinds: those which establish principles, rules, or laws for the co-ordination and direction of human activities to achieving an end outside of and objective to man; and those which establish norms by which human activities are regulated and directed to realization of an inner and subjective end proper to the nature of the faculty that originates them.[5] Political economy, for instance, exposes the laws that govern the production and distribution of wealth, and Logic fixes the rules which the reasoning powers should observe to attain their appropriate object. Practical sciences of this latter class are called *normative.* Now, Ethics determines the end that the will by its volitional act ought to aim at, and the good that it ought to desire, in order that volition may fulfil its appropriate purpose. It is, therefore, a normative science.

BASED ON REASON. The principles on which a science is based may be derived from one of four sources: they may be communicated by a divine revelation; they may be immediately known; they may be inductively inferred from psychological experience; or they may be generalizations from the facts of history and ethnography. All four methods have been used in constructing sciences of conduct. Only the three last, however, need be noticed, for no one contends that the Ethics with which we are engaged derives its principles from a divine revelation.

So far, therefore, as the source of ethical principles are concerned, there are two main schools, the Intuitionists and the Empiricists. The Intuitionists teach that at least the fundamental principles of Ethics are intuitively known, or are immediately perceived as self-evident. The Empiricists derive their first principles from the data supplied by psychological observation or from the facts of anthropology. By tracing the genesis and development of moral conduct and moral ideas in the individual or in the course of history, they attempt to fix standards or norms by which right may be discriminated from wrong.

EMPIRICISM. Empirical sciences of conduct have their value. They may supply Ethics with subsidiary information of importance, but obviously, so long as they confine themselves within the barriers of Empiricism they can reach no conclusion regarding the ground of obligation. As a consequence they have either logically deprived the imperatives of Ethics of their unconditional character, confounding the ought with the expedient or the befitting; or they have in fact openly disavowed it. That "every man is thinking about interests," and necessarily subordinating duty to them, as Bentham[6] assures us; or, as Spencer maintains, that "there exists a primordial connection between pleasure-giving acts and the continuance or increase of life,"[7] and that "experiences of utility have been transmitted through nervous modifications, and augmented from generation to generation";[8] or that certain ways of doing and acting came to be approved or disapproved for one reason or another in primitive groups, and that these approvals and disapprovals finally came to be organized and consolidated into custom—these are assertion of facts to be proved. Even should they be proved, we are as much in the dark as ever as to *why* we *ought* to put our conduct in accord with them. We seek for a justification of the moral imperative, and are given personal, evolutionary, or sociological speculations on its origin and history. There is no logical device by which we can induce from experience the primary principle of Ethics. The validity and authority of the principle "one ought to do right," which is involved in every secondary principle and is the ultimate major premise of all moral reasoning, is not proved by showing from what primitive emotions it arose, or what experiences of utility fixed it into a conviction. The imperatives of empirical sciences of conduct can at best be only optatives; their prescriptions are to all intents and purposes only those of moral hygienics.

INTUITIONISM. Intuitional theories of Ethics may be classified in various ways: according to the ground which they assign for the binding power perceived in moral imperatives; according to the objective range claimed for the intuitive faculty; and according to the nature assigned to that faculty itself. We are at present considering only the last classification; the others will be discussed in their proper place. All intuitional theories of Ethics, therefore, insofar as they attempt to determine the faculty that is perceptive of moral imperatives which are known immediately, and not as the result of discursive reasoning may be reduced to two classes: those that demand a special faculty distinct from intellect, and those that make intellect the only faculty perceptive of truth, whether of the speculative or practical order. It must be confessed that intuitional Ethicians in exposing their views are not always careful of coherency. Accordingly they will not in every case be contained within the confines of a logical classification. Some, for instance, are Empiricists insofar as they make the faculty which perceives the moral quality of an action an acquired habit or system of habits; and they are intuitionists insofar as they hold that this habit or system of habits, once acquired, becomes a principle of immediate perception. Our purpose then is to define types of theories, not to criticize individual theorists.

Theories assuming a *special faculty* by which right is discerned from wrong are various, but only two classes need be noticed: one asserting that it is a faculty of feeling; the other that it is a faculty superior to other faculties, which is at the same time emotional and cognitive.

AFFECTIVE INTUITIONISM. The advocates of moral feeling, whom we shall call Affective Intuitionists, differ in the detailed working out of their theories. These differences, however, regard mainly the specific and qualitative object of intuition rather than the intuition itself. They agree in teaching that good conduct is in harmony with man's natural feelings, affections or sentiments, and that consequently on seeing others do actions of a certain kind, or on being conscious of having done them ourselves, or on anticipating the doing of them by ourselves or others, there arise within us certain agreeable or disagreeable feelings. This faculty of experiencing liking or dislike for a contemplated way of acting they call the "moral sense." The earlier exponents of this theory were Shaftesbury,[9] Hutcheson,[10] and Hume.[11]

Shaftesbury's explanation of what he terms "the sense" of right and wrong is briefly this. Objects on being presented to us by the senses give rise to certain affections which induce to action or deter us from acting:

But the very actions themselves, and the affections of pity, kindness, and gratitude, and their contraries, being brought into the mind by reflection, become objects. So that by means of this reflected sense there arises another kind of affection towards these very affections themselves which have already been felt, and are now become the subject of a new liking and disliking.

Hutcheson also describes this faculty as a reflective affection:

There is in man a natural and immediate determination to approve certain affections and actions subsequent upon them, or a natural sense of immediate excellence in them not referred to any other quality perceivable by our other sense or by reasoning. When we call this determination sense or instinct, we are not supposing it of that low kind which even brutes possess.

And in the introduction to the *Inquiry* he lays down the thesis,

. . . that some actions have to men an immediate goodness; or that by a superior Sense which I call a Moral one, we perceive pleasure in the contemplation of such actions in others . . . and much more do we perceive pleasure in being conscious of having done such actions ourselves, without any view of further natural advantage from them.

Just as, therefore, objects possess qualities that attract or repel us, and thus give rise to feelings of liking or disliking for the objects themselves; so actions that may result from these feelings are themselves objects of a higher feeling or affection by which we become aware of a higher quality in them that is independent of the primary sensuous feelings. This capacity for feeling these higher qualities is called the moral sense because of its analogy with sensuous feeling.

Hume calls this moral sense "a sentiment" or "an immediate feeling and finer internal sense," the activity of which is wholly distinct from that of reason. In order to meet the argument that we undoubtedly appeal to reason in order to prove that conduct is good or evil, he distinguishes between the simpler forms of good conduct and good conduct of greater complexity. The former, he says, immediately on being perceived commands our affection and approbation; and where they fail of this effect, it is impossible by any reasoning to adapt them to our taste and sentiments. With regard to the latter it is requisite to employ reasoning in order to correct a false relish, or to feel the proper sentiment. Reason simply enables us to discern the object correctly; it is through the moral sentiments that we become conscious of its virtuous or vicious character.

This theory of moral feeling is explicitly or implicitly taught by a succession of English moralists from Shaftesbury to Spencer. As, however, the affections are various, different systems have been elaborated according as predominance was given to a single radical feeling, such as benevolence; or a group of feelings, such as enlightened self-love with sympathy; or to the egoistic or altruistic affections. Again they differ insofar as they hold that the affection or affections which are the guides and standards of moral conduct are endowments of nature implanted in all men, or products of associated ideas, of social forces or of evolution. But these differences regard the psychology rather than the ethical standing of the affections. Generically they are at one in teaching that the faculty by which we are made aware of the moral worth of an action is not a cognitive faculty but an affective appetency. Cognition of good and evil there is, of course, but it is subsequent to affective states and is determined by them. Cognition records the fact that an emotion is felt. An action is known to be morally good, because upon its being brought into consciousness a consonance between it and our affections is felt; and it is known to be morally bad, because in like manner a dissonance is felt.

CRITICISM OF THEORY. The first difficulty that confronts us in estimating the tenableness of this theory is a psychological one. What precisely is feeling? The word is used in many acceptations, and covers a wide range of mental experiences both of a sensuous and intellectual kind.[12] Assuming that the moral sense is not a sensuous power,[13] but belongs to the higher grade of mental life, the word "feeling" is used to express a corresponding form of intellectual consciousness, which because of its immediate and vivid character is analogous to the sensuous feeling of pleasure and pain.

Now feeling in this higher sense is either a merely passive experience, and the moral sense is a susceptibility thereto, or it is an active experience, one, that is to say, in which a relation is constituted between mind and object.[14] In the first sense, feeling can testify to nothing. Martineau says:[15]

A state of sentiency, be its seat or be its cause what it may be—an emotion, a relish, a disgust—is something of which I am *recipient* in virtue of a passive susceptibility; it knows nothing, it does nothing, it is simply *felt*.

Hamilton, who popularized in English the tripartite classification of mental powers, concedes that feeling as such indicates no objective reality. He says:[16]

The peculiarity of feeling, therefore, is that there is nothing but what is subjectively subjective; there is no object different from self— no objectification of any mode of self. We are indeed, able to constitute our states of pains or pleasures into objects of reflection; but in so far as they are objects of reflection they are not feelings, but only reflex cognitions of feelings.

If, therefore, the Affective Intuitionists teach—and this seems to be their position—that moral feelings passively indicate right and wrong, and that only by contemplating them can the intellect know what conduct deserves approbation, and what disapprobation, they are logically Hedonists, though of a superior type, and are logically committed to the consequences of Hedonism. They make spiritual or morally esthetic pleasure and pain the norm of morality. A purely subjective state is taken as the basis of morality, and skepticism is induced regarding objective morality. Logically they should accept all reflective affections as indications of good or evil. If they do, they have no absolute morality, but one that varies with the "moral relish" of the age or individual. Contrary to the convictions of mankind, moral truths have neither validity nor fixity independently of the feeling mind.

If this conclusion is rejected, as in fact it is by the Affective Intuitionists themselves, then the feelings which do have a moral worth must be distinguished from those which do not, by some standard extrinsic to them. But the only faculty that can supply this standard is reason. Even Hume admits, at the expense, it is true, of consistency, that reason must be called upon to determine the proper sentiment that one should feel. Reid's genesis of the Feeling Theory is worth quoting here:[17]

The approbation of good actions and disapprobation of bad are so familiar to every man come to years of understanding, that it seems strange there should be any dispute about their nature. . . . Yet for half a century it has been a serious dispute what this approbation and disapprobation is, *whether there be a real judgment included in it, which like all other judgments must be true or false; or, whether it include no more but some agreeable or uneasy feeling in the person who approves or disapproves.*

He then traces the controversy to "the modern system of Ideas and Impressions."

Des Cartes (1596-1650) and Locke (1632-1704) went no farther than to maintain that the secondary qualities of body—heat and cold, sound, color, taste, and smell—which we perceive and judge to be in the external objects, are mere feelings or sensations in our minds, there being nothing in bodies themselves to which these names can be applied; and that the office of the external senses is not to judge of external things, but only to give us ideas of sensations from which we are by reasoning to deduce the existence of a material world without us, as well as we can.

Arthur Collier (1680-1732) and Bishop Berkeley (1685-1753) discovered from the same principles that the primary as well as the secondary qualities of bodies, such as extension, figure, solidity, motion are only sensations in our minds; and, therefore, there is no material world without us at all.

The same philosophy, when it came to be applied to matters of taste, discovered that beauty and deformity are not anything in the objects, to which men from the beginning of the world ascribed them, but certain feelings in the mind of the spectator.

The next step was an easy consequence from all the preceding, that moral approbation and disapprobation are not judgments which must be true or false, but barely agreeable or uneasy feelings.

If on the other hand the moral sense is a faculty through which exists a relation between the mind feeling and the object felt, it is either intellect or will, that is to say, the faculties the terms of whose activity are respectively knowledge and appetence. Now appetence is the responsive movement of the will subsequent to cognition by the intellect of an object that is good, or perfective in some way of the being of which will is a faculty. It cannot therefore be the faculty that discriminates between right or wrong.

In general these theories take little or no account of the fact that men are conscious of moral obligation. That certain actions are in harmony with the constitution of human nature and its implanted affections, may explain how the moral emotions can give satisfaction, and how their satisfaction manifests good taste, and exhibits "what is charming and lovely in temper and action"; but it cannot explain the concept of duty. Shaftesbury, it is true, insists on the reality of duty and Martineau[18] is at some pains to defend him from the consequences of the Feeling Theory of Morals. He succeeds in showing that Shaftesbury had not worked out a coherent system and that he admitted facts of the moral life which have no place in his system.

SPECIAL FACULTY THEORY. The most notable of the Intuitionists, who require a special faculty, distinct from reason and feeling, for the perception of moral values, is Joseph Butler (1692-1752). He calls this faculty indifferently "conscience," "moral reason," "moral sense," or "divine reason," and it is described as a "principle of reflection"; but usually the name Conscience is appropriated to it both by him and by his disciples. It is, he tells us,[19] "a faculty in kind and in nature supreme over all others, and which bears its own authority for being so. Through this natural supremacy of conscience over every other faculty men are a law to themselves." It was placed within us by our Maker to be our proper governor. "This is its right and office; thus sacred is its Authority." In his *Dissertation on Virtue,* he says that conscience is neither "a sentiment of the understanding," nor "a perception of the heart," but includes both. It is at once cognitive and emotional. It not only reveals the right, but reveals it magisterially, inspiring reverence and a sense of obligation.

Before evaluating this theory we must first notice the confusion, or at least the indistinction, that obtains among writers of this school between practical reason, which dictates the general principles of conduct, and conscience—using the word in the sense of faculty—which points out the right and wrong of individual conduct. The former, with regard to certain general principles of conduct, is intuitive and certain; the latter is always discursive and sometimes erroneous. The perception by which we attach the idea of rightness to a general class of actions is intellectual and may be intuitive; while the process through which we attach the same idea to a particular case of conduct is neither intuitive nor is it always purely intellectual; it may in fact at times be largely emotional. One may admit as self-evident that it is wrong to do an act of injustice to one's fellow man, and yet decide for reasons, in the formation of which will plays a prominent part, that a given way of acting is or is not just. Nor is this a peculiarity of moral reasoning. In the investigation of historical, economic, and even physical facts, men are liable to be swayed by feeling, and to reach conclusions which could not be justified by reason alone. If, therefore, there be a moral faculty, it is important to know which of these two functions is proper to it.

Butler in the *Sermons* seems either not to have perceived the problem or to have reached no clear conclusion regarding it. At any rate he leaves the question undefined. In the *Dissertation on Virtue,* influenced by the Affective Moralists, he identifies the moral faculty with conscience and lays stress on its emotional character. Reid (1710-1790) is more explicit. We have, he says,[20] a moral faculty which immediately testifies "the first principles of all moral reasoning, from which all our knowledge of our duty must be deduced." Such a faculty, however, "would be of no use, if we had not the power of applying it to particular actions." The application is made by conscience, the judgments of which "are not like those we form in speculative matters, dry and unaffecting, but from their nature are necessarily accompanied with affections and feelings" of approbation and disapprobation. "This approbation and disapprobation, when we come to analyze it, appears to include not only a moral judgment of the action, but some affection, favorable or unfavorable towards the agent." The moral faculty, therefore, is an original power of the mind, which first dictates the first principles of morality, and then "without the labor of reasoning," approves of actions that are good, and disapproves of those that are bad.

James Martineau,[21] the most notable among recent representatives of this school, inverts this process. Conscience first judges our particular acts and then by "an extending range of intuitive perceptions," "rules emerge from cases." The immediate object on which conscience passes judgment is the "inner springs of actions."

These natural principles which impel to action are manifold in human nature. "We are sensible of a *graduated scale of excellence* among our natural principles, quite distinct from the order of their intensity, and irrespective of the range of their external effects"; and among them accordingly there exists "*hierarchical* gradations of authority."

The sensibility of the mind to the gradations of this scale is precisely what we call Conscience. It is not its office, therefore, to pass judgment on the absolute moral quality of these springs of action, for their moral worth is *relative,* determined namely by their grade in the "hierarchy." Conscience in other words, does not exercise its function, until there is a "breach of the peace" in our nature, and a difference amounting to strife has arisen between springs of action; and its office consequently is to decide which is higher, worthier than the other, and in comparison with it, has the clear *right to us.*

The transition from the immediate knowledge of the better or worse, in an individual case, to rules or general principles is asserted to be, not an induction or generalization by inference, but an intuition, which however is not the same in all men.

CRITICISM OF THEORY. In criticizing this theory, we confine ourselves to the question whether a special faculty be required for the cognition either of the general principles of morality or of the morality of an individual act. There are in effect two questions, the first of which we might dismiss, since Reid virtually admits that knowledge of the general principles of morality is an act of the understanding, and Martineau virtually maintains that it is an induction. Martineau, it is true, says, "The progressive enlargement of the ethical view . . . I regard as an extending range of intuitive perception of relative worth." But this is a merely verbal evasion of the difficulty. General principles which enunatiate the abstract relations of subject and predicate are known from concrete cases only by inductive reasoning. However, meeting the issue directly, we contend that a special faculty for knowing the general principles of morality is superfluous, and a special faculty by which we are immediately made aware of the morality of particular acts is absurd.

In the first place, then, the advocates of a special faculty admit that practical reason is cognitive, and insofar agrees in function with speculative reason; but they urge furthermore that it is emotive; it not only knows, it impels to action. They concede also that both faculties perceive truth, but the truth perceived by practical reason is *sui generis.* That "two paralleled lines will never cross one another," and that "we ought to respect the rights of others" are both perceived by the intellect to be true; but in one case the truth is merely identity between an object and its predicate, in the other it is an ideal identity to be established between the subject perceiving and an end perceived. In one case it is only the truth, in the other it is the truth of goodness and rightness.[22]

Our answer to the first argument is that practical reason, or intellect, insofar as it perceives the general principles of morality, is not emotive but directive. It is not a spring of action, but it puts before the will a truth, which may be said to be objectively a spring of action. Emotion, which may with propriety be termed a spring of action, is subsequent to the perception of the truth. It arises, therefore, from the appeal of the apprehended truth to the will, or faculty that originates action. We do not feel the appeal or experience the emotion, whatever form it may be said to take, until we have perceived the object that appeals, and the qualities in it by reason of which it appeals. The mind may and undoubtedly often does perceive the truth of moral principles, and their obligatory character, unstirred by any emotion. Martineau's description of emotion, therefore, as "thought in a glow," though in accord with his theory, is in disaccord with the facts of psychology. Emotion is no more "thought in a glow" than the pleasure arising from the sight of an attractive object is vision in a glow.

The answer to the second objection is, that the truth of goodness or duty, precisely as truth, is not *sui generis*. That honesty is a duty, that a landscape is beautiful, that the angles of a triangle are equal to two right angles, are not three distinct kinds of truths calling for the existence of three distinct kinds of faculty. Nor is it true that in a general principle of morals an ideal identity is established between the subject perceiving and an end perceived. This is the office of conscience, into the ultimate act or imperative of which an emotional element does enter.

In the second place, then, conscience is not an intuitive faculty discerning right and wrong in individual conduct. For either these intuitive discernments are held to be infallibly certain or they are liable to error. The first alternative is at variance with moral experience. Men find it difficult at times to decide conscientiously what is the right or wrong of an individual course of conduct, and at times reach a conclusion, which they hold to be certain, but which on reflection they discover to be erroneous.[23] This alternative, therefore, could be held by those only who teach that the norm of morality is variable, and changes with different ages and even with "the extending range of intuitive perception" in the individual. And this charge is logically valid against Reid, McCosh[24] and Mansell,[25] as well as against Martineau.

The other alternative takes the ground from beneath any sane theory of knowledge. If we may concede that the immediate declarations of any one intuitive faculty may be false, we invalidate the claims of all the others, and logically we are committed to skepticism.

Reid tells us:

The faculties which nature hath given us, are the very engines we can use to find out the truth. . . . We are born under a necessity of trusting them. . . . Every man in his senses . . . believes his consciousness with respect to his own thoughts and purposes . . . his understanding with regard to abstract relation of things. . . . And he has the same reason and is under the same necessity of believing the clear and unbiased dictates of his conscience.[26]

Our moral discernment of what we ought, and what we ought not to do, is not so strong and vigorous by nature as to secure us from very gross mistakes with regard to duty.[27]

Our conscience must therefore be educated, he concludes. But what this means, except that it must "by proper culture" be brought to observe and reason rightly, is hard to say. The question as to whether Conscience is a special faculty need not, after what has been said, detain us in its solution. Any one who has practised the introspection which Catholic ascetical writers call examination of conscience, knows that it is discursive, and that the spiritual phenomena and experiences brought forward to prove the contrary are easily explained by the interaction of reason and will.

BASED ON REASON. We conclude therefore that Ethics is a science based on reason. This means that its first principles—or at least one primary first principle—are immediately known neither through feeling or conation, nor by a special faculty, but by practical reason, which is nothing more than a function of intellect; that they are admitted with certainty and accepted without proof; that principles more and more specific are the progressive application of a first principle, by obvious or increasingly complex reasoning, to classes of action more and more particular; that every dictate of reason commanding or forbidding an individual action is a conclusion of reason founded ultimately on a first principle.

First, therefore, in asserting that reason is the basis of Ethics, we do not maintain that all the general principles of morals are immediately known, or equally evident. On the contrary we admit that many of them are difficult of proof, and that the value of the argument by which they are proved may be more readily apprehended by some than by others. Speculative and practical reason are not two distinct faculties, but two functions of the same intellect. In the exercise of one function it is not more gifted than in the exercise of the other. There are certain primary truths of both orders which it knows to be self-evident on the apprehension of the terms. It must infer the others by reasoning processes that are identical, that may be more or less complicated, and that call for greater or less intellectual capacity, training, and labor.

Secondly, we do not maintain that our knowledge of the primary principles, which are intuitively known, is innate or that it is *a priori* in the sense that it is independent of, and logically prior to, all experience. The subject of a practical judgment between which and the predicate good or right, identity or diversity is affirmed, is ultimately known through some experience, real or imaginary. Nor are the ideas of good and right and their opposites, evil and wrong, which are predicated of the subject, original to reason. Like all our ideas, whether of a speculative or practical character, they are known from experience or through the operations of discursive reason. Moreover, it may be granted that it is on the occasion of some experience that we put the *nexus* or *copula* between the subject and predicate of a practical principle, but what we deny is that the necessity of the nexus is known by or through experience. In claiming, therefore, that Ethics is based on reason, we mean that some primary principles of morality are, on the clear apprehension of the terms, objectively self-evident, and are intuitively known by the intellect to possess a necessary and universal validity which is not due to the constitution of the mind, but is inherent in the objective reality of the moral order.[28]

DIFFERENTIATING ELEMENTS. Ethics, lastly, is distinguished from other sciences dealing with conduct as their subject-matter on three heads. First, as a *practical* science, it is distinct from psychology which investigates the nature of conduct in itself, or the factors involved in it, as ideas, emotions, desires, or the powers of mind from which it springs. It is distinct also from history, moral statistics, and anthropology, which view conduct as an aggregate of facts to be classified, and co-ordinated in an explicative system. Secondly, it differs from sciences which though practical are not *normative,* as political economy and jurisprudence, which directly regard conduct in its outward aspects, and which, insofar as they indirectly entail any inward control, are subject to the regulative pre-eminence of Ethics. It is for the same reasons distinguished from an empirical Ethics that estimates the moral worth of an action exclusively from the consequences in which it issues, or the external effects that result from it.

Lastly it is distinguished by its *formal object,* which is rightness, from sciences which assume the name of Ethics. To the question, why ought I do this and avoid that? two answers have been given. First, because it is reasonable or befitting my nature to aim at or to seek to keep what is *good,* and to avoid or seek to get rid of what is *evil;* and secondly, because I am obliged to do what is *right,* and to avoid what is *wrong.* The second answer necessarily includes the first; the first may conceptually exclude the second. One could, therefore, construct a normative science of conduct as related to a rational ideal, namely, to the end and the good, however diversely this end or good might be conceived in different systems. But one could also construct a normative science of conduct, which including the first, would relate conduct to rightness. Both might be called a science of Ethics. But the former would take only a partial view of the problem to be explained, could predicate only reasonableness of conduct; the other would take a complete view and could predicate oughtness of conduct. It would dictate not only that a certain course of conduct should be pursued in order to be reasonable and attain the end, but also that conduct ought to be reasonable and directed to the attainment of the end. The first would not, therefore, occupy the whole field of conduct; the second would.

Consequently, if there were no science of Ethics that interpreted the oughtness of conduct and sought the ultimate grounds of it, one should have to be constructed; otherwise an aspect of conduct of the highest moment is left unexplained. Such a science would supply an adequate norm, one namely by which conduct is to be regulated and prescribed in its highest and widest relations; and would accordingly be distinct from and superior to a science of conduct which avowedly excluded from its consideration the idea of obligation, or resolved it ultimately into a psychological or logical necessity.

Sidgwick names these two sciences of Ethics respectively, Esthetic and Jural. It would, however, be better to confine the adjective "esthetic" to the designation of those systems of morality in which moral goodness is likened to or identified with beauty, and the faculty of forming moral judgments is held to be analogous to the faculty by which we appreciate the fine arts. Such a theory is expressly taught by Hume, Herbart and others, and is sometimes attributed to Shaftesbury and Hutcheson. Nor does the denomination "jural" describe with sufficient accuracy the second school of Ethicists, many of whom, though conceding authoritativeness to the dictates of reason, do not ground that authoritativeness in the right (*jus*) of a superior. Without anticipating by our designations a solution of the problem these different theories present, it will be better to call Eudaemonistic those ethical systems which make well-being (ἡ εὐδαιμονία),[29] in whatever it may be said to consist, the ultimate category of Ethics; and Deontologistic those which make oughtness (τὸ δέον) such a category. The necessity of assenting arises in both systems from truth apprehended as evident or made manifest by reasoning. The obligation of consenting in eudaemonistic systems is either a natural necessity of the volitional faculty or it is groundless; in deontologistic systems it is imposed by authority. It must however be acknowledged that in some of these, though the oughtness of conduct is emphasized and the authoritative character of the dictates of reason is maintained, it is an implication rather than an explicit attribute of morality.

Notes

1. St. Thomas, *Com. in Post Analyt.*, Lib. I, Lect. I: "Sicut ratio formalis visibilis sumitur a lumine per quod color videtur; ita ratio formalis scibilis accipitur secundum principia ex quibus aliquid scitur. Et ideo quantumcunque sint aliqua scibilia diversa per suam naturam, dummodo per eadem principia sciantur pertinent ad unam scientiam quia non erunt iam diversa in quantum sunt scibilia; sunt autem per sua principia scibilia."

2. Balfour, *Philosophic Doubt*, Appendix, presents with sufficient clearness the reason for the opinion that Ethics is not a science. See also Henry Sidgwick, *The Methods of Ethics,* Ch. I, §1; Martineau, *Types of Ethical Theories,* Vol. I, p. xv.

3. *Types of Ethical Theories,* Vol. I, Preface, p. xv.

4. *S. T.,* 1, qu. 89, a. 11. "Secundum hoc differunt intellectus speculativus et praticus; nam intellectus speculativus est qui quod apprehendit non ordinat ad opus, sed ad solam veritatis considerationem; practicus vero intellectus dicitur qui hoc quod apprehendit ordinat ad opus." Cf. *S. T.,* 1, qu. 14, a. 16 and *DeVeritate,* qu. 3, a. 3.

5. St. Thomas, *Com. in Eth. Nicom.,* Lib. I, Lect. I: "Invenitur duplex ordo in rebus. Unus quidem partium alicujus totius, seu alicu-

jus multitudinis ad invicem, sicut partes domus ad invicem ordinatur. Alius est ordo rerum in finem. Et hic ordo est principalior, quia primus. Nam . . . ordo partium exercitus ad invicem est propter ordinem totius exercitus ad ducem.Ordo autem quadrupliciter ad rationem comparatur. Est enim quidam ordo quem ratio non facit sed considerat, sicut est ordo rerum naturalium. Alius ordo quem ratio considerando facit in proprio actu. . . . Tertius est ordo quem ratio considerando facit in operationibus voluntatis. Quartus est autem ordo quem considerando ratio facit in exterioribus."

6. *Deontology,* Vol. I, p. 9.

7. *Data of Ethics,* Ch. VI, n. 33.

8. Spencer's *Letter* in *Appendix* to Bain's *Mental and Moral Science.*

9. *Characteristics: An Inquiry Concerning Virtue and Merit,* 1711.

10. *An Inquiry Concerning the Ideas of Beauty and Virtue,* 1725; *Treatise on the Nature and Conduct of the Passions,* 1728; a posthumous work entitled *A System of Moral Philosophy,* which appeared in 1755, eight years after his death.

11. *An Inquiry Concerning the Principles of Morals* and an *Appendix Concerning Moral Sentiments,* 1751.

12. The value of the tripartite division of mental functions into cognition, conation and feeling is examined by Maher, *Psychology,* Introd., Ch. III; Bk. I, Ch. XI, and Ch. XX. We hold the scholastic doctrine that all the facts of consciousness can be traced to two ultimately distinct energies or faculties of the soul, namely, cognition and appetency.

13. Solimani, *Philosophiae Moralis Institutiones,* attributes to Robinet the theory that the moral sense is a sixth sense of the same organic kind as the five external senses. Such a theory is not worth examining.

14. This must be conceded, even though one held with Martineau that feeling was "an implicit knowledge" of that relation, which becomes explicit by reflection. *Types of Ethical Theories,* Vol. II, Bk. I, Ch. I.

15. *Types of Ethical Theories,* Vol. II, Bk. II, Branch II, Ch. III.

16. *Lectures on Metaphysics,* Lect. XLII.

17. *Essays on the Active Powers,* Essay V, Ch. VII.

18. *Types of Ethical Theories,* Vol. II, Shaftesbury.

19. Sermons II and III. Butler does not hold that "men are a law to themselves" in the sense that conscience is autonomous or the ultimate and independent source of obligation, though Dugald Stewart, one of his disciples, seems to do so; but only in the sense that man from the constitution or nature conferred on him by his Maker "hath the rule of right within."

20. *The Active Powers of Man* (Sir W. Hamilton, ed.), Essay III, Chs. VI-VIII.

21. *Types of Ethical Theories*, Vol. II, Bk. I, Ch. I, §2.

22. These arguments may be found presented and answered by St. Thomas in *S. T.*, 1, qu. 79, a. 12, and in *De Veritate*, qu. 3, a. 3. See also *S. T.*, 1, qu. 14, a. 16, for an exposition of the difference between speculative and practical reason.

23. Martineau's doctrine that conscience never errs, because its decision is given on the relative worth of compelling springs of action simultaneously present in consciousness, is a sophism unworthy of him. Even were his theory of conscience admitted, the only legitimate inference would be that conscience is always subjectively certain, not that it is always infallibly certain or objectively right.

24. *Intuitions of the Mind.*

25. *Metaphysics.*

26. *The Active Powers of Man*, Essay III, Ch. VI.

27. *Op. cit.*, Ch. VIII.

28. See St. Thomas, *Com. in Post. Analyt.*, Lib. II, Lect. XX, "ex sensu." Cajetan holds that "habitus principiorum praeexigit experimentum non solum ratione cognitionis terminorum, sed etiam ratione complexionis eorundem." *Com. in Post. Analyt.*, Lib. II, Lect. XIII. The passage is explained in *Neo-Scholastique*, Fevr. 1899, p. 20.

29. Ἡ εὐδαιμονία does not signify happiness except as a necessary consequence. See *Chapter X*.

CHAPTER III

The Postulates of Ethics

The fundamental postulates of Ethics are: (a) *that God exists, who made all things according to archetypal ideas and for His external glory;* (b) *that man, His only visible rational creature, has a free will and an immortal soul;* (c) *that man is endowed with certain primitive impulses to individual and social well-being, by which his nature is adjusted to the purpose of his creation.*

Postulates. By postulates we mean a premise which a given science claims as valid without demonstrating it; not because it cannot be demonstrated, but because the demonstration of it belongs to a science other than that which uses it. A postulate differs from an hypothesis in this that a postulate has been or can be proved, whereas an hypothesis is taken for granted or assumed without proof or on proof confessedly insufficient to produce the assent of certitude.

In the Aristotelian and Scholastic sense postulates are certain, and borrowed by one science from another that is preparatory to it. St. Thomas writes:[1]

Hoc quidem commune est eis quod cum sint demonstrabilia, tamen demonstrator accepit ea non demonstrans, et praecipue quia non sunt demonstrabilia per suam scientiam, sed per aliam ut supra dictum est. Unde et inter immediata principia computantur, quia demonstrator utitur eis absque medio, eo quod media non habent in illa scientia.

C. S. Peirce who contributed the article on "Postulates" to Baldwin's *Dictionary of Philosophy and Psychology* says: "It is plain that Aristotle makes a distinction between *hypotheses* and postulates," but that the distinction is irrelevant. "Omitting the distinction," he continues, "the two have this in common—that they are propositions not necessarily true, which are assumed as the bases of deductions." It is indeed undoubtedly true that Aristotle made no intrinsic distinction between postulates and hypotheses. But then Aristotle did not use the latter term in its modern acceptation. Both

49

hypotheses and postulates are propositions which though demonstrable are assumed without demonstrations. In its modern signification, an hypothesis is a proposition taken for granted because it seems to afford an explanation of facts already known and a provisional interpretation of their connection and dependence. They are therefore tentative assumptions, are relative to the science that employs them, and may turn out to be artificial abstractions. Much confusion obtains in the modern use of the word, due largely to prevalent theories of knowledge. Kant in the *Critique of Practical Reason*[2] defines a postulate to be "a theoretical proposition, not demonstrable as such, but which is an inseparable result of an unconditioned *a priori practical law.*" He admits three postulates of Practical Reason, namely, God, immortality, and freedom. Of these freedom alone is a condition or *ratio essendi* of the moral law:[3]

The only one of all the ideas of speculative reason of which we *know* the possibility *a priori,* without however understanding it.

The ideas of God and immortality, however, are not conditions of the moral law, but only conditions . . . of the practical use of our pure reason. Hence with respect to these ideas we cannot affirm that we *know* and *understand,* I will not say the actuality, but even the possibility.

Practically, however, they must be assumed; and as, in a practical point of view, they contain no intrinsic impossibility, they are *objectively* valid for pure practical reason, though for speculative reason the necessity of assuming them remains merely *subjective.* A recent philosophic tendency, called Pragmatism,[4] makes further inroads on the validity of the three ideas to which Kant granted at least subjective necessity. To the Pragmatist, God, immortality, and freedom are neither true in themselves nor necessarily, but only insofar as the acceptance of them involves consequences which have practical bearings on life and action.

Our postulates are not, therefore, beliefs which we have formed because "they help us to get into satisfactory relations with other parts of our experience,"[5] nor theoretical propositions incapable of proof, which the needs of pure practical reason necessitate us to assume. Nor are they truths which must logically be granted because without them an evident position cannot be explained. In this sense they would be the conclusion of a regressive argument. Granting indeed the undeniable fact that man is a moral being, one may by valid reasoning conclude that there is an ultimate source of the authoritative dictates of reason, and that such a source can only be God; that man whom it commands is capable of actively determining himself to obey or disobey it, and that in his higher nature he transcends the conditions of mere physical causality and the doom of things that are entirely subject thereto; that if his history be looked at in largest outline it will be found to manifest universal, constant, and uniform tendencies. But the argumentations by which such inferences are made do not belong to the province of Ethics. They belong to other departments of knowledge, nor are the conclusions established derived exclusively from study of the ethical fact. Our purpose, therefore, is not to prove but to expose and define the sense of these postulates.

NEED OF POSTULATES. Every science has need of the external assistance of postulates, for each individual science is cognate to others and, in varying degrees, is their debtor. But a science that is concerned with man must impetrate largely from other sciences. Especially must this be the case, when it treats of the highest and most far-reaching activity of man—his voluntary actions in their moral relations. Not improperly, therefore, has Ethics been called the final interpretation of nature; and it has been justly maintained that a system of philosophy that does not flower into a coherent and solid system of morals is blighted at the root. If its conclusions are obscure, or render insoluble the problems that involve the supreme agent among visible things, it is a sectarian hypothesis or an intellectual figment out of accord with the universe of interrelated and articulated truth. Therefore, in general, Ethics postulates a sound system of philosophy. In particular, it presupposes in the first place true principles and conclusions regarding man's origin and end, for if it have not ascertained for it the reasons, efficient and final, why he is, it cannot tell what he ought to do. Secondly, it presupposes like conclusions regarding man's composite nature, his faculties, their mode of exercise, and the mutual bearings of their higher and lower functions. Lastly, it must be rightly informed of the historical lines along which he has individually and socially given outward expression to the inward tendencies of his nature. Principally, it must rely on the sciences of natural theology, psychology, and anthropology for principles and facts which fall without the scope of its inquiry.

COSMOLOGICAL POSTULATE. This postulate is resolved into four distinct propositions: (a) a necessary, self-existing Being exists;

possessing the plenitude of being, and specifically the intellectual attributes of mind and the moral attributes of will in the highest conceivable degree; (b) this Being is the Creator of all other beings, which consequetnly are contingent; (c) rational contingent beings are images of the Creator's archetypal ideas; (d) the necessary self-existing Being freely bestowed existence on contingent beings for a purpose which could not be other than the procuring to Himself of external glory. Without attempting to transgress the limits of Ethics, we shall briefly unfold the import of these propositions.

NECESSARY BEING. A necessary being is one that neither can be, nor could have been, non-existent. A self-existing being is one of whose essence it is, that it should exist. The two concepts differ in what they expressly denote; the one puts the emphasis on a mode of existence, the other on a mode of essence. It we could conceive—and there have been philosophers who fancied they could—a being that depended for its existence on another, which, as its cause or source, produced it necessarily and from eternity, such a being would be necessary but not self-existing. But a self-existing being, if conceived at all, could not be conceived as ever being or having been non-existent, or as deriving its existence from another. No adequate concept of it can be formed that does not include inoriginated existence as an essential attribute. Furthermore, a being which, according to our finite way of speaking, is the source of its own existence, or in which, properly speaking, its essence is its existence, cannot be conceived as being conditioned by any degree of not-being, or as being limited in being. As it is absolute in existence, so it is in essence; it must by a necessity of thought contain the plenitude of essence and existence. It must possess in the highest conceivable grade those attributes of being in the concept of which limitation does not inhere. Every perfection, therefore, which of its nature does not intrinsically demand limitation must be attributed to a necessary self-existing being. Now intellect and will of themselves know no bound. We may think of given intellects and wills which are limited in energy and range for reasons that are extrinsic to the nature of these powers themselves. But to a necessary, self-existing being unconditioned intellect and will must belong; the power of knowing the fullness, the breadth and depth of truth, the omnipotence of will, the immutable indefectibility of its holiness must be essential attributes. Such a necessary, self-existing being possessing in a transcendent degree all perfection is God. That God exists is demon-strated in natural theology.

CREATED BEING. Everything else but God must be beings which can be and could have been non-existent, and which by receiving existence do not thereby become self-sustaining. Such beings are said to be contingent, that is dependent on another for nature and exist-ence and for continuance in existence and activity. Out of nothing they were brought by the Omnipotence of Will, and into nothing would they sink again if not sustained in existence by that same Will. To think otherwise, that is to say, to ascribe to contingent beings any self-sufficiency with regard either to initial being or continued being would be so far forth to grant them self-existence, and consequently its implication, the plenitude of being. The crea-tive act, therefore, presupposes no preexisting material out of which creatures are formed, nor seminal forces from which they are devel-oped, and it did not produce anything that, on the possession of existence, can endure without the sustaining power of the Creator.

Created things have received from the Creator the perfections by which thy are constituted each in its kind, and these perfections they do not possess in their fulness. Hence, they are said by the Schoolmen to have *participated* being, that is to say, they do not possess fully but only share in the perfections of being. They are analogues of Him of whom it is more properly said that He *is* exist-ence, will, and intellect, than that He *has* existence, intellect and will. Attributes predicated of the necessary, self-existing Being must be predicated by identity. Creatures, on the other hand, since they participate in these attributes, are said to *have* them. In every case, therefore, in which perfections of being are predicated of God and creatures, there is some want of equivalence in signification. The terms are identical, the perfections signified are truly predicated in both cases, yet in the case of creatures they are predicated with limi-tations that affect their intrinsic nature, and declare them to be analogues of the absolute reality.

The ethical significance of these truths lies in the conclusion that God's dominion over all things is universal, absolute, and es-sential. It is universal, in the sense that to it are subject all created natures, every faculty of each nature, and every single action and operation of these faculties; that it prevails in every circumstance of age, place or time; that it is supreme over any dominion possessed by creatures. It is absolute, because its exercise is unconditioned by creatures, and ordered solely by the divine attributes of wisdom and holiness. It is finally essential, since, founded in the nature of necessary and contingent being, God could not dispossess Himself of it, without making creatures self-existent and independent of Him.

ARCHETYPAL IDEAS. A being-by-participation is an imitation of a being that is such by its essence. The infinite plenitude of being must precontain in a transcendent degree every finite and limited perfection of creatures. Since they are contingent they depend on their Creator not only for being, but for being what they are. God is not only the cause that gave them existence and nature, He is also the exemplar according to which they were created. Every perfection of man's nature, therefore, is patterned on the perfections of the Divine Nature. Now as the Divine Nature, though infinite in perfection, is absolutely simple, It cannot be apprehended in one finite concept. The human intellect to form a notion of It must divide into a number of distinct concepts its ideas of a reality that in itself is absolutely one and indivisible. These distinct concepts are of course precisive, not negative. In his effort to apprehend an object that exceeds his comprehension man arranges according to his mode of thinking his precisive concepts in such a way that they follow one after another in logical series. Hence he conceives one attribute or action of God to be logically prior or posterior to another, without asserting thereby that there is division or sequence in the Divine Nature and activity.

Considering then the Divine Nature as creatures are related to it, we may distinguish four of these logical stages, to each of which corresponds a distinct imitative term. First, we conceive the Divine Nature as outwardly imitable, and as being the ultimate ground of all outward aptitude for existence, to which corresponds *possible being*. Secondly, we conceive the Divine Nature as known by the Divine Intellect to be imitable (a) in the essences or native constitutions of creatable being, and (b) in the natures or active powers inherent in essences. To this corresponds respectively (a) the *archetypal ideas* to which the intrinsic make-up of creatable essences are to be conformed, and (b) the *archetypal norms* which determine the modes of acting and working that should characterize creatable natures. Thirdly, we conceive the Divine Intellect decreeing that to one of the many orders of creatable beings, existence in time be given; the term of which is *the present universe* of things. Fourthly, we conceive Wisdom decreeing that in created natures principles of activity be implanted by which their operations and movements shall be directed in conformity with the archetypal norms of the present universe. The term of this logical stage is *natural law,* by which created things, each agreeably to its nature, are directed, necessarily if they are irrational, freely if rational, to their appointed ends. In a word, God created things in accord with His divine ideas, and fixed their actions and movements in keeping with eternal law.

EXTERNAL GLORY. Creation cannot be a necessary act, one namely to which the necessary self-existing Being was compelled by the exigencies of His nature or attributes. The necessity of creation may be understood in one of two senses: first, that the creation of the present universe was necessary; or secondly, that, although God freely chose to create the present universe rather than other possible universes, the creation of some universe was necessary. To assert either would be to deny the inward self-sufficiency of the self-existing Being, and to misconceive the plenitude of perfections possessed by an infinite Being. Neither could creation be a purposeless act, because as such it would be incompatible with supreme intelligence and absolute holiness of will. Creation, though free, must have been for a reason worthy of the wisdom and holiness of God. Strictly speaking, this reason, while exhibiting the purpose of the creative act, does not become the motive of it. With regard to finite wills, purpose and motive will be found to coalesce; not so, however, for the Infinite Will, which must ever have acted for a purpose, but could never have acted from a motive. A motive is causal, and, insofar as it moves, is independent of the will; and consequently implies what Kant calls "heteronomy of will." Autonomy of will, or independence of motive in the strict sense of the word, Kant wished to make the characteristic of even contingent and participated holiness, as it must undoubtedly be the essential mark of absolute holiness.

Now the only conceivable reason for creation worthy of a Being of infinite perfection, who cannot act because of desire, is the communication of being in such a way as to manifest through it His own perfections. This purpose necessarily entails the creation of beings capable of knowing Him from the truth, goodness, and beauty exhibited in participated being, and capable of loving and praising Him therefor; or in other words of glorifying Him. The glory given by His creatures is called *external* to distinguish it from God's own self-knowledge and self-love.

If the external glory of God is the primary purpose of creation, creatures will not only objectively manifest in orderly and graded sequence vestiges and likenesses of uncreated excellence, but some of them also must have the capacity of formally recognizing it. They must be endowed therefore with faculties adapted to and destined for this purpose, and must have an impulse so to employ them. They will as a consequence have an intellect capable of knowing the truth, and a will capable of loving the good, and a craving for the satisfaction of these capabilities which will leave them restless until it is sated.

PSYCHOLOGICAL POSTULATE. This enuntiates two attributes of an intellectual being, of which one is the logical and immediate antecedent of a moral act, the other a necessary though remote consequence. The first of these is freedom of the will, or as it is more precisely styled by St. Thomas and the Schoolmen, freedom of decision or choice (*liberum arbitrium*). The power of comparing alternative objects of desire, and of choosing between them when neither is apprehended as commensurate with the will's appetency for good is a necessary prerequisite of conduct. The other is immortality of the soul. The doctrine that the human soul survives its separation from the body, and lives endlessly is a necessary complement of the teaching of Ethics on the nature of the moral order.

FREEDOM. Apart from the inherent difficulties that beset the subject of free will, much of the confusion that involves the discussion of it is due to a want of precision in the use of the term "freedom." The word "freedom" has many senses. It seems primarily to apply to an agent that is the cause of its own action or inaction. In its widest sense, then, it means immunity from necessity in action, whether the necessity be negative, as restraint, or positive, as constraint. There are accordingly as many kinds of freedom as there are manners in which an agent can be unconditioned by necessity; so that of the same agent freedom and necessity may be predicated at the same time, and of the same act, though in different senses. A rational being, for instance, may be necessitated by the moral law to do what he is volitionally free to do or leave undone. To make clear the kind of freedom that is claimed for the will, we shall define the different species of necessity that may affect action.

EXTRINSIC AND INTRINSIC NECESSITY. In the first place, then, necessity of acting may arise from causes extrinsic to the agent, or from the intrinsic constitution of its nature. Extrinsic necessity imposed by an efficient cause is called *physical,* as when an agent is compelled by force to an action that is incongruous to its native appetency, or restrained from an action that is congruous thereto. Necessity of this kind is *coaction.* As is evident, coaction cannot be exercised on the will itself, constraining it to wish what it does not wish or hindering it from wishing what it does wish. A man may be coerced in respect of his outward actions, but no power can compel the immediate acts of the will. Immunity from coaction, or *freedom of spontaneity,* must therefore be conceded to the will. Extrinsic necessity of acting produced by a final cause is called *moral.* It consists in this that a necessary connection is apprehended to exist between an action of the will and an end to be obtained. In this case the will is morally necessitated to posit an action that leads to the realization of the end. This may occur in two general ways. First, when an end is, for whatever reason, absolutely wished, the will necessarily wishes the means by which the end can be obtained; for instance, if a man wishes absolutely to save his life, he necessarily wishes whatever will conduce thereto. Secondly, when an end is authoritatively assigned by a superior, the will is subject to the moral necessity of conforming its actions to the command of the superior.

Intrinsic necessity of action is of two kinds. In every created nature is implanted a tendency by which each is moved and directed to the end of its creation. This tendency is an impulse, and in a secondary sense a law. By it each created nature is impelled to those modes of activity which are peculiar to it, and by it its range of operations is circumscribed, and its functions in the scheme of the universe defined. Inherent in every nature there is a motive power that specifies it. It is as much an attribute of intellect as it is of matter, as distinctive of will as it is of a magnet. This necessity is named by the Schoolmen the necessity of *specification.* It does not drive the faculty to action, but when inclination or tendency is actuated, determines its specific mode of action. In cognitive beings, with which we are concerned, the appetitive tendency is enacted by sensuous or intellectual apprehension. The *necessity of actuation* is had, therefore, when a faculty in presence of its proper object, duly and rightly proposed, cannot withhold action, as for instance, the necessity of the intellect to assent to a self-evident proposition. Now the proper object of the will is good as such, or good without qualification. Regarding this good the will is not free, but, as has been said, is subject to the necessity of specification. If it acts at all, it must tend to an object, which, as presented in consciousness, is invested with the form of goodness, and when the object is unqualifiedly so presented it cannot abstain from volition. Freedom from the necessity of actuation is not, therefore, claimed for all voluntary acts. Free will presupposes as a condition of its exercise an indetermination on the part of the intellect with regard to the object, that is to say, either the object has not and is seen not to have a necessary connection with the specific satisfaction of the will's inherent tendency to good as such, or, if it have such a connection, is presented through false apprehension as not having it. It is as repugnant to the nature of will to be necessarily determined to volition by an object apprehended to be qualifiedly good, or good under some aspects and under others evil, as it is to the nature of intellect to give firm assent to a probable proposition. Nor can the excess of good over evil in the apprehended object necessitate the consent of the will, any more than the preponderance of reasons for one opinion over its opposite necessitates assent of the intellect.

FREEDOM OF WILL. The only act of the will of which freedom is therefore predicable as an intrinsic quality is the *elicit* act, or the immediate act of the will itself, by which choice is made between alternative objects of desire neither of which is unqualifiedly desirable. *Imperate* acts, or acts of other faculties which are subject to the control of will, are not said to be free, except by an ellipsis of language that gives them a denomination belonging to the elicit act which originated them.[6]

Freedom of will does not mean that the action of the will is irrational and motiveless. It is elicited for a purpose and because of a reason. The object apprehended as desirable is not a mere antecedent which in no wise moves the will. The causality of motive is not, it is true, reducible to the attractive power of a physical force; it is peculiar to the object of a faculty which is moved by cognition, and necessitates to action only when cognition does not or cannot present alternative solicitations. The will, as every faculty, needs the stimulation of some cause distinct from itself before it can act. This cause, an object present in consciousness and known to be desirable, arouses a will-movement towards the object. This was called by the

Schoolmen *actus primus*. It measures the attraction exercised by the object, and may or may not be followed by a corresponding volition called by the Schoolmen *actus secundus*. If other and undesirable aspects of the known object come into consciousness—as normally happens, unless the will hurries into action—a conflicting will-movement away from the object is aroused; or if an object, incompatible with the first, presents itself as desirable, a corresponding will-movement ensues. The will concurs or refuses concurrence with one or other of these movements and yields to the motive that initialed it. In this second act the will is not necessitated. Though it could not consent that either will-movement or first act should become a second or volitional act but for the motive to which the will-movement was due, its consent was not compelled by either motive. The consent—or *finalis sententia de agendis,* as St. Thomas describes it—was freely given, though induced by a motive.[7]

IMMORTALITY. It is proved in psychology that the individual soul, or the spiritual principle in man by which he is a rational and moral being, will survive the dissolution of the body, and continue endlessly to lead a life of intellectual and volitional activity. It is not, of course, claimed that the immortality of the soul implies self-existence; that the soul is immortal in the sense in which its Creator is immortal. Created spiritual substances never cease to be contingent beings. They are sustained in existence by the power of God, who concurs with them in all their operations. As God's sustaining act is free, it might conceivably be withheld, and the soul would then vanish into the nothingness from which the fiat of the Almighty called it. But as the purpose for which the Almighty freely gave it existence, demands its conservation in endless existence, and as this purpose is stamped on its nature's higher faculties and tendencies, the soul is said to be immortal by nature. This truth is here postulated as a necessary complement of the Moral Order, without which our existence as moral beings could have no ultimate rational meaning and would be irreconcilable with the primary purpose of creation.

ANTHROPOLOGICAL POSTULATE. Every created thing has its own mode of operation, and an innate inclination to perform those operations that agree with its nature. As we ascend in the grade of being the modes of operations peculiar to a nature become many, and are performed by many faculties, each of which has its own

corresponding natural inclination. Since all the faculties of a being
are radicated in the same nature, their inclinations are not unrelated; but, co-ordinated among themselves, and subordinated to a
dominant inclination, they produce one resultant which manifests
the inclination of the unitary nature as such. This appetency of the
unitary nature the Schoolmen called *appetitus naturalis,* and its
object *bonum naturae conveniens,* that is to say, the good that is
agreeable or naturally corresponds to the nature. In cognitive beings the subordination of diverse inclinations to the dominant inclination is effected through mind which apprehends an object not
as agreeable to one or other faculty, but as agreeable to the nature
as such.

Now man is a composite being in whom an animal nature is
informed by a spiritual substance, and in whom therefore are
formed appetencies analogous to those characterizing inferior creatures, but subserving the good of the whole man. Consequently as
each separate faculty of his nature has an appetency for an object
that is connatural to it, so the individual man has an appetency for
what is the congruous good of his nature as a whole or as considered
in all its essential relations. This latter appetency, according to St.
Thomas,[8] manifests itself in four fundamental directions: (a) in
the inclination man has in common with all creatures to resist disintegration or dissolution; (b) in the inclination he has in common
with other animals to perpetuate his species, and to care for and
train his progeny; (c) in the inclination he has, as an intellectual
being, to seek knowledge of the source and purpose of his being;
(d) in the inclination he has to live in the communion of endeavor
and thought with his fellowman. Of these the first and second inclination are common to man and inferior creatures only in an
analogous sense. They coincide in matter, at least remotely, one
looking to the preservation of the individual, the other to the preservation of the species. As existing in man, who is conscious of self
and of his essential relations to others, they take on a form which
is necessarily different from that which they have in the lower creation. A chemical compound or a quartz crystal, for instance, resists
disintegration by the physical forces of their nature, and a brute
animal propagates its species in response to an appetite that seeks
its satisfaction without thought of self or of progeny. The third
inclination is proper to rational beings, and finds its ultimate expression in man's recognition of his dependence on a transcendent

being to whom is finally referred his life and activities. The last inclination, though distinctive of man, is adumbrated in the instinct of animals to herd or flock together. Historically it is enacted in three distinct forms of natural societies—domestic, civil and religious—through which the objects of the three first inclinations are adequately secured. These inclinations manifest indeterminately the end or good of our nature. The determination of the concrete forms they must take in order to realize harmoniously the unitary good of nature is the office of reason. The dictates of nature, therefore, which they disclose are to be construed on rational principles and in the light of an ultimate regulative end.

The other inclinations of human nature are extensions, derivates, or complexes of these four.

SOCIAL INCLINATION. The social propensity or impulse discloses a twofold intention of the Creator. They are the radical tendencies by which human nature is driven to seek the well-being of the individual and the advancement of the race. Neither of these ends can man compass except in organized union with his fellow man. In isolation he is incapable of acquiring the physical, intellectual, and moral development for which nature intended him; and race perfection, which is the result of the acquired and transmitted development of the individuals which constitute it, cannot be reached by men segregated from one another. Man has therefore constantly exhibited natural traits which reveal his fitness for, inclination to, and need of fellowship with other men. It is a fact to which the records of history testify, that men under normal conditions are always associated in some form of domestic, civil, and religious society; that in spite of the restrictions on liberty and the limitations of rights which membership in these associations entail, they everywhere endure; and that civilization advances as these associations are better adjusted to their specific purposes and their stability more firmly secured, and on the other hand retrogrades when their mutual relations are disturbed and their endurance threatened.

St. Thomas, following Aristotle, says that those who by natural inclination are outside of society have either fallen below or risen above the normal conditions of human nature. He who cannot contract social union with others or has no need of their society, says Aristotle,[9] is either a wild beast or a god—ἢ θηρίον ἢ θεός. St. Thomas[10] finds evidence of man's sociability in the fact that he has capacities which are useless outside of society, and needs that can be satisfied only in society. As an instance of the former he mentions the faculty of speech. Brute animals, he says, have vocal organs, but their use is confined to the expression of pain or pleasure. Man alone can use his voice to express ideas. Such a faculty would be purposeless outside of society. Since nature, therefore, does nothing aimlessly—*nihil facit frustra*—the faculty of speech, which attains its full development only in society, declares man to be a social being. The latter he illustrates by contrasting the natural needs of brute animals, and the equipment bestowed on them by nature for meeting those needs with the physical and rational wants of man, for the relief of which nature has made no immediate provision. It gives him instead a practical intelligence through the exercise of which he may surpass the brute by adapting the gifts of nature to the requirements of his bodily and intellectual life. The practical intelligence, however, of the individual man would be unable to satisfy the exigencies of a rational being's life, if not stimulated, assisted, supplemented, and complemented by the practical intelligence of other men. But this cannot be had outside society. Man is therefore by nature a social being, one, namely, fashioned by nature for intercourse and communion with his fellow men and borne by a natural impulse to form stable unions with them. In this social impulse, as much an essential quality of his nature as are his individual impulses, is formed the *genetic origin* of domestic, civil, and religious society.[11]

SOCIAL VERSUS GREGARIOUS INSTINCT. The impulse to act with other men, to interchange with them material or intellectual goods, to combine with them for the attaining of a common good, bears a resemblance to the gregarious instinct of animals, yet differs from it in important respects. (a) The social impulse transcends the gregarious instinct, since it is accompanied by self-consciousness; is reduced to actuation by the self-conscious exercise of reason; and is subject to the control of will. (b) It is more far-reaching in effect, since it regards not only the preservation of the individual and the species, but their well-being and perfection as well, and results in the development and advancement of the race. (c) Its imperiousness is moral rather than psychological. It induces man to its actuation through an idea of a congruous good which reason presents, and not through a compelling intrinsic impulse.

NOTES

1. *Com. in Post. Analyt.*, Lib. I, Lect. XIX.

2. Kant's *Ethics*, Abbott's translation, pp. 219 and 96, note.

3. *Ibid.*, pp. 88-89.

4. The term "Pragmatism," as the designation of a philosophic method, was first used by C. S. Peirce. In an article, entitled "How to Make Our Ideas Clear," which was published in the *Popular Science Monthly* for January, 1878, he proposed a principle or maxim that would, he believed, on application to an object of thought enable one to conceive it clearly. The maxim which he was led to adopt by reflection upon Kant's *Critique of Pure Reason* is enunciated thus: "Consider what affects, that might conceivably have practical bearings, we conceive the object of our conceptions to have. Then our conception of these is the whole of our conception of the object." He did not apparently intend to deny the validity of speculative truths; yet the last sentence of his maxim contains in germ the philosophic method which today is known as Pragmatism—a method which does not aim merely at clarifying our ideas, or even attesting the truth of them by their practical consequences but at subordinating logical thinking to the ends of practical life. To decide the truth or falsity of a conception or theory we must examine the practical consequences, "either in the shape of conduct to be recommended, or in that of experience to be expected," which may conceivably result from it. Apart from these, the conception has no significance, and is neither true nor false. "Truth is one species of good," and is determined on grounds of utility. "The true," as James says in *Pragmatism* (p. 222), "to put it briefly, is only the expedient in the way of our thinking, just as the right is only the expedient in the way of our behaving," and it is therefore relative and variable. For a refutation of Kant and the pragmatist the student is referred to the exponents of scholastic Epistemology.

5. James, *Pragmatism*, p. 58.

6. The present editor adds here a footnote from a loose sheet of Father Brosnahan's MS, judging that the definitions may advisably be inserted here.

The acts of the will are:

1. *Elicit*, i.e., the immanent act immediately proceeding from the will.

2. *Imperate*, i.e., the transient act or the act elicited by some faculty subject to the control of and moved by the will.

1. *Voluntary*, any act of whatever kind that springs from the will, whether necessary or free.

2. *Volitional,* any act that springs from the will after deliberation, i.e., one posited from a motive and freely directed to the realization of a purpose.

3. *Non-Voluntary,* an act performed quite independently of the will, as acts which are the result of automatic vital impulses.

4. *Involuntary,* an act which occurs in spite of a volition to the contrary.

1. *Appetitive,* insofar as it is responsive to the attraction of a good.

2. *Conative,* insofar as it is an effort to acquire the good. Every conative act is appetitive, but inversely an act may be appetitive without being conative, e.g., an inefficacious desire or mere wish.

7. See Maher's *Psychology,* Ch. XIX and Rickaby's *Free Will and Four English Philosophers.*

8. *S. T.,* 1, 2, qu. 94, a. 2.

9. *Politics,* Bk. I, Ch. 2.

10. *De Reg. Princ.,* L. I, C. 1; *Com. in Pol.,* Lib. I, Lect. I.

11. In a private note to the present editor answering a difficulty concerning this use of the word "genetic," Father Brosnahan wrote as follows:

1. Genesis implies (a) a beginning (b) due to natural impulses, which are radical, and which underlie all concrete and specific actuations. The genetic origin of conjugal society, e.g., is to be traced to the physiological and psychological inclinations and aptitudes that impel to its formation. But the genetic origin will not explain the specific forms that conjugal societies have taken, nor the individual society into which Socrates and Xantippe entered. Historical causes of many kinds must be introduced to explain this. The same may be said of the institution of property. The genetic impulses to acquire and hold as one's own material goods has been through historical causes enacted in manifold ways.

2. A juridical origin accounts for juridic effects, that is for effects that arise from a cause which confers a right (*jus*) and imposes a duty (*officium*). The juridical origin of civic society must account for the right that the community (i.e., people collectively) has to social peace and well-being, and for the duty that is incumbent on the people taken singly of furthering the purpose of the community.

3. The family is the *immediate* element of civic society, since it (i.e., civic society) has its immediate raison d' être in the fact that the family though perfect in respect of its end, is imperfect in respect of the means conducive thereto. The extrinsic purpose of both family and state is the good of the race. The state is utterly incompetent to promote the good of the race except through the family. Every deteri-

oration of the family renders the state less effective for its extrinsic purpose. The higher the family the more effective the state.

This question is not to be confounded as it sometimes is, with the question of the right of suffrage. When we say that the family is the immediate element of the state we mean (a) that it is the proximate basis of the state, (b) and that the proximate purpose of social or civic activities is to be regulated by their effect on the family, or that the well-being of the family is the regulative norm of state activities. The right of suffrage—which is a political, not a civic right—however exercised and to whomever granted—must always keep in view the fact that the intrinsic well-being and extrinsic aim of the state is realized in *tantum quantum* the family is secured in its right and assured of its development in physical, intellectual, and moral progress.

If these distinctions are kept in mind many difficulties can be solved: (a) the *intrinsic end* of a person, individual or corporate, is the fullest perfection that nature destines and fits it for; the *extrinsic end* is that which the intrinsic end when acquired realizes outside the person, or which, when in process of being acquired, it furthers; (b) the primary intrinsic purpose of a corporate person (family, state, or church) is the attaining of its intrinsic completion or finish. The secondary purpose is the attaining by the individuals of the well-being which the society of its nature can confer and which renders them fitted for the primary purpose; that is, the primary purpose is social, the secondary is personal. The latter is directed to the former and both to the extrinsic purpose. For instance, the secondary purpose of conjugal society is mutual love and help; and of the state, domestic and individual material prosperity for the individual citizen. The primary purpose of the first is the procreation of children, of the second collective peace and permanence. The extrinsic purpose of both is the good of the race which nature intended each to promote according to its functions. If these distinctions are clearly apprehended and the subordination understood, I think that all the ethical fumbling with difficulties that are found in books would be avoided.

CHAPTER IV

CONDUCT

Conduct is volitional action of whatever kind, whether internal or external.

Conduct insofar as it is ethical implies a certain psychological reality due to the faculties from which it proceeds, and a certain quality because of which it is denominated moral. Two questions therefore arise: (1) what is conduct in itself? (2) what is morality?

CONDUCT. Though conduct in the proper sense of the word is ascribed only to man, not all actions performed by men, even when they are peculiar to him, necessarily fall under the head of conduct. Many actions elicited by the faculties of his rational nature, and therefore characteristic of him, may not be so denominated; as, on the other hand, many actions of his animal nature, if they proceed from motive and are directed to the attainment of a purpose, are denominated conduct. Thus assent to a self-evident proposition, though an exclusively human act, is not conduct; whereas the act of eating which is common to man and brute is conduct. Only those actions, says St. Thomas,[1] are properly called conduct (*actus humani*)[2] over which man has control. But he has control over his actions through reason and will; hence freedom of choice (*liberum arbitrium*) is said to be a function of will and reason. Those actions, therefore, are properly conduct which are deliberately willed. In other words it is the mode of activity peculiar to man, not the substance of the act that makes it conduct. Now the modal attribute of acts of conduct by which they are wholly distinguished from the actions of irrational creatures is that they are volitional; that is to say they are voluntary actions, which presuppose knowledge of an end and the means thereto, are subsequent to deliberation regarding the means, and are consequent on choice. Voluntary acts inasmuch as they are acts of the rational appetitive faculty do differ substantially from the appetitive acts of the brutes,[3] but when they are

66

necessary, as happens, they agree with them in their mode of production. But volitional acts are not only voluntary, and so distinct in kind from the appetitive acts of an animal nature; they are also free, and therefore differ also in their mode of production.

Spencer[4] defines conduct as "either—acts adjusted to ends, or else—the adjustment of acts to ends; according as we contemplate the formed body of acts, or think of the form alone." And he adds, "conduct in its full acceptation must be taken as comprehending all adjustments of acts to ends, from the simplest to the most complex, whatever their special natures, and whether considered separately or in their totality." Conduct so defined, that is, acts adjusted to ends, he confines to living creatures but extends it to all, to the lowest mollusc as well as to highest intelligence. The reason for this arbitrary extension in the application of the term is to be found in the needs of his evolutionary theory. We must first, he says, form a universal concept of acts adjusted to ends as exhibited by living creatures before we can frame a conception of the evolution of conduct. Now Spencer is perfectly justified in contemplating all acts adjusted to ends, and of arranging these in graduated and serial sequence according to their increasing complexity; such a sequence may undoubtedly be found in the universe of things. But usage does not justify him in designating the content of this universal concept as conduct. We do not speak of the conduct of an oyster. The sophistry, not uncommon in evolutionary philosophy, consists in applying to the generic element of a specific concept a name that belongs to the species only.

ELEMENTS OF CONDUCT. Since conduct is, as we have seen, action springing from motive and adjusted to purpose or end in view, it is the outcome of various acts of the intellect and will, some of which are concerned with the end and some with the means conducive to the attainment of the end. The logical order and sequence of these acts is given by the Schoolmen as follows: First there is an act of the intellect by which an object is apprehended as good in itself, and responsive to this there arises in the will a *liking* for the object, or a complacency in its goodness without any wish to possess it. If, however, the object is presented as good to the agent, liking becomes *wish,* and the intellect is instigated to examine whether the object is attainable. Thereupon follows a second act of the intellect by which it judges the object to be a good that may be striven for and not impossible of attainment. This judg-

ment moves the will to an act that is called *intention,* literally the
tending towards or stretching forth toward an object. Intention
may accordingly be defined as a movement of the will to gain a
particular object, in virtue of which it desires in an undefined way
the means that lead to the realization of the end. It should be
noted that intention as such does not include the desire of any
certain means, since one may have the purpose of acquiring a particular good, and realize in a general way that it can be obtained,
before possessing adequate knowledge of the means to be employed.[5]
These three acts of the will, liking, wish and intention regard the
object as an end.

When the intention of gaining an end is formed or when an
habitual intention becomes actual, a third act of the intellect ensues, and the first that is concerned with the means. Reason inquires
into and investigates how and in what manner the intention may
be carried out, and the intent realized, or examines the disparate
or conflicting procedures by which the intention might be executed.
This act, by which the reasons for or against the adoption of a particular set of means are compared and weighed in the light of the
intended end, and with a view to a decision, is called *deliberation*
(*consilium*).[6] This act, however, is not necessarily a prolonged
process. One who deliberates is said to stop and think, it is true;
to weigh facts and reasons cautiously and without haste. And undoubtedly in matters of great moment, and when action is not urgent, deliberation should have these qualities. But when the problem
to be solved is of lesser importance, or the need of quickly reaching
a decision is pressing, alternative courses of action and their relative
values may be compared and estimated in a moment. Through the
deliberative act of reason which discovers and defines the means
suitable for gaining the end, the intention itself is known to be
definitely realizable.

Consequent on deliberation, the will puts an act by which the
conclusions of reason are accepted and action is finally decided on.
This act, regarded as an acquiescence in the deliberate judgment of
reason is called *consent* (*consensus*), and is described by St. Thomas
as the *finalis sententia de agendis;* regarded as the preference of
one out of many examined ways of proceeding it is called *choice*
(*electio*). Choice and consent are identical when deliberation immediately reveals one means pre-eminently adapted to the attaining
of the end in view. If, however, after deliberation, two or more

means are perceived to be suitable for carrying out the intention, between consent and choice, a discriminate judgment intervenes which asserts that for some practical reason, one rather than the other is to be used. In both cases the decision (*arbitrium*) to act is free, and though in form it is an act of reason, substantially it is an act of the will. Consent and choice, therefore, are acts neither of reason only nor of will only, but complex acts proceeding from both at once.[7]

It may not be out of place to observe that this explanation of the series of acts issuing in volition is not to be understood in a mechanical way. The Schoolmen were aware—none more so—that the actions of a spiritual being are not produced with the time-succession of actions that are material; that liking, wish, and intention might in entity be one act, and that deliberation, consent, and choice might be practically instantaneous. The purpose of their analysis was to define the psychological elements that entered into the formation of a volitional act and their relations of priority and dependence. Volition therefore is a free conative act toward a determined end through chosen means. The other acts that integrate conduct are those by which the will carries or attempts to carry its volition into execution, acts, namely, of the intellect, of the senses, or of the muscular power, insofar as these are subject to the control of the will. Volition itself is called an elicit act of the will, since it proceeds immediately from the will; the other acts that are under the control of the will, and posited through the mediation of volition are called imperate acts.

KNOWLEDGE OF THE END. Since conduct springs from motive, the agent not only apprehends the thing which is an end, but also knows that it is an end, and that his acts have a practical bearing on its attainment. Knowledge of an object as in some way suitable to the agent and obtainable by him is not only the antecedent and concomitant of volition, it is also the reason of it. An appetitive act following after and because of knowledge of this kind is a voluntary act. Only voluntary acts are elements of conduct. The reverse however is not true, for conduct is always under the control of will, and some voluntary acts are necessary. First, if the object is, and is apprehended to be, absolutely good, and secondly, if the object is apprehended to be good without qualification, though in reality it be not so, the will necessarily follows the lead of reason and elicits an act in accord with its knowledge. In the first case the necessary character of the act implies perfection both in the object known, and in the intellection by which it is known, but in the second case, since the object is not unqualifiedly good, the necessary character of the act is due to defects in the intellectual processes by which it is apprehended. The conditions under which an object is known determines the manner in which it is embraced by the will. It cannot be more firmly desired than it is apprehended to be desirable. What reason, therefore, apprehends to be desirable under every aspect, the will of necessity desires; and what reason recognizes to be desirable in some respect and undesirable in others, the will freely embraces or refuses. In order, therefore, that a voluntary act be volitional, its object, whether it terminates intention or choice, must be presented by reason as good with qualifications.

ADVERTENCE TO WILL-MOVEMENT. When the first liking and wish for an object arise in the will, either the agent slips or is hurried into action, or, simultaneously with the will-movement, doubts regarding the desirableness of the object present themselves to reason, and action is stayed by a counter movement of the will. Thereupon motives for different or conflicting procedures emerge into consciousness. The mind becomes aware of reasons for the desirableness of action, of abstention from action, or of different or contrary action; and hence competing or irreconcilable will-movements ensue. In this the action of reason, which we have already described as deliberation, intervenes, and the value of motives for alternative actions is examined. Now it is evident that fulness of deliberation depends primarily on the attention given by the mind to the substance and qualities of the alternative actions. Some of the adjuncts which go to complete the action objectively considered may escape advertence, and even where the action is fully apprehended in all its physical bearings, its desirableness as a good from one point of view may be noticed without advertence to its undesirableness from others. Advertence, therefore, may be incomplete or complete, and consequently deliberation may be partial or full. These variations in advertence and deliberation will effect corresponding variations in the character of conduct. The same action may in some regards be fully volitional, and in others partially volitional or non-volitional.

DECISION AND CHOICE. The act of determining the practical question whether to do or what to do, with which deliberation is concerned, partakes of the nature of a judgment and a volition, and may under different aspects be attributed to reason and will. Aristotle, apparently in doubt as to which faculty prominence should be given, calls it an act of appetitive intellect or of reasoning appetite.[8] Butler may have had some similar idea when he describes the moral faculty as being neither "a sentiment of the understanding," nor "a perception of the heart" but a combination of both.[9] The rival claims of heart and head give rise to two extreme schools. We have first the Moral Sense Hedonists, who, observing that our moral perceptions are suffused with an emotional quality that is wholly absent from our perceptions of purely speculative truths, invented an affective faculty the office of which was to feel the truths of conduct. St. Thomas notices a like controversy regarding the faculty of free decision or choice. He says:[10]

Quidam dicunt liberum arbitrium esse tertiam potentiam a voluntate et ratione distinctam propter hoc quod vident actum liberi arbitrii, qui est eligere, differentem esse ab actu simplicis voluntatis et ab actu rationis. Nam rationis quidem actus in sola cognitione consistit; voluntas autem actum suum habet circa bonum quod est finis; liberum vero arbitrium circa bonum quod est ad finem. Sicut ergo bonum quod est ad finem egreditur a ratione finis; appetitus vero boni a cognitione finis; ita dicunt quodammodo naturali ordine ex ratione voluntatem procedere, et ex duabus tertiam potentiam quae est liberum arbitrium. Sed hoc convenienter stare non potest.

The extreme rationalist, on the other hand, contends that moral judgments are given on purely intellectual grounds. Such in effect is the position of Clarke, Kant, Green and others who make "absolute reasonableness," as such, a motive power over the will. We do not of course deny that it is the same faculty which tells us speculative truths and moral truths. But the truths themselves belong to different orders. The mind rests in the possession of the former, and is impelled to action by the apprehension of the latter. The former are merely rational, the latter are rational and affective.

SUBJECT MATTER OF DECISION AND CHOICE. Decision and choice, then, are concerned: (a) with judgments that have a relation to will, the truth of which consequently consists in the objective identity of the subject, i.e., conduct, and the predicate, i.e., good or right; (b) with judgments which are derived from a ratiocination in which a necessary principle of conduct is applied to concrete circumstances; (c) with a particular judgment in which the objective identity of right or wrong with an individual act of conduct is asserted; (d) with a judgment, finally, which pronounces that a given volitional act is to be or may be posited. Evidently, therefore, decision and choice involve the activity of reason and will, the difference between them being one merely of connotation. Decision lays stress on the rational side of the act, choice on its volitional side. St. Thomas brings out this distinction in his definition of free decision (*liberum arbitrium*), and in his analysis of the act of choice. *Liberum arbitrium,* he says, is freedom in passing judgment:

Intellectualia non solum sunt liberae actionis; sed etiam liberi judicii, quod est liberum arbitrium habere;

Judicium igitur intellectus de agibilibus non est determinatum ad unum tantum, habent igitur omnia intellectualia liberum arbitrium.[11]

Homo . . . non solum est causa sui ipsius in movendo sed in judicando; et ideo est liberi arbitrii, ac si diceretur liberi judicii de agendo vel non agendo.[12]

Liberum arbitrium est potentia qua homo libere judicare potest.[13]

Solum quod habet intellectum potest agere judicio libero in quantum cognoscit universalem rationem boni, ex qua cognoscit hoc vel illud esse bonum.[14]

He tells us that choice is a preference by the will of one rather than another of the judgments formed in deliberation:

Practicae inquisitionis duplex est conclusio; una quae est in ratione, scilicet sententia, quae est judicium de consiliatis; alia vero quae est in voluntate et hujusmodi est electio, et dicitur conclusio per quandam similitudinem; quia sicut in speculativis ultimo statur in conclusione, ita in operativis ultimo statur in operatione.[15]

Judicium est quasi conclusio et determinatio consilii. Determinatur autem consilium primo quidem per sententiam rationis et secundo per acceptationem appetitus. . . . Et hoc modo ipsa electio dicitur quoddam judicium a quo nominatur liberum arbitrium.[16]

The object preferred in choice is the one finally judged to be more useful than others for obtaining the end that is intended. But this must not be understood too narrowly. The object of choice, it is true, precisely insofar as it is an object of choice, is merely a means, and is not desirable in itself. In the actual experiences of our volitional life, however, such objects usually have a goodness of their own by which the will is attracted. If the problem of deliberation were concerned only with means, which, apart from their bearing on the end, made no other appeal to the will, practical reason alone, supposing the will's fixed resolve to gain a particular end, could give the decision and determine choice. Nor is it to be understood that an end which is now intended may not itself have been a matter of previous choice. Intention is the will to gain an end regarding the desirableness of which there is at present no intellectual indetermination. This does not mean that it was not in prior stages of appetition a means chosen for the realization of some further end. In fact every good except goodness itself can come into deliberation and be a matter of choice. *"Quae sunt ad ultimum finem, in quantum sunt ad finem, sub consilio cadunt,"* says St. Thomas.[17] Moreover in the process of deliberation if the only means available to reach the end should prove undesirable of itself or on other grounds, the intention of gaining the end may be abandoned, and abstention from all action chosen.

INTERNAL AND EXTERNAL ACTS. The word "conduct" is usually employed with a tacit reference to the outcome of volition in external actions. The reason is obvious; it is usually the outer manifestation that reveals to us the quality of the inner act. But neither in our own case nor in the case of others do we regard voluntary activity as susceptible of a moral predicate through its outer side.[18]

Morality may be predicated of those acts only which are subsequent to deliberation, and are accordingly posited under the guidance of practical reason, and subject to the control of will. Every act, therefore, which, dictated or authorized by a judgment of practical reason, is within the power of the will to originate or inhibit as it pleases, is conduct.[19] Now acts of this kind may be internal, i.e., acts of the imagination, of the intellect, or of the will itself; and external, i.e., acts of the sense organs, or of some muscular or locomotive faculty of the body. For the volitional act becomes normally an imperate act, and is completed either inwardly through the exercise of a mental power, or outwardly through the senses, the faculty of speech, or some bodily movements. Conduct therefore comprises both internal and external acts.

CONDUCT AND BEHAVIOR. Conduct is distinguished from behavior precisely in this, that we judge behavior by its outward conformity with accepted social canons of propriety or legality; whereas we judge conduct by the motive power from which it springs and which the outer action reveals. Deeds done from ignorance, inadvertence, or under the influence of intense and uncontrolled feeling, though condemned as behavior, may be excused as conduct. Our moral verdict is pronounced on the volitional act itself, and on other actions because they are recognized either to have taken their rise from a deliberate act of the will, or, if they owe their origin to an impulse antedating deliberation, have become volitional by being approved and accepted by such an act. Actions done from a sense of social behavior, propriety, honor, or legality, often bear a resemblance to those done from the moral imperatives of reason, and are not infrequently confounded with them. Moreover the mandates of social behavior are often allied to moral imperatives of reason. Social sanctions do act as incitements to moral conduct that comes or may come under the notice of others and so indirectly influence personal morality. The differences, however, between behavior and conduct are well-defined. First, the approbation or disapprobation consequent on one's observance or violation of the social proprieties results even if he who experiences them is conscious that his success or failure is accidental. Secondly, they have special relations to the esteem of others, to respectability or disrepute; and regard primarily a social tribunal and the outward aspects of actions. Lastly, they do not affect unconditionally, but relatively, in the supposition that one values as an end and so far as one values it as such, the advantages of good repute in the social class to which he belongs.

With conduct it is otherwise. First, if one has fallen into any immorality, his sense of self-disapprobation is conditioned only by his consciousness of responsibility. Secondly, though the morally wrong action be tolerated or condoned in the society in which he is a member, or be known to himself alone, he is shamefaced in his own presence; as, on the other hand, he is conscious of self-approbation when his action is morally good, even if it meets with the disfavor of others. Lastly, he recognizes that the approval or condemnation of self is determined by a law of his reason that is absolute and final, independent of his personal interests or inclinations, superior to the canons of society, and more binding than legality.

NOTES

1. *S. T.*, 1, 2, qu. 1, a. 1.

2. The Schoolmen styled volitional acts *actus humani*. It should be noted that *humani* does not signify *human* in the English sense of the word, that is, of or pertaining to man alone, but characterizes the preeminent habitude of his free activity.

3. St. Thomas, *S. T.*, 1, 2, qu. 6, a. 2, ad 1, concedes, in order to explain the words of St. Gregory of Nyssa and St. John Damascene,

that the movements of the sensitive appetites in brute animals may be denominated voluntary because of their likeness to the act of the will in being posited subsequent to cognition. This usage of the word has ceased with later Scholastics.

4. *Data of Ethics,* Ch. I, §2.

5. The Scholastic sense of the word *intention,* which applies to the act of the will, is to be clearly distinguished from the utilitarian sense in which it signifies only the intent or the purpose of the act. Intention, according to John S. Mill, is the willed consequences of his action. Other utilitarians, as Bentham, define it to be the actual consequences or results of the action. It is important to keep these distinctions in mind in view of the fact that a school of utilitarians determine the moral quality of a volitional act exclusively by its external consequences. By English usage the word is used both in a subjective and an objective sense, the subjective being, according to lexicographers, the primary sense, and the objective an occasional and derivative sense. It is characteristic of psychological Utilitarianism to use the term exclusively in an objective sense.

6. *S. T.,* 1, 2, qu. 14.

7. *S. T.,* 1, 2, qq. 13-15; Suarez, *De Ultimo Fine Hominis,* Tract. III, D. VIII, Sect. 2, n. 5.

8. *Ethic. Nich.,* Bk. II, Ch. VI: διὸ ἢ ὀρεκτικὸς νοῦς ἡ προαίρεσις ἢ ὄρεξις διανοητική, καὶ ἡ τοιαύτη ἀρχὴ ἄνθρωπος.

9. Whewell corrects the texts of the *Dissertation on Virtue,* making Butler say, "a perception of the understanding or a sentiment of the heart," and adds, "I think it cannot be doubtful that Butler intended to write as I have printed." But to one who knows the difficulty, it may well be very doubtful.

10. *De Veritate,* qu. 24, a. 6.

11. *Contra Gentiles,* XLVIII.

12. *De Ver.,* qu. 24, a. 1.

13. *Ibid.,* a. 4.

14. *S. T.,* 1, qu. 59, a. 3.

15. *De Ver.,* qu. 22, a. 15, ad. 2.

16. *S. T.,* 1, qu. 83, a. 3, ad. 2.

17. *S. T.,* 1, 2, qu. 15, a. 3.

18. Martineau's analysis of conduct in its relation to a moral predicate is worth quoting. "James Mill," he says, "is fond of laying out its elements into three stages: (1) the sentiments whence it springs; (2) the muscular movements in which it visibly consists; (3) the consequences in which it issues. Of these cut off the first, and the other two lose all their moral quality; the muscular movement becomes a spasm or sleep-walking; the consequences become natural phenomena, pleas-

ant like fine weather, or terrible like an incursion of wild beasts. But cut off the other two, and in reserving the first alone, you save the moral quality entire: though paralysis should bar the passage into outer realization, and intercept the consequences at their birth, still the personal record contains a new act, if only the inner mandate has been issued." *Types of Ethical Theories,* Vol. II, Bk. I, Ch. I, §1.

19. "Actus autem susceptibilis est bonitatis secundum quod aliquatenus ratione deducitur; quod contingit in illis actibus tantum qui imperantur a voluntate quae consequitur deliberationem rationis." *2 Dist.,* 40, qu. 1, a. 5.

CHAPTER V

MORALITY OF VOLITIONAL ACTS

The morality of a volitional act consists in its conformity or deformity with that norm to which volitional acts of their nature and in all their essential aspects ought to be conformed.

THE SUBJECT OF MORALITY. Used in its general sense as referring to right and wrong, morality is predicated of many subjects. Not only is conduct said to be moral, but also will and character, laws and principles, motive and purpose, imputability and sanctions. Evidently the predication, though in none of these cases figurative, is not formally the same in all. To one of them it belongs by priority, to the others because they bear to the first some causal, final or dependent relation. The denomination *moral* belongs primarily to that subject to which other subjects receiving the same denomination are referred by one or other of these relations.

Now this subject is volitional action or conduct. The will is said to be good when it is the psychological cause of virtuous actions; looked at merely as a faculty it is neither morally good nor morally bad. Character is recognized to be morally good when it is the effect of, or has been produced by repeated volitional actions that are good, or when after formation it is the co-operative cause, with the will, of good conduct. A motive or purpose is said to be good, when it exhibits an end in accord with the nature and essential bearings of a volitional act. Laws and principles receive the denomination, when they express the harmony that ought to exist between a volition act and its norm. Imputability and sanctions are called moral, because they are consequences and indications, respectively, of the moral attribute of conduct and the moral efficacy of law. Morality is therefore predicated principally and in strict propriety of the volitional act, and of other moral entities insofar as they bear a relation to this.

77

MORALITY A RELATION. We must define the general notion attaching to the term "morality," before we can determine what it is that makes conduct moral. Is morality a fiction of the mind or has it objective reality? The question involves, of course, the fundamental problem of Epistemology regarding the nature of knowledge. That problem we assume to be solved in accord with the principles of Scholastic Realism. Starting then from the psychological fact that men have moral ideas and that they accordingly ascribe morality to certain modes of action, our inquiry concerns the reality of this attribute of conduct.

Now any theory that makes it a conventional figment, created by the human mind to meet varying social or civil needs, belies by implication the fundamental fact on which Ethics is based, and gives morality a mutable and conditional character, and inevitably leads to moral skepticism. To assign as the basis of morality an arbitrary institution fostered by the cleverness of politicians[1] or a traditional and hereditary way of looking at conduct is to identify it ultimately with behavior, and to empty the ethical verb "ought" of its specific content. If, therefore, morality has a reality antecedent to and not derivable from legality or historical custom, the further question arises as to whether it is an absolute quality of conduct or an intrinsic relation of it. That morality is absolute in the sense that it is not contingent on our inclination or desires, or on the customary or formal ordinances of human society, is manifest from what we have already declared. But is it absolute in the sense that it is a quality that belongs to conduct independently of any relation? The Schoolmen following St. Thomas maintain with practical unanimity that it is a relation. Even conceding the position held by some of them that a volitional act and a moral act were in fact coextensive, these, they contended, differ in their objective concepts. A volitional act as such, St. Thomas teaches, takes on the moral attribute only when another idea is added by which it is specifically narrowed.[2] The volitional act, considered merely as having a certain physical reality received from the conative faculty from which it freely proceeds, is indetermined in morality.

This is quite clear with regard to imperate acts, as studying, conversing, walking, any of which may have the same perfection of physical reality, whether they are morally good or morally bad. The action of a man, for instance, justly defending his life and that of an enemy attempting unjustly to deprive him of it may be equally perfect volitionally, though one is good and the other evil. With regard to elicit acts the distinction is not so concretely evident, but can be inferred from an analysis of the ideas. The volitional character of an elicit act arises from its dependence on the free will. This dependence is equally present and may be equally complete in acts of opposite moral character. The elicit act is volitional whether it be right or wrong; it is not moral, however, until it is disjunctively either one or the other. Its moral character, therefore, is determined by another relation superadded to its relation of dependence on free will. As, however, every volitional act is always and actually either good or bad, its dependence on the will may be reckoned the generic element of morality, of which good and bad are the supreme species.

Briefly, the elicit act has a relation to a subjective principle, or the faculty from which it proceeds and by reason of which it is volitional; and to an objective principle which fixes the moral value that it ought to possess if it is to attain its appropriate end. It is this latter relation that constitutes morality. But the further question arises: Is this relation to be conceived as inhering in the volitional act itself, or as residing in the outward conduct? If the first, then morality is intrinsic to the elicit act, and in the strictest propriety attributable to man himself as the agent; if the second, it would be extrinsic to it, and not the agent but what the agent did could properly be said to be moral.

Now admitting the fundamental fact which Ethics professes to interpret, it is man himself to whom through his elicit acts moral goodness and badness are properly imputable. It is the elicit act, then, which by accord or disaccord with its objective principle receives a moral denomination. In any other supposition praise or blame would belong to the deed and not the doer; the proverbial dog that bit the stone which struck him would be logical, and the common judgment of mankind which looks on man himself as morally responsible would be highly illogical. The relation therefore constituting morality is intrinsic to man's volitional act and refers to an objective principle or norm to which it ought to conform.

CONFORMITY TO NORM. The objective principle that determines morality is universal, affecting all free activity; supreme, transcending every other regulative principle of conduct. Now such a principle is a norm to which volitional acts of their nature and in all their essential aspects ought to be conformed. The terms "right" and "wrong," by which we designate opposite moral attributes of conduct, confirm this truth. The word "right" is derived from a root meaning to rule or keep straight. Etymologically it applies to the movement of a material body towards a mark or goal without deflections in lateral directions. Thence by a natural extension of meaning it came to be applied to movements of higher kinds, those, namely, involved in the activities of intellect and will. In every signification it connotes a term which as norm determines the aim of the movement, and keeps it within its proper boundaries. We declare reasoning to be right, for instance, when, precisely as reasoning, it is in keeping with the nature of the faculty that originates it. In like manner the morally right is the conformity of volitional actions as such to the norm which is by nature appropriate to the will. The term "wrong" gives the same evidence. Allied by etymology with the participle "wrung" it primarily signifies that which is wrung aside or twisted from its direction, scope or type.

UTILITARIANISM. Utilitarians are usually credited with holding that morality is extrinsic to the agent, and that it resides in the results or consequences of his actions without regard to motive. These results or consequences, foreseen and sought as desirable, they call *intentions,* using the word exclusively in its objective sense.[3] By *motive* they understand the subjective affections which move the agent to will an action. Bentham's exposition of the doctrine is characteristically clear:[4]

A motive is substantially nothing more than pleasure and pain operating in a certain manner. Now pleasure is in itself a good, nay even, setting aside immunity from pain, the only good. . . . It follows, therefore, immediately and incontestably, that there is no such thing as any sort of motive that is in itself bad.

If, then, actions were evaluated by motive, all actions would be good. But we know for a fact that some actions are condemned as bad, and others approved of as good. Consequently, if actions are termed good or bad, "it is only because of their effects." The examples by which Bentham in the same chapter illustrates his theory leave little doubt as to his meaning, and could in fact justify us in concluding on the principles of his theory that all actions, whether their consequences are foreseen or not, are according to the external effects they produce either good or bad. Bentham's doctrine, therefore, may be summed up in these propositions: 1. Motive is of its nature always good; 2. The elicit act is in itself always good; 3. Between motive, or why one acts, and intention, or what one means to do or does, there is no moral connection; 4. The morality of an overt act lies wholly in the consequences in which it issues.

BENTHAM'S EXPLANATION. Admitting this theory, we cannot with propriety predicate moral badness of any man. The motive of Judas' action in betraying Christ was good; Nero in persecuting the Christians acted from a motive that was in itself good. Their actions were vicious undoubtedly but only because of their consequences, since "vice may be defined to be a miscalculation of chances, a mistake in estimating the value of pleasure or pains." [5] Yet Bentham, it may be objected, concedes that a man "can be termed good or bad, when on such or such an occasion he suffers himself to be governed by such and such motives." [6] His explanation, however, deprives his concession of any value. That quality in a man by reason of which he may be termed good or bad is his disposition. But his disposition is good or bad according to the intentions it is apt to form and the effects it is apt to produce. [7]

Again he admits that "the causes of intentions are motives." "If on any occasion," he says, "a man forms either a good or a bad intention, it must be by the influence of some motive." [8] Now this admission is either an abandonment of his whole system, or the influence here attributed to motive is purely physical and we shall be compelled to admit, as he says elsewhere, that "from one and the same motive, and from every kind of motive may proceed actions that are good, others that are bad, and others that are indifferent." Furthermore, Bentham confounds the criteria of morality or the standards by which we can determine whether a particular act is objectively good or bad, and morality itself, i.e., the attribute of an agent because of which he is formally worthy of praise or blame. The former are the end of the action or the consequences in which it naturally results, and the end of the agent or that which he aims to achieve. (These do, as we shall see, determine the morality of the act.)

Finally, Utilitarians give to the word "motive" a meaning by which it is wholly dissociated from intention. Motive they conceive to be a feeling or an affective movement of consciousness, the generic aspect of which is an impulse to pleasure or an aversion from pain. Intention is of the intellect and will, namely the end foreseen as desirable and then attempted. It may be conceded to them that the generic impulse to pleasure is interpretatively good, though in the concrete it may be actually evil. But it must be denied that this impulse is a motive until it is actuated by the apprehension of a particular pleasure. When so actuated it is an individual end foreseen as pleasurable, and differs from what they call intention only as the apprehended end moving and the apprehended end aimed at.

MILL'S THEORY. J. S. Mill is not so straightforward as Bentham. There is necessarily a certain degree of incoherency in Mill's Utilitarianism because of the Stoic element with which he attempted to hybridize its Hedonism. He is however equally emphatic in asserting that "Utilitarian moralists have gone beyond almost all others in declaring that the motive has nothing to do with the morality of an action, though much to do with the worth of the agent."[9] Again he says:[10]

There is no point which Utilitarian thinkers (and Bentham pre-eminently) have taken more pains to illustrate than this. The morality of an action depends entirely upon the intention—that is, upon what the agent *wills to do*. But the motive, that is the feeling that makes him will so to do, when it makes no difference in the act, makes none in the morality, though it makes a great difference in our moral estimation of the agent, especially if it indicates a good or bad habitual disposition—a bent of character from which useful or from which hurtful actions are likely to arise.

Now if motive can make a difference in the morality of the act, as Mill implicitly admits, how can it be said that it has *nothing to do* with the morality, or that the morality depends *entirely* on the intention, understanding by intention the overt act when willed by the agent? And again, if the motive can make a great difference in our moral estimation of the agent, though it makes none in the morality of the action, motive itself, it would seem, may be the immediate subject of morality. The apparent contradiction may be partially removed, if we bear in mind that Mill assigns two distinct subjects which may receive the predicate good or evil, namely (a) "intentional" acts, and (b) habitual disposition; yet judges the moral worth of the latter from the likelihood of its relation to the former. The "intentional" act derives its morality from the effects it produces; and habitual disposition, from which motive (in Mill's sense) springs, merits our moral approbation or disapprobation, in proportion as it is likely to issue in intentional acts productive of happiness or unhappiness. In every case, therefore, the morality lies in the outer effect produced. The whole trend of his *Essay on Utilitarianism* confirms this conclusion, and shows that he is at one with Bentham in maintaining that the overt act is primarily and directly the object of our moral judgments.

KANT'S THEORY. Kant goes to the other extreme. "In order that an action be morally good," he says, "it is not enough that it conform to the moral law, but it must also be done for the sake of the moral law." [11] Now if the meaning of this and similar passages is that volition as immediately proceeding from the will can be conformed to the moral law and at the same time not be done for the sake of the moral law, Kant egregiously fails to show it, even though we should admit his narrow conception of the moral law. For the internal act of the will that is conformed to the moral law, is necessarily elicited for the sake of the moral law. One may, it is true, will an imperate or an overt action, which in fact is in accord with the moral law, and yet not done for the sake of that law, but from a motive that is in disaccord with it. But in this case neither is the elicit act conformed to the law. For instances, a tradesman, to take the first of Kant's illustrations, may deal honestly with his customers solely from a motive of commercial prudence, and accordingly his outer act would be conformed to the moral law; while his inner act, granting that Kant's norm of morality is the true one, would be elicited from a wrong motive, and therefore would neither be done for the sake of the moral law, nor be conformed to it. The only legitimate conclusion that can be drawn from the examples[12] by which Kant tries to conciliate assent to his doctrine that the morality of volition is independent of what the will performs or effects, or of the aptness of its act for the attainment of some proposed end, amounts to the obvious truth, that one may do what is good for a motive that is evil, or in other words that the end of an action may be morally perverted by the further end of the agent.

But Kant seems to go further. He is sometimes understood to deny unqualifiedly that moral goodness consists in a relation. He does in fact maintain that a good will must be out of all relation to any object of inclination or desire, or any law unidentified with itself. "Freedom," he says, "is the *ratio essendi* of the moral law . . . were there no freedom it would be *impossible to trace* the moral law in ourselves at all." [13] Freedom, however, in Kant's sense, is immunity of the will from any determination by causes extrinsic to it. Moral goodness, therefore, in this system is incompatible with any

relation of the volitional act to an extrinsic norm, whether that norm
be happiness, an authority distinct from rational will, or a perfection or state of well-being conceived of as an object of attainment.

Nevertheless, he cannot exclude all relation from his concept of
morality. He distinguishes between the rational will (*Wille*) and
the elective will (*Willkür—arbitrium*). The latter is the appetitive
faculty in relation to action, or inasmuch as it is combined with
the consciousness of power to produce action. "Rational will is the
appetitive faculty not (like the elective will) in relation to action
but rather in relation to what determines the elective will (*Willkür*) to the action; and it has properly itself no determining
ground." Rational will, Kant says, is not for this reason lawless.
It is subject to immutable laws, otherwise it would be absurd. It is
the property of the will to be a law to itself. As it is identical with
practical reason the law is the principle of contradiction as applied
to volitional activity. That is to say, by the law of practical reason
one should act only from such subjective principles (maxims) as
may be universally applied without involving practical contradiction.[14] "Insofar as it can determine the elective will it is practical
reason itself."[15] Assuming this dualism of will, action is immoral
when it is determined by relation to any object independent of the
rational will; and it is moral when it is conformed to the law of
pure practical reason. This law in its last analysis is without content,
and is simply the rational necessity of universal self-consistency in
volitional activity:

Pure practical reason "is not provided with the matter of the law;
there is nothing which it can make the supreme law and determining
ground of the elective will except the form, consisting in the fitness of
the maxim of the elective will to be a universal law."[16]

Morality of action, therefore, consists in a relation of agreement
or disagreement with the principle of contradiction as applicable
in the world of volitional activity.[17]

SELF-REGARDING ACTS. In the history of ethical vagaries two
extreme positions are on record regarding the subject-matter of
morality. The first places the regulative principle of conduct in the
good of self; to this, social well-being must on rational grounds recognize its subjection. Morality, therefore, is concerned with self-
regarding action, and with other-regarding action only insofar as
they further the interests of self. The doctrine of this school finds

expression mainly in Egoistic Hedonism. Hobbes is usually accredited to this school and regarded as its modern originator; and undoubtedly he attempts to resolve all virtue into a principle of self-love. But with Hobbes consistency is a jewel, in that he thought it too rare and precious for ordinary wear. In the *Leviathan* he says: [18]

> Moral philosophy is nothing else but the science of what is good and evil *in the conversation and society of mankind.* [Italics mine.] Good and evil are names that signify our appetites and aversions which in different tempers, customs, and doctrines of men are different . . . from which arise disputes, controversies and at last wars. And therefore as long as man is in a condition of mere nature (which is a condition of war) his private appetite is the measure of good and evil.

But when man has succeeded in getting out of a condition of mere nature—which he must do, if he and his fellow men are not to become the victims of egoistic morality—the civil laws are

> the rules of good and evil, just and unjust, honest and dishonest. . . . Legitimate kings, therefore, make the things they command just by commanding them, and those they forbid unjust by forbidding them. [19]

J. S. Mill in his *Dissertations,*[20] describes Bentham's moral outlook:

> Bentham's idea of the world is that of a collection of persons pursuing each his separate interests or pleasures, and the prevention of whom from jostling one another more than is avoidable may be attempted by hopes and fears derived from three sources—the law, religion, and public opinion.

Hobbes and Bentham are generally regarded as the typical exponents of this theory; to which the name of Egoistic Utilitarianism has been given. Other prominent advocates of it are Locke (1632-1704) in *Essay on the Understanding,* Bk. II, Ch. 21 and Ch. 28; Helvetius (1715-1771), *De l'Ésprit;* James Mill (1783-1836) *Analysis of the Human Mind,* and *A Fragment on Mackintosh.*

OTHER-REGARDING ACTS. The other doctrine places the subject-matter of morality in social well-being, and restricts morality to other-regarding actions, or at least universally subordinates to them self-regarding actions, so that these latter have moral worth only insofar as they contribute to the former. The first of these ethical views has gradually lost caste, but the second is becoming almost habitual in the moral estimates of the present day. Both are extreme and partial interpretations of the fundamental fact of Ethics. We do pass a moral judgment on our conduct, whether its direct term be self or others. We may in the utmost privacy perform an action which is of no benefit or harm to any human being but ourselves—except in the indefinite sense that all our personal conduct does ultimately and indirectly affect others—and yet be vividly conscious of having done right or wrong. As, on the other hand, if our conduct have an exclusively social bearing we approve or reprobate it morally, independently of any advantage or utility gained or sacrificed by us. Again, since the primitive impulses by which our nature is adjusted to the purposes of its creation are both egoistic and altruistic, morality cannot be based on the preponderance of either over the other. Unity of nature cannot be had by the suppression of one in favor of the other; if the nature is to be kept intact they must be harmonized by an objective regulative principle, which determines the scope of each, and in particular cases of apparent conflict the prevalence of one over the other. To assume that they cannot be harmonized is to assume that nature is unbalanced and irrational. A morality based on such an assumption merits the predicates of the assumption itself.

The theory that confines morality to other-regarding actions, received its systematic setting from Auguste Comte (1798-1857), who coined as a designation of it the term "Altruism."[21] His theory may be briefly summed up in the following propositions:

1. The functions of life are three, the affective, speculative, and active, belonging respectively to heart, intellect, and character.

2. Of these the affections, or the feelings prompting us to action, constitute the preponderating element of human nature, giving it unity, and standing out as the essential center of moral existence. They precede both intellect and activity, and unlike them are never intermittent.

3. Affective life which governs and harmonizes the whole of existence falls into two principal divisions: personal and social.

4. Between these two there is a permanent antagonism, and there cannot be a perfect balance. Equilibrium of the whole is possible only by one of the two gaining the preponderance.

5. The essential condition of individual and social worth and happiness is the adequate ascendency of the altruistic sympathies.

6. The first principle of morality, therefore, is the subjective supremacy of the social over the personal affections, and the expression, "Live for others," is the summary of the whole moral code.

CRITICISM OF THEORY. The theory is disproved first by the arguments already adduced against making the affections superior to reason as the regulative principle of morality; and secondly, because as just shown it does not interpret the fundamental fact of Ethics, and disrupts the unity of human nature and re-establishes a unity that is external and artificial.

As elaborated by Comte it is open to further objections. It is founded on a biological theory and a theory of localized cerebral functions which have no scientific standing. By assuming such a theory as a basis of Ethics the distinction between the moral and the unmoral is destroyed, since the sympathetic instincts are both wider and narrower than duty. As functions of brain organs they are found in brute animals, and as found in man are not coextensive with moral judgments. Lastly, conceding as he does that the egoistic impulses are more energetic and universal than the altruistic impulses no reason can be found within the limits of his system for giving ascendency and moral supremacy to the latter.[22]

The philosophy of Comte was introduced to English students in 1853 by George H. Lewis[23] and has exercised a notable influence on subsequent ethical speculation. J. S. Mill attempted to ingraft Altruism on the Hedonism of Bentham. The result was, as we shall see, Altruistic Utilitarianism.

Modern socialists have appropriated the altruistic theory and applied it to their materialistic concept of man's destiny and their principle of class consciousness. They place outside the sphere of morality all self-regarding actions. "Personal morality is a contradiction in terms"[24] and judgments declaring them good or bad are esthetic not ethical.[25] In like manner morality based on the relation of man to God is disavowed: "What we have to do on behalf of the ethics of the social-democratic State is to separate them from precepts enjoining duty to God."[26] Social conduct alone, they hold, is within the province of Ethics. Hillquitt says:[27]

To be ethical or unethical[28] human actions must have some bearings on beings other than the actor himself; they must be tested by their social effects. . . . Ethics remains indifferent to the conduct of the individual towards himself, as long as that conduct does not directly or indirectly affect the well-being of his fellow men or the human race.

Similar quotations from other socialistic authorities could be multiplied.[29] According to the tenets of some of the leading exponents of Socialism, Altruistic Ethics is further restricted by the principle of class consciousness. That is to say, not all other-regarding actions lie within the boundaries of morality, but only those that regard the members of the socialistic organization, or that regard others insofar as they are of advantage in promoting the aims of Socialism.

NOTES

1. Mandeville, *The Fable of the Bees,* 1714.
2. "Actus humanus in quantum est actus nondum habet rationem boni vel mali moralis nisi aliquid addatur ad speciem contrahens." *De Malo,* qu. 2, a. 4.
3. One regrettable source of confusion in modern philosophic English is want of precision in the use of allied words like action and act, relation and relative, intention and intent.
4. *Principles of Morals and Legislation,* Ch. X, §2. This work, which was published after the author's death and by Sir J. Bowring, may be, as James Martineau says, a less authentic treatise and possibly tinctured by the rhetorical manner of its editor, yet probably exhibits not unfairly the outpourings of Bentham's unguarded moments.
5. *Deontology,* Vol. I, p. 131.
6. *Principles of Morals and Legislation,* Ch. II, §1.
7. *Ibid.,* Ch. XI, §3.
8. *Ibid.,* §18.
9. *Utilitarianism,* Ch. II.
10. *Utilitarianism,* Ch. II, note.
11. Kant's *Ethics,* translated by Abbott, pp. 5ff.
12. *Ibid.,* pp. 13, 14, 15.
13. *Ibid.,* p. 88, note.
14. *Ethics,* Abbott's transl., pp. 65, 66.
15. *Ibid.,* p. 268.
16. *Ibid.,* pp. 2ff.
17. Illustrations of the applications of the principle may be found in Kant's *Ethics,* pp. 18, 39-42.
18. Pt. I, Ch. XV.
19. *Philosophical Rudiments,* Ch. 12, n. 1.
20. Vol. I, p. 361.
21. *A System of Positive Polity;* see especially Ch. 3. That the norm of morality is benevolence or sympathy for others is of course not original with Comte. A predominantly altruistic coloring is given to morality by Cumberland (1632-1718) in his work *De Legibus Naturae,* written against Hobbes' egoistic interpretation of morality; by the early

Affective Intuitionists Shaftesbury and Hutcheson, and by others, even of hedonistic schools.

22. See Caird's *Philosophy of Comte*, Ch. IV.

23. *Comte's Philosophy of the Sciences.*

24. Ladoff in the *International Social Review*, February, 1905, p. 449.

25. Bax, *Ethics of Socialism*, p. 126.

26. Leatham, *Socialism and Character*, p. 43.

27. *Socialism in Theory and Practice*, pp. 37, 38.

28. He means "moral or immoral." This inexact use of the term "unethical" is not infrequent with socialistic and evolutionary moralists.

29. See *Socialism, The Nation of Fatherless Children*, by Goldstein and Avery, and *The Morality of Modern Socialism*, by Ming.

CHAPTER VI

The End

The end of man is known from the final tendency of his nature as exhibited by his rational appetitive faculty.

The first of the three elements contained in the concept which is expressed by the word "ought" is THE END. *Regarding this, four questions may arise:* 1. *How can we know the end of man?* 2. *What is the ultimate end of man realizable by his volitional activity?* 3. *What is the object through the possession of which his ultimate end is realized?* 4. *What are the specific activities of man by which this object is possessed?*

MEANING OF NATURE. The word "nature" is one of great ambiguity. It is used principally to signify the native constitution or very being of a thing, the material universe, the energy that is intrinsic to matter, a system of related phenomena. Usually modern philosophies restrict its meaning to the world of matter in the sense of something constitutive, dynamic, or phenomenal. In this meaning it excludes from its comprehension the supersensible and spiritual, and consequently puts outside man's nature whatever pertains to, affects, or proceeds from the immaterial principle of his being.

We understand the word in the sense which the Schoolmen have adopted from Aristotle: "Nature is primarily and properly the essence of things which, by reason of what they are, have in themselves a principle of action."[1] Two notions make up the idea of nature according to Aristotle: (a) the essence or constitutents of the being; (b) a principle of activity which is in the things themselves, and belongs to them, because they are such beings. The nature of man, therefore, is his essence or the reality of which his being is constituted, so far as that essence is the radical principle of the activity that is peculiar to him.

MAN'S NATURE. Now we know from psychology, first, that man's essence is composed of two parts, a spiritual soul and a mate-

90

rial body, bound together in substantial unity; that as a nature it is endowed with certain faculties or powers of acting, each of which has a tendency to an appropriate object; and that on due presentation of its appropriate object, each faculty is called into action, and elicits an operation that is proper to itself. Between these three, therefore—faculty, action, and object—there is a correlation; the faculty is adjusted to its object, the object is adapted to the faculty, and the action of the faculty is fitted to bring about the union of the object and faculty. That is to say, the faculty by its enacted tendency towards its object receives its complementary perfection, and, in being actuated, reaches its object. We know, secondly, that since the nature in which these faculties are radicated, from which they emanate, and of which they are specific capacities and powers, is one in being, its unitary character entails the co-ordination of its different tendencies and their subordination to a principal tendency, which, like the resultant of many forces, indicates the tendency of the whole nature.

There is, however, with regard to human nature a special difficulty which does not obtain for natures composed of homogeneous parts and acting through physical necessity.

The tendencies of man's nature are not only many and complex, but because of his composite being they are proximately directed to terms of essentially diverse, and it may be of conflicting, character. When St. Paul says: "I am delighted with the law of God according to the inward man; but I see another law in my members, fighting against the law of my mind,"[2] he is declaring a psychological fact. Moreover, because of his free will, man may in practice give precedence to one class of tendencies in preference to another. The cravings of the animal compart may clash with, and prove more attractive than the solicitations of the spirit. Anticipation of the pleasurable feelings that accompany the exercise of the sensuous faculties may effectively allure, even when reason discloses their discordance with human nature as such. Again, as man through intellect is capable of viewing certain attributes or aspects of a thing dissociated from others also pertaining to it, the abstract deliverances of reason may defectively express the tendency of the unitary nature and disagree with the equally important indications of that nature's tendency as revealed in its emotional instincts.

It must be conceded, then, that the final tendency of human nature is not the *resultant* of many tendencies that coalesce in a

homogeneous system. Nevertheless, however numerous and disparate the tendencies of man's nature may be, they are not independent
and unrelated. They must, when in action, have mutual bearings
and reciprocal adjustments, driven to act now by one impulse, now
by another, now by a resultant of many. If the unity of his nature
is to be preserved in conduct, the different tendencies of his faculties
should be co-ordinated in accordance with their respective values
and subordinated to a supreme tendency, to which they are subsidiary or to whose control they are either directly or indirectly subject. This supreme tendency, therefore, exhibits the tendency of the
man's nature as such, gives worth to his actions and unity to his
character.

TENDENCY AND END. The supreme or dominant tendency of a
nature cannot be objectively indeterminate or indefinite in scope.
It must necessarily direct to an appropriate term which specifies it,
and defines its aim and goal. All activity and growth, whether
physical, intellectual, or moral, must have a limit beyond which it
cannot go. The very concept of a finite nature, which is a specific
essence with capacities and functions that are peculiar to itself,
defines not only its range but also its reach. The purpose of its
existence, then, must be to do the work that it has the power of
doing. When this is fully done, the nature has been brought to that
final relative perfection for which its faculties fit it and which is
distinctive of it. Between the tendency of a nature, therefore, and
its final perfection there exists the relation of design to purpose.
Now we may distinguish between the *end of the action,* and the
end of the agent, or between the result in which an action of its
nature terminates, and the purpose which the action is made to
subserve by the free will of the agent. These two ends may be
identified, that is to say, the rational agent may desire nothing but
what is the natural result of his action; or with regard to defectible
wills they may be distinct and even incongruous, that is to say, the
agent may arbitrarily direct his action to an end between which
and the natural result of his action there is no intrinsic connection,
or there may be discordance. The end we are concerned with in the
proposition is the end of the action, or that natural result which
in the design of the Author of nature is the purpose of man's activity
as revealed by his specific tendency.

SUPREME TENDENCY AND WILL. In man, because of his composite nature four grades of being are found united in one: the an-

organic, vegetal, animal and rational. It is quite clear that these are so related that the lower are auxiliary to and subservient to the higher. We may, in fact, dismiss from consideration the anorganic and vegetal forces since they are merged into the animal life, and are of physical necessity subordinated to it. Hence only two main classes of tendencies need be examined, those, namely, that are proper to the sensuous and those that are proper to the rational life. Now the faculties that perform the functions of these two lives and their respective tendencies may be classed under two general heads: the apprehensive or cognitive faculties and tendencies, and the appetitive or conative. We know from psychology[3] that the object of a faculty, on being rightly presented, rouses the mind to some sort of activity; that, in other words, the tendency of the mind which was potential becomes actuated and that the mind thereby takes on a relation to the object which did not exist before. By every mental act there is established between the mind acting and the object of the act a relation, the ground of which is in the mind itself. But this relation is constituted either by an act that is receptive, by which namely the object is vicariously brought into consciousness, or by an act that is subsequent to the psychical presence of the object in consciousness and is active in its attitude towards it. By an act of the first kind a mental image of the object is produced through which the mind knows the object; by an act of the second kind the mind responds through liking or desire to the attractive aspects of the object as known. The apprehensive faculties, therefore (*ad—prehendere*) are those by which the mind receives the object within itself through a psychical image and there re-presents it; and the appetitive faculties (*ad—petere*) are those by which the mind reaches out for the object as known through its mental representation. The tendency of the apprehensive faculties is directed to knowledge of the object, of the appetitive faculties to possession of the object known.[4] As found in the same nature they are mutually adjusted, so that apprehension is the condition and measure of appetency, and appetency the completion and *ratio essendi* of apprehension.[5] By the first we know, by the second we do. The final tendency of the nature, therefore, is found in its appetitive tendency.

APPETENCIES IN MAN. Now in man there are two classes of appetencies, the lower or sensuous, which he possesses in common with the brute creation, and the higher or rational which is peculiar

to him. But in the unitary nature of man it is the higher that subordinates the lower. As St. Thomas says, although it is natural for
the sensuous appetence to seek what is pleasant or agreeable to the
senses, it is not natural to man, as man, to do so in abstraction from
his rational appetence. On the contrary he does not act as a man,
but as an animal when he yields to his sensuous appetites without
regard to the exigencies of his rational nature.[6] The rational appetitive faculty, therefore, exhibits the final tendency of human nature.

In what sense this conclusion is to be understood will be made
clearer by again quoting from St. Thomas. He tells us that in every
appetible object we may consider (a) the thing itself that is the
object of appetence, and (b) the ground of its appetibility, as for
instance the study of Ethics and the profit, satisfaction, or pleasure
derivable therefrom. Now the will or *rational* appetitive faculty
tends directly to the ground itself of appetibility; its seeks primarily
and principally the good, the satisfying, or the pleasant; and secondarily this or the other object, but solely insofar as it is apprehended to embody to some extent the common ground of appetibility. The lower or *sensitive* appetite tends concretely to the appetible
object which is presented to it by sense cognition. Its primary object
is not the satisfying or the pleasant, but this individual object, which
is apprehended to be satisfying or pleasant. The extent of its tendency is circumscribed by the scope of the sensuous faculty that
proposes its object.

On the other hand, the will's tendency is as universal as the
intellect's capacity to know. In whatsoever object the intellect can
perceive the ground of appetibility, to that the will has a natural
tendency.[7] The adequate and appropriate object and end of the
will's tendency, therefore, is that common and comprehensive
ground of appetibility—the *ratio boni,* as St. Thomas calls it—
which the intellect can apprehend; and only in an object in which
the whole ground of appetibility is present will the rational appetence find complete and perfect satisfaction. The rational appetitive
faculty, therefore, exhibits the final tendency of man's nature inasmuch as in each and every elicit act, while freely moved by the
desirability of a particular object, it is necessarily moved by an
innate appetence towards a common and comprehensive ground
of appetibility.

NOTES

1. *Metaph.*, 1015, 6.
2. *Rom.* 7:22.
3. Maher's *Psychology*, Introd., Ch. III.
4. St. Thomas, *De Ver.*, qu. 22, a. 10, says: "Dicitur aliquid esse objectum animae secundum quod habet aliquam habitudinem ad animam. . . . Res autem ad animam invenitur duplicem habitudinem habere: unam secundum quod ipsa res est in anima per modum animae, et non per modum sui; aliam secundum quod anima comparatur ad rem in sua esse existentem. Et sic objectum animae est aliquid dupliciter. Uno modo in quantum natum est esse in anima non secundum esse proprium, sed secundum modum animae, id est spiritualiter; est haec est ratio cognoscibilis, in quantum est cognoscibile. Alio modo est aliquod objectum animae secundum quod ad ipsum anima inclinatur, et ordinatur secundum modum ipsius rei in seipsa existentis; et haec est ratio rei appetibilis, in quantum est appetibilis."
5. *2 Dist.* 39, qu. 1, a. 2.
6. *2 Dist.* 30, qu. 1, a. 1, ad 4: "Quandocumque multa conveniunt ad constitutionem alicuius, alicui eorum potest aliquid secundum se convenire naturaliter secundum *naturam propriam,* et aliquid convenit sibi secundum *naturam* totius. . . . Secundum hoc ergo dico, quod vis concupiscibilis naturale habet hoc, ut in delectabile secundum sensum tendat, sed secundum quod est vis concupiscibilis humana, habet ulterius ut tendat in suum objectum secundum regimen rationis; et ideo quod in suum objectum tendat irrefrenate, hoc *non est naturale sibi in quantum est humana,* sed magis contra naturam ejus in quantum hujusmodi."
7. *De Ver.*, qu. 25, a. 1.

CHAPTER VII

BLESSEDNESS

The absolutely ultimate intrinsic end of man's volitional activity is blessedness or the final perfection of his rational nature with the happiness consequent thereupon.

THE END. In its primary meaning, end signifies the terminal part of a material body. Thence by an easy analogy it came successively to designate: (a) the close and natural outcome of any continued operation or series of actions; (b) the result of conative activities which before achievement is in some manner foreknown by the agent, and which on achievement leaves the conative faculty relatively at rest; (c) the mental representation of this result as desirable, and as such inducing to action which may lead to its realization. In this last sense the end is a final cause, the immediate effect of which is to move the appetitive faculty to action. It may be defined as that on account of, or for the sake of which anything is done; and may be looked at from two points of view: first, as the *motive,* or that which induces to action; secondly, as the *purpose* or the object or state which the action is intended to attain or effect. The former is first in intention, directs the agent's action, and rules in subordination to itself intermediate intentions and actions; the latter is last in execution, that namely which is the outcome and close of the successive operations originated by motive. Motive and purpose are, of course, correlative for created wills; yet it should be noted that the actual motive of a created agent may be out of relation with the purpose in which nature, or rather the Author of nature, intended the action to issue. That is to say, the present explicit motive for acting may in defectible wills intend a result which differs from that to which the action of its nature tends. Our proposition regards the absolutely last intrinsic purpose of man's volitional activity, designed by the Author of his nature and manifested in the tendencies of that same nature.

DIVISION OF ENDS. As an end is that on account of or for the sake of which anything is done, every object is an end which is *in itself* desirable, and the reason why other objects are chosen and used as means. But it is clear that some things may be desirable in themselves, and at the same time be a means to a more desirable object. Hence we distinguish *proximate, remote* and *last* ends, according as the desirable object is the immediate, intermediate or ultimate term of volition. Furthermore, an end may be last within a certain province or sphere of activity, or *relatively* last, or last for the whole unconditioned range of volitional activity, or *absolutely last*. There may be as many relatively last ends as there are departments of human activity in which a special object is sought. But there can be but one absolutely last end, which must be the same for all men. We do not assert that the ultimately last end is necessarily simple. It may be complex, composed of many elements, but it must be a single whole. The very concept of an absolutely last end as the correlative of the final tendencies of a unitary nature compels us to admit that there can be but one object which fills the measure of its capacity and in the possession of which all appetitive tendencies are completely satisfied and rest. To this all other ends must necessarily be subordinated and from their relation to it they must receive their worth.

Another distinction which obtains in this matter is that which exists between the *intrinsic* end of a nature and its *extrinsic* end. The former is an end realized within the nature itself through the attainment of the fullest development and perfection for which its faculties fitted it, and towards which consequently its appetencies directed it. The latter is an end outside of the nature, to which its final state of perfection is ordained by the Author of the nature. These two ends are of course intimately related, so that a nature realizing its intrinsic end fulfils its extrinsic end, and can promote its extrinsic end only insofar as it furthers its intrinsic end. An intrinsic end of a plant, for instance, is to bear seed; its extrinsic end is the use which in the economy of creation its seed was designed to serve. Now it is proved in natural theology, and we assume it as a postulate of Ethics,[1] that the formal extrinsic glory of God is the last extrinsic end of man. Ethics is directly concerned with the intrinsic end of man's volitional activity and consequently of man himself. This we assert is blessedness.

BLESSEDNESS. On its subjective side blessedness is the complete satisfaction of the rational desire that expresses the unitary tendency of human nature. The objective ground of this satisfaction includes two elements: (a) supreme and perfect well-being in life and activity, and (b) full and unalloyed happiness. It is inconceivable that it should consist in happiness apart from well-being, or that happiness should be full and unalloyed if well-being were partial or less than capacity demanded, since well-being is the ontological ground of happiness; besides, well-being is itself an object of rational desire. Until obtained, therefore, it would leave rational desire unsatisfied. Nor, on the other hand, can it consist in a well-being which brought no final happiness, for undoubtedly happiness is an object of rational desire, without which there could be neither contentment nor cessation of appetitive tendencies. And in fact no one, either Stoic or hedonist, who admits that man has a last end, denies that it comprehends well-being and happiness, as we shall see later. Their dissensions regard rather the logical priority to be given to one or other of these elements, their connection, or the causal relation existing between them.

Blessedness, therefore, is a state of existence, (a) in which man possesses the full measure of well-being for which he has a capacity and need, or in other words, the final perfection of his rational nature; (b) in which he enjoys an abiding pleasurable consciousness springing from the fact that the supreme tendencies of his nature energize in the full possession of their objects, or in other words, final happiness. And as a corrollary of these attributes, it should be stable and unending. For it could be subject to change only on one of two suppositions, namely: (a) that the capacity of human nature for well-being and happiness was indefinite, or could be continuously and progressively enlarged; (b) that the capacity of human nature having once been sated, it might thereafter diminish. But in the first case there would be no last end, and consequently no goal that could determine the direction of man's moral development; in the other case, having a degree of possession adequately responding to the capacity of the nature, that possession could lessen and decline only through a change in the nature itself. Neither could it be terminable, because, as St. Thomas argues, desire naturally follows cognition.[2] But the intellect unlike the senses apprehends being unlimited in duration. The rational appetite, therefore, seeks permanence in blessedness. In fact, if the state of blessedness were transitory and impermanent, the blessed would either be aware of it, or be in doubt regarding it, or be ignorant of it. But the knowledge that they were going to lose what they have, that their state, however satisfactory, was fleeting, would embitter present possession; the fear that they may lose it would arouse constant anxiety as to the future; and ignorance as to whether they would or would not lose it would make error an essential element of their final happiness.

KNOWLEDGE OF FINAL END. The absolutely last intrinsic end of man's volitional activity is known, (a) from the innate tendency of the will to its adequate and appropriate object, since this is, as it were, the essential gravitation of the faculty towards that for which it has capacity and need, and which reciprocally responds adequately to the one, and fully satisfies the other; (b) from the elicit acts of the will which are actuations of its innate appetence through knowledge of the desirability of particular objects. In the first place, the intrinsic object or state that responds to the innate appetence of the will must be one in which the full ground of appetibility is realized and consequently as comprehensive as the will's faculty of rational desire. This can be nothing else than complete well-being or final perfection and the happiness consequent thereupon. In the second place the elicit appetence is only the innate appetence in act, particularized by the individual object presented to it. This individual object may or may not be exhaustive of the natural appetence; it may be one in which the ground of appetibility is only partially found or in which it is fully found. Now the formal element in every desire, *qua* desire, is the natural inclination of the will towards an object that shall be repletive of its innate tendency, just as the formal element—making due allowance for the defects of the comparison—in the attraction, whether chemical, magnetic or molar, exercised by one substance over the other, is the specific power of the attracting substance; or borrowing a metaphor from the physical sciences, we may say that the will in all its acts seeks saturation by its object. In every actual volition, therefore, the fulness of well-being and happiness is either explicitly or implicitly sought. This is confirmed by the experience of our inner life. We may be indefatigable in our pursuit of fortune, pleasure, honors, yet no attainment or possession brings surcease of desire. All of us, in fact, are occupied with some interest, whether trivial or important, yet no measure of success brings permanent content. On the contrary, we are conscious that the satisfaction sought generally loomed larger in anticipation than it proved on realization, or that even if it met our expectations, it was always followed by a new desire urging us to further activity. It is a commonplace of secular and spiritual literature, that man "never is, but always to be blest"; that "we have not here a lasting city, but seek one that is to come"; that only in the final perfection of our rational nature will the innate appetency of the will cease and give place to happiness.

LAST END REALIZABLE. That the ultimate end or purpose of any being's existence must be realizable in some manner and in some mode of duration might seem so obvious as scarcely to need proof. So far, however, as man is concerned it has been denied by philosophers of note. It cannot be proved *a posteriori*. If our knowledge of man is confined to the experience of this life, we may grant that we cannot find in it what it does not contain—anything that can give him his ultimate intrinsic perfection; and we may admit that Taylor's[3] alternative way of putting the question is valid:

Make your account of the ethical ideal which you propose for realization within your own experience and that of your immediate circle adequate, and you will find that your ideal has *ipso facto* become unrealizable under the given conditions; content yourself with a statement of what is realizable, and you will find that, as an account of an ideal, it is most deplorably low and inadequate.

Now as a matter of fact, mankind never has and cannot content itself with the second alternative. History and language testify that it never has contented itself with a "deplorably low and inadequate" ethical ideal. The science of Ethics itself is proof that an adequate ethical ideal is ineradicable from the human mind. The only practical question is, whether the ethical ideal of an ultimate state of final well-being and happiness is attainable, or whether it is an illusory phantasm, mendaciously luring us towards a goal that is inaccessible, and tantalizing us unto reaching out for what is eternally in advance of attainment.

Now it is an indispensable condition of our knowing and doing that we believe the world to be a rational system. It is moreover a necessary consequence of the cosmological postulate. Convince us that the universe is incoherent and not governed by law, and life, philosophy, and science become rambling and muddled dreams. The first law of a rational system is that it should be teleological insofar as its parts have a purpose, and insofar as between their powers and purpose there is a mutual relevancy and consonance. In the vegetal and animal world we find that between organ and function and between function and purpose there is correlation. Keeping within the proportion of analogy, these principles are applicable to the higher faculties of intellect and will. If these have capacities which transcend their purpose, then man, the highest visible being of the universe, is an unproportioned extravagance, his distinctive faculties aimless and his existence a useless torture. But this conclusion would be valid, if the last intrinsic end of man were unattainable. He is a self-conscious being, and therefore capable of rational self-love. He is a moral being, and therefore conscious of obligatory ideals of holiness, justice, and charity. Between this sense of duty and the rational love of self there must be an ultimate adjustment and harmony. This can be had only in the realization of his final perfection and happiness.[4]

Nor can the rationality of man's capacities and powers in the scheme of things be served by assigning him an ultimate extrinsic end, which may be attained though his ultimate intrinsic end is frustrated. To endow him with cravings, needs and capacities in order that he might be a mere means for realizing the good of humanity, the state, the absolute spirit, or other abstraction, would be to make a fool of him and an analogy of the system of which he is a part. Lastly, if men could be intimately convinced and persuaded that this was their office in life, that there was no correlation between rational love of self and their moral impulses, they would, except perhaps in cases of fanatic heroism, treat these latter as embarrassing conditions of existence to be tolerated, evaded or overcome, as are physical or social inconveniences. The practical tendency, therefore, of any theory which denies the possibility of man attaining an ultimate intrinsic end is destructive of morality.

The argument is strengthened by invoking the truth of the cosmological postulate. The wisdom, holiness, and justice of the Creator has "ordered all things in measure, and number and weight." [5] But the Divine Wisdom would be impugned by maintaining that the Creator implanted in our rational nature an essential and insuperable tendency towards a goal that could never be reached. Disproportion between power and purpose in the works of man marks a want of intelligence and foresight. We cannot admit the possibility of this in the works of the Creator. Again Divine Veracity would belie Itself, if the promise which the essential tendency of our nature expresses were false. For if the essential tendency of our nature were a radical source of deception to us, such deception should ultimately be traced to the Author of Nature. Finally the Divine Goodness would defeat Its own purpose, if Its highest visible creature should be rendered more wretched than the brute by those qualities through which he excels them.

PURSUIT THEORY. That the ultimate intrinsic end of man is not a term of attainment but of pursuit, is a theory that has found a place in widely different schools of Ethics.[6] Hobbes, a hedonist, holds that felicity does not consist "in the repose of the mind satisfied; but in a continual progress of the desire from one object to another; the attaining of the former being still but a way to the latter."[7] Kant, a Stoic, almost repeats the assertion of Hobbes, substituting moral perfection, for hedonistic desire: "For a rational but finite being," he says, "the only thing possible is an endless progress from the lower to the higher degrees of moral perfection."[8] The difference between them is, that Kant postulates immortality as a condition of indefinite advance in moral perfection or toward holiness; while the hedonists as a class make the ultimate end of man consist in a temporal existence "exempt as far as possible from pain, and as rich as possible in enjoyments," or practically concede that the individual man in the present stage of evolution cannot realize his end.[9]

There are certain presumptions which may be alleged in favor of these positions. For the hedonist it may be said that blessedness cannot consist in rest, as our doctrine would seem to imply, but in activity; that therefore the pursuit of the objects of desire must be a component of happiness. The pleasure of pursuit may be described with Spencer as a successively renewed consciousness of personal efficiency made vivid by actual successes and partially excited by impending successes.[10] Our doctrine is, first, that blessedness does not consist in inaction, but in cessation from conative tendency. Conation denotes only a phase of the will's activity, namely, its effort (*conatus*) to do or get something. The joy and delight of the will in the possession, union with and dilection of the object that was sought through conation may entail an inner activity which exceeds in intensity and perfection any activity of pursuit. Outward activity is always an index of interior want; inward activity the exponent of an inner grade of perfection. The former is a process towards the attainment of an end and is incompatible with the attainment itself; the latter is the highest and completive activity of the will.[11] Secondly, it may be doubted whether pursuit, as such, is pleasurable. Certainly no argument adduced by any school of Hedonism proves it so. Apart from the anticipated or imagined satisfaction of the desire that impelled to pursuit, it seems to be neutral. The pleasure that accompanies it in mundane experience arises either from progressive attainment[12] or the expectation of it, or the consciousness of skill or efficiency.[13] Our experience in this life shows, it is true, that in striving we frequently find satisfaction, and disappointment on attainment. But this is explained, first from the subjective fact that an object of desire is presented by reason in an alluring light, and when obtained is discovered to be less desirable than imagination pictured it; and secondly by the objective fact, which we shall presently prove, that no finite object can give complete content of will.

Kant's position might be understood in one of two intelligible ways: either man is indefinitely capable of moral growth, and consequently no limit can be assigned to the perfection which he may acquire; or there is a limit, but it is an ideal term of perfection which it is impossible to reach, though approach to it be continuous and unceasing. What Kant does in effect is to modify one of these interpretations by the other. He holds that man's final perfection is the totality of endless progress to absolute goodness: "Nothing can possibly be conceived . . . which can be called good without qualification except a Good Will."[14] "Absolute goodness is holiness or perfect accordance of the will with the moral law."[15] This perfect accordance is realized only in "a will whose maxims [subjective principles of acting] necessarily coincide with the law of autonomy."[16] The law of autonomy is that man in his volitional acts or the acts of his elective will should be free from, independent of, and unconditioned by any relation of whatever kind to any other being:[17] "The idea of freedom is inseparably connected with the conception of autonomy." If man were a member of the world of understanding only, he asserts, his will would of necessity be pure, that is, conformed to the principle of autonomy; as on the other hand, if he were a part of the world of appearance only, his actions would necessarily be heteronomous, that is, conformed to the natural laws of desires and inclinations.[18] As, however, he is and presumably shall remain throughout the everlasting reaches of existence a dual being of the noumenal and phenomenal order, he may not hope here nor at any imaginable point of his future existence to be perfectly adequate with his rational will. Nevertheless, though this progress be directed to a goal infinitely remote, yet in God's sight to whom the conditions of time are nothing, the endless progress is a whole of accordance with the moral law, and in its totality may be regarded as a possession.[19]

CRITICISM OF THEORY. The presumptions of this theory are many. We shall notice two that directly impugn our proposition. The first is, that man's ultimate intrinsic end or blessedness does not consist in union with an object which will satiate the natural cravings of his highest faculties, but in a subjective condition of self-purity by which he shall finally have put himself out of every relation of dependence on any object of the universe. Granting the presumption, Kant's conclusion that final beatitude is actually attainable follows as a matter of course. The state of Kantian beatitude could be reached only after man has despoiled his nature of its essential attributes. Kant's conclusion therefore is a *reductio ad absurdum* of his premises; no rational being, as long as his intellect retains an innate tendency for the fulness of objective truth, and his will for the fulness of objective good, could find unaltered contentment in a self-centered void. The second presumption is that human nature is divided into two parts which are irreconcilable. This crude dualism pervades Kant's entire system. There is of course an apparent dualism in our nature, familiar to readers of St. Paul, by which the lower is said to war against the higher. But this dualism is not essential, nor is it removed by the extinction, suppression, or ignoring of desire, but by directing it to an end in the possession of which it will be satisfied to the limit of capacity. The Kantian position on the contrary divorces man's rational from his emotional nature, creates a natural and necessary insubordination of one to the other, and renders a unitary end of actual life impossible.

It may be objected that Kant does admit happiness as a consequence of final holiness and as a constituent of the *summum bonum*. A rational being, he concedes, needs happiness, and if he is truly holy deserves it.[20] But the concession seems to be verbal. After rejecting the error of the ancient Epicurean and Stoic schools, which misapplied their acuteness, he says, in trying to trace out identity between "two extremely heterogeneous notions," he proceeds to explain the sense in which happiness is to be taken in order that it be a homogeneous consequence of holiness. Have we not, he asks, a word which does not express enjoyment as happiness does, but indicates a satisfaction in one's existence, an analogue of the happiness which must necessarily accompany the consciousness of virtue? Yes! this word is *self-contentment,* which in its proper signification always designates only a negative satisfaction in one's existence in which one is conscious of needing nothing.[21] This consciousness of needing nothing, arising not from the positive satisfaction to the full of rational desire, but from the negative satisfaction of being free from and independent of desire, must, therefore, be the happiness which "in exact proportion to morality" is acquired by man in his interminable journey to an infinitely distant goal. The fact is that Kant never wholly cast off the influence that Hume exerted over him, and whom he undertook to refute. He admits the latter's phenomenal world, and takes refuge from it in another or noumenal world of his own construction, between which and Hume's world there is no ultimate connection. Happiness, understood as being a pleasurable state springing from the possession of good, is in Kant's system phenomenal; holiness is noumenal. They are therefore "two extremely heterogeneous notions."

NOTES

1. Ch. III.

2. *Com. in Eth. Nich.,* Lib. I, Lect. X; where he explains Aristotle's teaching that blessedness is had only ἐν βίῳ τελείῳ.

3. *The Problem of Conduct,* p. 393.

4. An illustration of the style of reasoning by which this almost obvious truth is obscured, is supplied by Sully, *Pessimism,* p. 167. "If an end is known to be in the nature of things *unattainable,* it is not *disproved;* it still remains the ideal direction for which we should make were the order of things changed, so as to allow of its attainment. Nevertheless it is shown to be *unsuitable* to be the supreme end of action in the existing order of things." An end that is unattainable and therefore unsuitable to be the supreme end of action in the existing order of things is by the very fact disproved for the existing order of things, unless the existing order of things is irrational. It is absurd to assert categorically that "it *still remains* an ideal direction," when its only use would be in an hypothetical order of things. An ideal that may not be actualized in a given order of things is not real for that order of things, but figmental.

5. *Wisdom* 11:21.

6. Dr. Cronin, *Science of Ethics* very appropriately gives the designational *elpistic* (ἐλπιστικός) to theories of this class. Plutarch mentions a sect whom he calls the Elpistics, who made hope the only way of life.

7. *De Homine,* Ch. XI. As for an ultimate end beyond this life Hobbes says: "There is no such *finis ultimus* (utmost aim) nor *summum bonum* (greatest goal) as is spoken of in the books of the old moral philosophers." *Leviathan,* XI.

8. *Ethics,* Abbott's tr., p. 219.

9. To objectors who "doubt whether human beings, if taught to consider happiness as the end of life, would be satisfied with such a moderate share of it," as falls to the average man, Mill's answer is, "that great numbers have been satisfied with less." He evades the difficulty by an equivocation. He passes from one meaning of the word "satisfied," i.e., "to rest content with" to another meaning, i.e., "to be resigned to." "A highly-endowed being," he says, "can learn to bear the imperfections of the world, if they are at all bearable." But what if they are not bearable, or if one is not a highly-endowed being, or if a highly-endowed being can find in his philosophy no rational grounds for bearing with them? Spencer refers the complete solution of the difficulty to a future predicted age, when, evolution having completed its work, conduct shall be perfectly adjusted to the completion of life. In the meantime, until this earthly paradise shall have been evolved, we must be satisfied to aim at making the surplus of happiness over misery as great as we can. In other words individuals living in the present stage of evolution can never attain their ultimate intrinsic end.

10. *Data of Ethics,* 58.

11. As Rickaby remarks (*Of God and His Creatures,* p. 14, note) our idea of life derived from experience involves change. We more readily conceive eternal death than eternal life. Yet we predicate eternity of a living God.

12. Mackenzie, *Manual of Ethics,* Ch. VI, n. 1.

13. Sidgwick, *Method of Ethics,* Bk. I, Ch. IV, p. 47 (7th Ed.).

14. *Ethics,* p. 9.   15. *Ibid.,* p. 218.   16. *Ibid.,* p. 58.

17. *Ibid.,* p. 72.   18. *Ibid.,* p. 73.   19. *Ibid.,* pp. 218-20.

20. *Ibid.,* p. 206.   21. *Ibid.,* pp. 207-14.

CHAPTER VIII

INADEQUACY OF FINITE OBJECTS

No finite object or combination of finite objects can confer final blessedness on a rational being. Nor can blessedness consist in any self-realization absolutely considered.

ULTIMATE ENDS. Another distinction of ends must be introduced in order to make clear the precise question which the proposition answers. Ends, then, may be objective (*finis qui*), subjective (*finis cui*), or formal (*finis quo*); or in other words, the object *which* is desired, the subject *for whom* it is desired, and the action or quality *by which* union between object and subject is effected, may each with propriety be designated ends of volition.[1] One may, for instance, desire a knowledge of the science of medicine for oneself; and under different aspects, self, the science of medicine, and knowledge of it would be the ends of one's studious endeavors.

Accepting this distinction of ends, we are met by a difficulty which is seldom expressly presented but is always latent in many modern systems of Ethics. That these three ends are intimately connected is evident. But is there a relation of sequence and dependence between them; and if so, which of the three is the principal end? With regard to formal end there is no difficulty. It may be identified with the objective or subjective end according as it is looked at on its objective or subjective side. The possession of an object by man is from different points of view the same as the thing possessed or the subject possessing.[2] But a difficulty does arise if objective and subjective ends are compared. Is the object which is desired and sought, or the person for whom it is desired and whose satisfaction is secured through its possession, the principal end to which the other is subordinated? It may, for instance, be argued, that the object of desire, though intrinsically possessing qualities which render it desirable, is not ultimately desirable because of itself, but because of its fitness to give satisfaction to the subject; that therefore between the object of desire and the person desiring there is the relation of means to an end. If the argument is valid, we must admit that man is unqualifiedly an end to himself, and that all other ends desirable by him are mediate and referable to him as an ultimate end. Such a conclusion in its full logical import leads to extreme egoism. It would justify each individual in looking on himself as the central *ego* of the universe.

THE PRIORITY OF ENDS. A categorical answer cannot be given to the difficulty just raised. We must first define in what sense a rational being may be said to be an end to himself; and, moreover, distinguish between the respective worths of various objects of desire as compared with man himself.

Now man is an end to himself, first in the negative sense, that being a person and *sui juris,* he cannot be regarded as subordinated in worth, or as a means to any other created being or collection of created beings. Secondly, in a positive sense, he is an end to himself in the sense that his own final blessedness is the ultimate intrinsic end of all his volitional activity, and cannot be sacrificed or disregarded for the sake of any other assignable end of his nature. On the other hand, he is not an end to himself in the sense that his final blessedness or the approaches thereto are not referable to the purposes of his Creator, whether ultimate or proximate; or in the sense that any grade of perfection proper to him as a rational being can be attained out of relation to the purposes of his Creator. Between man's intrinsic end, therefore, and his extrinsic end there is mutual adjustment not precisely of means to an end, but of indissoluble phases of a unitary objective end, one of which regards the creature, the other the Creator, so that every grade of attainment of the intrinsic end is simultaneously a corresponding grade in the attainment of the extrinsic end. Systems that miss this correlation drift, or logically tend to drift, into one of two extremes: either they make man an end to himself in an unqualified sense and terminate in extreme egoism, or they make him a means to Humanity, to the ideal State, the Absolute Spirit, the Eternal Self, or to some other abstraction, and deny the dignity of personality.

Next, if a comparison be instituted between man himself and the objects of his desires, these fall into three classes: they are in worth and dignity of nature inferior, equal, or superior to him. The first are subservient to him; they are for his sake, not he for theirs. With respect to him, therefore, they are the means of acquiring some secondary or accessory perfection of person, as for instance health, honor, wisdom or virtue. They may indeed be desirable in themselves, but not ultimately of themselves. The second class of objects, those namely which are equal to him in worth, are his fellow men. They possess, as he does, the same inalienable dignity of personality, and as such are ends to themselves in the negative and positive sense already explained, and exist primarily for the purposes of the Creator. Now desire is love for an object viewed as unattained but attainable. The unattained object may be loved either for its own sake, and in this case the only thing that can be desired for the subject is union with the object; or it may be loved for the sake of self in any of its manifold aspects, and in this case that which is desired is one or other of the various personal satisfactions that the object may be the means of bringing. A person, therefore, as an object of desire may be sought for either with a disinterested love, which is called the love of benevolence or of friendship, or with an interested love which may be designated the love of egoism or of self-seeking. Now the only way that a person as such may rationally be an object of desire for another person is by the love of benevolence or of friendship. It is not contended of course that the love of benevolence or friendship positively excludes all regard to self; but only that the personal satisfaction and delight that will follow on the realization of disinterested desire is not included as an element in the direct object of volition. It is true one may have an interested desire for a person, not precisely as a person, but as an agency by whose operations one may profit either in outward benefits or inner self-complacency. But interested desire of this kind can never rationally be pushed to such an extent as to lose sight of the essential attribute of personality in another. Neither the person who is the subject of desire nor the person who is the object of desire, can be subordinated one to the other. Lastly, if the being who is the object of desire is one of transcending excellence, it is quite clear that its subordination in any sense to the one desiring is contrary to reason. The only teleological relation existing between them is that of a rational being seeking union with its ultimate objective end.

Object. In a wide sense, the word "object" may mean whatever is cognized as a term of conative tendency. It would therefore comprise a state or condition of the agent to be achieved or produced by personal endeavor (*finis qui efficiendus*), and an actual reality distinct from the agent by the acquisition of or union with which conative tendency is satisfied (*finis qui obtinendus*). We have already shown that the state or condition which man ultimately seeks to establish is blessedness, and that this is compassed by the cessation of conative tendency in the possession of an actual reality distinct from and not subordinate to self, by union with which rational appetence is gratified to the limits of its capacity. Our present inquiry, therefore, concerns this reality.

FINITE OBJECTS. It may be doubted whether any school of Ethics ever made finite objects distinct from man himself the ultimate objective end in the sense in which we have explained it. On the contrary even those which reject our proposition, if rightly interpreted, regard these objects as instrumental and subservient to man, that is to say, as aids and means by which he may reach his highest perfection and happiness. In the last analysis these theories mean that the individual man, or the race, namely—putting aside abstractions—the aggregate of men who will exist in some future state of development, is the ultimate objective end. The latter interpretation we dismiss from consideration. It denies what we have already proved and asserts by implication what we have already disproved. It denies that each individual man can obtain the last end that his nature craves; and it asserts that past and present rational beings are only means in a process, which when completed will accrue to the blessedness of some future and more or less remote rational beings, the intrinsic demands of whose nature is not essentially different from those of human nature today and in the past. There is in fact no rational alternative between making man, who is the ultimate subjective end of his volitional activity, at the same time the ultimate objective end, or in seeking that objective end in a supreme being, transcending man in excellence. Our question, therefore, reduces itself to this: Can man by the use or help of finite objects finally come to full realization of himself in perfection and happiness?

DIVISION OF FINITE OBJECTS. Now finite objects may be grouped under three heads: (a) the outer goods of life, as wealth, honor, power; (b) the inner goods of the body, as health, beauty, sensuous pleasures; (c) the inner goods of the soul, as knowledge, love, virtue. Can the human soul find final blessedness in or through the possession of any of these? Not assuredly in goods of the first group. For they are wanting in the essential characteristics of an ultimate end for a rational nature; they are not obtainable by all men, millions having lived and died who never had an opportunity of acquiring them; between their possession and a morally meritorious life there is no teleological connection, as they may be the fruits of unrighteousness as well as the rewards of virtue; when acquired they are as often the source of misery as of happiness, of deterioration of character as of its ennobling; if pursued as the main interest of life, they progressively whet an appetite which they can never satisfy; lastly they are extrinsic and incidental to the inner life of man, and can never appease the "heart's desire."

A similar judgment can be passed on goods of the second group: they belong to a level of existence which is common to us with the brute animal. Even if they could be secured in any satisfying degree they would not perfect the higher life of the soul, nor quench its craving for a beatifying object. Besides, many of the limitations and defects native to the first group of goods are discoverable in them. Like the goods of fortune they are inculpably beyond the reach of many, they are often fortuitous and insecure, and are morally neutral.

The third group of goods might seem to fulfil the requirements of the problem. Knowledge is a perfective act of the intellect as love is of the will, and the latter faculty through virtue is developed in efficiency and rectitude of aim. It might be maintained, therefore, that through the final perfecting of these distinctive powers of the soul man could realize the fulness of being and life of which he is capable. But the reasoning misses the point at issue. In the first place *knowledge* and *love* are formal ends; by them the subject knowing and loving is put into union with the object known and loved. But the question is not whether knowledge and love are elements of formal beatitude—this as we shall see in the next proposition must be admitted—but by what kind of knowledge and love is subjective beatitude obtained. The character of the fruition that they bring varies with the worth of their object and their functional perfection. An object of supreme worth may be known and loved imperfectly, as on the other hand an object of inferior worth may be thoroughly known or intensely loved. Before we can affirm, therefore, that knowledge is beatifying we must know whether, in the order of truth, the worth of the object is such that it adequately responds to intellectual capacity, and whether the mode of apprehension fills capacity to completion. Now no mere knowledge of created things will satisfy the intellect's appetence for truth. The acquisition of any given degree of knowledge about created things opens up and allures to deeper truths; every riddle of the universe solved reveals a new one asking for solution. *Felix qui potuit rerum cognoscere causas,*[3] but knowledge of any finite cause induces to a quest of a further cause; and the human intellect will not rest in the possession of beatifying knowledge until its cognition of the first cause equals its capacity. In like manner it may be shown that love cannot beatify if engaged with beings of finite perfection. Love, it is true, differs from knowledge in this respect, that because of our emotional nature its intensity, and the exaltation consequent thereupon may exceed the worth of the object. This happens, however, only when knowledge is narrowed and the functions of reason are usurped by imagination. Rationally and normally love is commensurate with knowledge. When it is in excess of knowledge it is unstable, and with broadening knowledge is doomed to perish. The only love therefore that can give final beatitude is one that follows upon knowledge of a beatifying object.

In the next place *virtue* also is a formal end, and moreover, unlike knowledge and love it is not an element of formal beatitude, but a means of attaining it, or a disposition to seek it, and a power of progressing towards it. Virtue, therefore, under whatever formula proposed—whether as hedonistic discernment, which enables one to choose the surest and most lasting pleasures, or "bent of character" from which useful rather than hurtful actions are likely to arise; or the wisdom of the Stoic by which one overcomes the passions through self-discipline and will-power;[4] or the acquired inclination and facility in acting rightly of the Schoolmen—is in no case ultimate, and belongs not to the goal or haven, but to the journey of life.

INADEQUACY OF FINITE OBJECTS. It follows as a consequence that no combination of created objects can confer beatitude. First, because the imperfections by which they are, singly or in groups, inefficient are qualitative not quantitative; they do not supplement one another, but at best give partial satisfaction in distinct planes of life. Secondly, because they do not collectively measure up to the highest and ultimate needs of man. Thirdly, because, unless subject to the ordinating pre-eminence of an object transcending them, they may become incompatible, and respectively lose value. The contention sometimes advanced that reason can exercise a regulative function in their choice is futile, until a supreme object, whatever it may be, is proposed for reason itself, by which values are estimated and subordination determined.

SELF-REALIZATION. In view of the conclusions established, it will not be difficult to deal with the recent forms of the doctrine that *self-realization is the supreme end of life*. The formula, which of itself is sufficiently ambiguous, is rendered more so by speculations on the content of the notion *self*. Its prominence in English Ethics is due to the Neo-Hegelians of whom T. H. Green (1836-82) was the leader.[5] Green's theory is that immanent in man there is a divine self-realizing principle. An illustration, which he himself indicates[6] will afford a concrete exposition of the theory. We can, he says, state the truth about a living and growing organism, an oak-tree, for instance, by the help of two conceptions, which we shall try in vain to reduce to a third. One is the end in which the growth terminates, or the form of life realized in the oak. This end must be real and present in the oak, because it is operative throughout its development, yet it is not identified with any stage of the development. The other is the complex of material elements that go to make up the particular oak in its individuality and as progressively modified by the form of life which determines it. The oak as a "particular living being" is not less one and indivisible because we cannot dispense with either of these conceptions, if we would understand it aright; or because it is sometimes one sometimes the other of them that is predominant in our usage of the term "living being." In like manner, as the oak form of life is realizing itself in the organism of individual trees, so the divine mind is realizing itself in man. If we are to understand the self-conscious reality one and indivisible in each of us, it must be by conceiving both an end eternally complete which is gradually realized in the organic processes of sentient life, and that organic process itself with its history and conditions.

SELF. To understand, therefore, what is meant by "self," we must distinguish between the *primary* and unreflective self, considered simply as a subject of mental experiences, and the *personal* or reflective self capable of consciously reflecting on itself as an object.[7] The essential thing in personality, Green tells us,[8] is self-objectification. We are persons insofar as we are consciously objects to ourselves. It is in the analysis of this consciousness that the true self is to be found, the self that we should strive to realize. Now our conscious experience contains two phases, of which neither admits of being reduced to or explained by the other. We experience a series of phenomena and events in succession, and are accordingly subject to change and modifications in time. Again we are conscious of ourselves as the enduring subject of these mental experiences, holding them together in a synthesis that is outside of time. All knowledge, that is, all distinctively intelligent and moral experience, is timeless. If for the sake of convenience we distinguish between a temporal and a timeless self, we do not commit ourselves to the unjustifiable assumption that there is a double consciousness, but hold that the one indivisible reality of our consciousness cannot be comprehended in a single conception.[9] There is, therefore, within us a spiritual principle by which we are conscious of the various stages in our process of knowing, which itself is not a process nor subject to succession. Such a principle is neither in time nor space, is other than the world of phenomena, is immaterial, immovable, and eternally at one with itself.[10] This can only be explained by supposing that "the eternal Spirit or self-conscious subject, which communicates itself, in measure and under conditions, to beings which through that communication become spiritual," is gradually realizing itself through the vehicle of our phenomenal nature[11] just as the oak form of life gradually reproduces itself in the individual trees.

But if, granting that this "eternal Spirit," "this mind for which the world exists," this divine self-realizing spirit is at work in the persons of men, we ask in what does its *realization* consist, the theory vacillates just where one might reasonably expect it to be unhesitating. In virtue of the divine principles in him, man, we are told, has definite capabilities, the realization of which can alone satisfy him; but what they are he does not know. They are not realized in any human life that has been or is, nor, it would seem, can they be realized in any life that can be lived by man as we know him.[12] Nevertheless they are relative to a definite end; they issue in a process of development, and such a process cannot be *ad infinitum*.[13] Nor can we take refuge in solutions that play fast and loose with the notions of "person" and "spirit." If an eternal Spirit, in the only sense in which we have reason to think there is such a being, realizes itself at all, then it can only have its being in persons, that is in self-conscious subjects. We are disguising the difficulty, not escaping it, by seeking the realization of the eternal Spirit in some development of mankind, as distinct from the persons who are developed in that development, or by supposing that the Spirit which is in man could fulfil its capability in some organization of society, unless personal perfection is attained by the individuals who are members of the society.[14] Unless, therefore, the capabilities of man admit of fulfilment in individuals, he is merely a means to an end which is not himself, to some impersonal Humanity, some ideal State, or other absolute and all-embracing end. A conclusion of this kind cannot be accepted; it denies personality to man. The end of a self-conscious subject must really exist not merely *for* but *in* a self-conscious subject.[15]

GREEN'S DILEMMA. Green is too intellectually honest not to recognize "that there are capacities of the human spirit not realizable in persons under conditions of any society that we know, or can positively conceive, or that may be capable of existing on earth." In other words, self-realization is the supreme end of man; but self-realization cannot be reached under any conceivable conditions of temporal society. What then is the solution of the difficulty? One thing is clear: "the *negative* assurance at any rate must remain, that a capacity, which is nothing except as personal, cannot be realized in any impersonal modes of being." His *positive* solution is problematic. He presents us three optional answers to the difficulty.[16]

First, we may accept "the supposition that the personal life, which historically, or on earth, is lived under conditions which thwart its development, is continued in a society with which we have no means of communication through the senses, but which shares in and carries further every measure of perfection attained by men under the conditions of the life that we know." But this seems to be only a generalization of the Kantian theory.[17] Unless the perfection attained in time is carried not only further, but so far that realization of the "eternal self" is finally reached by the individual, the solution is elpistic—a solution which, as we have seen, Green will not entertain.

Secondly, "we may content ourselves with saying that the personal self-consciousness which comes from God is forever continued in God." Before consenting to content ourselves with this saying we would like to know what intelligible meaning it has; what for instance is "God," and what does it mean to continue forever "in God"? The Divine Name is mentioned for the first time at the end of the first chapter of book first, and there it is used to designate the spiritual principle which is immanent in nature or the unifying self-consciousness which is the organizing principle of the world. Now in Green's theory, man is now and continues *in* "God," and yet, though his personal consciousness is timeless, he has not attained "an eternally complete consciousness." If the point of the solution is in the word "forever," we are again, though in a vague form, committed to the Kantian notion that an endless duration is required in order to fill out the endless progress towards the moral destination of our nature. If this is the solution, final self-realization is not for each of us individually, but *for* and *in* the divine self-consciousness which must be conceived to be the organizing principle in all processes of cosmic development, to whom the end to be attained is already real and present—the "one far-off divine event to which the whole creation moves."

And, in fact, Green seems finally to take refuge in this solution, "playing fast and loose" with the notion of personality which he had so laboriously constructed. He defines "the true notion of the spiritual relation in which we stand to God" to consist in this:[18]

That He is not merely a Being who made us in the sense that we exist as an object of the divine consciousness . . . but that He is a Being in whom we exist; with whom we are in principle one; with whom the human spirit is identical in the sense that He *is* all which the human spirit is capable of becoming.

Thirdly, "we may pronounce the problem suggested by the constant spectacle of unfulfilled human promise to be simply insoluble." That is to say, if we cannot understand how we individually, who will never acquire "an eternally *complete* consciousness," are not identical and in principle one with the divine mind to whom such consciousness is ever real and present, we can only say, *ignorabimus.* But a theory that ends in *ignorabimus* is certainly not a solution of the difficulty. And when the difficulty is an essential outcome of the theory, we are justified in treating the theory as the difficulty has been treated.

MONISM. In the next proposition we shall present the scholastic doctrine of "self-realization," and expose the true nature of man's "eternally complete consciousness." Before beginning that exposition, however, we shall notice two philosophical errors which are fundamental in self-realization theories that are based on pantheistic or naturalistic conceptions of the immanence of the Deity in nature. The first of these is a monistic conception of "being," or rather of spiritual being.[19] If the Monists do not tacitly assume that the goal of philosophic effort is to find a unity for the universe which would annul the fundamental and irremovable distinction between matter and spirit, they seek at least a unitary concept of spirit which will do away with the difference between a necessary being (*ens a se*) and a contingent being (*ens ab alio*). The consistent ideal of philosophic thought is, they believe, to find in the manifold manifestations and workings of the universe a single principle which is not merely the cause of all things, but is all things. Being is conceptually one: therefore the unity of being is real, they conclude.[20] The Schoolmen do not admit the real identity of all actually existing things. They hold that there is one self-existent Being, infinite in the sense that He is the plenitude of being, yet simple in the sense that He is sheer actuality, in whom components or composition can neither be nor be conceived to be; that all other beings are contingent, have received and continue to receive from Him existing essence and nature, and are finite in the sense that singly they have received but one species of being, and do not possess that so exhaustively as to exclude others from possessing it also, and that collectively they do not include all the modes of being that are. Socrates, to use St. Thomas' illustration, is finite first because he has human nature only, and furthermore because as *a* man he is not humanity itself, but one having or sharing in humanity. An apparent difficulty suggested by the teaching of St. Thomas regarding the angels[21] affords a further illustration. He held that there cannot be more than one angelic spirit in its own species, that consequently another could not participate in its specific grade of spiritual being. But admitting the theory of St. Thomas, the Schoolmen would still hold that an angel participates in "being" with all creatures, and in the generic angelic nature with all other angels; but that no individual angel shares its *specific* angelic nature with any other angel.

All created things, therefore, are in their very being dependent and participating. This mode of being is essentially involved in the concept of being itself as predicable of created things. On the other hand the being of God is self-existent and imparticipable. This mode of being is also essentially inherent in the predicate of being as applied to Him. It follows in the Scholastic system that being is truly and intrinsically attributed to creatures as well as to God, but that we can form no unitary or generic concept of being which is applicable to both. But if the being of God and the being of creatures cannot be even conceptually identical, much less can there be any kind of real identity between them. Now this doctrine of the analogy of being is fundamental in the metaphysics of the Schoolmen, and applies to every attribute that is predicated of both God and creatures. Spirituality, therefore, personality, self-consciousness, intellectuality, goodness, are attributed to God and man not by conceptual identity but by analogy. It alone reconciles two truths, neither of which can be denied without degrading our concept of God, namely, the immanence of the Divine Nature in the universe and Its transcendence above it.

The Scholastic doctrine is *monistic* in teaching: (a) that there is a First Cause from which all else derives its origin; (b) that this First Cause is present in the universe sustaining created causes in existence, and as a supereminent cause concurring with them in their activities. It is *dualistic* in teaching that the First Cause, who is immanent in the being and working of the universe, at the same time transcends that universe not merely in a spatial or temporal sense, but in His being, nature and attributes, and is consequently really distinct from it.

In conclusion we may draw these inferences: (a) The Divine Self, who is already transcendently real in the plenitude of being cannot have as the purpose of His working in and through the world of consciousness His own self-realization. To deny this would be to degrade the concept of God. (b) Man cannot have as the goal of his moral endeavor the realization or reproduction in himself of an "eternally complete consciousness," if by this "eternally complete consciousness" is understood the transcendent consciousness of God. To assert that such is the ideal of his volitional activity would be to make self-deification the ultimate end of life. (c) Although man may be said to have an "eternal self" in the sense that his conscious duration shall be endless, he has not now, nor shall he ever have an eternal or timeless self in the sense that his duration is or will become conceptually identical with that of God.[22]

REALITY AND THOUGHT. The other error on which these "self-realization" theories are based regards the nature of reality and thought, and their relations.[23] So far as this error bears on our present subject, it first confounds the mode in which a thing is known with the mode in which it exists. In effect the medieval controversies regarding "universals" appear in a new guise. Now, our knowledge is abstractive; in a given concept we view reality under an aspect only, which, though true, does not exhibit a complete correspondence between thought and object. The psychological fact, therefore, that in conceptually constructing a universe of related objects we can prescind from time, or from other phenomenal qualities which common sense tells us are realities, does not prove that the thing so considered is timeless, and much less that it is eternal.[24] What the mind does not assert in a given concept, it does not necessarily deny. From the nature of the human mind knowledge cannot be a replica of reality. Secondly, it is a gross fallacy to conclude that, because the conscious self is permanent and, in thinking, makes abstraction of the time in which it is, the thinking and the thinker are out of time. The actual self of which we have knowledge comes into existence at a certain time, experiences an order of succession in its life which it cannot help thinking is real, can recall its past, and anticipates a future when it shall cease to have bodily existence. It is conscious of its permanent identity through all these changes, but it is not conscious of being timeless or eternal. Lastly, the more a concept abstracts from the differences in its object, the smaller are the notes of reality which it presents. The thinnest of these concepts is "being," which may mean anything that is one remove from mere nothing, but which as such can have no actual existence at all.[25]

By adding to this concept that of "self-consciousness," the Neo-Hegelians construct the Universal Self. By so doing they must either deny the reality of all else but self-conscious beings, or admit a dualism for which there is no single ultimate ground. Now, acknowledging as we must the reality and existence of an individual self-conscious being, the transition by abstraction to the reality and existence of a universal self, which is and is not the same as the individual self, has no validity. Internal experience does not justify it, nor does any necessary demand of thought. The reality of the universe and the relation of knowledge to it are adequately and consistently accounted for by the scholastic doctrines of the analogy of being and the origin of universal ideas. A theory of self-realization, therefore, which necessitates one to think of himself as at once an individual and a universal, imposes conditions which could be fulfilled only by obliterating the distinction between a concrete, conscious, and incommunicable reality and an hypostatized abstraction to which the designation "self" cannot be applied by any rational use of language.

GENERAL PRINCIPLES. Other forms of self-realization theories may be disposed of by keeping in mind the general principles which we have already established: 1. The ultimate intrinsic end must be perfective of man in his highest and specific faculties. Many of his capacities are merely means to other capacities, and are worthy of development only insofar as in progressive subordination they minister to the dominant capacities, which exhibit the final tendency of his nature considered as a whole. 2. It must be attainable by all men individually. It cannot be an end which can be attained only by future members of the race, or only by some especially gifted individuals. Nor, for the same reason, can it consist in the full and rounded development of all man's physical, intellectual, and emotional capacities; such a development would be impossible in all the three orders named, or in any of them singly, besides, as already noted, destroying the subordination of capacity to capacity which is essential to the unity of man's nature. 3. Lastly it must harmonize the proximate ends of man as a social being, and be correlated to an ultimate end, for man cannot be an end to himself in an unqualified sense.[26]

NOTES

1. Suarez, *De Ultimo Fine Hominis,* Disp. I, Sect. 6, nn. 4-8.
2. *S. T.,* 1, 2, qu. 11, a. 3, ad 3.
3. Vergil, *Georgics,* II, 490.
4. Kant in his Ethics defines virtue as "a rightful disposition arising from *respect* for law" (p. 225), or as "a moral strength of the will" (p. 316). It is however identified with "holiness" only in a "being in whom no opposing impulse counteracts the law of his rational will" (p. 316), "whose maxims necessarily coincide with the laws of autonomy" (p. 58). Now God alone is such a being (p. 222). Actual holiness, therefore, is not in Kant's theory, as we have already seen, the ultimate formal end of man. "This perfection being an ideal, demands approximation to this end, but not the attainment of it, which surpasses human powers" (p. 316, footnote). We have already proved that the holiness proper to a created being, namely complete possession of its last end and fixity in adherence thereto, is an attribute of beatitude.
5. *Prologomena to Ethics.*
6. *Ibid.,* n. 68.
7. See *Dictionary of Philosophy and Psychology, sub voce* "Self," where this simple distinction is painfully elaborated into a mystery. "In reflective consciousness the self is not only subject—the subject-self—but it is also object of its own reflection—object-self. The object-self [the self?] however, when thus made object, is at the same time

identified with the subject-self, which is said to reflect. This peculiar fact, that the subject that reflects is at once also its own object of reflection, is the great mystery of philosophy and the basis of systems of speculative thought." In plain English an intelligent being may be not only a subject thinking, but may know that it is a subject thinking and in this sense become an object of thought to itself. Neither the self nor the intellect is in itself and for our present mode of knowledge an immediate object of thought, but only as performing some of its functions. Now it is hard to see where there is any mystery in this, except to one whose thought is limited by imagination, and to whom the unthinkable is the mentally unpicturable.

8. *Prol. to Ethics,* n. 182.

9. *Ibid.,* nn. 58-68.   10. *Ibid.,* n. 54.

11. *Ibid.,* nn. 67, 180, 184.   12. *Ibid.,* n. 180.

13. *Ibid.,* n. 189.   14. *Ibid.,* nn. 183-185.

15. *Ibid.,* n. 187.   16. *Ibid.,* n. 185.

17. Ch. VII above.   18. *Op. cit.,* n. 187.

19. Green (n. 42) confesses that after all our protests against Dualism we are at last left with an unaccountable residuum—call it the *matter* of sensuous experience, the phenomenal, or what one pleases —which is an essential element of the real world of experience, and which we cannot trace to what we regard as the organizing principle of that world.

20. Only the general principle of Monism is given. Its application has varied in thoroughness with different schools. Some have found that the universe as we know it would not fit into the formula, and have satisfied themselves with a partial application of it. Others, refusing to recognize those aspects of the world that proved recalcitrant, have reduced everything to matter or spirit, distilling spirit out of matter in the one case, and making matter some sort of a by-product of spirit in the other. Others again, ascending into regions of thought into which the world as we know it never enters, have discovered an abstraction called the Absolute which alone is the Being that truly is and which holds in a higher synthesis the infinite and the finite, the necessary and contingent, spirit and matter, and the diverse and contrary manifestations of each. For the elaborations of Monism along spiritualistic, materialistic or other lines, the student may consult Maher's *Psychology,* Ch. XXIII. Our present concern is only with spiritualistic Monism. Its materialistic forms can provide no theory of self-realization that is ethically worth considering. Absolute or Transcendental Monism will be noticed later.

21. *S. T.,* 1, qu. 50, 2. 4.

22. Speaking philosophically, only the duration of God can prop-

erly be called eternal. But Green and his disciples confound a consciousness which shall be everlasting or which is timeless in a precisive sense with an eternal consciousness.

23. The student is referred to Walker's *Theories of Knowledge* for an exposition and refutation of the different theories of Absolutism, or theories which hold that the only explanation of knowledge and reality, of subject and object of consciousness is to be found in an Absolute, which is the immanent ground and final synthesis of all differences and contrarieties. The "self-realization" theories makes this Absolute self-conscious. We shall discuss later another theory which makes it blind will.

24. In attaching a meaning to the Neo-Hegelian use of the word "timeless" the student must keep in mind the Kantian doctrine that time is an *a priori* form of sense intuition—a product of the activity of the subject which gives a perspective order to objects of experience. It has consequently no significance for the conscious self or in general for things-in-themselves. The use of the word "eternal" as a synonym for "timeless" is probably due to Spinoza (*Ethics,* p. I, def. 8, and p. V, prop. 34, scholion) and confounds the conceptual with the real.

25. Rickaby, *Of God and His Creatures,* notes on pp. 20-21.

26. For discussions of the metaphysics of this subject the student may consult Cronin's *Science of Ethics,* Ch. XIII; Rashdall's *Theory of Good and Evil,* Book II, Ch. 3, §1, and Book III, Ch. I, §3; Taylor's *Problem of Conduct,* pp. 59-83; Sorley's *Recent Tendencies in Ethics.* Aristotle in refuting Plato's Idea of Good (*Eth. Nic.,* Bk. I, Ch. VI) and St.Thomas in his commentaries thereupon (Lects.VI-VIII) supply principles which are applicable to monistic theories of self-realization.

CHAPTER IX

ULTIMATE BLESSEDNESS

The specific activities of his spiritual faculties by which man comes into possession of and union with his ultimate objective end are perfect knowledge and perfect love of God. Wherefore ultimate blessedness cannot be obtained in this life.

FORMAL BLESSEDNESS. If blessedness is the final perfection of a rational being, it must *formally* consist in the highest phase of being of which he is capable. This is necessarily some form of life. But life, as St. Thomas says,[1] may be understood in two senses: either as the very mode of being that differentiates the living from the non-living (*ipsum esse viventis*), as when we say that an animal has life and that a stone has it not; or as the activity, by which the living principle passes from mere potency to actuation, and which differs in kind for various modes of being, and within its kind reaches various grades of perfection (*ipsum operare viventis*), as when we speak of a man leading a spiritual or sensuous life, a literary or a business life. Evidently it is in the latter sense that man's formal blessedness can be said to consist in life. Of God alone can it be said that His very being is His blessedness. For man, therefore, formal blessedness must consist in the highest attainable activity of his rational nature.

ESSENTIAL AND UNESSENTIAL BLESSEDNESS. If formal blessedness be considered in its entirety, many activities are required to complete it. Man's final perfection must comprise the highest activities of every faculty essential to his nature. It might, therefore, be claimed that certain activities of sense belong, at least as accessory and subordinate elements, to his entire blessedness. But such a claim would entail the admission that blessedness is realizable either in our present state of existence, or in some future state, in which the soul after its separation from the body by death would again be reunited to it, a question which we shall consider later. In any case, it could not be claimed that those activities of our sensuous nature which proceed from want were requisite to a state of final perfection; the function of these is evidently transitory and temporal. Nor can it be maintained that any sensuous activity whatsoever was an essential constituent of blessedness; first, because the essence of formal blessedness must consist in the highest attainable activity of man's spiritual and distinctive nature, and secondly, because the senses deal with objects which we have already proved to be intrinsically insufficient to confer essential blessedness. Again, it might be claimed that, since man by his rational nature is a social being, certain intellectual and emotional activities by which he knows and loves other blessed beings, and by which he delights in intercourse and association with them, necessarily belong to any complete blessedness. Nor can we demur to this claim. Undoubtedly the blessedness of a rational being when looked at as a whole includes the satisfaction of all rational capacities and cravings, even of those which indicate intermediary and subordinate purposes of his nature.[2] But neither do these activities enter into the constitution of essential blessedness.

Between *essential* and *unessential* blessedness there is this difference, that the former is completive of rational life as such, and involves an object which is adequate to the faculties that disclose the final tendency of that life, capable therefore of sating desire to the limit of capacity; while the latter perfects a faculty insofar as it manifests a proximate or mediate tendency of the nature, and is concerned with objects which partake analogously of the attributes of the essential object. Bearing in mind that comparisons are not parallels, we may illustrate the difference between the objects of essential and unessential blessedness by the example of one who knew and loved a friend, and because of attachment to his friend would prize anything that was a revelation of his personality, his portrait, the books he wrote, or even his signature. This secondary blessedness is not said to be unessential in the sense that it is merely incidental and fortuitous, but in the sense that, though necessarily linked with essential blessedness, it is dependent on it, and has no worth out of relation to it.

Essential blessedness, therefore, contains in a supereminent degree the analogous forms of unessential blessedness, and would remain undiminished, even if by an hypothesis these should cease to be. Could we, to use another illustration, find an artist who enjoyed the unclouded contemplation of his ideal, he would still experience satisfaction from envisaging partial views of it, which reproduced, in color, form, or sound, different aspects of it as perfectly as the material used would permit. This satisfaction, however, would be but a reflection of his essential enjoyment. It would neither enrich the essential enjoyment by its presence, nor would the essential enjoyment be attenuated in the hypothesis of its absence. It might be a necessary concomitant, it would not be a constituent of the essential enjoyment.

OBJECT OF ESSENTIAL BLESSEDNESS. The faculties in the activities of which essential blessedness consists are either intellect or will or both, since these are the specific faculties of man's rational nature, and indicate its final tendency. Consequently the object of activities essentially beatifying must be one which (a) is accordant in nature with these faculties; (b) suffices of itself to meet adequately the demands of their appetencies; (c) and embraces, though transcending, the universality of their objects. Now the specific activities of man are immaterial and spiritual; their appetencies are towards everything in which truth, the ground of cognoscibility, and good, the ground of desirability, are found; and definitely to an object in which these grounds are comprehensively and superlatively realized. But God alone, as infinite truth and goodness is such an object; and therefore He alone is the object of essential blessedness.

St. Thomas presents this argument succinctly :[3]

Blessedness is perfect good which entirely appeases desire, otherwise it would not be the last end, if something still remained to be desired. But the object of the will is universal good, as the object of the intellect is universal truth. Hence it is clear that nothing can set the will to rest but universal good. This is not found in anything created, since they have participated goodness, but in God alone. Therefore God alone can fill the heart of man.

CAJETAN'S DIFFICULTY. Cajetan proposes against this argument the difficulty that the object of the will, and likewise of the intellect, is universal in predication, that is to say, that everything of which the notions good and truth can be predicated are respectively objects of will and intellect. But it is a fallacy to argue from a universal in predication to a universality in being. Suarez,[4] however, considers the argument valid, if rightly understood. For in the first place, if the object of the will and of the intellect is as extensive as the notions good and truth, it clearly includes God, who is the universal good and truth, not in the sense that He is a notion predicable of all things, but in the sense that He is in a transcendent and supereminent degree all good and truth. And, secondly, since the objects of will and intellect are coextensive with good and truth, it follows that the tendencies of these faculties will give place to the fruition of possession only on the attainment of the supreme good and truth.

St. Thomas' Difficulty. St. Thomas himself raises and answers a more serious difficulty against the proof.[5] It is true, he argues, that the blessedness of an intellectual being consists in knowing and understanding the best intelligible; still this admission must be taken relatively. An object may be so highly intelligible in itself as to be beyond the understanding of a given grade of intellect. Just as, to use a sensuous illustration, the sun may be so brilliantly visible as to be invisible to a bat. Hence an intellect such as man's is not able to know the absolutely highest intelligible object, but some lower intelligible object, which is at the same time the highest that can be known by it.

The preceding difficulty bears on the kind of knowledge that we can have of God rather than on the knowledge itself. Man's intellect is a spiritual faculty, and therefore between it and all spiritual truths, God included, there is some cognoscitive proportion. As a matter of fact, man does know God even in his present existence, though that knowledge is analogous and inadequate. Although God is in Himself the absolutely highest intelligible object, the knowledge of Him by His creatures is relative to their grade of intelligence. Comprehensive knowledge of Him is beyond the compass of any created intellect. An infinitely intelligible being can be comprehended only by an infinite intellect. Moreover we concede that man cannot by his unsuccored intellect look face to face on Him who "inhabiteth light inaccessible." An intuitive knowledge of God exceeds man's natural powers of intelligence. But if man cannot fix his eyes unblinded upon the midday blaze of the sun, he can nevertheless know it from its effects in nature, from its energizing heat and life-giving warmth, as well as from the radiance with which it suffuses and reveals the visible world. Conceding, then, that the vision of God is beyond the reach of the human intellect, unless elevated by an added endowment, the objection does not prove that man is not capable of attaining a height of abstractive knowledge, which would completely satisfy his natural capacity.[6]

ACTIVITIES OF ESSENTIAL BLESSEDNESS. The activities by which formal blessedness is essentially constituted are, in the first place, those which are proper to the faculties which of their nature are fitted and destined for union with and possession of the essential object of beatitude, and secondly, those which are directly concerned with that object. Man cannot be said to be essentially blessed, until he attains his ultimate objective end through every activity through which he is capable of attaining it. Now the nature of both intellect and will indicate that they are made for the possession of and union with God. The receptivity of one is for supreme truth, of the other for supreme good; and the fulness of life, therefore, in which the soul's want is superseded by the rest of blessedness, will be enjoyed only when its twofold receptivity has been repleted. But the possession of the supreme truth is through knowledge, and union with the supreme good through love. Therefore the specific activities that essentially constitute the life of blessedness are perfect knowledge and perfect love of God. This perfection is, of course, to be understood relatively, that is to say, it is commensurate with the soul's powers of knowing and loving.

SCHOLASTIC CONTROVERSIES. The conclusion that we have just established is that of Suarez[7] and his followers. Some recent writers have asserted that it is an eclectic opinion, in which the real point of the question is missed. A brief exposition of the two principle opinions which divided the medieval Schoolmen on the subject may help to put the meaning of Suarez' opinion in a clearer light. The first of these is that of Scotus[8] and the Scotist doctors generally, who held that the essence of formal blessedness for our rational nature as such consists in an act of the will alone, namely, in the perfect love of God, for which the presentation of God through perfect knowledge is a necessary prerequisite. The other is that of St. Thomas[9] and of the Thomists who hold that it consists in an act of the intellect alone, namely, in perfect knowledge of God, upon which as a necessary complement follows perfect love of God. This divergence of views is not to be confounded with that which obtains today between Intellectualists and Voluntarists with which it is often identified. Neither attempted to interpret the intellectual or cognitive functions in terms of the emotional or affective functions, or these latter in terms of the former. Both admitted that intellect and will had each its peculiar activities. Nor did they disagree on which was the more radical faculty. They both taught that will was a metaphysical consequence of intellect. The idealistic theory that the universe was mind and that nature and history were merely applied logic, and the theory that blind will was the ultimate principle of the universe would have been rejected equally by both as foolish. The question at issue between them therefore was whether intellect or will by its activity exhibited more perfectly the rational life of man.

SCHOLASTIC AGREEMENT. The major premise of both schools was that the essence of formal blessedness consisted in a unitary act, and that this act was the most perfect act of the most perfect faculty. This principle is denied by Suarez who maintains that every activity, by which the soul is directly joined to the ultimate objective end, enters as an essential constituent of formal blessedness, since formal blessedness is nothing else than the final perfection of a rational creature through those activities which put it in possession of and union with its beatifying object. He sees no more reason for asserting that an ultimate formal end should consist in one rather than in many activities than that any intermediate formal end should be so constituted. Even granting that one activity, that of intellect for instance or of will, considered metaphysically and out of relation to the other, should be proved to be more perfect than the other, the fact still remains that each is engaged with the beatifying object in itself; that from the nature of the soul, it is endowed with various powers none of which grasp the entire object, but each under some formal aspect; that consequently complete conjoinment with its object of which the soul is capable results from the consonant and mutually proportioned activities of all the faculties that were made for directly attaining it. The essence of formal blessedness is not therefore determined by the entitative perfection of one or other beatifying act, but by the perfection of the bond established between the soul and God, by the activities that directly conspire to produce it.[10]

It was on the minor premise that Scotist and Thomist divided, one holding that love and the other that knowledge was the most perfect act of the most perfect faculty. The fundamental arguments by which they proved their minors are equally disparate. The superiority in perfection of one faculty over the other may be inferred either from their proper acts, and hence the nobler the act which a faculty is capable of eliciting, the nobler is the faculty; or from their formal objects, and hence, the more elevated the formal object of a faculty, the higher in perfection is the faculty. The Scotist argued from the former principle, the Thomist from the latter, and each denied the validity of the other's criterion.

SCOTISTS. The Scotists maintain that the love of God is a higher and nobler act than knowledge of God. Although an act of the intellect is prior to an act of the will in uniting man to God, this priority, they argue, is not one of perfection but of process. The perfection of union is had only through an act of that faculty, whose object is first in intention and last in attainment. But this object is God as the supreme good; and the act by which man is perfectly united to the supreme good is love, an act of the will. Passages may be cited from St. Thomas in which he seems to assent to this opinion. For instance he says: [11]

There are two powers in man, by which he can adhere to God, namely, intellect and will. . . . But the adhesion that is through the intellect receives its completion through that which is of the will, because through the will man attains rest in that which the intellect apprehends. . . . Therefore the adhesion of love to God is the chief way of adhering to Him.

Again, in discussing the superior excellence of one choir of angels over another in the angelic hierarchy, he puts this difficulty to himself: Knowledge is prior to love, and intellect seems to be a higher power than will. But, the order of the Cherubim is taken from knowledge and that of the Seraphim from love. Therefore, the order of the Cherubim is higher than that of the Seraphim. In rejecting this conclusion he lays down the principle that by knowledge the thing known is in the subject knowing, but by love the subject loving is united to the object loved.[12] From this principle he infers that love is more excellent than knowledge, when the object of these activities is superior in being to the subject exercising them, as on the other hand knowledge excels love when their object is lower in being than the subject knowing and loving.[13]

THOMISTS. The Thomists maintain that the higher perfection of one faculty over the other is not determined by their proper acts but by their respective formal objects or the specific aspect under which each reaches the beatifying object. It is indeed the Supreme Good that beatifies; but it is as truth that man first reaches and perfectly possesses it. Perfect knowledge, therefore, of God or the Supreme Good is the essentially beatifying act. They admit with St.

Thomas that love of God is higher and better than knowledge of God, but refuse to accept the Scotists conclusion that the faculty eliciting this love, namely will, is a higher faculty than intellect, or that it is the distinctive faculty through whose activity man attains formal blessedness.

In the articles referred to above, St. Thomas makes two comparisons of intellect and will. First, compared as faculties, each of which has its own peculiar perfection because of its relation to its formal object, he finds intellect a higher faculty than will. The formal object of the intellect, he says, is more abstracted from the individuation of the thing than the formal object of the will, and therefore more elevated. Furthermore it is intelligence, or the power by which we know truth, and not will, or the power by which we embrace truth presented to us under the aspect of goodness by the intellect, that differentiates man from lower beings. Will, as a grade of appetence, depends on, and is in nature posterior to intelligence; while intelligence, as a grade of cognition, does not depend on will, and in nature is prior to it.

Lastly it is by intelligence and under the aspect of truth that the object of the soul's activities is first brought into union with it; the union through will is based on the prior union and measured by it. The Thomists conclude, therefore, that formal blessedness must consist substantially and principally in an activity peculiar to man, as having intelligence, and only consequently and dependently on those that are peculiar to him, as having rational appetence. The second comparison between intellect and will regards their relation to one or other things in which their formal object is found; and so compared, he concedes that because of the qualities of the particular thing with which the faculties are engaged, the activity of one may be nobler than the other. This perfection, however, is not intrinsic to the faculty, but belongs to it by reason of the particular thing on which its activity is here and now exercised. This he illustrates by the example of the faculties of sight and of hearing. Assuming the former to be intrinsically higher than the latter, it may yet happen that an act of the latter is, because of the particular object that it perceives, more elevating than an act of the former. A bird may not be a thing of beauty to look at, though its song be a joy forever.[14]

SUAREZ. The judgment of Suarez[15] on these opinions may be reduced to these propositions. 1. The arguments of St. Thomas prove that the essence of formal blessedness consists primarily and radically in the perfect knowledge of God; so that, if by essence is understood that attribute of blessedness which is the root of all its other attributes—or which is called the metaphysical essence—then undoubtedly the opinion of St. Thomas seems alone tenable. 2. A perfect act of the pure love of God is, however, absolutely necessary in order that the essence of formal blessedness be had in its completeness, and this, he thinks is the opinion of St. Thomas.[16] 3. The opinion of Scotus, if understood in an exclusive sense to assert that the essence of formal blessedness is constituted solely by a perfect act of the pure love of God, scarcely seems probable. 4. The delight of possessing God, or any self-regarding love of Him, though following necessarily from the perfect knowledge and the perfect love of Him, are not essential constituents of formal blessedness.[17]

TEMPORAL BLESSEDNESS. It needs hardly be proved that in this life no stage of blessedness can be reached beyond which there is no further stage reasonably desirable. Whatever the perfection we may attain in our present existence, it is not final. It does not equal the capacity and the demand of the soul; through the warp of it runs a weft of imperfections and tangles; it is not unalterably fixed, but varying constantly, as a thing in the process of making; however finely wrought it may be, it will in fact and effect vanish wholly at death, except insofar as it is or may be an earnest of a future blessedness that is full, faultless, unchangeable, and everlasting. One might indeed acquire the contentment of Stoicism by learning to endure the ills that must be borne, or the complacency of culture by starving higher appetencies; but the final satisfaction of every rational desire cannot be achieved during our earthly existence. Final blessedness is therefore reserved for a future life, in which the conditions that render it unattainable here do not obtain. Now if our ultimate end is beyond our reach here, it follows evidently that this present life is but a prelude to an ampler life hereafter. The blessedness which it can afford must consequently be initial and partial, and consist in attaining the proximate and mediate ends that are preambulatory and conducive to the final possession of complete blessedness. Now all men desire final blessedness, that is, the highest perfection and happiness of which they are capable. This desire is the loadstone and loadstar of all their voluntary activities. But under the spur of unregulated desire they seek it often where it cannot be found, and their quest of it is often aberrant or retrograde.

They pervert the order of ends, making the proximate the ultimate, and the mediate the final, or in seeking an intrinsic end, preclude the extrinsic end that gives it worth. The two conditions, therefore, of temporal blessedness are, that the ultimate intrinsic end of life, and consequently its extrinsic end, should be known and acknowledged; and that the subordinate ends of life should be sought insofar as they are approaches to the complete realization of self by the perfect knowledge and the perfect love of God. We may conclude, then, that our present span of life is not only prolusory but probationary as well. Within it is discovered the ideal of attainment that will guide us, but not the goal; the ideal of good that draws us on, but not the end that gives us rest.

RESURRECTION OF THE BODY. If final blessedness cannot be realized on earth, two alternative suppositions present themselves. It will be realized (a) either in a future state in which the disembodied soul lives the life of a spirit free from the trammels of sense, or (b) in one in which it is again united to the body, and lives again, though in a more exalted way, the composite life of intellect and senses. Scholastics of eminence may be alleged for either opinion. Their disagreement turns on the questions whether the soul after its separation from the body by death, and as long as that separation lasts, is in a natural or unnatural state.[18] In other words, is the soul existing in the body, and existing after death incorporeally, in two successive stages equally natural to it; or once having been made, and by its grade of spiritual being adapted for union with the body, does it forever retain a natural exigence for that union?[19]

INDIRECT DIFFICULTIES. The acceptance of either opinion involves us in difficulties. Some of these are indirect; and, for both suppositions, regard the mode of existence and mental life which the blessed shall possess, or, for the latter supposition, the physical qualities of the bodies that souls of the blessed shall reanimate. Many of these difficulties are unanswerable from any sources of knowledge which are ours naturally. We can know that a future life of blessedness is attainable; that is consists formally in the perfect knowledge and perfect love of God; that it will, when attained, be an everlasting possession; and that the physical and intellectual conditions under which it will be led must be such as befits the state of final perfection. But the manner of it all must remain largely a matter of speculation as long as we are on this side of the veil that separates the here from the hereafter, except insofar as that veil is lifted by revelation. We may indeed on the principles of scholastic philosophy hold: (a) that the knowledge of God which we should have in a state of natural blessedness is not intuitive but abstractive, yet perfect in its kind and therefore not analogous as in this life; (b) that, in the supposition of a future resurrection, the body would not possess the endowments which from revelation we know will be attributes of glorified bodies, that, nevertheless, it would have an integrity of constitution in keeping with the state of the soul, and no longer hampering it in the fullest exercise of its native activities.

DIRECT DIFFICULTIES. The other difficulties are direct, and if valid, would prove the impossibility of man attaining by his natural faculties an ultimate state of blessedness. First it may be contended that intellect and will, being faculties illimitable in range, always retain a capacity for further attainment. Any given grade of attainment is limited; therefore no attainment exhausts capacity and fully satisfies desire. Beyond each plane of perfection that is reached, there rise higher peaks, but there is no summit where striving shall cease in final contemplation of a cloudless heaven. The blessed may be compared to Shelley's wild-eyed charioteers who[20]

> . . . lean forth and drink
> With eager lips the wind of their own speed,
> As if the thing they loved fled on before,
> And now, even now, they clasped it.

The difficulty is the latent first premise of every system of Ethics which, since the Stoics set up their ideal wise man as the inimitable exemplar of moral endeavor, makes conscious striving, self-discipline, and moral progress the end of any life that man shall ever enjoy. It implies either that death closes our career as moral beings, or that if we continue to live hereafter, progress, which is the law of the soul's life on earth, may by analogy be presumed to be the law of its life in that future state. Its obvious fallacy lies in assuming that our intellectual powers are capable of indefinite enlargement, because their object is infinite in perfection. Now every human intellect, since it is created, is finite; since it is individual, its actual or potential powers are definite. It may acquire a higher development than it has at any given instant in time, but there is a limit beyond which it cannot be developed. That limit is reached in blessedness, and is distinctive and peculiar for each of the blessed. We may not, therefore, confuse perfect subjective possession of God with perfect objective possession. The same sunset, for instance, is seen by the poet, the scientific man, and the rustic, and each sees what he is capable of seeing. The same God will be known and loved by each of the blessed as fully as each is capable of knowing Him and loving Him, but not with the same measure of knowledge and love. Perfection in a faculty's mode of attainment can equal the perfection of attainability in the object only when the faculty is as illimitable in powers of comprehension as the object is in perfection. If it be urged that those who are less blessed than others, seeing that higher blessedness, will ineffectually desire it, and so fail in entire satisfaction, the answer is that their perfect knowledge and love of God reveals to them the utmost capacity of their faculties and stifles irrational desire.[21]

The other difficulty may be put in the words of St. Thomas:[22]

The knowledge of effects kindles the desire of knowing the cause. . . . Therefore, the desire of knowledge naturally implanted in all intelligent beings, does not rest unless, after finding out the substance of things made, they come also to know the cause on which these substances depend. By the fact, then, of pure spirits knowing that God is the cause of all the substances which they see, the natural desire in them does not rest unless they come also to see the substance of God himself.

The argument evidently is as applicable to the souls of the blessed as to pure spirits. The conclusion, then, is that no abstractive knowledge, however perfect, will give final satisfaction to the soul's natural desire for knowledge. Only by intuitive knowledge of God himself can its yearnings be set at rest. But intuitive knowledge of God transcends the natural powers of created or creatable intelligence. Man, therefore, was not made to attain essential blessedness.

The last conclusion cannot, of course, be attributed to St. Thomas;[23] and yet the premises are his. The apparent contradiction may be solved on the following principles. 1. Man has an *innate* appetence for blessedness. 2. He has, therefore, an *implicit* appetence for the object of blessedness. 3. The innate and implicit appetence is actuated, or becomes *explicit* and *elicit* appetence or desire, through knowledge. 4. If, therefore, man knows God, or the object of blessedness, only through his natural powers, the innate appetence becomes a desire of knowing him with the highest *abstractive* knowledge of which his natural powers are capable. 5. If man knows by revelation that he is elevated to a supernatural destiny, that the means of fulfilling his destiny are bestowed on him, and that he will be endowed with a supernatural faculty by which the knowledge of God appropriate to that destiny can be had, the innate appetence becomes a desire of knowing God *intuitively*. 6. On the principle of St. Thomas, therefore, that *"omne prius salvatur in posteriori,"* [24] the desire of the vision of God is now natural, first, in the sense that human nature, as at present constituted, is destined for that vision; secondly, in the sense that for man once elevated to the supernatural state no other blessedness is possible; and thirdly, in the sense that in view of his destination any abstractive knowledge of God, however perfect, would leave some void in desire. [25]

NOTES

1. *S. T.*, 1, 2, qu. 3, a. 2.
2. *S. T.*, 1, 2, qu. 4, a. 8.
3. *S. T.*, 1, 2, qu. 2, a. 8.
4. *De Ult. Fine Hom.*, Disp. V, Sect. 1, n. 7.
5. *S. T.*, 1, qu. 12, a. 1. and *Contra Gentiles,* III, 25, *Potest autem aliquis.* In these and similar places St. Thomas is speaking of the supernatural blessedness of man, that, namely, which will be had through the vision or intuitive knowledge of God. Our study of the question is purely rational. On principles of reason the blessedness of man is what he could have attained, had he been left to the natural and unaided powers of intellect and will. The principles by which the difficulties are solved in one case are, with due allowance, applicable in the other.
6. Another difficulty arises to a student of St. Thomas from *Contra Gentiles,* III, 50, the title of which is, *That the natural desire of spiritual substances is not set at rest by the natural knowledge which they have of God.* We shall consider this difficulty after completing our proof.
7. *De Ult. Fine Hom.*, Disp. VII, Sect. 1, nn. 29-42.
8. *4 Dist.* 49, qu. 5.
9. *S. T.*, 1, 2, qu. 3, a. 4, and *Contra Gentiles,* III, 25, 26. The first passage may be found translated into English in Rickaby's *Aquinas Ethicus,* and the second in his *God and His Creatures.* The author uniformly translates *beatitudo* and *felicitas* by the word "happiness"— a translation which we cannot help thinking unfortunate, since it lays stress on the pleasurable and consequent aspect of *beatitudo,* rather than on its perfective and primary aspect.

10. Suarez, *De Ult. Fine Hom.,* Disp. VI, Sect. 3.

11. *Contra Gentiles,* III, 116.

12. See Ch. VI above.

13. *S. T.,* 1, qu. 108, a. 6, ad 3. See also *S. T.,* 1, qu. 82, a. 3, and *De Ver.,* qu. 22, a. 11.

14. The whole controversy may be dismissed as futile by some modern thinkers on the ground that it assumes the existence of distinct faculties. The word "faculty" finds disfavor with them, because of their mechanical conception of the Schoolmen's doctrine on the subject. The soul assuredly has the power of knowing and loving, and these are distinct mental activities. Now, whether these powers are called faculties or no, and are conceived of as really distinct, in no wise affects the basic point of medieval controversy. The question still remains whether the soul insofar as it is a power of knowing, or insofar as it is a power of loving, is the higher and more distinctive presentation of man.

15. *De Ult. Fine Hom.,* Disp. VII, Sect. 1, nn. 29-36, and Disp. XV, Sect. 1, n. 6.

16. He refers to *S. T.,* 1, 2, qu. 1, a. 8, and qu. 4, a. 8, ad. 3; 2, 2, qu. 27, a. 6, ad 3; and *De Ver.,* a. 11, ad 11.

17. A full exposition and defense of the Thomistic opinion will be found in the *Salmanticenses,* Tom. V, Tract. IX, Disp. I, dub. 4. The Scotist doctrine is exposed by Mastrius, *Disp. Theol.* in I Lib. Sent., Disp. VI, qu. 12.

18. St. Thomas sometimes speaks of this state as being *contra naturam,* for instance in *Contra Gentiles,* IV, 79; sometimes as being *praeter rationem suae naturae, S. T.,* 1, qu. 89, a. 1.

19. For a discussion of the subject, which belongs to another department of philosophy, the student is referred to Urraburu, *Psychologia,* P. II, Disp. XI.

20. Shelley's *Prometheus Unbound,* Act II, Scene IV.

21. Dante in the *Paradiso,* Cant. iii, 64ff., puts a seemingly Scotistic solution in the mouth of Piccarda. He asks "But tell me, ye whose blessedness is here, do ye desire a more loftly place, to see more, or to make yourselves more dear?" She answers: "Brother, the virtue of love stilleth our will, and maketh us long only for what we have, and giveth us no other thirst. Did we desire to be more aloft, our longings were discordant from his will who here assorteth us, and for that, thou wilt see, there is no room within these circles, if of necessity we have our being here in love, and if thou think again what is love's nature. Nay, 'tis the essence of this blessed being to hold ourselves within the divine will, whereby our own wills are themselves made one. So that our being thus, from threshold unto threshold throughout the realm, is a

joy to all the realm as to the king, who draweth our wills to what he willeth; and his will is our peace; it is that sea to which all moves that it createth, and that nature maketh." The translation is that of *The Temple Classics.*

22. Rickaby, *Of God and His Creatures,* p. 222.

23. *Contra Gentiles,* III, 51, 52; *S. T.,* 1, qu. 12, a. 4, and 1, 2, qu. 5, a. 5.

24. *S. T.,* 1, qu. 62, a. 7. Cf. also Suarez, *De Ult. Fine Hom.,* Disp. IV, Sect. 3, nn. 2-4.

25. The subtler points of the question are treated by Dr. Sestili in a theological disquisition on *S. T.,* 1, qu. 12, a. 1, entitled *De Naturali Intelligentis Animae Capacitate, atque Appetitu Intuendi Divinam Essentiam.*

CHAPTER X

THE GOOD

Goodness is the attribute of an object by reason of which it has a relation of fitness to an appetence. It is perfective, delectable, and useful; real and apparent. In every volitional act man seeks, at least interpretatively, supreme perfective goodness, though the object in which he seeks it may be only apparently good.

GOOD. The second of the three elements involved in the concept which the word "ought" expresses is *Good*. Regarding it the following questions may be asked: 1. What is the good, what are its kinds, and to which of them does the denomination by preeminence belong? 2. What is the norm by which good is distinguished from evil? 3. What are the determinants of good and evil? 4. Can a volitional act be indifferent, i.e., neither good nor evil? 5. What are the subjective conditions of imputability, and when are the good or evil consequences of actions imputable to us?

Taken in its widest application the notion of good, as presented to us *a posteriori,* has the same extension as the notions of the desirable, the likable, or the appetible. Hence good may be generically described as that which is the object of appetence. This, however, is only a description; it does not tell us what good is. If we could advance no further we should be logically impounded in the tautology of J. S. Mill and other Utilitarians for whom the desirable and the good have the same comprehension. We might indifferently, and with equal precision, say that the reason why a thing is good is because it is desirable, and the reason why it is desirable is because it is good. But an easy analysis of the desirable will enable us to find a definition of good, and obviate the necessity of reasoning in a circle.

Confining our examination to human actions, whether voluntary or volitional, we know that desire is an act of the rational appetence involving a relation to an object, the ground of which is want on the part of the appetitive faculty. This want, however, is not to be understood too narrowly as though it were always need. It may indicate a subjective imperfection due to physical or mental defect, or one due similarly to excess. One may want food or information, because one is hungry or ignorant; and on the other hand one may have vital energy beyond comfort, and need exercise, or information beyond one's powers of assimilation, and need intellectual rest. One may have not enough and want more, or too much and want less. But furthermore it may arise from a perfection the consciousness of which impels to self-development, as in the case of one who wishes to advance in the esteem of a friend or in the love of God. It always, however, involves a relation to an object which, insofar as it is apprehended to be suitable for satisfying want, is said to be desirable. Desirability is, therefore, reciprocally a denomination of the object expressing its relation to the appetitive faculty, the ground of which is it fitness to appease desire. It is this ground that constitutes the goodness of the object. Hence desirability is not conceptually goodness but a denominative relation to appetence supervening on it. Goodness, as the ground of desirability, is therefore the attribute of an object by reason of which it is fitted to satisfy appetence, and consequently become desirable. St. Thomas says :[1]

That to which an agent definitely tends, must be fitting to it; since, except for some fitness of the thing to itself, it would not tend to it. But *what is fitting to an agent is good for it.*

A thing is said to be good, therefore, when it has the attributes which befit its kind, and which would be desirable if they were absent, or when it has attributes which are fitted to satisfy the wants of another, consequently desirable to that other. For instance, we say that an act is good when it is in keeping with the nature of the agent, or when it is capable of bringing to the agent a desirable state of being.

FIRST CLASSIFICATION. Between an appetitive faculty and good there is an intrinsic correlation. The faculty is made to reach out for, and bring the agent into union with the objective attribute of being which we call good; and good itself, therefore, as the Schoolmen say, extrinsically specifies the faculty. To want on the part of the faculty responds an attribute of things which is fitted to satisfy want. This want arises primarily from the absence of a perfection which the agent needs, or to which it aspires, or from the presence of a positive imperfection, or superfluity that is inharmonious with nature. The good that satisfies this want is *perfective good*. Concomitant with the absence of desired perfection or the presence of undesired imperfection, there is a conscious feeling of being unsatisfied, which may range through all the gamut of the unpleasant from mere discontent to pain.[2] This feeling of unsatisfaction is a secondary want necessarily incident to the primary want. It is a psychological symptom of the primary want, and nature's stimulus to satisfy it. The relief of it consequently becomes itself an object of desire. The good that brings this relief is *delectable good*. Like the affective state which it replaces, it may vary from the mere assuagement of feeling to the glow of delight. Lastly an object may be a pure means to the attainment of perfective and delectable good, that is to say, the ground of its desirability is wholly extrinsic to it, and, outside of its usefulness to obtain one or other or both the goods described, it is not desirable. The means that serve this purpose is *useful good*.

Everything that is desirable is desired on one or more of these three grounds. But if it be asked to which of them does the term "good" apply by priority, the answer is to the perfective good. It is quite clear that they are not all good in precisely the same sense; they have not all the same relation of fitness to appetence. The useful is denominated good much in the same way as climate is denominated healthy; it has no intrinsic fitness to appetence, but is conducive to that which has. Both the perfective and the delectable are good in themselves, that is, they have qualities intrinsic to them which render them desirable. They differ, however: the delectable, though good *in itself*, is not good *of itself*; whereas the perfective is good *in itself* and *of itself*. The intrinsic qualities by which the former is desirable depend on the latter's real or apprehended fitness to satisfy the primary impulse or appetence towards that which will bring the agent a congruous perfection or relieve it of an incongruous imperfection. Good, therefore, primarily and intrinsically designates the perfective, secondarily and intrinsically the delectable, while the useful, as such, is denominated good for reasons that are extrinsic to it.

SECOND CLASSIFICATION. Since good is appetible in itself, when it is fitted to satisfy the want of an agent, there may be as many sorts of goods as there are specific wants to be satisfied. As a matter of fact man is conscious of many disparate wants. He may desire bodily well-being, or sensuous pleasures, the evolved power of acquiring truth and truth itself as a possession, the graces of life, literature or art, the companionship, esteem, or happiness of his fellow man, the prestige and power of successful enterprise or ambition, the quiet and approval of conscience, the realization of an ennobling and heroic enthusiasm. His wants are as numerous as are the contacts of his many-sided nature with reality. They are physical, intellectual or affective; individual or social; commonplace or magnanimous; mundane or heavenly. But various, divergent, and conflicting though they be, the objects that satisfy them are in every case sought because they are apprehended as capable of appeasing desire either partially or fully.

Now desire is set at rest when the nature reaches that to which it is driven by its final tendency. Tendency is enacted by the consciousness of some perfection of being which is needed, or some development of an actual perfection which is wanted. It is therefore perfective good, or that which is good in itself and of itself, which is the ultimate ground of desirability of whatever kind, even when through false apprehension it is sought in a thing in which it does not objectively exist. Furthermore, a good may be perfective of the nature as such, considered, namely, in all its essential relations, or perfective of some part or faculty of the nature, but in subordination to the nature as such; or again it may be perfective of one or other part or faculty of the nature but in such a way as to be discordant with the nature as such. Good is *real,* therefore, when it is perfective of the unitary nature, or so perfective of a part of the nature that this part retains its proper relation of inferiority or preeminence to other parts, and of subordination to the whole. Good is *apparent* when, though perfective of a part of the nature, it throws it out of its natural relation to other parts, or gives disproportioned worth in the economy of the whole. The good is *moral* when it superadds to the concept of real good a relation to the norm of volitional activity. An object, therefore, is morally good, when the desire of it is an appropriate perfection of the free will. An object considered out of all relation, actual or potential, to the will, though it may be physically good or bad, cannot be said to be in any sense moral.

INTERPRETATIVE INTENTION. The last part of the proposition is a corollary from what has been established. In his volitional activity man does indeed seek this, that or the other particular object, many of which are only apparently good. His choice of the object on which he fixes desire may be erroneous, but the desire itself is an individual actuation of innate tendency of his will toward perfective good. A body of water controlled by numberless sluice-gates may be used judiciously or injudiciously, for the betterment, injury, or ruin of the fields into which it is discharged, but it always seeks equilibrium. Whatever direction man's desires may take, he always intends at least interpretatively the appropriate and adequate object which, responding to the capacity and need of his rational nature, can set desire and tendency at rest.

We say this intention is at least interpretative, for there are four ways in which the will can intend an object: actually, virtually, habitually or interpretatively. Its intention is *actual* when the end intended by an elicit act is explicitly present in consciousness at the time that the imperate acts proceeding from the elicit acts are performed. Its intention is *virtual* when the end intended is not explicitly present in consciousness, but the efficiency (*virtus*) of the elicit act previously formed and unrevoked is transmitted through the serial mediation of imperate acts steadily leading to the attainment of the end. Its intention is *habitual* when the end intended by the elicit act previously formed and still unrevoked is neither explicitly nor virtually present in consciousness. From such an intention imperate acts may or may not proceed. An example will illustrate the latter case. One who sets out with the actual intention of posting a letter may fail to do so, not because he changed his intention, but because he has been distracted by intervening interests. Yet he cannot be said *not to have* the intention, as is evidenced by the fact that a mental association will rouse it to activity. An habitual intention of this kind may last for years. When imperate acts leading to the end do follow upon such an intention two cases may arise. Either the actual intention has degenerated into a kind of habit, as when one begins an operation with an actual intention but continues it even to completion, while occupied with other thoughts; or the actual intention has formed an attitude of will toward an end, by reason of which imperate acts conducive to the end may be imputed, though neither the end nor the bearing of the imperate acts on it are thought of at the time the action is performed. In general, virtual and habitual intentions are weakened forms of a former unrevoked actual intention. Finally an intention

is *interpretative* when the imperate acts are directed not in virtue
or by habit of a previously formed actual intention, but by their
very nature to an end, which, though negatively, is not positively
excluded by an elicit act of the agent.

It is quite clear that in every volitional act man intends a particular good, or the complex of a concrete object and of goodness;
that the goodness, either truly or falsely apprehended to invest the
object, is the formal motive of volition; and that the will, though it
may, following the erroneous judgment of the intellect, negatively
reject the object, it cannot positively exclude goodness from its aim.
But any particular good is an object of volition only insofar as it
is apprehended to be inchoatively or partially related to supreme
good. The will, therefore, in every volitional act intends at least
interpretatively supreme goodness.

EUDAEMONISM. The word "happiness" is usually accepted as an
English equivalent for the Aristotelian word εὐδαιμονία, which St.
Thomas and the Schoolmen generally translated *beatitudo* or *felicitas* understanding by these terms the ultimate perfection of a rational creature. Sir Alexander Grant, whose invariable rendering of
the Aristotelian term is "happiness," acknowledges[3] that with Aristotle pleasure is not a primary part of the concept, but rather inferentially implied in it. The error of attributing to Aristotle the
theory that happiness is the highest good of man may be traced to
the author of the Eudemian Ethics. Kant in modern times gave a
new vogue to the error, and by usage Eudaemonism has become a
superfluous and misleading synonym for Hedonism.

The doctrine of Aristotle on the subject is contained in Books
First and Tenth of the *Nicomachean Ethics.*[4] He begins his investigation by noting that learned and unlearned alike understand by
Eudaemonia, the well-being of life and its activities—τὸ εὖ ζῆν καὶ
τὸ εὖ πράττειν.[5] Starting from this common notion he finds that the
characteristics of *eudaemonia* are: (a) It is a final end—τὸ τέλος
τέλειον—one which is desirable in itself always, and never on account of anything else. Other ends, as honor, pleasure, knowledge,
virtue, are desirable in themselves, it is true, but are sought for the
sake of *eudaemonia,* which they are assumed to produce.[6] (b) It is
an end sufficient in itself—τὸ τέλος αὔταρκες—that is to say, suf-
ficing man in all his essential relations, and not to be reckoned
among other goods, as the most desirable of a class, but to be regarded as outside of comparison and supreme.[7] (c) It must be

something intrinsic to man—τὸ ἔργον τοῦ ἀνθρώπου—to be found in the exercise of his distinctive and specific functions, namely, in the activity of his rational life—ἀνθρώπου δὲ τίθεμεν ἔργον ζωήν τινα, ταύτην δὲ ψυχῆς ἐνέργειαν καὶ πράξεις μετὰ λόγου. *Eudaemonia,* he concludes,[8] is the energizing of the principle of life in man in conformity with the law of his own excellence, or as having the perfection of its kind—ψυχῆς ἐνέργεια κατ' ἀρετήν. He adds to complete his concept that *eudaemonia* must be perfect in duration— ἐν βίῳ τελείῳ—for as one sparrow or one day does not make a spring, so neither does a brief time suffice for man's blessedness.

The nature of pleasure and its relation to *Eudaemonia* touched on in Book First[9] is fully discussed in Book Tenth. In criticizing certain theories he first establishes some preliminary conclusions. These are: (a) Pleasure is natural to man; all men seek pleasure and fly pain, following an impulse that ranges throughout life's activities.[10] (b) Pleasure, as such, is in itself desirable, though not of itself.[11] (c) Pleasures are divided into two classes, namely, mixed and unmixed. The former are those that are preceded by or accompanied with discomfort or pain; the latter, those to which no degree of unpleasantness is annexed.[12] The theories of the Platonists that pleasure is a transition to one's natural state (κίνησις), a process of becoming something better than one was (γένεσις) or a replenisment of want (ἀναπλήρωσις) are untenable.

ARISTOTLE'S DOCTRINE. Having disposed of erroneous opinions, Aristotle proceeds in the next chapter to present his own doctrine. This may be summed up in the following propositions. (a) Pleasure is fruition; like vision, it is at any given moment finished in its kind. It is not the flower producing or produced, but its fragrance; not the feeling of that which promotes life, but the feeling that supervenes at the moment on some stage of vital activity. (b) Pleasure arises whenever a faculty obtains its proper object. Like the bloom of health to youth it is the natural consummation of the faculty's healthy energizing. (c) Pleasure is inseparably connected with the consciousness of vital activity and the exercise of vital functions. The desire of it is as natural as the desire of vital energizing. (d) Pleasures differ in quality; these differences, however, do not inhere in pleasures as such. Since pleasure is attendant on the act of every faculty, whether sensuous or intellectual, it receives its excellence from the excellence of the faculty that is exercised, from the perfection of its activity, and from the perfection of the object with which it is engaged. The higher, therefore, the faculty, the more effective its activity, and the more elevated its object, the higher the pleasure.

In chapter fifth he gives his reasons for holding that pleasures differ in kind. (a) As our several mental activities differ from each other in kind, the respective pleasures that are appropriate to them must likewise differ. (b) While the exercise of a particular faculty is strengthened by its own pleasure, it is impeded by the pleasure of another. (c) As pleasures accompany virtuous and vicious actions alike, they must necessarily differ as the actions of which they are issue. (d) Creatures differing in kind, as a brute animal and a man, have each their appropriate pleasure; and therefore the pleasures that belong to the nature which man has in common with the brute's must differ in kind from those which belong to his higher nature. (e) Men have different temperaments and tastes, and consequently what is pleasant to one may be unpleasant or painful to another.

Aristotle's conclusions briefly recapitulated are: that the highest good of man consists in the highest activity or perfection of his rational nature; that the happiness which is the appropriate pleasure of this good is desirable in itself, since it is the finish of the perfection attained; that it is not desirable of itself, since in being and quality it depends wholly on a specific energizing of the soul.

HEDONISM. The theory that makes pleasure desirable in itself and of itself, and consequently happiness the supreme good for the sake of which and with reference to which all else is desirable, has played a leading part in English ethical thought since the time of Hobbes. In principle it can be traced to Aristippus, the Cyrenaic, and Epicurus, but has received various modifications in modern times. However, the fundamental tenet of all forms is that the desirable is identical with the delectable. This may be understood in two distinct senses. One may hold that as a matter of fact it is psychologically impossible to desire anything unless pleasure in some form is its ultimate determinant. Or one may admit as a psychological fact that some desires are not pleasure-seeking, but maintain that they would be unworthy of a rational being, if their ultimate determinant were not the promotion of happiness. The theory based on the former view is called by Sidgwick *Psychological Hedonism,* and is egoistic in character; that based on the latter view he calls *Ethical Hedonism,* and is universalistic or, as it has been infelicitously styled, utilitarian in character. Now the core of either theory is not expressed by saying that happiness is ultimately desirable, for undoubtedly as the efflorescence of final perfection it is ultimately desirable, but by saying that happiness rather than perfection is the ultimate determinant of desire. Both, insofar as they are definite and distinctive theories, hold that pleasure, either as a matter of fact or as a matter of reasonable aim, is desirable in itself and of itself.

PSYCHOLOGICAL HEDONISM. Our first concern is with Psychological Hedonism, which directly impugns our proposition. The doctrine on which it is based is clearly presented by J. S. Mill:

All desirable things (which are as numerous in the utilitarian as in any other scheme) are desirable either for the pleasure inherent (*sic*) in themselves, or as means to the promotion of pleasure and the prevention of pain.[13]

Desiring a thing and finding it pleasant, aversion to it and thinking of it as painful are phenomena entirely inseparable, or rather are two parts of the same phenomenon; in strictness of language, two different modes of naming the same psychological fact: that to think of an object as desirable (unless for the sake of its consequences), and to think of it as pleasant, are one and the same thing; and that to desire anything, except in proportion as the idea of it is pleasant, is a physical and metaphysical impossibility. So obvious does this appear to me, that I expect it will hardly be disputed.[14]

Oracular certainty is not convincing, when we recall that ethical thinkers since the time of Aristotle have denied what Mill called obvious; that Sidgwick, his disciple, denied it; that even Hume, with whose writings he was familiar, concedes that the distinction between the desirable and the pleasant is at least an hypothesis "conformable to the analogy of nature"; and that it has been philosophically exploded by Green, Rashdall and Taylor, not to mention others. But if the dogma of Psychological Hedonism is neither obvious nor proved, to what does it owe its plausibility, and why does it still retain a standing in many ethical text books and in popular thought? Immediately to a defective analysis of desire and an ambiguous use of the word pleasure. When they say that what we desire is pleasure, they use the word sometimes in a subjective sense to signify an agreeable feeling, and sometimes in an objective sense to signify the thing that gives an agreeable feeling. The passage from Mill just cited illustrates this confusion of thought. Again, in its objective sense, the object which gives pleasure is confounded with an object insofar as it gives pleasure. Desire clearly refers to two features of a thing, namely, to a well-being which its possession is capable of conferring, and to an agreeable feeling consequent in the realization of the well-being. It will readily be admitted, provided the word "pleasure" is not restricted to agreeable feelings of a sensuous kind, that the gratification of any desire through the attainment of its object is accompanied by pleasure—at least by the pleasure of having gratified desire—without being committed to the admission that the agreeable feelings themselves, whether sensuous, intellectual or moral, or that the object precisely as it is thought of as capable of affording these feelings is the end of desire. It seems foolish to contend for instance that a student desires knowledge merely for the sake of and in reference to pleasure.

COMPUTATION OF PLEASURES. Before offering reasons for rejecting Psychological Hedonism, we premise that the questions as to whether and how we may measure and compute pleasures, or as to what pleasure or sum of pleasures is more eligible than others is irrelevant; until we have decided that—to use the words of James Mill[15]—"pleasure in a general way, or speaking generically, i.e., in a way to include all the species of pleasures, and also the abatement of pain, is the end of action." With this understanding of the question at issue we adduce in disproof of the hedonistic theory three classes of facts: psychological, social, moral.

(a) PSYCHOLOGICAL FACT. There is the *psychological fact* that the idea of pleasure is often evoked by the desire, not the desire by the idea of pleasure; in other words we first desire the object in response to sensuous or intellectual tendency, and then it is imagined or thought of as pleasant. The anticipated pleasure is the resultant of desire, not the motive that excited it. The very possibility of intellectual pleasure, for instance, presupposes desire of knowledge. It were as reasonable to say that the thought of such pleasure is the exciting cause of the volitional appetency which we call desire, as it would be to say that the imagined pleasure of satisfying hunger is the exciting cause of the sensuous craving for food. The fact that an object may become pleasant to us only because we have set our desires on it, is evidenced in the case of those who pursue an object of desire with the clear consciousness that no enjoyment, which can result from their efforts, is at all comparable with the sufferings which they must endure in the prosecution of their desires, or the pain they shall experience in its realization. Aristotle's example in illustration of this truth is classical. In the *Nicomachean Ethics*[16] he discusses the nobleness of bravery which, he declares, depends on the sacrifices it calls for; the brave man by facing death in battle consciously runs the risk of losing his life. He then draws the inference, that "it is not true of every virtue that the exercise of it is attended with pleasure, except insofar as one attains the end sought." The literature of all ages, embodying the instinctive wisdom of the race and reflecting its moral estimates, the history of the sufferings endured for freedom, truth, or religion, confirms this psychological truth. Assent to it can be evaded only by cynical subterfuges, some of them of a degrading kind, and others perversive of the impulses that make for moral progress and civilization. When men have submitted to privations, physical or mental pain, for the sake of a worthy object which could not give, and at the time was not thought of as capable of giving, a compensating amount of pleasure, they have been praised if they received any commendation from their fellow men, not for the intensity of their love of pleasure or the cleverness of their hedonistic calculus.[17] The error of Psychological Hedonism arises from its ignoring the correlation between appetence and its object, and between appetence and the corresponding perfective energizing of the faculty. Its fallacy is, as Rashdall terms it, "a hysteron-proteron; it puts the cart before the horse";[18] from the fact that pleasure is consequent on desire, it concludes that it is the antecedent of desire.

(b) SOCIAL FACT. The *social fact* that many of our desires are other-regarding—that is to say, regard the satisfaction of impulses implanted in our social nature—likewise militates against the hedonist theory. Illustrations of this fact are the impulse to benevolence and friendship, the parental impulses, and the civic and humanitarian impulses. That acts consciously performed in response to these impulses are not directed to the attainment of our own pleasure, and are indeed in many cases incompatible with it, is an assertion which one would fancy hard to challenge. It is in fact simply equivalent to saying that some of our acts are unselfish. There is pleasure of course in doing unselfish deeds, at least the pleasure of having done what was noble; but to maintain that unselfish deeds are done for the sake of this pleasure is nonsensical. We can deny that any human being ever performed an unselfish act, and so deny the fundamental fact of Christianity, and the convictions of mankind as embedded in language. But we cannot concede that men have performed self-denying actions, and contend at the same time that they were done from a motive of personal pleasure or interest. It is beside the question to claim, as the hedonist does, that acts of benevolence, of parental devotion, of patriotism or of loyalty to some beneficient ideal have each their own peculiar pleasures and delights, because this has been admitted by every moralist who has written sanely on the subject.

But the question is whether the benevolently disposed is capable of being ultimately interested in any thing except his own feelings: whether a father is incapable of seeking his children's good except for the sake of and in reference to his own gratification; and whether a citizen can love his country for any other reason except that the exercise of such love is pleasant to him, or is the means of obtaining prospective emolument or honor. Introspection gives but one answer to the question. Benevolent conduct does not of itself give pleasure either actually or in anticipation, unless previously desired. The pleasure does not create the desire which the friend, the father, or the patriot feels; it is the desire to do disinterested deeds that creates the pleasure that springs from their performance.

Two experiences against which ascetic science constantly warns the student of perfection may obscure this truth, but an exposition and disclosure of them will confirm it. The first is that when other-regarding desires are thwarted, consciousness of discomfort or pain results, and the aggressive passions (*passiones irascibiles*) come into play. Thus a secondary and self-regarding desire arises which may dominate the primary desire or even supersede it; and so become— unless we are on our guard—an egoistic stimulus towards gratifying the desire. The second experience is that, when the other-regarding desire is progressively expedited, the pleasure attending on success may overbear the primary desire; and again, an action begun from benevolent motives may end in being performed from motives of self. But it is evident that the self-seeking motive is in both cases subsequent to the disinterested motive.

(c) MORAL FACT. The *moral fact* that on other than hedonistic grounds we discriminate between virtuous and vicious pleasure is the palmary argument against Psychological Hedonism. There are pleasures that are recognized to be not merely less eligible than others but intrinsically evil, i.e., not worthy of being desired at all. It is not denied, of course, that such pleasures have been desired, and are therefore desirable in the sense that they *can be* desired. This however does not imply the principle that they *are worth* desiring.[19] Nothing but the exigencies of a theory can hide the fact that men have despised pleasure, comfort, material well-being and life itself at the bidding of conscience and for the sake of duty. Bentham's confident assertion that "it is in fact idle to talk about duties"; that "every man is thinking about interests"; that "to interest duty must and will be made subservient,"[20] does more credit to his consistency than to his intelligence. A mediocre knowledge of history might have informed him, that when a conflict arose between pleasure and duty, the highest types of manhood have renounced the former; and that on such renunciation have the stable foundations of our civilization been laid. In confirmation of this truth it is not necessary to appeal to the heroism of the Christian martyrs; humbler illustrations may be found in every walk of life: in the case of men who have chosen the burden of the right in preference to the pleasures of the alluring wrong, who have done their duty at the price of physical pain or mental anguish. The labored attempts to trace the motives of these actions directly or indirectly to hedonistic feelings is a sophistry which, as Rashdall says, rarely imposes upon any but the very immature student of Psychology or Ethics.

AFFECTIVE INTUITIONISM. This doctrine is radically a species of Hedonism. It constitutes the good of conduct in a special kind of beauty, and makes the cognitive pleasure arising from its contemplation the determinant of moral desire. "What is *beautiful*," says Shaftesbury,[21] "is harmonious and proportionable; what is harmonious and proportionable is *true;* and what is at once beautiful and true is of consequence agreeable and *good*." And elsewhere he says,[22] "there is no *real good* beside the enjoyment of beauty." It is true that Shaftesbury denies that pleasure is desirable, but he understands the word in the sense "of our modern Epicures who are taken up with pleasure of a more substantial kind."[23] It should be borne in mind that Affective Intuitionism is a species of Hedonism, differing from the Hedonism of Bentham first in making the beautiful in conduct, or what it is pleasant in conduct to behold, the end of moral desire; and secondly demanding a special faculty by which the attractiveness of moral action is immediately perceived.

PSYCHOLOGICAL UTILITARIANISM. The distinctive tenet from which this ethical school derives its name is that the morality of an action is constituted by its utility.[24] In other words, an action is good insofar as it is a means to the realization of an end, which is of itself desirable, and evil insofar as it tends to frustrate that end. But utility is a relative term; an action may be useful for many different ends. Conceivably there might be as many different systems of Utilitarianism as there are ends deemed ultimately desirable by various schools of Ethics. We might have eudaemonistic, esthetic, Nietzschean, or pragmatic Utilitarianism as well as hedonistic Utilitarianism.[25]

Furthermore "the principle of utility" may be understood in two senses. In the first place it may be taken as a criterion or test by which the morality of an act can be known. The effects producible by an act may be indicative of its goodness, and the intellect considering these can discern whether a given act does or does not fall under a class of acts commanded, permitted, or prohibited by a moral principle. So understood, it is not the usefulness of the act which constitutes its goodness; on the contrary its goodness renders it useful for observing a law of morality. Or, again, when one resolves on a specific act of virtue, as for instance an act of benevolence, the means by which to execute the act are chosen after weighing the usefulness of various alternatives of conduct. Neither in this sense does the usefulness of the act constitute its goodness, but because it is either good itself, or because, though indifferent itself, it is capable of being good by the direction given it by the will, it becomes useful for the intent of the agent. In neither case does its usefulness constitute its morality, but its actual or potential morality renders it useful. "The principle of utility" understood in this sense is employed in every school of rational Ethics. It is not distinctive of empiric Ethics.

Secondly, understood in its utilitarian sense it is not merely a criterion for discriminating between good and evil; it is the norm by relation to which the action is given morality insofar as it is receptive of it. "By the principle of utility," says Bentham, "is meant that principle which approves or disapproves of every act whatsoever according to the tendency which it appears to have to augment or diminish the happiness of the party whose interest is in question."[26] These two meanings assignable to "the principle of utility" are often confused by students of Utilitarianism.[27]

MILL'S DOCTRINE. The most noted exponent of Psychological Utilitarianism is J. S. Mill.[28] Starting from the common tenets of Hedonism that pleasure or happiness is not only desirable in itself, but of itself, that it alone is ultimately desirable, and that every

action possesses moral worth or is devoid of it, in proportion as it is
or is not useful in furthering happiness, he assigns, as the subject for
whom this happiness was to be obtained, mankind at large. Putting
the theory in our terminology, the ultimate extrinsic end of all
volitional acts is to promote the happiness of man in general, the
ultimate intrinsic end of the individual man is to secure his own
happiness, but only in proportion as it conduces to the general
happiness, and consequently the regulative norm of conduct is "the
greatest happiness of the greatest number." We need not delay to
refute these principles. We have already shown that morality is
intrinsic to our acts, that happiness is not ultimately desirable *of
itself* neither for the individual man, nor for the aggregate of men
called society or mankind; and that, although the well-being and
consequent happiness of his fellow man is one of the proximate and
important ends of conduct, it is not the ultimate and all-embracing
end. We are concerned rather with those phases of Psychological
Utilitarianism by which it became a distinctive species of Hedonism.
In three important respects, then, does it modify sheer hedonism in
its attempt to accommodate itself to the psychological, social and
moral facts to which reference has been made in a preceding section.

HARTLEY'S MODIFICATION. The first modification was introduced by Hartley.[29] Without relinquishing the principle of Hedonism that love of sensuous pleasure originates all desire, he refuses to
admit that "rational self-interest," which is the same with "the
abstract desire of happiness and aversion to misery," is the actual
motive of every intelligent being's conduct during the whole course
of his existence.[30] On the contrary he maintains: [31]

> There are certain tempers of mind, with the actions flowing from
> them, as of piety, gratitude . . . towards God; of benevolence, com-
> passion . . . towards men; of temperance, patience . . . in respect of a
> person's own private enjoyments or sufferings; which when he believes
> himself to be possessed of and reflects on, a pleasing consciousness and
> self-approbation rise up in his mind, exclusive of any direct explicit
> consideration of advantage likely to accrue to himself from his pos-
> session of these good qualities. In like manner the view of them in
> others raises up a disinterested love and esteem for these others.

These "tempers of the mind," however, are not primitive but
derivative affections, that is to say, traceable ultimately to sensuous
pleasures and pains, and evolved therefrom by the law of mental
association. Children are early taught to associate mentally pleasure,

reward and praise with actions which their elders esteem good; and pain, punishment and blame with those they esteem evil. Later and during the whole progress of life experience teaches us that agreeable consequences attend the exercise of many virtues and unpleasant ones the practice of many vices. The many immediate, or at least obvious though remote, benefits that follow from the virtuous actions of others lead us first to love the persons themselves by association, and then by a further association to love the virtues that endeared them to us apart from any connection these virtues may have with our own interest. These associations are further reenforced by the factitious pleasures of sympathy, ambition and religion. On this theory all our emotions, love of parents, social affections, friendship, loyalty to country, reverence for law and authority, and religious sentiments, are ultimately derived from sensuous pleasures with which they were in past experience mentally associated.

The objections to this theory are many and obvious.[32] (a) It does not account for many judgments reprobating vicious pleasures, the evil consequences of which are not evident, when indulgence is controlled by prudence. (b) The mental associations formed in childhood will not explain their steadfastness and strength in later life when reason has developed and experience has dispelled other illusions. (c) It does not account for their early formation, for their identical prevalence, nor for their transmission from generation to generation. (d) It begets a falsehood, since we are misled by these associations into accepting as pleasant what was originally and is in itself unpleasant. Let us grant that it was a deception in our early life to fancy that we loved virtue, whereas we really loved the pleasure that was somehow connected with it; and again let us grant that, by an equal deception, we hated vice, whereas actually we hated the surplus of pain over pleasure,[33] which had somehow issued from over-indulgence. Granted all this, we still assert that it would be senseless in mature years to carry on these self-deceptions. Once we have discovered the pedigree of our "disinterested" sentiments the fraud should no longer deceive us. (e) It gives no rational worth to virtue over vice. The love of virtue is not any more reasonable than a miser's love of money, as both are due to mental associations. He first loved money for the pleasure he hoped to procure by it, and then he loved it for its own sake. (f) It attempts to derive pleasures which are the accompaniment of one class of mental activities from pleasures that belong to another, and specifically distinct, class; the higher from the lower; the intellectual and moral from the sensuous. (g) It makes an instruction and a discipline that is pedagogical for a process that is creative. Because education, training, and experience lead us to perceive the truths of conduct, it concludes that emotional states fabricated by past mental associations have originated those truths.

SPENCER'S EVOLUTIONARY THEORY. The difficulties urged against the opinions of Hartley and James Mill, [34] who tried to explain by associationism conduct which does not arise from the individual's desire of pleasure or his aversion to pain, are in some respects lessened by the evolutionary hypothesis which Spencer and his followers have applied to Ethics; and in other respects are increased. Retaining the hedonistic principle that the primary spring of all conduct is pleasure, Spencer first concedes that certain emotions responding to right and wrong conduct "have no apparent basis in the individual's experience of utility." He then remounts to the dawn of sentient life where the experiences of the utility of pleasure and the harmfulness of pain began, where, namely, a connection between pleasure-giving actions and the increase of life, and between pain-giving actions and the decrease of life was first established. These experiences produced cerebral modifications by which the connection between pleasure or pain and their correlatives, the increase or decrease of life, became through physiological associations permanently fixed. The cerebral modifications in turn were transmitted by heredity, continually augmented through successive generations, and finally consolidated in emotional tendencies to forms of conduct that are beneficial to the individual and the race, while the experiences on which they were based and from which they sprung have passed out of consciousness. Their imperious promptings seem now something connatural, and are sometimes mistaken for an immutable characteristic of our intellectual and volitional faculties, impressed upon them by a divine authority.[35]

SPENCER AND DISINTERESTEDNESS. We are not at present discussing Spencer's opinion on the origin and nature of moral obligation. That subject belongs to a later proposition. Nor is his opinion on the ultimate intrinsic end in question; this he asserts is happiness, though he holds that it is not or should not be the immediate aim of conduct.[36] At present we have to do with his explanation of the psychological fact that some of our actions are "disinterested," i.e., not posited for the sake of pleasure. Now, while it removes one of the difficulties against Hartley's theory, it increases another. Hartley accounts for the formation of "disinterested" motives by introducing mental associations operating within the span of a few years. Spencer transfers the problem from the region of verifiable evidence and appeals to physiological associations working through evolutionary periods. The deception involved in the hedonistic paradox, which in the theory of the older Associationists arose from causes that might have been counteracted, in the evolutionary theory has now become imbedded in the frame of our mind. Our emotional tendencies, whether advantageous, useless or harmful to us, cannot now be obliterated. Through some obliquity in the evolutionary process pleasure has been dissociated from many of our desires. Tendency is no longer enacted by a craving for an agreeable feeling. We are governed by the prejudications of ancestral ghosts. Yet we ask: Why should a bull, for instance—if he had the use of reason—permit himself to be affected by a violent prejudice against a red rag, because his forebears once associated the feeling of pain with the color of red and transmitted to his progeny through modifications of the nervous system this ancestral association? Spencer, when asked what in his theory prompts him to denounce the unjust treatment of inferior races, answers:[37]

I am prompted by a feeling which is aroused in me quite apart from any sense of duty, quite apart from any thought of Divine command, quite apart from any thought of reward or punishment here or hereafter. . . . If you say that my theory gives me no reason for my interest in asserting this principle, the answer is that I cannot help being interested.

But neither can the bull help feeling irritated at the sight of a red rag; and if he could give a reason, it would be as satisfactory as Spencer's. If we have no other guide to determine the good of conduct except that the primitive craving for pleasure has by accumulated and transmitted experiences been metamorphosed into non-hedonistic desires, we are at the mercy of a rule that is contingent, vague, and, for all we know, is arbitrary and meaningless, and we are being individually cheated for the sake of the ultimate temporal happiness of future members of the race, who, we have no assurance except a mere dogma of evolutionary philosophy, will ever reach the earthly paradise that we are blindly sacrificing ourselves to obtain for them.

The fact is that Spencer's genesis of moral emotion is not the basis of his theory of morality; but his theory of morality performed his hypothesis of its evolution. Accepting Hedonism he had to make a place for it in his scheme of evolution. Had he been an Aristotelian Eudaemonist, he could as successfully have made his morality eudaemonistic. He probably fancied that he was working forward from primitive data, while as a matter of fact he was working backward from the principles of Hedonism and arranging the steps of this retrogression, as well as he could, to accord with the incontrovertible facts of moral consciousness.[38]

MILL AND DISINTERESTEDNESS. The second modification consists in recognizing altruistic or other-regarding affections as unqualifiedly distinct from egoistic or self-regarding affections, and aims at giving an account of them which will be consistent with psychological Hedonism. J. S. Mill is the representative exponent of this modification. It is the last redoubt of a theory of morality that makes pleasure the ultimate determinant of desire. Psychological Hedonism presents three distinct phases. First, Hobbes and his followers frankly and vigorously repudiated any attempt at harmonizing egoistic and altruistic affections, or rather they maintained that every other-regarding act when analyzed was resolvable into self-love.[39]

The gross extravagance of this position, which even ordinary introspection will contradict, hindered its general acceptance. It was superseded after a long period of protest and ethical speculation by another position which under various guises prevailed for a long time. Bentham, who may be taken as the representative of this phase of Psychological Hedonism held, that among the pleasurable motives inducing to action were benevolence, friendship and the like; that these are not resolvable into the pleasures of self-love, but constitute a distinct class of pleasures. Nature or custom has so fashioned us that we derive pleasure not only from the satisfaction of personal feelings but also from the contemplation of another's happiness. He differed from Hobbes in asserting that, although the motive of a benevolent action is the pleasurable feeling that the anticipation of its performance excites, its direct object is the happiness of another; whereas Hobbes held that the pleasure of self was always the motive and object of the action.[40] Hume says:[41]

Nature must by the internal frame and constitution of the mind, give an original propensity to fame ere we can reap any pleasure from that acquisition. . . . Now where is the difficulty in conceiving that this may likewise be the case with benevolence and friendship, and that, from the original frame of our temper we may feel a desire of another's happiness or good, which by means of that affection becomes our own good and is afterwards pursued from the combined motives of benevolence and enjoyment?

Why may we not allow, he continues, to humanity and benevolence, what must be allowed to vengeance, which "from the force of passion alone may be so eagerly pursued as to make us neglect every consideration of ease, interest and safety?" The "great *hysteron-proteron* of Psychological Hedonism," as Rashdall styles it, is glaringly manifest in this passage. Hume unconsciously admits the incontrovertible fact that in seeking the happiness or welfare of others, as well as in seeking their misery or destruction, pleasure is not the motive of desire, but desire, realized in fact or in prospect, is the source of the pleasure. In the third phase of Psychological Hedonism, J. S. Mill makes a final attempt to account for this fact.

MILL'S ILLOGICALITY. One of the difficulties of dealing with Mill's views is that they were never logically coordinated. He oscillates between psychological and rational Hedonism, as it suits the purpose of his argument. His *Essay on Utilitarianism* consequently abounds in contradiction and fallacies. An exposition of them in detail would be an almost interminable task. It is however not needed, as the principles by which they may be detected have already been given. We deal with him here only insofar as he departs from or refines upon Bentham. In an early essay[42] he points out the defects of temperament and experience which disqualify Bentham as a philosophic moralist. The first of these was his incapacity to appreciate, or even to attach any value to anybody's view but his own.[43] The other was his limited knowledge of human nature.[44] Mill does not profess to reject Bentham's principles; his censure regards the narrow range of human emotions within which those principles are applied. He claims that the highest forms of self-sacrifice, of benevolence, and of devotion to the common good may be inculcated on utilitarian principles. He says:[45]

I must again repeat, what the assailants of utilitarianism seldom have the justice to acknowledge, that the happiness that forms the utilitarian standard of what is right in conduct is not the agent's own happiness, but that of all concerned. As between his own happiness and that of others, utilitarianism requires him to be as strictly impartial as a disinterested and benevolent spectator.

If these assertions could be proved, the problem that had vexed Utilitarians would have been solved. Mill in his zeal to remove some of the reproaches that had been brought against his system, expresses sentiments, which—apart from some extravagances—do him credit as a man, but which in spite of his fervid insistence, and their appeal to the moral judgment of men, leave the logical inquirer unsatisfied. There are no moralists, except perhaps some pessimists of Schopenhauer's school, who would deny that the general good and the happiness of other men is one of the ends of life; that it is an important end; and that it is to be secured to the greatest extent possible. Even von Hartman admits this. What the philosophic student of Ethics want to know is: why the Psychological Utilitarian should regard the happiness of others desirable apart from any pleasure thence accruing to self; or why he should be an impartial spectator as between his ultimate intrinsic end and that of another.

MILL'S REASONS. Mill gives two reasons. The first of these is purely logical:[46]

No reason can be given why the general happiness is desirable, except that each person, so far as he believes it attainable, desires his own happiness. This however being a fact, we have not only all the proof the case admits of, but all which it is possible to require that happiness is a good, that each person's happiness is a good to that person, and the general happiness, therefore, a good to the aggregate of all persons.

Then, reverting to the associationist theory, he proceeds to show that other things which are objects of desire, as virtue, power, fame, are desirable either as means to or parts of happiness; and concludes that "happiness is the sole end of human action, and the promotion of it the test by which to judge all human conduct." The presentation of his argument in logical form is a sufficient refutation of it. It may be put as follows: Assuming as proved by the principles of mental association that for each person the ultimate determinant of all desires is happiness, it follows that to all persons their happiness is ultimately desirable. Now a happiness that is ultimately desirable to all persons is the general happiness. Therefore the general happiness is ultimately desirable to each and every person. It puts a strain on one's credulity to believe that the author of a *System of Logic* did not perceive the illogical character of this transition from the collective to the distributive use of the word "all."

His second reason is drawn from our social nature. It may be presented in two propositions. (a) Our moral feelings "are not indeed a part of our nature in the sense of being in any perceptible degree present in all of us" but are acquired faculties. Human nature is "susceptible by a sufficient use of external sanctions, and of the force of early impression, of being cultivated in almost any direction" whether mischievous or utilitarian, egoistic or altruistic. As a matter of fact it has been developed to entertain moral feelings of a utilitarian character. (b) He perceives however that this explanation, based on the associationist theory, is open to the objection already adduced, namely, that such a genesis of our moral feelings renders them factitious:

But moral associations which are wholly of artificial creation, when intellectual culture goes on, yield by degrees to the dissolving force of analysis: and if the feeling of duty, when associated with utility, would appear equally arbitrary; (*sic*) if there were no leading department of our nature, no powerful class of sentiments, with which that association would harmonize, which would make us feel it congenial, and incline us not only to foster it in others (for which we have abundant interested motives), but also to cherish it in ourselves; if there were not, in short, a natural basis of sentiment for utilitarian morality, it might well happen that this association also, even after it had been implanted by education, might be analyzed away.

But there *is* this basis of powerful natural sentiment; and this it is which, when once the general happiness is recognized as the ethical (sq. on. p. 30) standard, will constitute the strength of the utilitarian morality. This firm foundation is that of the social feelings of mankind; the desire to be in unity with our fellow creatures, which is already a powerful principle in human nature, and happily one of those which tend to become stronger, even without express inculcation, from the influences of advancing civilization.[47]

The deeply-rooted conception which every individual even now has of himself as a social being, tends to make him feel it one of his natural wants that there should be harmony between his feelings and aims and those of his fellow creatures. . . . This conviction is the ultimate sanction of the greatest-happiness morality.[48]

The sufficient basis of Psychological Utilitarianism is "the subjective feeling in our mind"[49] that the happiness of others is "a thing naturally and necessarily to be attended to, like any of the physical conditions of our existence."[50]

Now everything that Mill contends for regarding man's social nature is admitted by a follower of Aristotle, except his conclusion. It is true that there is implanted in human nature impulses looking to the happiness of others. It is more exactly true however to say that these social impulses are directed to the well-being of our fellow men and welfare of the race, or to that which is the source of happiness which we should reasonably desire for them. It is also true that it is man's destiny as a social being to promote the well-being and happiness of his fellow man; but it is not true that this is his ultimate destiny, as it is not theirs, merely to enjoy temporal happiness. The distinctive principles that Mill should have established, if his system is to stand, are two: (a) that happiness or a pleasurable state of being is the *ultimate determinant* of desire, and (b) that the promotion of the greatest happiness of the greatest number of men is the *ultimate purpose* of each one's existence. He presents us with no premises from which either principle follows, and at best merely veils by the persuasiveness of his exposition "the profound discrepancy," as Sidgwick admits, that exists between them. The prepossession that well-being and happiness are simply two sides of the same psychological fact and that they are conceptually interchangeable pervades and vitiates all his arguments. And the assumption that the ultimate end of man must be realized during his temporal existence is accepted as a truth that no one will challenge, though unsubstantiated by either reason or experience.

MILL'S HIERARCHY OF PLEASURES. The third modification consists in recognizing the superiority of the higher over the lower pleasures, and in claiming that, precisely as pleasures, one differs in kind from the other, and is intrinsically, as a pleasure, more desirable than the other. This position, Mill assures us, may be taken by a Psychological Utilitarian "with entire consistency." Yet in the same paragraph he acknowledges that Utilitarian writers in general have not taken it, but have placed the superiority of mental over bodily pleasures in their circumstantial advantages, and that to draw out the consequences of the utilitarian principle "in any sufficient manner many Stoic, as well as Christian, elements require to be included." It would be useless to discuss philosophically an eclectic position of this kind. Under Mill's treatment, Utilitarianism ceased to be a system. Leslie Stephen says that Mill tried to remedy "the really weak points of the old Utilitarianism." But these really weak points were, as we have seen, essential elements of Psychological Utilitarianism. Mill's application of Stoic and Christian principles to the system was not sanative, but at best sedative; he did not cure but concealed its weaknesses. Though his bias continued to be hedonistic, he had abandoned more completely than he was aware of the fundamental principles of his predecessors.

MILL'S WEAK POINTS. We shall, therefore, merely make a brief examination of Mill's effort "to remedy the weak points of the older Utilitarianism." In the first place he asserts that it would be absurd to estimate pleasures by quantity alone, i.e., by their intensity and duration,[51] while in estimating all other things quality is to be considered as well as quantity. And indeed it would be quite absurd. But it is an absurdity necessarily involved in a theory that makes pleasure or happiness the ultimate determinant of desire. If the delectable is only another side of the desirable, the more desirable is simply the more delectable. That pleasures differ in kind and that the more delectable may be the less desirable is, as Aristotle shows, undoubtedly true; but when Mill furthermore asserts that this distinction of kinds is, as a norm of desire, "quite compatible with the principle of utility," i.e., of Utilitarianism, the only evidence he offers is emphatic affirmation. If pleasure is differentiated in kind from pleasure, it cannot assuredly be by what is common to pleasure as such. A Utilitarian, therefore, who admits that higher and lower, intellectual and sensuous, virtuous and vicious pleasures differ in kind and that the former are intrinsically more desirable than the latter, must logically admit also that the ultimate determinant of desire is a quality superadded to pleasure.[52] The error of the Hedonist does not consist in making a pleasurable state ultimately desirable, for this is held by all Eudaemonists; but in making pleasure the determinant of that state, instead of making the perfection of being proper to the state the determinant of pleasures that are or are not desirable.

Mill next proceeds to set up a canon by which we may discern "which is the best worth having of two pleasures, or which of two modes of existence is the most grateful to the feelings, apart from its moral attributes and from its consequences." He recognized the necessity of establishing some canon of conduct, if his Utilitarianism was not to vaporize into meaningless rhetoric. His mental bent rendered him incapable of accepting an eudaemonistic canon, and his social modification of Bentham's Utilitarianism precluded the personal pleasure of satisfying other-regarding impulses. "Mill perceiving that something was wanting," says Leslie Stephen, "makes the unfortunate attempt at supplying the gap by his assumption of an imaginary consensus of better minds." But furthermore be it noted, it must be a consensus of "better minds" who have had experience of both kinds of pleasures. "Of two pleasures," he says, "if there be one to which all or almost all, who have experienced both, give a decided preference, irrespective of any feelings of moral obligation to prefer it, that is the more desirable pleasure." From the verdict of these, the only competent judges, he continues, "I apprehend there can be no appeal." The incoherencies of Mill's position are obvious and we shall let the utilitarians settle that phase of the matter among themselves. What concerns us is that an external tribunal of widely experienced pleasure-seekers is set up, which alone is competent to decide what mode of existence is "the most grateful to the feelings." This is the last word of Mill on Psychological Utilitarianism; authority has superseded psychology.

ETHICAL UTILITARIANISM. Sidgwick recognized that Utilitarianism was an intellectually discredited system unless a rational basis could be provided for it. Mill's introduction into Bentham's "moral arithmetic" of qualitative differences in pleasures which were not resolvable into differences of degrees, though in thorough accord with the moral consciousness of mankind, was fatal to Psychological Hedonism. If one pleasure was intrinsically higher than another it must be by something outside of its pleasantness. This something, therefore, must be revealed by reason and not by feeling. Accordingly retaining the Utilitarian principle that "the greatest happiness of the greatest number" is the ultimate end of conduct, Sidgwick seeks its justification in the moral intuitions.[53] He is, therefore, a Hedonist in his conception of the ultimate good, a Utilitarian in his conception of the ultimate end of conduct, and an Intuitionist in method. *The Method of Ethics* professes to base Utilitarianism on moral dictates of reason rather than on the conclusions of experience. Now in the commonly recognized principles of prudence, benevolence and justice we discover, he thinks, elements that are self-evident or intuitively known. These are: rational self-love which dictates that one should aim at his own good on the whole; rational love of others which dictates that one should regard the good of any other individual as much as his own; and rational impartiality in the application of general rules, the rules namely of prudence and benevolence.[54] Apart from the question as to the origin of our moral intuitions, these principles, as reflection shows, possess ultimate validity.[55]

The problem Sidgwick set himself to solve was to define the relation of self-love to love of others on rational grounds, and on the same ground to derive Ethical Utilitarianism from the relation thus established. He encumbered his task with three difficulties. First, he sought to find a rational relation between two principles equally axiomatic and opposite without having recourse to a higher and distinct principle which could harmonize them. The relation between self-love and love of others can be rendered rational either by subordinating the worth of one to the other, as do respectively the egoist and altruist, or by subordinating both to the regulative preeminence of a wider and more exalted principle through conformity with which they become rational.[56] Sidgwick chose the former alternative and involved himself in an ethical dualism from which there is no escape.

It is true that at the close of the concluding chapter of his work he practically confesses that unless certain theological postulates are admitted, there is "an ultimate and fundamental contradiction in our apparent intuitions of what is Reasonable in conduct." But this confession forms no part of the argument by which he attempted to reconcile Utilitarianism with reason.

Secondly, by making happiness of itself the ultimate good, he entangled himself in an indefinite subjectivism to which he vainly tried to give a definite objectivity. From the proposition, "his own happiness is the ultimate aim of each man," he endeavored to reach the conclusion "the greatest happiness of the greatest number is the supremely reasonable object of each man's desire." Happiness, undefined by the perfection of which it is the outcome, is simply an agreeable state of consciousness. It is one thing for the student, another thing for the merchant or athlete, one thing for the ascetic, another for the sensualist. "The greatest happiness of the greatest number" receives accordingly as many interpretations as there are classes of individuals who, each rationally desiring happiness for himself, should rationally desire the same for others. Thirdly, by making the happiness of self the ultimate intrinsic end of each man, and the general happiness his ultimate extrinsic end, to which if need be the intrinsic end was to be sacrificed, he divorced man's psychological nature from his ethical nature. The older utilitarians, whatever their defects, never led their followers into a blind alley in order to disclose to them an irreconcilable incompatibility of an essential impulse of their rational nature and their ultimate extrinsic end.

SIDGWICK'S ARGUMENT. This, in effect, is nothing more than an elaborated and developed exposition of Mill's bald presentation.[57] Syllogistically the argument may take this form. 1. Whatever is reasonable for each one to seek is objectively reasonable. It is reasonable for each man to seek his own happiness. Therefore, to seek happiness is objectively reasonable. 2. Whatever is objectively reasonable should be impartially sought. In an impartial quest the happiness of one is not preferable to that of another. Hence, it is objectively reasonable to attach as much importance to the happiness of another as to our own. 3. To our mind impartial reason tells us that happiness diffused among many is greater than happiness confined to the individual self. The happiness diffused among the many is the greatest happiness of the greatest number. Therefore— summing up antecedent consequences—impartial reason tells us that it is objectively reasonable to seek the greatest happiness of the greatest number in preference to the happiness of the individual self.

The major of the first syllogism is untenable by a Hedonist. "Objective" is a protean term. A thing may be said to be objective either because it has reality independently of a subject knowing or desiring it, or because, though intrinsically a modification of a subject, it may when non-existent be apprehended as something that it would be desirable to induce. Again this modification may be definite, that is, fixed by the very nature of the subject, as for instance, health; or indefinite, that is varying with the faculty it affects and the temperament and tastes of the subject, as pleasure. Pleasure is attendant on the energizing of every appetence, and is not merely a modification of the subject, but one that is peculiar to him. As such it cannot be reduced to one objective category. The major is true therefore only in a tautological sense. Hence the conclusion is wider than the premises. The only legitimate conclusion would be: "Therefore to seek one's own happiness or pleasure is objectively reasonable, namely in the second sense of the term 'objective' just defined."

The second syllogism, besides laboring under the equivocations that vitiate the first, introduces other fallacies. "Impartially sought" may mean that, in adjudicating the respective claims of self and of another to pleasure or happiness, prejudice or prepossession does not influence one. Sidgwick's principle of "justice" so understood would recognize that individual claims may clash, but that in reason one has precedence over the other. In this sense the rational claims of self need theoretically never come in conflict with the rational claims of another. If the self-evident deliverance of reason can run counter to one another we may as well cease philosophizing. We cannot admit that the ultimate intrinsic end of self may become incompossible with the ultimate intrinsic end of another, though we may admit that proximate ends sought by self and by another may conflict. But when such a conflict arises one or other claim rationally prevails. Practically the decision may at times be difficult; but if an ethical system necessitates the theoretic admission that two equally rational claims may be positively irreconcilable, the only legitimate conclusion to be drawn is that the system itself is not a rational interpretation of the facts of moral consciousness.

Again the phrase may mean that detached from rational love of self and viewing one's own happiness irrelatively to self, one should on principles of reason regard another's happiness of equal importance with one's own, both being alike in intensity and duration. But we instinctively ask: Of equal importance to whom? "From the point of view (if I may so say) of the Universe" answers Sidgwick. But again, what is "the Universe" to which a point of view is dubiously attributed? It may be the present or a future aggregate of human, or in fact of all sentient, beings, or it may be the sum total of happiness that can exist, which Sidgwick calls the Universal Good, using the term "Universal," consequently, in an arithmetical sense. The later seems to be the sense intended, though the former is necessarily implied. In either sense his principle of "justice" begs the position which he has so laboriously undertaken to prove; and in neither is it, as he assures us, a rational intuition. Reason does not compel one to assume an attitude of justice or fairness towards a summation, unless it can be shown whether and to whom it is important that the summation be greater or less. This other, on Utilitarianism principles, can only be "the Universe" of one's fellow men. That we should seek our own good so as at the same time, as far as may be, to promote the good of others is a moral truth which reason can prove, but it is not a rational intuition. But that we should in direct opposition to rational love of self impartially contemplate our own and another's happiness as equal ciphers in a sum total of happiness is not a rational intuition and neither can it be proved as long as we are persons and not pawns in the game of "the Universe."

Of the third syllogism little need be said. An agreeable state of consciousness multiplied among many is assuredly greater numerically than that same agreeable state when enjoyed by one or a few, but it is not greater in intensity and duration. The multiplication of units possessing an attribute does not increase the attribute itself. It is not in fact easy to see why it would not be rational on purely utilitarian principles to neglect or sacrifice the happiness of the many, if by so doing the happiness of the few could be prolonged or intensified. A practical Utilitarian has said, apparently with the view of justifying economic conditions that brought material prosperity and happiness to his own class: "The American Beauty rose can be produced in all its glory only by sacrificing the early buds that grow up around it." The utilitarian who is morally better than his system would repudiate such a conclusion, but could he disprove it on utilitarian principles? He cannot show that the happiness of a minority should not be sacrificed, if thereby the greatest happiness of the majority be obtained; or that the happiness of the many today should not be deliberately frustrated in order to produce a class of men who could enlarge future happiness. He can on no logical ground pass from intension to extension, or justify a less intension for the sake of a wider extension. On the contrary, if he estimate happiness in a spirit of impartial aloofness to individuals, he must perceive that the supremely great happiness of a select class is "from the point of view of the Universe" of more value than a mediocre happiness diffused among the multitude. If he can put aside rational love of self while impartially seeking happiness he may for the same reason hold in abeyance rational love of others.

IDEAL UTILITARIANISM. Rashdall realizes that an ethical system based on hedonistic principles must, when submitted to analysis, result inevitably in radical contradiction, and to that extent refuses to accept the Utilitarianism of Sidgwick. But he accepts as "a priori or immediate deliverance of reason" the axioms of prudence, benevolence, and equity. He says: [58]

It is self-evident to me that I ought (where it does not collide with the greater good of another) to promote my own greatest good, that I ought to prefer a greater good on the whole to a lesser, and that I ought to regard the good of one man as of equal intrinsic value with the like good of any one else.[59]

The fundamental principles then of Rashdall's system are: first, that the ultimate end is well-being or εὐδαιμονία, which includes, but is not determined by, happiness; secondly, that actions are good or evil only in proportion as they tend to produce the greatest amount of happiness for society in general; and thirdly that "the axioms of Prudence, Benevolence, and Equity possess a clearness, definiteness, and freedom from contradiction which other alleged intuitions so conspicuously lack."[60] He escapes, therefore, the incoherencies intrinsic to the hedonistic utilitarianism of Sidgwick, by taking as the ultimate aim of conduct a generically definite end. But his Ideal Utilitarianism is as open as is Sidgwick's to the difficulties that reason brings against any ethical system which sets up the good of society, humanity, or the race as the ultimate extrinsic good of each individual. The first premise of utilitarianism, that society or humanity is an end in itself, in the sense that it has no purpose beyond itself, seems an absurdity, is not at any rate self-evident, and has not been proved.[61] We cannot determine how far a soldier is for the sake of the army until we have determined what the purpose of the army is. Neither, in like manner, can we determine how far an individual is for the good of society or the race, until we have clearly determined whether society or the race themselves have any purpose, and what relation that purpose has to the good of the individual.[62]

In conclusion we call the student's attention to the importance for clear thinking of the distinction which we have made between the extrinsic and intrinsic ends, between the objective, subjective, and formal ends, between an end to be possessed and an end to be produced. These may seem to be mere scholastic refinements, but neglect of them has given to Utilitarianism of whatever kind its intellectually muddled and inconsequential character.

SCHOPENHAUER'S PESSIMISM. The theory that directly contravenes our proposition is that of Pessimism.[63] It is as old as human philosophy, but in modern times Schopenhauer has attempted to give it a scientific cast.[64] The leading tenets of his teaching insofar as they bear on our subject are these.

(a) The ultimate reality of the world is unconscious Will or blind conation. Kant had left the "thing-in-itself," or noumenon that underlies all phenomena, unexplored; Schopenhauer finds it to be, what we should call appetence, to which however he gives the name "Will." This unitary, indivisible, irrational and unconscious Will is not the cause but the innermost essence of individual things, manifesting and "objectifying" itself in all forms of being from the lowest to the highest.

(b) Its distinctive activity is craving for what it has not or is not. This Schopenhauer calls "desire." Will, of its very nature, is always desiring. But desire supposes want, and want is necessarily painful. Will is, therefore, essentially unhappy. This unhappiness increases as Will objectifies itself in consciousness and reaches its maximum in man.

(c) Pleasure is merely neutral, being the relief that follows on the temporary cessation of desire; and consequently pain, which is the essential evil of the universe, preponderates in life over respite from desire.

(d) Freedom from pain is possible only when desire is lulled or extinguished. A temporary release may be found in artistic enjoyment, but final escape from the misery of life can be effected only by the extinction of the will to exist.

The metaphysical postulates of this philosophy of misery do not fall within the scope of our discussion. We simply note that its starting point is the idealism of Kant, and its termination a pantheistic materialism which denies the immortality of the soul. Its assumption that all the value of life is measured in terms of pleasure or pain we have already disposed of.

REFUTATION OF SCHOPENHAUER. To the ethical side of Schopenhauer's Pessimism we oppose the following contentions.

(a) The ultimate principle, that is to say the first cause, not the ultimate ground in a pantheistic sense, of the universe of things, is a will indeed, but not a will devoid of consciousness, separated from intelligence, and acting without purpose.[65] This contention is a necessary inference from our cosmological postulate.[66] The manifestation of this will in the world through creation is rational, both in the sense that the world is a coherent system of parts combined by the interdependence and mutual bearings of countless forces into a physical whole, and also in the sense that it is an ordered system of ends reciprocally coordinated, and ultimately subordinated to one end which gives meaning and value to the moral whole.[67] The rejection of these contentions would reduce science and morality to chaos. And in fact what moral principles Schopenhauer advocates are wholly extraneous to his system. An ultimate reality which, as it gradually objectifies itself in higher and higher forms, becomes continuously more evil until it reaches a maximum in a self-conscious being, must be essentially evil itself. A world-ground that is evil at the root is either rational or irrational. If it is rational, it would certainly be irrational on the part of individual objectifications of it to make the end of their conscious existence consist in negating its activity. The only reasonable procedure for them would be to recognize and accept their identification with the ultimate reality, and to seek their well-being and blessedness in misery. If it is irrational, then any science of conduct that is in accord with the universe of things must also be irrational. The condemnation of the ultimate reality that objectifies itself in the conscious individual, when pronounced by that individual is utterly absurd. The craving to be reasonable is only one of the absurd phases of the world's misery. And an attempt by self-conscious beings to correct the evils which arise from the objectification of the world-will is as futile as would be the rebellion of rays of light against their source. If the world-will is evil and irrational at the root, then Schopenhauer has no right to appeal to reason; he is appropriating what is extraneous to his system. If it is evil and rational, then reason points out evil as our good.

(b) That the distinctive activity of the will is desire indicating want (even if it be accepted as a psychological truth) proves that the will essentially seeks that which will bring it happiness. It proves not that the will is essentially unhappy, and that surcease of misery can be attained by extinction of desire, but rather that it is temporarily unhappy, and will gain happiness by fulfilment of desire. Its present actual want of complete happiness is a spur by which it is guided and induced to seek its essential happiness hereafter.

(c) The theory that pleasure is merely negative while pain is positive is so grotesque that it has been abandoned by subsequent Pessimists. It has no foundation, either rational or experiential, outside of the temperamental pessimism of its author.

(d) That pain immeasurably preponderates, or that it preponderates at all over pleasure in this life in incapable of proof or disproof. The *a priori* arguments advanced are based on an incoherent metaphysics, or on an erroneous psychology. Nothing can be established *a posteriori,* until we have invented an hedonistic unit. This unit would involve the two elements of intensity of feeling, and duration as estimated in consciousness, both of which elude scientific measurement. Moreover, in order that the hedonistic balance be of scientific value, we should have to calculate the exact amount of pain there is in the world from the very nature of things, and discriminate from it the pain caused by the volitional activity of man, which, since it is remediable, should be deducted from the sum total of pain experienced by sentient beings. This would be a problem of maddening complexity. But it would be enormously more complicated, if we include in our computation, as pessimists do, the pains and pleasures which the lower animals experience. In their regard we cannot even surmise what the hedonistic balance would be. Pessimists usually vitiate their conclusions, first by reading into brute consciousness the feelings which they fancy according to their various sensibilities they would have in similar circumstances, and secondly by unscientifically bestowing their sympathy more largely on those that suffer than on those that enjoy. The pain of the tiger's prey in the jungle may have been intense, but the pleasure of the tiger may also have been intense, besides being longer in duration.

(e) Pessimistic blessedness would consist in a full denial of the will to live, or a state of quiescence in which all desire is extinguished, and out of which no object however alluring can entice. Attaining to this, one sinks to an attitude of passivity towards life and its interests. Towards the severest pain of being and its most ennobling pleasures he is equally indifferent. This condition Schopenhauer describes as a state of peace. When every member of the race shall have attained it, the perversity of the world-will shall at last be conquered.

PESSIMISM IMPOSSIBLE. Many and obvious difficulties can be raised against the possibility of realizing the aim of Pessimism, even granting that it be rational. If the blind striving of the world-will to objectify itself in miserable self-conscious beings will not be frustrated until all of them in concert have reduced themselves to a state of unemotional coma, there is no likelihood of it ever being frustrated. And if it were, we have no certainty that it would not begin over again to objectify itself in beings more capable perhaps of misery than we are. But the point that directly concerns us is that in this system the end of man is not the blessed expletion of rational desire, but its atrophy. The purpose of existence is not to be, the aim of will is not to will, and of nature to become callous.

Why all this should be brought about by a long and painful struggle instead of by suicide or drugs is hard to see. Schopenhauer's reasons are worthless. The suicide, he says, affirms his desire of happiness, whereas he should have denied it. If he had hastened his death by painful and ascetic practices he would have denied the will to live. But why, if he escapes from the worst possible world, should he be so meticulous about the method? It is ridiculous to say that one method is right and the other wrong, since there is no right or wrong in a world that is evil at the root. Schopenhauer then betakes himself to the covert of all bewildered philosophies, the good of the race. The suicide, he says, takes thought of himself only, the complete frustration of the world-will entails consideration of the species. But his philosophy can assign no reason whatsoever why the individual should interest himself in the race. Unless the intrinsic end of men, whether it be escape from misery or possession of happiness, can be synthesized in a higher purpose, no rational motive can be given why one man should neglect his own interests for the sake of another.

VON HARTMAN'S PESSIMISM. Von Hartman[68] differs from Schopenhauer in his metaphysics and psychology, and modifies in some respects the extreme Pessimism of the latter. He holds that the ultimate reality of the world is not only will but also intelligence, both of which, however, are unconscious. The world, as we know it, is the work of will, instinctive reason merely guiding it in its blind instinctive craving for life, much as a somnambulist correlates his movements into a united act. When the underlying nature of the universe has through its striving evolved itself into consciousness, the two elements of its being, reason and will, come into conflict. Conscious reason perceives that the irrational will in its eagerness for life has produced an existence, the essential characteristic of which is hopeless misery. Differing from Schopenhauer he concedes that pleasure is positive, but agrees with him in maintaining that the surplus of pain over pleasure is incalculable. Man, he tells us, has been the dupe of three successive illusions: (a) the illusion that happiness is attainable in this life; (b) the illusion that happiness, though not to be found in this life, will be realized in a life after death; and (c) the illusion that, disregarding existing individuals, happiness will come through the amelioration of humanity at some future time. These illusions he contends have one after the other proved vain. The purpose of conscious intelligence, therefore, should be to undo the irrational work of the unconscious. The last intrinsic end of life, in other words, is to bring about by accumulating the energy of will under the direction of conscious intelligence, the annihilation of the will to live.

The first illusion must be proved to be such, if any system of Pessimism is to stand; yet we have seen that a balance sheet of essential cosmic misery or happiness is not possible. Such proofs as are given are based on a metaphysics that begs the question by assuring that the world is evil at its root, and therefore evil in its flowering. If proof could be offered at all, it would lie in an appeal to the lives of those who, eliminating from their lives, as far as may be, the evils due to volitional irregularities, have conformed their actions to the designs of their Creator and found thereby a measure of happiness in excess of life's sufferings. The second illusion postulates the negation of immortality and the position of Pantheistic Materialism. It is equally necessary for any form of Pessimism that it should be proved, for even should we admit that in individual lives there were a preponderance of inculpable suffering over present happiness, the assured hope of a blissful immortality renders nugatory a pessimistic interpretation of life. In attempting to establish this illusion von Hartman argues from the nature of the Unconscious, out of which we emanate and into which we sink again at death—an argument which has no validity outside of his philosophy. The third illusion might be granted if the first and second were proved; but it is impossible to tell what the Unconscious is capable of doing under the direction of von Hartman.[69]

In one important point von Hartman differs from Schopenhauer. The latter made the denial of the will to live the immediate aim of the individual, the former makes it the remote aim of the race. When the general growth of intelligence shall have brought men to recognize the misery of living, and sympathy of each man for all other men shall have become universal, then by one concerted act the world of consciousness can be destroyed and the Unconscious reduced to its original amorphism. In the meantime, until the remote day shall dawn, it is every one's highest duty to promote the world process by living as joyously as he may. The more eagerly men seek pleasure, the sooner they shall perceive the essential misery of existence. If the captious student asks for a guarantee that the Unconscious will not again start into activity and reproduce another world of consciousness and misery, von Hartman's answer is that on the theory of probabilities, the likelihood of its doing so will gradually become less with each successive repression by enlightened beings, until the absolute end of life is practically assured. One suspects at times that von Hartman was an unconscious humorist.

NOTES

1. *Contra Gentiles,* III, 3.

2. Hedonist psychologists have attempted to give to all these affective states as a generic designation the name of pain. The comprehension of all unrest and dissatisfaction arising from physiological want under pain is a common but discreditable sophism. It consists in conferring on the genus the designation and attributes of the species. It becomes more logically offensive when the formulae derived from physiological pain are applied to the unpleasant affective states of the intellectual nature.

3. *Ethics of Aristotle,* Vol. I, Essay IV. (Cf. *ante,* Ch. IX, note 9.)

4. The authorship of Books V, VI and VII is disputed. The least that can be said against them is that if they are the work of Aristotle they have been so changed by editorial recension as to misrepresent the teaching of Aristotle, known to us from his undoubted writings. For a review of the evidence, see, Sir Alexander Grant's *Ethics of Aristotle,* Essay 1.

5. Bk. I, Ch. IV, n. 2.   6. Bk. I, Ch. VII, nn. 4, 5.

7. *Ibid.,* n. 8.   8. *Ibid.,* nn. 10-15.

9. *Ibid.,* Chs. VIII-X.   10. Bk. X, Ch. I.

11. *Ibid.,* Ch. II.   12. *Ibid.,* Ch. III.

13. *Utilitarianism,* Ch. II, p. 10.   14. *Ibid.,* Ch. IV, p. 36.

15. *Fragments of Mackintosh,* p. 389.

16. Bk. III, Ch. IX.

17. "Vice may be defined," Bentham says, "to be a miscalculation of chances, a mistake in estimating the value of pleasure and pains. It is false moral arithmetic." *Deontology,* Vol. I, p. 131.

18. *The Theory of Good and Evil,* Bk. I, Ch. II.

19. Mill says (*Utilitarianism,* Ch. IV) that "the sole evidence it is possible to produce that any thing is desirable, is that people do actually desire it." In other words: men do desire every thing they seek; therefore every thing they seek is desirable. This piece of dogmatism

is, as we shall see, abandoned later by Mill himself in a most ludicrous fashion.

20. *Deontology*, I, pp. 9-10, 31-32.

21. *Miscellaneous Reflections*, Vol. III, p. 183. (Italics are mine.)

22. *The Moralists*, Pt. III, Sect. 2.

23. *Ibid.*, Pt. II, Sect. 1.

24. For the historical origin of the name, see Leslie Stephens, *The English Utilitarians*, Vol. I, p. 178, n.

25. The indeterminate meaning of the principle does not escape Bentham. He thought the idea conveyed by it vague, and found that the want of a sufficiently manifest connection between it and happiness operated as a bar to the acceptance that it might otherwise have gained. Mill, however, fixed its use, though he did not succeed in confining its application to hedonistic lines.

26. *Principles of Morality and Legislation*, Ch. I.

27. See Ch. V above.

28. John Stuart Mill did not of course originate the utilitarian movement, nor in fact give any special development to the ethical principles of which the movement was the outward political expression. He had been indoctrinated in these by his father, James Mill, who in turn had been a fervent disciple of Bentham. What he did do, however, was to conciliate favor for it by qualifying the doctrines of his father and Bentham, and by overlaying it with moral teachings which had no logical connection with it, but which were in accord with the common moral persuasions of men.

29. *Observations on Man*, 1749.

30. *Ibid.*, Prop. XCVI.

31. *Ibid.*, Prop. XCIX.

32. It may not be superfluous to note that the facts of mental association are not rejected, but the efficacy attributed to it by the utilitarians. For an exposition of the nature of mental association, and the theories regarding it consult Maher's *Psychology*, Bk. I, Ch. IX.

33. According to Hartley, *Observations on Man*, Prop. VI, pain is "nothing more than pleasure itself carried beyond its due limit." Later however in analyzing his six classes of intellectual pleasures, he admits that his physiology of pleasure and pain "seems of little importance" and that it matters little "whether it be adopted or not."

34. *Analysis of the Human Mind*, Chs. XVII-XXIII.

35. *Data of Ethics*, Vol. II, nn. 33, 22; Spencer's letter in the Appendix of Bain's *Mental and Moral Science*.

36. In the *Data of Ethics*, Vol. I, n. 57, he says: "It is quite consistent to assert that happiness is the ultimate aim of action and at the same time to deny that it can be reached by making it the immediate

aim. . . . I then go further, and say that throughout a large part of conduct guidance by such comparisons (i.e., of pleasures and pains) is to be entirely set aside and replaced by other guidance." In this passage, and elsewhere too, Spencer reveals while trying to conceal the hedonistic paradox, namely, that "the more a cultivated reason," as Kant puts it, "applies itself with deliberate purpose to the enjoyment of life and happiness, so much the man fails of true satisfaction." In order to attain happiness the hedonist must immediately aim at something entirely different. Between the supreme end of life and the immediate purpose of his action there must be no qualitative similarity. We have Spencer's assurance that this is "quite consistent." It may be in his system; it would not be though in a consistent system.

37. *Principles of Ethics,* Appendix C.

38. Rashdall in *The Theory of Good and Evil,* Vol. II, pp. 357-358, makes some observations that are very much to the point: "No true account of what the moral consciousness actually is can possibly be vitiated by any true account of its genesis. No doubt accounts are sometimes given of the genesis of morality, which do seem to be destructive of the authority claimed for the moral faculty. Where this is the case it must be due to one of three causes: (1) Either the facts are true as far as they go, but will not by themselves really explain the ideas which they are supposed to explain, or (2) the moral historian must be mistaken in the facts upon which the theory is supposed to rest, or (3) what purports to be a mere statement of historical facts really implies already a theory about the actual nature of morality and the developed moral consciousness, which goes beyond the mere statement of historical or psychological facts.

39. Hobbes in the *Leviathan* defines religion as "fear of a power invisible, feigned by the mind or imagined from tales publicly allowed; if the tales are not allowed it is *superstitition;* and if the power imagined is truly such as we imagine it is *true* religion." Similar views may be found in Manderville's *Fable of the Bees,* in Rochefoucald's *Maximes,* and in the writings of Helvetius. Waterland (1683-1740) in a sermon on "Self-Love" sums up the doctrine of early Hedonism: "It is with references to ourselves and for our own sakes that we love even God Himself. . . . All virtue and piety are thus resolvable into a principle of self-love."

40. *Principles of Morals and Legislation,* Ch. X. There are passages in Bentham's works, especially in *Deontology,* published some years after his death by Sir John Bowring, which are thoroughly Hobbesian; but there can be little doubt that the trend of his doctrine is as I have exposed it.

41. *An Inquiry Concerning the Principles of Morals,* Appendix II.

42. *Essay on Bentham,* first published in the *London and West-minster Review,* August, 1838, afterwards included in the "Dissertations."

43. *Ibid.,* pp. 375-6 (Holt edition) : "Bentham failed in deriving light from other minds. His writings contain few traces of the accurate knowledge of any schools of thinking but his own; and many proofs of his entire conviction, that they could teach him nothing worth knowing. . . . He had a phrase, expressive of the view he took of all moral speculations to which his method had not been applied, or (which he considered the same thing) not founded on a recognition of utility as the moral standard: this phrase was 'vague generalities.' . . . He did not heed, or rather the nature of his mind prevented it from occurring to him, that these generalities contained the whole un-analyzed experience of the human race."

44. *Ibid.,* pp. 378-380: "In many of the most natural and strongest feelings of human nature he had no sympathy; from many of its graver experiences he was altogether cut off; and the faculty by which one mind understands a mind different from itself, and throws itself into the feelings of that other mind, was denied him by his deficiency of imagination. . . . No one, probably, who, in a highly instructed age, attempted to give a rule to all human conduct, set out with a more limited conception either of the agencies by which human conduct *is* or of those by which it *should* be, influenced."

45. *Utilitarianism,* Ch. IV.   46. *Ibid.,* Ch. IV.
47. *Ibid.,* Ch. III, pp. 29-30.   48. *Ibid.,* pp. 31, 32.
49. *Ibid.,* p. 27.   50. *Ibid.,* p. 30.

51. Bentham, besides intensity and duration, enumerates other at-tributes of pleasure which should be taken into account by the Utilitarian, namely, the certainty or speed with which they can be obtained, their freedom from pain, their power of producing other pleasures, and the extent to which they can be shared by others. But it is clear that these are simply aspects of intensity and duration. Gassendi in his *Philosophiae Epicuri Syntagma,* P. I, C. IV, formulates four rules for the moral guidance of the Hedonist: 1. That pleasure with which no annoyance is connected is to be chosen. 2. That annoyance with which no pleasure is connected is to be rejected. 3. That pleasure which hin-ders a greater pleasure, or engenders a greater annoyance, is to be rejected. 4. That annoyance which prevents a greater annoyance, or produces a more abundant pleasure, is to be chosen. These rules with change of application, express the morality that is peculiar to Utili-tarianism.

52. Kant says (*Ethics,* p. 109, Abbott's tr.) : "It is surprising that men, otherwise acute, can think it possible to distinguish between

higher and *lower* desires, according as the ideas which are connected with the feeling of pleasure have their origin in the *senses* or in the *understanding;* for when we inquire where are the determining grounds of desire, and place them in some unexpected pleasantness, it is of no consequence whence the *idea* of this pleasing object is derived, but only how much it *pleases.* Whether an idea has its seat and source in the understanding or not, if it can only determine the choice by pre-supposing a feeling of pleasure in the subject, it follows that its capability of determining the choice depends altogether on the nature of the inner sense, namely, that this can be agreeably affected by it."

53. *The Method of Ethics,* 7th ed. In the preface to the 6th edition he gives an interesting account of the growth and formation of his conviction that Mill's system could not be final in philosophy.

54. *Op. cit.,* Bk. III, Ch. XIII.

55. As we are merely examining Sidgwick's argument, we pass over for the present his conceptions of prudence, benevolence and justice.

56. Spencer in *Data of Ethics,* Pt. I, Chs. XIV, XV, dreams of and predicts a final evolutionary stage in which the "apparently permanent opposition between egoism and altruism" will disappear. But for the philosopher dreams are a poor substitute for facts, and human predictions are not even a makeshift for reasons. Besides what shall we do in the meantime—except live as best we may according to the principles of Spencer's relative Ethics? When we ask for bread Spencer reaches us a stone.

57. The proof of Ethical Utilitarianism is put as cogently as perhaps it can be put, by Rashdall in *The Theory of Good and Evil,* Vol. I, pp. 44ff. Dr. Cronin in *The Science of Ethics,* Vol. I, pp. 327ff., cites the passages, and, commenting on it, thoroughly exposes its fallacies.

58. *The Theory of Good and Evil,* Bk. I, Chs. IV, VII.

59. *Ibid.,* p. 85. It should be borne in mind that Rashdall, though he holds that these axioms are *for him* self-evident, immediate, intuitive, or (if we like to say so) *a priori* moral truths, does not maintain that they are evident to every one. "There are degrees of moral illumination as there are degrees of musical sensibility or mathematical acuteness" (p. 85). This contention and admission gives a subjective aspect to his theory which puts us in a quandary. If we deny the intuitive character of these axioms we lay ourselves open to the charge of being wanting in moral sensibility and acuteness. For the present we must be prepared to incur the risk, reserving for a later proposition the question of the evidence that belongs to different kinds of moral judgments.

60. This last principle he illustrates by showing that, because of its consequences to the well-being of society, "veracity should always give way to Benevolence, wherever there was the slightest collision between them" (*op. cit.*, p. 89).

61. Dr. Cronin in his *Science of Ethics,* Vol. I, pp. 334-351, exposes the arguments that have been adduced to prove it. We do not delay on them, because they are either mere assertions, generalizations from social facts which are wider than the facts justify, misrepresentations of the facts, or regressive reasonings from a theory which implicitly assumes the conclusion to be proved.

62. Like Sidgwick, Rashdall too writes his palinode in Bk. III, Ch. I, where he exposes, more clearly though than Sidgwick, the necessity of admitting, as an ethical postulate, the existence of God, possessing intellect and will, and really distinct from the individual minds to which He has given being.

63. "Pessimism" is a word with various shades of meaning. It may be used to designate a temperamental or philosophic valuation of life and its experience. In the latter sense it is a theory of the world directly opposed to the optimism of Leibnitz, who contended that this was the best possible world—not necessarily the best imaginable. Schopenhauer was the first to advance with some show of philosophic method the theory that this is the worst possible world. His position however is taken in direct opposition to Hegel, for whom he entertained an intense and profound contempt. He later held that if the world were looked at statically, or at any historical moment, it is evil; if looked at as a process or movement, it is good. Accordingly Schopenhauer maintained that the world process was essentially evil. Later pessimists modified this extreme position, and are content to hold that though this is not the worst possible, it is one in which evil so preponderates over good as to make its final extinction desirable. Cf. *Enc. Brit.*, "Pessimism," by W. Wallace.

64. 1788-1860. His work, entitled *The World as Will and Idea,* contains his fundamental doctrine.

65. To Schopenhauer acting for a purpose and from a motive meant the same thing; nor is this philosophic limitation peculiar to him.

66. See, *ante,* Ch. III, under "Cosmological Postulate."

67. *Ibid.,* under "Cosmological Postulate," *sub finem.*

68. 1842-1896. He published the *Philosophy of the Unconscious* in 1869, and ten years later *The Phenomenology of the Ethical Consciousness.*

69. See, Sully's *Pessimism,* especially Chs. VII-X, and Barlow's *Ultimatum of Pessimism.*

CHAPTER XI

NORMS OF GOODNESS

The proximate norm of goodness is our rational nature, looked at in all its essential relations; the ultimate norm is the Divine Nature as known to the Divine Practical Reason.

NORM OF GOODNESS. We distinguish between the norm and the criterion of goodness. By the former we understand that by conformity with which an action or object of volition takes on the attribute of goodness; by the latter that by which the conformity is known and tested. A norm is an objective rule which determines; a criterion is a subjective rule by which we judge and discriminate. The distinction is of importance; disregard of it has given rise to many superficial theories and useless ethical controversies. All ethical speculations which aim at deciding what is the good or evil of volitional actions merely by their consequences or effects substitute criterion for norm. Conduct is good or evil not because it has or has not a certain utilitarian, pragmatic, or esthetic value, but on the contrary because it is good or evil it subserves or frustrates our highest utility, gives the finest or most worthless practical meaning to life, and renders it beautiful and noble or ugly and degrading. Until we have discovered a norm of conduct, attempts to set up rules for discerning good from evil must manifestly be ineffectual.

Now every science of Ethics admits a real distinction between good and evil, although the theories elaborated to explain the nature and origin of the distinction may in effect invalidate it. Such a distinction cannot be denied without denying that there is a fundamental fact, which Ethics undertakes to analyze and interpret, and consequently that there is any science of Ethics properly so called. No science proves its fundamental fact. The fact that we are conscious of a real distinction between good and evil may indeed be individually verified by introspection, may be inferred in others from manifestations similar to those that characterize its workings

179

in ourselves, and is testified to by the literature and laws of all ages. We have, therefore, such verification of its universality as we have of any other mental quality. We know that others perceive color, possess reason, dislike pain, reverence uprightness only from the unchanging similarity of their judgments and actions with ours.

AMORAL INDIVIDUALS. If it be objected that history would seem to afford us examples of men, who were absolutely unconscious of any real distinction between good and evil, our reply is that if such men are or have been, they are not subjects of Ethics; but at the same time we may observe that they would be universally regarded as abnormal and unfit for human society. Moral perversion or hebetude is only a species of mental derangement. If the logical processes of a lunatic do not disprove the facts on which the science of logic is built, neither does the moral alienation of the vicious negate the fundamental fact of Ethics.

OBJECTIVE DIFFERENCE. But if the difference between good and evil is real, it is in the first place objective, namely, not dependent as an effect on thinking or feeling of men taken either individually or collectively; and secondly it is intrinsic, that is to say, the conceptual content of the idea of good wholly and necessarily excludes that of evil. But a difference between good and evil, which is objective and intrinsic, presupposes a norm by which these generic types are essentially fixed; and on the other hand the existence of such a norm involves a real, i.e., an objective and intrinsic, difference between good and evil.

INTRINSIC DIFFERENCE. The reality of this difference is, therefore, nullified by theories which, though conceding it to be objective, deny it to be intrinsic, as well as by those which deny both its objective and intrinsic character. Descartes is the representative of the first class of theorists.[1] He held that the difference between good and evil arises exclusively from the free will of God, and that consequently had God so willed it, what we now consider good might have been evil, and, reciprocally, what is now evil might have been good. In other words, actions are not commanded or prohibited by God because logically prior to His command or prohibition He knew them to be intrinsically good or evil, but they are good or evil solely because of His eternal and immutable enactment. The same opinion is attributed to Puffendorf,[2] who, however, seemed to hold in some unintelligible way that, although the good or evil of our actions depends on their relation to a natural law, God was free to give us another nature than that which we have.

Both theories are founded on erroneous theological concepts. Descartes misunderstood the relation between the divine omnipotence and the divine freedom. Puffendorf absurdly supposes that if God acts necessarily, that necessity could not spring from the nature of His infinite perfection, but must have been imposed on Him by an extrinsic and coeternal principle. The only interest that attaches to these theories today arises from the fact that Spencer[3] attributes indiscriminately to all religious creeds, pagan, Hebrew and Christian, the belief that good and evil, right and wrong are such "simply in virtue of divine enactment." His inferences deal mainly, it is true, with the conception of right and wrong; but from the doctrine of a creed which asserts that right and wrong depend from the will of God, he seems to infer that those who profess the creed should also maintain that good and evil are such by divine decree. To interpret the tenets of your adversary in terms of your own philosophy, and then to credit him with the tenets so interpreted, is not an uncommon method of argumentation. Spencer might, assuming his philosophy, have rejected the moral tenets of religious belief as untenable, or having mastered the philosophy which he was refuting, might have endeavored to show that its teachings were contradictory, but he had no justification for attributing the incoherencies that followed from his philosophy to those with whose philosophy he had no acquaintance. As we shall see, right and wrong, if understood in their precise sense as entailing obligation, have their source in the will of God, who having *freely* created man, must *necessarily* have willed and decreed that man's volitional activity ought to be in conformity with his nature and the archetypal norms of conduct. This may be held in perfect consistency with the position that, logically prior to the divine decree, good and evil are such from the constitution of man's nature, and from the Divine Nature of which it is an imitation.[4]

FALSE THEORIES. Both the objective and intrinsic differences between good and evil are obliterated in theories which trace our moral ideas to the educational forces of human society, or to the trend of evolution. Mandeville and Hobbes attribute the distinction to civil laws; but the former need not be taken seriously, and the latter contradicts himself according to the exigencies of his argument. Hobbes tells us that "as long as man is in this condition of mere nature (which is a condition of war) his private appetite is the measure of good and evil";[5] that "civil laws were the rules of good and evil . . . that, therefore, what the legislator commends must be held for good and what he forbids for evil";[6] that there are fundamental laws of nature, "as justice, equity . . . and in sum the doing to others as we would be done to."[7] In the *De Corpore Politico, passim,* he speaks of the natural duty of obeying rules.

The theory of Hobbes was taught also by Rousseau and Von Kirchman, and is in principle involved in the statolatry to which Hegelian philosophy has given rise. Wundt[8] and Levy-Bruhl[9] assign custom as the root of law and morality, and insofar as they distinguish between moral or immoral customs, they attribute the differentiation to historical development. Evolutionary theories which affirm that the human soul has been evolved from lower vital principles and ultimately from the blind forces of nature must derive the distinction between good and evil from the changing and unfolding appetencies of man as he adjusted himself to his environment. Logically, advocates of these theories should hold that between contempt and adoration of God, between filial love and parricide, between benevolence and hatred, beneficence and robbery, between treachery against country and patriotism, between sensuality and spiritual self-mastery, there are no moral differences which are not effects of the causes enumerated, and which, in the conceivable supposition that these causes had acted otherwise than they have, might have been reversed or abolished. The sciences of ethnology and zoology will supply examples of the lines along which these causes have worked and along which there is no reason for supposing they might not work again, if there were no absolute and objective norm of goodness. (We shall, of course, discuss later the obscuration of certain moral principles of good and evil due to social degradation or to want of moral development.) If they admit the conclusions logically involved in their theories they must hold that moral goodness is relative, varying with different ages, races, and climes and having only an extrinsic worth; that the fundamental fact of Ethics is a delusion, and that there is no science of good and evil except one that is purely empirical. If on the contrary they repudiate them, they must admit that there is an intrinsic and objective norm of good and evil. The error that underlies all these theories consists in confusing the growth of the race in knowledge of good and evil with the growth of good and evil themselves. Because the subject knowing varies, they implicitly infer that the thing known varies also.

PROXIMATE NORM. The appropriate and fitting perfection of an agent is its good. The norm of its perfection is therefore the norm of its goodness. But the proximate norm of man's perfection is his rational nature looked at in itself and in all its essential relations. In fact the proximate norm of perfection for any nature is that with which its activities should be consonant in order that they be perfect. This evidently is the nature of the agent; the vegetal activities of a plant or the sensuous activities of an animal are perfect, when they further the proximate end of the agent from which they proceed, and befit its nature considered as a whole. The proximate norm of goodness for man, therefore, is his rational nature insofar as it is the primary principle by which his actions, whether they be elicit or imperate, are produced, and the immediate subject modified by them.

But this principle and subject, if adequately considered is (a) in itself a composite nature in which faculties and tendencies, mutually adjusted and subordinated to rational will as a regulating and dominating faculty, constitute an *individual order;* and (b) in view of its essential relations is a social nature, which, allied by innate impulse, needs and destiny with other natures equally social, constitutes in union with them an *order of rights and duties;* and (c) a created nature, which owing its origin and perpetuation to a Supreme Being, and its meaning and value to His design, is a member of a *universal order,* which embraces, unifies, and consummates all other orders. Briefly, man's nature in its individual entirety as a complex of cognitive and emotional tendencies rationally reducible to order, taken in its relation to other men as a unit intrinsically adaptable to the social order, and in its relation to its Creator as an agent capable of promoting and made to promote the purpose of the universal order, is the proximate norm of goodness for this volitional activity.

Erroneous systems of Ethics spring from disregard of this three-fold aspect of human nature. If one of these aspects is taken as the exclusive basis of morality, or if any one is rejected, systems of morality may be elaborated, which, however coherent they may be, will not fit our rational nature as it is, and will consequently be subversive of the only morality to which that nature is intrinsically adapted. Distorted views of man's nature involve distorted views of his purpose in the universe. Errors therefore regarding the proximate norm of morality may be reduced to three classes.

EMOTIONAL OR RATIONAL NORM. Looking at human nature in itself, the emotional or rational side of it may be taken exclusively as the norm of goodness. The Emotionalists, though belonging to various schools of Ethics, agree in making feeling—either the feeling for pleasure, for the beautiful, or for well-being—the motive of conduct, and consequently human nature, considered exclusively as the subject of these feelings, the objective rule of good and evil. The functions of reason they accordingly hold to be subservient to feeling. Feeling reveals what is good; reason, perceiving the revelation, examines and evaluates the means of producing the most lasting and fullest satisfaction of feeling. Hedonistic, affective, esthetic, and pragmatic moralists belong to this class.[10]

STOICS. The Rationalists hold reason, independent of all emotional or affective states or experiences, to be the determining principle of goodness. For them, therefore, our rational nature exclusive of its emotional side is the norm of goodness. The older adherents of this opinion were the Stoics. They taught that universal nature, of which individual human nature is a participation, was the objective rule of conduct. This nature looked at in itself as an objective order of things and in abstraction from any relation to human needs and desires was accordingly the norm of goodness. Whatever was conformed to this norm was good in itself; all else was neutral, i.e., neither good nor bad. The good man, or what was the same thing, the wise man was he who rose superior to happiness and misery, content to live in accord with "nature," and in indifference to emotional experience.

KANT. Modern Stoicism, the typical exponent of which is Kant, has degenerated into philosophic Formalism. Starting from the proposition that only a good will (*Wille*) can be called good without qualification, he concludes that elective will (*Willkür*) is good only when conformed to rational will (*Wille*). By rational will is understood practical reason, which is "the appetitive faculty not (like elective will) in relation to action, but rather in relation to what determines the elective will to action." By goodness is understood freedom; and freedom is a property of will by which it can be efficient independently of any purpose extrinsic to it, and irrespective of any end that has an emotive causality, however reasonable that causality may be. Elective will or the faculty of action is therefore good when determined by rational will, which in its turn has no determining ground, but is self-determined by the laws of its own being. The law of its being is that it determines only to actions, the subjective principles of which are without contradiction universally applicable to all actions of the same mind.[11] Our rational nature is denied any attribute by which it is a norm of goodness; we are left merely with an *a priori* form, the principle of self-consistency in the world of volitional activity. Any action motived exclusively by the attraction of a good extrinsic to us, whether it be a good fitted to give perfection or to bring pleasure, is entirely without moral worth.[12] Obedience to God, fair dealings with our neighbor, love of country, which normal reason pronounces to be intrinsically good, are in Kant's theory good only when prompted by respect for the principle of self-consistency in action, or as it is designated, the law of practical reason.

Now the norm described—if in any proper sense it can be called a norm—evidently can provide us with no content for the concept of goodness. There is nothing, as Kant concedes, which it can make the determining ground of the will except the *a priori* form that a personal reason for acting must take in the mind before action befits a rational being. Furthermore, the principle of self-consistency can hold in regard to good no other position than that held by the principle of contradiction with regard to truth. It is merely a negative, though necessary, condition of good. Undoubtedly good, like truth, must be consistent with itself, and with every other good; but the question, what is that by reason of which good is so consistent, and evil is not? still remains unanswered. Lastly, it seems impossible to find consistency in Kant's method of getting the matter of a moral principle out of the *a priori* form of practical reason. Generalizing from his own illustrations, referred to above, the method is this: Take any action whatsoever, conceive it to become a universal mode of action; if the conception is practically consistent, the action is good; otherwise it is evil.

Kant's first example illustrates his method. A man reduced to despair by a series of misfortunes contemplates taking his own life. But adverting to the *a priori* law of practical reason, he asks whether his own volitional activity would become contradictory by so doing, and whether his personal reason for such an action could be a valid one for all men. The first question he answers by bringing in the end for which self-love was given us by nature, namely, to impel to improvement of life, a consideration that is foreign to his system, and apart from which or from cognate teleological principles suicide cannot be shown to be intrinsically self-contradictory. The other question he does not explicitly answer. The answer would be, that if taking one's life in the conditions described were a universal law, the law would necessarily contradict itself, for it would be a contradiction that all should commit suicide with the result that there would be no one to observe the law. The conclusion of course does not follow. Only those who were wearied of life would in Kant's supposition commit suicide. There would always remain a goodly number of cheerful or at least of contented survivors. Among these would be found from time to time some to whom life had become intolerably wretched, and who, uninfluenced by the heteronomous "feeling whose special nature it is to impel" to the preservation of life, might obey without contradiction in universal volitional activity, the categorical imperative: Commit suicide, when life is no longer worth living. On merely *a priori* Kantian principles, and dismissing all consideration of the end and purpose of life, as assigned by a Creator and manifested in the rational impulses of our nature, their action would be highly moral. The student who will examine the other illustrations given by Kant will discover that the irrationality of specific courses of conduct turns not on an intrinsic inconsistency that would exist in its adoption, but on considerations of ends of our rational or social nature, the emotive causality of which Kant condemns as destructive of "freedom"[13] and morality; or he will find that the irrationality, on Kant's principles, does not exist at all.[14]

EGOISM AND ALTRUISM. Human nature, viewed in its relation to others, gives rise to another pair of mutually exclusive systems, namely, Egoism which holds the personal self to be the norm of goodness, subordinating thereto all social impulses and assigning them moral worth insofar as they tend to further the preservation, well-being, or pleasure of the individual agent; and Altruism, which holds the social nature of man to be the norm of goodness, and that only conduct having for its end the interests and advantage of others for their own sake can be said to have moral worth.[15] Both systems are usually hedonistic and emotional in their interpretation of the good of life. Although Altruism owes its present vogue to Comte, it is not novel. The older moralists, who taught that sympathy, benevolence, or other social sentiment, quite apart from any expectation of personal advantage or loss, certified the end of conduct, necessarily held that our social nature was the exclusive norm of goodness.

The defects of both theories have already been exposed; they partition man's nature into two conflicting elements irreducible to a moral whole; they assign it an ultimate end, either intrinsic as the Egoists, or extrinsic as the Altruists, which is incompatible with the rational dignity of his personality, and each banishes from the domain of morality conduct which the other admits exclusively, but which in both cases the moral consciousness of mankind pronounces to be good.[16]

THEISM AND ABSOLUTISM. The problem of the universe and the solutions offered of it, give rise to two sharply contrasted moral theories. If our rational nature is essentially related to a first principle of things, that relation must enter as a constituent of the norm of goodness. Now the first principle of things is God, who is the first cause, the archetypal norm, and the final cause of everything distinct from Him; or the Absolute—I use the word in its ontological sense—which is the all-comprehensive ground of reality, and of which all that has actuality is a predicate, aspect, modification or attribute. Between these two concepts of a first principle of things there is a difference that cannot be bridged. The first involves a dualism in being itself, namely, the existence of a self-existent, self-conscious Being, who is in Himself and in a transcendant way the plenitude of all possible being, and the existence of produced beings, whose being is some analogue of the transcendant Being, and some of whom are self-conscious individuals. The second exacts Monism in being, and entails the ultimate identity of every form of matter, life and consciousness, which are "manifestations" of a single reality.[17]

The relations that exist between man and God or man and the Absolute are as diverse as are the first principles themselves, or the dependence of a creature on his Creator and the identification of "manifestations" with the reality from which they proceed. Unless we recognize a real distinction between the first principles of things and the individual self-conscious beings to which it has given existence: (a) we cannot attribute good or evil actions to the individual without attributing them likewise to the first principle of things; (b) we cannot maintain that there is an absolute distinction between good and evil; (c) and we must maintain that the relation of a bad man to the supreme Reality is as much in accord with the objective order of the universe as is that of a good man. Briefly, if the first principle of things, under whatever form or designation presented, is indistinguishable in reality from the self-conscious beings who compose it, if furthermore it is free to act only in the sense that it acts from the necessity of its own nature undetermined by any cause but itself, then to save its perfection, we must affirm that good and evil are relative and phenomenal, and that the Absolute itself overtopping these distinctions is super-moral, or is neither good nor bad. This position, though an inevitable development of the Absolutist theory, has found expression and defense only within recent years. It is professedly held by F. H. Bradley and A. E. Taylor.[18]

BRADLEY'S THEORY. Bradley is not as uncompromisingly logical as Taylor. Good and evil are, he tells us, appearances, the opposition between them is not absolute; yet at the same time he says:[19]

The Absolute is perfect in all its details, it is equally true and *good* throughout.

The good is not the whole, and the whole as such is not good. And viewed thus in relation to the Absolute there is nothing either bad or good. . . . But such a *truth* is in itself partial and *false,* since the Absolute appears in its phenomena, and is *real* nowhere outside of them. And so regarded from this other side it is *good,* and it manifests itself throughout in various degrees of goodness and badness.

In a sense, therefore, the Absolute is actually good. . . . Since in ultimate Reality all existence and all thought and feeling become one, we may even say that every feature in the universe is thus *absolutely good.*

This sounds like sheer nonsense; but one thing is clear, that in spite of good and evil being appearances, Bradley, claiming absolute goodness for the ultimate Reality, accepts the absolute validity of a category of being of which morality is the expression. If then the ultimate Reality is absolutely good, why, it will be asked, is it super-moral? Morality, it will be answered, consists in a positive strife and opposition between an idea or end in a self-conscious subject which strives to gain reality, and the existence of the same subject with its divergent mental states. This he illustrates by the example of a machine, in which a motive power is driving to the realization of an end but meets resistance from the pressure and friction of parts. This resistance, which may be called a lower good or a sheer evil, subserves an end beyond any of its parts, and the discord as such disappears and is taken up in an all-inclusive perfection.[20] A good action therefore is one by which the end is tending to realize itself, and a bad action one in which a conflicting inclination opposes. Both are essential to morality.

All this seems to be a confusion of the conditions in which morality usually obtains with the essence of morality. The question whether a virtuous action, one namely that is perfective of will in its active relation to its appropriate end, is a morally good action, is answered affirmatively if performed in conditions of volitional conflict with evil, and negatively if such a collision did not exist. The more ease or, in other words, the less friction one found in the practice of what men call virtue, the less moral one would become in Bradley's sense of the word, until finally holiness or absolute goodness would be the negation of morality.[21] This is in fact Bradley's opinion. Hypostatizing morality he says:[22]

> Morality desires unconsciously with the suppression of evil to become wholly non-moral. It certainly would shrink from this end, but it thus unknowingly desires the existence and perpetuity of evil. . . . Morality itself makes evil, desires in evil to remove a condition of its own being. It labors essentially to pass into a super-moral and therefore a non-moral sphere.

Now if there is any fact of moral experience more patent than another it is that the virtuous or truly moral man desires the suppression of evil and desires it consciously and that he does not shrink from this end. Who therefore or what is this bemused morality which unconsciously desires the suppression of evil and unknowingly desires its perpetuity? An excrescence apparently of a supposititious reality called the Absolute, which can retain its monistic character only by becoming self-contradictory.

TAYLOR'S THEORY. Taylor[23] frankly faces the issue that Bradley seems to evade. He distinguishes between morality in a comprehensive sense, which is a "name for all the practical side of life, including every experience in which an ideal can be detected," and morality in a restricted sense which "is the current name for those forms of activity which, as being at once essential to the well-being of the community, and not dependent for their existence upon a peculiar professional training, are expected of every member of society." To morality in this narrowed sense he allows the name goodness. This use of language, he thinks,

is naturally suggested by the current application of the name "goodness" to the spirit which prompts acts of natural kindness and humanity
—acts, that is, which need no professional training . . . for their conception and execution, and of which the sufficient prerequisites are
normal social feelings and such a degree of insight into the consequences of our conduct to others as is normally possessed by sane
human beings.

We need not delay on the altruistic and extrinsic nature of
morality thus described. We have disposed of that question. For
the intrinsic and personal morality which we are discussing, the
theory of the Absolute makes no provision. As Taylor puts it, such
a conception of morality involves an "insuperable duality of the
moral ideal," namely, a thesis—"My end must be capable of attainment," and an antithesis—"My end, in so far as it is an ethical
end at all, is of its very nature incapable of attainment."[24]

Nor need we again dwell on this subject. The point that deserves
notice is that "morality in the more extensive," and, as it is suddenly assumed to be, "the more accurate sense," presents us an
ideal derived from the whole content of the world-system by which
present existence is judged, and conduct and emotion connected
with it are judged. Of this content goodness is not the supreme or
regulative aspect but merely a partial side of life. The practical
ideals of life are inclusive of, but more ample than morality in its
popular sense. Morality itself, i.e., in its comprehensive sense, though
occupying a common ground with "religion" is in respect of it partial
and relative. For religion, the concepts and categories of morality
are secondary, subordinate, unsatisfactory, and superficial. Ultimately, all acts and characters, whatever moral designation they
merit within the subordinate and secondary domain of Ethics are,
each in its own place, fulfilling and, at the same time, failing to
realize the perfect world-system. The outcast and the sinner, equally
with the man of rigid virtue, are already, as members of the perfect
world-order, really perfect, if they only had the *faith* to perceive it;
and at the same time are equally imperfect in presence of the Absolute, or, as Taylor says, "equally guilty before God."

It is quite clear, without argumentation and in spite of the subterfuges of "aspects" and "appearances," that these systems of the
Absolute—and unfortunately they are widely accepted in substance
by those who profess to have profound insight into the nature of
the universe—destroy the recognized distinction between good and

evil, render morality ultimately worthless, and make it of only relative present worth. A system which issues in these conclusions can only be regarded as a *reductio ad absurdum* of the premises from which it is drawn, and of the method of thought by which it is constructed.

ULTIMATE NORM OF MORALITY. The objective, intrinsic, and absolute difference between good and evil necessarily entails a norm of morality which of its nature is ultimate, that is to say, which is the ground of subordinate norms, and is itself original, stable, and unchangeable. This norm is either our rational nature considered adequately, or a supreme nature from which it derives existence and of which it is an analogous likeness. The first alternative is untenable; for if his nature were the ultimate norm of morality, man would be unqualifiedly an end to himself—he himself would be his own supreme good. The other alternative is the only one that can reasonably be held, for the norm to which man's volitional actions should ultimately be conformed is a nature that is at once the source of his nature and archetypal of it.

Now the Divine Nature is: (a) first efficient Cause of all finite, contingent and temporal natures, since these as such are not self-existing, either in the sense that they came into existence independently of a first cause or in the sense that having existence their being no longer depends for continued existence on the being from which it was originally received; (b) first archetypal Cause of all grades of contingent being, since, possessing Itself the plenitude of being, all analogous forms of being must be related to It as to an exemplar, and insofar have reality as they re-present It in higher or lower stages of finite perfection, or are resemblances or traces of Infinite Being. It follows then that the Divine Nature known to the Divine Practical Reason as outwardly imitable is the archetypal norm to which the activities of finite natures are to be conformed in order that they be perfective of these natures, and is consequently the ultimate norm of morality or volitional activity.

NOTES

1. *Meditations,* Resp. 6, nn. 6 and 8.
2. *De Jure Naturae et Gentium,* Lib. I, c. II, sect. 6.
3. *Data of Ethics,* nn. 18 and 112.
4. The Scholastic doctrine may be found clearly exposed in Suarez, *De Bonitate et Malitia Actuum Hum.,* Disp. VII, Sect. 1. After relating the opinion of some medieval Nominalist, who held that volitional acts were evil solely by reason of a divine prohibition, that God in willing this prohibition was free, and that consequently no act is so evil that it might not have been good, he asserts that there are some volitional acts evil of themselves and of their nature, antecedently and independently of the will of God, whether free or necessary. He cites as holding this doctrine St. Thomas, *S. T.,* 1, 2, qu. 100, a. 1 and 8, and Scotus 3, *Dist.* 37, a. 1, qu. 1.
5. *Leviathan,* Pt. I, Ch. 15.
6. *Philosophical Rudiments,* Ch. XII, n. 1.
7. *Leviathan,* Chs. XIV and XVII.
8. *The Facts of the Moral Law.*
9. *La Morale et la Science des Mœurs.*
10. Aristotle uses the phrase καλὸς κἀγαθός to describe a man whose conduct and character was not only good in itself but a source of moral delight to the beholder. He emphasizes a consequent aspect of the morally good, which esthetic moralists have made the dominant one. The beautiful, whether physical, intellectual, or moral, supposes an harmonious perfection of object and superadds a special congruity to sensuous or intellectual vision which excites esthetic emotion.
11. An illustration may throw some light on this theory of goodness. May one, Kant asks, make a deceitful promise, when he finds himself in a difficulty from which he cannot otherwise extricate himself? The answer is that, though I may, for a motive, will (elective will) to lie, I cannot will (rational will) that lying should be universal, for in that case there would be no promises at all. The subjective principle of my elective will, should it become universal would involve my volitional life in self-contradiction; and for this reason and for no other my action would be wanting in goodness. (*Ethics,* pp. 18ff. and pp. 39ff.)
12. I say "without moral worth," because Kant is sometimes said not to have condemned actions of this kind as morally evil. But in the First Part of the "Philosophical Theory of Religion" (*Ethics,* pp. 329ff) he is emphatic in declaring that no action proceeding from elective will can be neutral (*adiaphora*). He does, it is true, speaking of actions of this kind, say (*Ethics,* p. 24) "I am willing to admit out of love for humanity"—a very heteronomous will, and unbecoming the apostle of autonomy—"that even more of our actions are correct." If so, they

can scarcely be morally evil. [EDITOR'S NOTE: Cf. "The Kantian Ought" which is printed as Appendix A to the present volume.]

13. The use of the term "freedom" by Kant in two different senses is exposed by Sidgwick in an Appendix to *Method of Ethics*. This equivocation, together with the equivocation on the word "will" is responsible for much confusion of thought.

14. In defense of Kant certain writers have maintained that Kant's *a priori* form does not give the essence of goodness, but a criterion by which it may be tested. "That this criterion is formal only and therefore empty," says Abbott, "is hardly of itself a valid objection. The test of valid reasoning, the syllogism, is equally empty." This defense is an abandonment of Kant's system. A test supposes matter, having or not having certain properties antecedent to the application of the test; Kant taught that the *a priori* form constituted an action good. The example of the syllogism is singularly unhappy. The syllogism does not guarantee the truth of the conclusion. This depends on the truth of the premises. If Kant's ethical edifice was constructed to give us merely a negative test of goodness, it seems highly overwrought, valuable as it may be conceded to be.

15. The use of the term Altruism is due to Auguste Comte (*Système de Politique Positive*, 1851), who formed it on the Italian or Provençal adjective *altrui*, and was introduced into English by George H. Lewis (*Comte's Philosophy of the Sciences*, 1853). It was adopted by Spencer, who predicted a reconciliation of it with Egoism, when the last stage of evolution had come. It has since popularized a vague designation of benevolent, or unselfish conduct. Etymologically it should signify actions which directly tend to benefit or injure others, but philosophic usage confines its meaning to the former.

16. Egoism and Altruism may be of course take other than hedonistic forms. One might be an egoist and believe that the ideal of conduct is self-assertion for any purpose, or an altruist and believe that self-sacrifice for any good of others was the ideal. But without stopping to discuss the psychologic tenets that would assign one end rather than another for conduct, we note that both self-assertion theories and self-sacrifice theories set up ideals of life which are subject to the objections presented in the text.

17. The modern policy or tendency to babelize language descriptive of religious or moral concepts, leads many writers to apply to the Absolute, the divine name and attributes. But the Absolute is either the sum total of reality known to us through phenomena, of which plenitude of being cannot be coherently predicated from any experiential knowledge that we possess, or it comprises the phenomenal universe and a Being the existence of whom we infer as the First Cause

of the phenomenal universe, and as infinite—not in a spatial or an indeterminate sense—but transcendently and positively. In either case to use language of the Absolute which conceptually and by historical associations is applicable only to God is a fraudulent appropriation of intellectual associations against which philosophy must protest. If the Absolute is a sublimation of the world of experience in which all differences and contrarieties are absorbed and reduced to harmonious unity it is not God. If it is a higher synthesis of the phenomenal universe and God it is impossible to say what it is.

18. The doctrine of the super-moral sphere of activity is by both writers involved in the question of what conscious attitude man should hold towards the Absolute, or, as it is called, the religious consciousness which can rise superior to the phenomenal point of view to which the moral consciousness is restricted. But we defer to its proper place a discussion of the religion of the Absolute.

19. *Appearance and Reality,* Ch. XXV, §iii. (Italics are mine.)

20. *Ibid.,* Ch. XVIII, §iii.

21. Aristotle's virtuous man who abstains from evil joyously and with pleasure and does good with facility and from formed inclinations would not be moral. *Eth. Nich.,* Bk. II, Ch. III.

22. *Op. cit., loc. cit.*

23. *The Problem of Conduct,* Ch. VIII, which significantly enough is entitled, "Beyond Good and Evil."

24. *Ibid.,* Ch. VII, where the assumptions from which this autonomy arises are exposed. Taylor disposes of the question of the future in a footnote. The positive evidence for a "future life," he says, "appears hardly sufficient to justify our resorting to the conception as a way out of our ethical difficulties."

CHAPTER XII

DETERMINANTS OF MORALITY

The determinants of morality are three: (a) the end of the action, which, when it is not indifferent, morally and objectively specifies the action; (b) the end of the agent, which morally and subjectively specifies the action; and (c) the circumstances of the object or agent, which either give an added specific morality to the action or modify its essential morality.

KINDS OF MORALITY. In the last proposition moral actions were classed generically as good and evil. It is quite clear, however, that there are kinds of good and evil. To worship God, to bestow alms on the needy, to preserve an inward temperance of thought and affection in a trying occasion, are all good actions; but good actions which differ in kind. Viewed objectively, they have each special relations of conformity to the norm of morality, and when performed they endue the will with distinctive perfections. And inversely there are kinds of evil action. Indulgence in degrading thoughts is not lying, nor is lying murder. Each has a malice of its own arising from its peculiar difformity from the norm of morality. Our present inquiry concerns the differentiating elements in good and evil actions by which they are constituted in kinds.

OBJECTIVE MORALITY. Every action proceeds from a specific faculty and issues in a result that is proper to the faculty. Whenever an action or a complex of actions immediately proceeding from a faculty other than the will is or normally would be subject to the will's control, or in other words, be an imperate act of an elicit volitional act, it falls within the range of morality; and viewed in relation to a judgment of reason regarding its congruity or incongruity with the norm of volitional activity, it is called in a restricted sense of the term an *object* of morality. Now an imperate act of the will is an elicit act of some specific faculty subordinated to it. The result that immediately springs from the exercise of this faculty, or that to which the imperate act is immediately directed by the will's elicit act, apart from circumstances adventitiously connected with it or consequences contingently following upon it, is the *end of the action*. This comprises not only externalized acts, as acts of beneficence or cruelty, but also interior acts, as kindly or malevolent thoughts, saintly or vicious imaginations.

The question, therefore, is whether the imperate act or the object of volition may have a goodness or badness of its own, independently of the motive of the agent, and of its circumstances or consequences. We maintain that it may, and that such morality is determined by the end of the action. It is quite clear that the end of the action may be in conformity with or in difformity from the purpose assigned by nature to the specific faculty from which it proceeds. This purpose is, as we have seen, adequately defined by the subordination of the faculty's functional activity to the good of the unitary nature considered in itself and in all its essential relations. Thus the faculty of speech, the natural purpose of which is to communicate to others what we think to be true, may be used in or out of harmony with the personal, social, or ultimate relations of the intellectual nature, whose instrument of expression it is. The end of the action, therefore, determines the morality of the imperate act or the objective morality of volition.

This conclusion, however, needs qualification. The end of the action may be in conformity with the purpose of the faculty either positively or negatively. The conformity is *positive* when the end of the action is so in accord with the nature of the agent, that its alternative is in discordance therewith. The conformity is *negative* when neither the end of the action nor its alternative is out of accord with the nature of the agent; for instance, one may use one's eyes either to read a book, or to view a piece of scenery. Before either end becomes definitely good or bad, it must receive further determination from adjuncts of the object with which the action is concerned, or from the conditions of the agent. An imperate act, generically considered, may be morally indifferent, while taken in its entirety it is good or evil. The use of the faculty of speech is in itself indifferent; but as the Apostle St. James says: "By it we bless God the Father, and by it we curse men who are made after the likeness of God."[1] Again, an object may be in itself neither good nor evil, yet on account of the proclivity of human nature, be *per se* a source of evil to men generally, or on account of age or a peculiar tempera-

ment be *per se* a source of evil to an individual. These same distinct-
tions obtain for an elicit action of the will, alternative effects of
which are the position or omission of an imperate act.

OBJECTIVE SPECIFICATION. With these explanations we may
argue: (a) that as every movement is objectively specified by the
result in which of its nature it issues, the will-movement which we
are considering, namely, volitional action, is objectively specified
by the end of the action; and (b) that when the end of the action
is not morally indetermined, the objective specification received is
in the order of morality.

OBJECTIONS. Two objections of some importance may be
urged against the conclusion. The first denies to the object of volitional actions any morality whatsoever. The objection is based on a
false analogy between truth and goodness, which is expressly taught
by Kant, and though not openly formulated, underlies nonetheless
much modern theorizing of a pantheistic sort on the nature of
morality. It is assumed that, as truth, i.e., logical truth, is purely
formal, moral goodness is equally so. The assumption mistakes the
functional activities of the two faculties, the respective objects of
which are the true and the good. The activities of intellect and will
aim, it is true, at the union of subject and object; but the logical
perfection of the intellectual union comes from the intellect itself,
independently of the nature of the reality with which it is psychically
conformed, whereas the moral perfection of will comes not from
the perfection of its conation, but from the character of the reality
with which it seeks union. Hence St. Thomas says, accepting Aristotle's doctrine, that truth is in the mind, while goodness is in things.
Even in the ontological order it is the intelligibility of an object that
makes it true, whereas it is not its appetibility that makes it good,
but on the contrary its goodness that makes it appetible.[2]

The second objection denies that the distinction between natural
and unnatural affords a determinant of conduct.[3] The reasons for
this denial are: (a) "The conception of human nature regarded as
a system of impulses" cannot be accepted as a practical guide, "since
in a sense any impulse is natural"; (b) when a conflict between
these impulses of our nature arises, no logical process of inference
from the actual physical life of man will enable us to decide which
of them should be followed; (c) it will not help us to say that the
supremacy of reason is natural, for "the nature that we are to follow
must be distinguished from our practical reason, if it is to be a guide

to us." Sidgwick's intention is not to prove that there is no real distinction between the natural and unnatural in conduct, or, as he would say, between the reasonable and unreasonable—such an intention would be an admission that there is no science of Ethics—but to show that no method of discovering what is reasonable or unreasonable can be based on consideration of the result in which volitional action naturally issues.

REFUTATION OF OBJECTIONS. The first objection has been proposed and answered by St. Thomas.[4] The answer is that a good and a bad act are equally natural in respect of the efficient cause from which they proceed, but are not equally in accord with nature in respect of the purpose for which the efficient cause was designed. Sidgwick disapproves of this distinction for the reason that it gives "a special precision to the meaning of 'natural'." But surely there can be no philosophical impropriety in using a word with special precision when discussing a matter in which the precise meaning legitimately obtains. Ethics cannot be treated without discussing ends, and, ethically considered, ends are not merely results but purposes also. If the application of the term *natural* is confined to the empirically known effects of efficient causes, every result of volitional activity is natural; the acts of the vicious or degenerate are as much in accord with nature as those of the virtuous and morally balanced. But if the faculties of a nature have their appropriate functions which fulfil in respect of the nature a peculiar purpose, it seems a narrow play upon words to say that it is as natural to abuse as it is to use them.

The second objection does not advance us beyond the first, except that it denies the possibility of reason logically inferring from the actual physical life of man the proper purposes of the faculties that subserve that life. This at least seems to be Sidgwick's contention. But the illustration which he gives exposes its weakness. "We can infer from the nutritive system that we are intended to take food. . . . But this carries us a very trifling way." Now we may logically infer more. Not only does the nutritive system impel us to take food, but as a part of the animal body to which it belongs, its impulse is purposive. It is impossible to see why we may not logically infer from the relation of our nutritive system to our physical life that we are intended to take food for the purpose of nutrition, and that the taking of food of such a kind or in such a way as to further or frustrate this purpose is in or out of accord with our nature.[5] What is said of the nutritive system may be said of our other faculties and functions, if considered in relation to our unitary nature. So far as they are subject to the will, the result produced by their use may be consistent or inconsistent with the purpose of nature.

The third objection gives Sidgwick's basic reason for rejecting conformity to nature as a norm of morality. He had, as he confesses, failed to find in psychology any coherent and harmonious ground for Utilitarianism, and on the other hand, though recognizing the defective method of Mill, he still held that the maxim of aiming at the general happiness was the supreme directive rule of conduct. His perplexity was removed finally after a study of Butler and Kant by which he was led to accept as the fundamental principle of morality an intuition of practical reason: Act in such a way as to promote universal happiness. This principle, which he fancied he derived from Kant's categorical imperative, is known, he says, *a priori* by practical reason. To Sidgwick's objection we answer, that neither our nature as distinguished from our practical reason, nor our practical reason enuntiating principles independently of our nature is our guide, but our practical reason passing judgment in accord with the exigencies and purposes of our faculties insofar as these are related to the synthetic purpose of our nature considered as a whole, or as the Schoolmen call it, "right reason," is the guide of our volitional activity.

But right reason must have something to reason on. The most elementary principle of morality, *Do good,* can have no application until reason has determined what is good. There are but two ways of doing this. An action is good either because it is suited to the nature of the agent, as St. Thomas teaches, or because, as Kant held, looked at as a universal manner of acting it is self-consistent. The first determination is psychological, and necessarily supposes a distinction between the natural and unnatural in conduct; the second is logical and is made independently of any relation of the action to an end, other than self-consistency. Now Sidgwick uses neither. His departure from Kant is as wide as possible. The categorical imperative of Kant is without content and must necessarily be so, if the will is to remain autonomous. The fundamental moral intuition of Sidgwick pronounces universal happiness to be the end of conduct—an end that Kant would regard as heteronomous. On the other hand the content of the moral intuition cannot, as Sidgwick acknowledges, be derived from the psychology of human nature. He is driven therefore to raise it to the rank of an intuitive judgment of practical reason, known apart from any relation of conformity or difformity which volitional action may bear to rational nature. Such an intuitive judgment imports innate ideas. If this be denied, it must be conceded that the ideas composing it are gathered from experience, and that the judgment would be intuitive only in the sense that the connection between the subject, i.e., a nature or faculty, and the predicate, i.e., an activity, is immediately perceived to be what it should or should not be. But this brings us back again to the psychological determination, and the distinction between what is in or out of accord with nature. If the first principles of good and evil have any content, that content is obtained either from psychological experience or is given *a priori* in consciousness. The latter supposition is too absurd to merit attention; yet Sidgwick's position logically precludes him from holding the former.

SUBJECTIVE MORALITY. The end of the agent, or the purpose sought by the agent, the desire of which moved it to originate imperate actions, may coincide with or exceed the end of the action; in other words the agent may have no purpose beyond that supplied by the end of the action, or he may direct or subordinate it to the attainment of a further end which is extraneous to the end of the action. One may, for instance, give alms to the indigent for the purpose of alleviating the want of a fellow-creature or of getting rid of the painful feeling aroused at the sight of suffering, or even for a purpose which has no intrinsic connection with almsgiving and which may either vitiate or ennoble it. In either case it is clear that the end of the agent subjectively specifies the morality of the volitional act, since it is the principle purpose aimed at by the agent and the motive that induced him to act. Whenever, therefore, the end of the agent is identical with the end of the action the subjective morality of the elicit act is the same as the objective morality of the imperate act. But when the end of the agent is distinct from the end of the action, the subjective morality is indeed derived from the end of the agent insofar however as this is affected by the end of the action, which falls within the compass of the integral volitional act, and which is proportioned or disproportioned to the final purpose of the agent.

Hence (a) if the *end of the agent* is *evil,* then, whatever be the moral quality of the end of the action, the volitional act is morally bad, since the principle and dominating purpose that moved to action is morally bad. The subjective morality is specifically that of the end of the agent, when the end of the action is indifferent or good;[6] and is twofold, i.e., specifically that of both ends when the end of action is also evil, the reason being that the end of the action, though desired only as a means, is an object of volition, and consequently affects the volitional act with its special malice.[7]

Hence (b) if the *end of the agent* is *good,* we have three suppositions: the end of the action is indifferent, or if good it is chosen purely as a means, or it is good and not only chosen as a means, but desired because of its intrinsic goodness; or finally it is evil. In the first case the subjective morality is solely that of the end of the agent,[8] since it is this alone that moves the will to action. In the second case, the specific morality is twofold, that namely inherent in the act, because of the end of the action, and that superadded by the purpose which the agent seeks to obtain through the end of the action.[9] "The act of one virtue may be directed to the act of another virtue," as St. Thomas says, "as when one gives of his goods to another in order that he may have his friendship. In this case the act is specifically" (i.e., from the end of the action) "one of liberality, but by the end of the agent one of friendship."[10] Lastly if the end of the action is evil, the volitional act is morally bad, even when the end of the agent is good. In order that a volitional action be morally good it must be in conformity with right reason. Evidently the choice of a means that is evil to realize an intention that is good violates the principle of right reason; it is an attempt to relate to goodness what is incompatible with it. Besides if an end apprehended by the agent to be good is so desired that its attainment is sought through a means apprehended to be evil, such a desire is necessarily inordinate. The bestowing of alms on the needy is a good action. But if one so ardently desired to perform such an action, that he would not hesitate to steal in order to satisfy his desire, obviously the individual and concrete desire has, because of its immoderation, ceased to be good. The saying, therefore, "the end justifies the means" is contrary to the principles of right reason, and therefore immoral.

Hence (c) if the *end of the agent* be *good,* yet *inferior in moral worth* to the end of action, the volitional act may be morally bad.

Whenever an end of the action, which has an intrinsic goodness of its own superior to that of the end sought, is subordinated as a mere means to the obtaining of this end, there exists a disproportion between the final purpose of the agent and the act through which it is sought. One may, for instance, lawfully, and in cases laudably, try to win the especial esteem of one's fellow men. But one may not perform acts of virtue, attend divine service, give alms, or practise abstinence, solely with this end in view, without perverting the order of reason.[11]

MORAL CIRCUMSTANCES. A volitional act of the simplest kind involves four principles. It proceeds from an agent or efficient cause, who for its production must be possessed of certain powers of intellect and will, and exercise them under determinate conditions; it is necessarily concerned with a special object, or subject-matter, which may be completed in a single imperate act or be a composite of many; it may be intrinsic to the agent, as his appetites or passions, or extrinsic to him as the material or social goods of life; it must be directed to a purpose, which may be identified with the end of the imperate act, or be distinct from it; and finally it must be elicited from a motive which formally determines and indicates the moral attitude of the will.

These four principles enter into the very substance of the moral act, since they are the concurrent causes essential to its production and constitution. They do, however, admit of modifications, which, on the analogy of local relations, are said to be *circumstances* of it or *to stand about it* (*circumstare*), and which are called *accidents* in the sense that they are concomitants, which are outside the substance of the act, and the presence or absence of which leave the morality of it substantially unchanged. Now circumstances may modify the act merely in its physical features (*in esse naturae*), as for instance that one should kill another with a bludgeon or with poison; or they may modify it in its moral relations (*in esse moris*), as for instance that one should lie for the purpose of injuring another or of defending one's father. We are of course dealing with moral circumstances only. These may be defined as accessory relations of a moral act, which, although incidental to its substantial morality, increase or decrease its accord or disaccord with the norm of goodness.

Again the modification arising from moral circumstances may be one of kind or one of quality; they may superadd a new species of morality, or intensify or diminish the good or evil of an existing species. In a sense the end of the agent may be said to be a circumstance with respect to the end of the action, when the former is distinct from the latter, as in the case of one who gives alms for the purpose of expiating his sins; but since the end of the agent is the final intent of the almsgiving, it cannot be said to be a circumstance with respect to the substantial act of volition.[12]

Lastly then our inquiry regards circumstances which may attend the moral act as constituted primarily by the end of the action, and finally by the end of the agent. Our contention is that these either superadd a new specific morality or vary the quality of the existing morality. Moral circumstances have been variously classified.[13] In general they may be classed under four heads, according as they affect the four principles of the moral act, that is to say, they may attach to the agent in his personal relations, to his purpose, to his elicit act itself, or they may belong to the object, whether person, thing, or function, on which the act is exercised. Of these some clearly are of such a character as to superinduce a special conformity or difformity with the norm of goodness. Thus to tell the truth, when by doing so one runs a risk of incurring serious loss, is an act not only of veracity but of fortitude as well, and to murder a person who is one's father is a twofold crime. Circumstances of this sort are called *specifying* circumstances. There are other circumstances which modify the virtuous or vicious character of the action without changing it in kind. For instance, to bestow alms out of one's abundance or out of a mere competence is in either case an act of beneficence, but in the latter case the benevolent motive is stronger; and, on the other hand, the evil of theft varies with the amount stolen and the economic need of the person from whom it is stolen. These are called *qualifying* circumstances; they aggravate or extenuate the specific evil of the action, or increase or lessen its goodness.[14]

The brocard of St. Dionysius, *Bonum ex integra causa, malum ex quocumque defectu,* is to be understood therefore in the light of these conclusions. An action is good, only if the three causes to which it owes its specific morality are good; namely, the end of the action, the end of the agent and the specifying circumstances; it is evil, if any one of these is evil. The reason is that every element required for the full accord of an act with right reason must be present, and every element that would introduce disaccord must be absent.

St. Thomas, commenting on the saying of Aristotle, that there are many ways of doing wrong but only one way of doing right, uses the illustration of bodily health and illness. Just as the harmony of all the functions of a living organism is required for health, and any derangement brings illness, so in order that an action be good, there must be a due proportion between the elements which enter into it, and to render it evil it suffices that any disproportion whatsoever should obtain, arising either from defect or excess.

MORALITY OF THE EXTERNAL ACT. It was a controverted question among the earlier Scholastic moralists whether formal morality belonged exclusively to the elicit act. Scotus and Alexander Hales seemed to have held that to a certain extent it was an attribute of the imperate act also, which accordingly increased specifically the morality of the volitional act. St. Thomas and subsequent Schoolmen generally maintain that formal morality is peculiar to the elicit act. They argue that formal morality is a property of the act which is intrinsically free, by which goodness and badness are imputed to the agent and by reason of which he is primarily responsible for the outcome of his volition. These predicates are verifiable only of the elicit act. The elicit and imperate acts therefore are in the order of morality not two distinct but one integral volitional act, the morality of which is single, when the end of elicit and imperate acts are the same. In the case of a manifold morality arising from the ends of the action and of the agent, and from specifying circumstances, the formal morality is that which is apprehended by the intellect and freely chosen or admitted by the elicit act of the will.

It may be asked, furthermore, in what sense the morality of a volitional act is increased by being externalized, for assuredly there is a difference of some sort between two volitional acts identical in object or intent, of which one is expressed outwardly in conduct, and the other fostered in the mind only. It is true that "whosoever shall look on a woman to lust after her hath already committed adultery in his heart"; but it is also true that he who finally consummates his adulterous desires is in some sense more vicious than he who has not gone beyond entertaining them in his heart. We answer: (a) that the exterior act gives no specific increase of morality; (b) that the absence of the exterior act from lack of opportunity does not *per se* diminish the morality of the volitional act; (c) that *per accidens* the exterior act may increase the morality of volitional act by prolonging it, by entailing its repetition, or by intensifying it.

The first assertion is proved from what has already been advanced regarding the moral specification of the volitional act and its formal morality. The second is clear from the nature of a perfect volition, which intends execution. If the execution fails of accomplishment because of hindrances, the lack of the exterior act is against the intention of the agent. But if in spite of one's intention and effort one fails to do the good or evil intended, the failure cannot affect the formal morality of the volitional act. What is involuntary cannot be imputed. The third assertion admits that the exterior act may indicate or induce an accidental augment in the formal morality. This may happen, as St. Thomas says, in three ways. The exterior act may show or cause a prolongation of the inner act of the will; when for instance

one wills to do a thing for a good or evil end, but leaves off on account of some obstacle, while another continues the will-movement, until he carries the work through, it is clear that this volition is prolonged in good or evil, and in that respect better or worse.

Again, the performance of the exterior act may call for a repetition of the elicit act:

If one wills to do a thing for a good or evil end, but deferring action for the time being, afterwards wills and does it, the elicit act is duplicated, and so a double good or evil is done.

Lastly, an exterior act may manifest the intensity of the elicit act:[15]

There are some exterior acts which, in so far as they are pleasurable or painful, naturally intensify or slacken the will movement. It is clear that the more intensely a will tends to good or evil, the better or worse it is.

NOTES

1. *St. James* 3:9.
2. St. Thomas, *De Ver.*, qu. 21, aa. 1-4; 2 *Dist.*, 39, qu. 1, a. 2; Harper, *Metaphysics of the School*, Props. XCVIII and XCIX.
3. Sidgwick, *Method of Ethics*, Bk. I, Ch. VI, §2.
4. *S. T.*, 1, 2, qu. 18, a. 5, ad. 3.
5. Later, in Bk. III, Ch. IX, Sidgwick concedes the principle which in Bk. I he seems to challenge. "In the case of the appetites for food,

drink, sleep, stimulants, etc., no one doubts that bodily health and vigor is the *end naturally* subserved by their gratification." (The italics are mine.)

6. Suarez, *De Bon. et Mal. Act. Hum.,* Disp. VIII, Sect. 1, nn. 1-6, 13-19.

7. Suarez, *op. cit.,* Disp. VII, Sect. 9.

8. Suarez, *op. cit.,* Disp. VI, Sect. 3, nn. 1-8.

9. Suarez, *op. cit.,* Disp. VI, Sect. 3, nn. 9-16.

10. *Contra Gentiles,* III, 38. Cf. Salmanticenses, *De Bonitate Act. Hum.,* Disp. VI, dub. 3.

11. Salmanticenses, *De Bon. Act. Hum.,* Disp. V, dub. 2.

12. *De Malo,* qu. 2, a. 6.

13. *S. T.,* 1, 2, qu. 7, a. 3; Suarez, *De Volunt. et Involunt.,* Disp. V, Sect. 2.

14. *Contra Gentiles,* III, 139; Salmanticenses, *De Bon. Act. Hum.,* Disp. IV, dub. 3.

15. *S. T.,* 1, 2, qu. 20, a. 4; Suarez, *De Bon. et Mal. Act. Hum.,* Disp. X, Sect. 2; Mastrius, *In Lib. 2, Sent.,* Disp. V, *De Act. Hum.,* qu. 5.

CHAPTER XIII

MORALITY OF VOLITIONAL ACTS

Every volitional act, taken in its individual entirety, is definitely either morally good or morally bad.

THE CONTROVERSY. The controversy on the possibility of an individuated volitional act being morally indifferent, or of conduct being in certain situations non-moral, is intimately connected with the nature of morality. Nor is it one of merely scholastic interest. Though more intelligently and thoroughly treated by the Schoolmen, it has engaged the attention of modern moralists. The Schoolmen are divided into two opposing camps on the question. St. Thomas[1] whom Suarez,[2] the Salmanticenses,[3] St. Alphonsus Liguori, the Thomists and Catholic moralists generally follow, affirm our proposition. But Scotus,[4] St. Bonaventure, Vasquez and others deny it. The two schools, though agreeing in their respective conclusions, often differ widely in their premises. The question at issue is whether a human act posited by an individual from a motive and directed not only to an end but by a preconceived idea of the end, can in view of the end of the agent and the circumstances which individuate it be indifferent or non-moral. It necessarily entails an inquiry into the essential conditions of formal morality, which is always individual, and may consequently be independent of the opinion one holds on the prior question, whether namely the object of a volitional act is always either good or evil. Scotus taught that the object was always either good or bad, while the individual act might be indifferent; St. Thomas on the contrary taught that the object might be indifferent, but that the individual act was definitely either good or bad.

ST. THOMAS. The doctrine of St. Thomas is expressly presented in the *Summa Theologica*[5] and in the *Quaestiones Disputatae*,[6] and is variously illustrated and enforced in his treatment of the virtues. His argument may be outlined as follows: Whenever an action proceeding from deliberate reason is directed to an end which right reason decides is an appropriate end of the agent, employs means which keep the proportion of reason, and uses these means in a manner and in circumstances befitting the agent and the end, such an action is morally good; and on the other hand, whenever an action proceeding from deliberate reason is in disaccord with the principles of right reason in respect of either the end, or the means, or the circumstances of agent or end, the action is morally evil. But every volitional action individually considered preserves or fails to preserve the symmetry and harmony of reason just described; and is therefore either good or bad morally.

Every agent who acts deliberately necessarily intends an individual end, and directs his imperate acts to the attaining of a determinate purpose. Now this end has been formally apprehended to be morally good or evil, and the imperate acts are either actually, virtually or habitually referred to its realization under this aspect, or it has been apprehended merely as suitable to satisfy some human need, intellectual, hygienic, or esthetic. The controversy centers on acts that are directed to ends of the latter sort. These we claim are never morally indifferent. First, the *purpose* of such acts are befitting or unbefitting the individual who performs them, and, whether or not referred by a previous actual intention to an end formally apprehended as moral, are in fact of their nature referable to it. But such acts are in positive conformity or difformity with our rational nature; and are therefore either good or evil morally. St. Thomas, speaking of supernatural acts, says:

He who has charity . . . acts meritoriously, whatever he does . . . unless he is thwarted by an irregularity in the act by which it is not *referable* to God.[7]

It happens sometimes that a man does not actually refer his act to God; since however the act does not in itself contain any irregularity by reason of which it is not *referable* to God, and since the mind of the man is habitually related to God as to his end his act is not only not sinful, but is even meritorious.[8]

And commenting on the text of St. Paul, "whether you eat or drink, or whatsoever else you do, do all to the glory of God,"[9] he says that this relation of whatever we do to the glory of God is understood either of the act of being referred or of the aptitude to be referred, because of the supernatural principle which elicits it.

Without assuming an absolute parallelism between acts proceeding from a natural faculty and acts proceeding from the same faculty when elevated by grace, we may assuredly on analogical grounds contend, that, if one's attitude of mind while performing a deliberate act is in accord with reason, his act, if not otherwise inordinate, is by the very fact that it is referable to a norm of morality ethically good. Whatever one does, therefore, if the purpose of the agent is some justifiable need of self or kindly service to another, and if the conditions heretofore prescribed are kept, his act is morally good independently of an actual and formal reference of it by him to a norm of morality.[10] Secondly, the *result* in which an action naturally issues either agrees or disagrees with the bodily or mental well-being of the agent, or promotes or impairs his proper relations to others. If, therefore, in the exercise of such acts the moderation of reason is preserved, they possess the goodness of the natural virtues from which they spring or to the formation of which they lead.[11] An apt illustration of the doctrine of St. Thomas is afforded by his article on the virtue of sprightliness (*eutrapelia*).[12]

Again, speaking of the virtue of temperance, he says:[13]

There are two ways of taking the phrase *necessary to human life.* In one way we may call that necessary without which the thing cannot be at all, as food is necessary to an animal; in another way we call that necessary without which the thing cannot be in a suitable condition. Now temperance regards not the former necessity only but also the latter. Hence the Philosopher says "the temperate man goes after pleasant things in view of health or of a good habit of body." But other things, that are not necessary to these ends, may be of two sorts. Some there are that are positive hindrances to health or a good habit of body, and these the *temperate* man in no way uses. . . . Others there are that are not hindrances to these ends, and these he uses in measure according to place, time and company. And, therefore, the Philosopher adds that "even the temperate man goes after pleasant things," that is, things not necessary to health or a good habit of body, "when they are not obstacles to these ends."

In the text referred to by St. Thomas, Aristotle says that he is a temperate man who seeks the pleasures that aid to health and good habit of body, in measure, and as he should, and in like manner other pleasures not injurious to either, which are not unbecoming or beyond his means:[14]

Sensible goods are connatural to man; and therefore when the mind soars above the things of sense, and is intent on works of reason, the result is a certain psychical fatigue. . . . But as bodily fatigue is thrown off by rest of the body, so must psychical fatigue be thrown off by rest of the mind. Now the mind's rest is pleasure or delight. And therefore a remedy must be applied to psychical fatigue by some pleasure. . . . But sayings or doings, wherein nothing is sought beyond amusement, are spoken of as sport or jest. And therefore we must at times make use of such things to rest the mind. . . . In the matter of games and sports there can be a virtue.

Actions therefore in which nothing beyond needed recreation is sought are, when the moderation of reason is preserved, morally good.

Lastly, "it cannot happen that an individual act be done without *circumstances* which make it right or wrong. For whatever it be, if it be done when, where, and as it should be done, etc., it is a well-regulated and therefore a good act; but if it be defective in any of these respects it is an ill-regulated and therefore a bad act." [15]

In conclusion, therefore, every volitional act is posited for a purpose that is either befitting or unbefitting the agent, issues in a result that either agrees or disagrees with the reasonable exigencies of the nature of the agent as an individual or in his social relation, and is done under circumstances that are in or out of keeping with the estate and purpose of the agent, that render the act itself seasonable or mistimed, or that make it helpful or injurious to others. Now a volitional act of this kind is in itself and irrespective of its actual reference to a further end either good or bad morally.

SCOTUS. The doctrine of Scotus seems on the surface to be inconsistent. He holds that every volitional act is objectively either good or bad, but that formally some of them are neither. The inconsistency disappears, however, if we advert to his distinction between objective goodness, which consists in the conformity of the act at least negatively with right reason, and moral goodness, for which it is necessary that the act should have the qualities of one proceeding from a habit of reason, i.e., it should be done readily and from inclination. Acts not so performed, though objectively good, are morally indifferent. Acts, therefore, preserving the moderation of reason, and having the conditions of object, end, and circumstances which we have required, are not morally good unless moreover they are performed with the firm steadfastness of a habit of virtue. Scotus is apparently supported by Aristotle,[16] who says that the intrinsic requisites for constituting an act virtuous are: that the agent have knowledge of what he is doing; that he do it by choice and from the motive of the virtue; that he do it by a formed and settled stability of will. The first two conditions are requisites of every volitional act, the last is peculiar to a virtuous, or, in the Scotistic sense, a morally good act.

Our direct answer to the Scotistic theory is: (a) Any action to which one is morally obliged, is a morally good action. There are many actions which are matters of moral obligation antecedently to the possession by the agent of the corresponding habit of virtue.[17] (b) If the mode of virtue were required for moral goodness, many acts of self-control, through which a habit of virtue is finally formed, would not be morally good. (c) An action may be virtuous or morally good in the sense that it conduces to the formation of a fixed internal character in the heart and mind of the agent, as well as in the sense that it proceeds from such a character already formed.

ARISTOTLE. This is in fact the teaching of Aristotle in the passage to which reference has been made. After showing in the opening chapters of the second book of the *Ethics* that habits of virtue are acquired by repeatedly performing virtuous acts, and that once formed they enable a man to practice virtue easily and joyously, he proposes and answers in the fourth chapter a difficulty against his theory. How can it be said, he supposes some one to inquire, that we become virtuous by performing virtuous actions? If our actions are for instance just or temperate, we ourselves are already just or temperate, as he that produces music is already a musician. His answer is, first, that both the artist and the virtuous man are alike in having acquired their respective habits by practice; but secondly, they differ in their relation to the artistic work and the virtuous deed. The work is artistic when outwardly it is such as the canons of art demand; a deed however is not virtuous if only outwardly it conforms to the norm of morality. It must furthermore have proceeded from an inner principle which is itself morally good. The artist, therefore, is one who has acquired knowledge of what is beautiful, and technique in giving expression to his knowledge. The habitually virtuous man not only has knowledge of what is good, but always, steadfastly, and gladly chooses the good. Knowledge of what should be done, and how to do it, is the least part in the equipment of the habitually virtuous man, since it can be possessed by those who have not acquired a habit of virtue; but it is the essential and exclusive qualification of the artist. Consequently an artistic work cannot be done by one who is not an artist, except by chance or under the guidance of a master. One, however, who has not as yet formed a habit of virtue, may do actions which, proceeding from a knowledge of what is good, and directed to a purpose that is good and moderated by rule of reason, are of the same kind as those performed by the habitually virtuous man. It can be rightly said, therefore, Aristotle concludes, that by the repeated performance of acts that are actually virtuous the habit of virtue is finally established.[18]

This passage of Aristotle has been misunderstood by some modern writers on Ethics. Sir Alexander Grant in his interpretation of the text clearly misrepresents the Greek philosopher's mind,[19] for he says that according to Aristotle:

These "just acts" by which we acquire justice are on nearer inspection not really just; they want the moral qualification of that settled internal character in the heart and mind of the agent, without which no external act is virtuous in the highest sense of the term.

Yet nothing can be clearer than Aristotle's position. He shows in chapter second that a habit of virtue is the product of reiterated acts, and that these acts are virtuous in the sense that each individually preserves the moderation of reason or the measure of virtue. In chapter fourth he answers the difficulty derived from the analogy of virtue to an art, by exposing the defects of the analogy, and concludes the chapter by reasserting the conclusion of chapter second.

Rashdall says:[20]

To Aristotle the man was not good until the "virtuous habit" was fully formed. He assumed that the imperfectly virtuous acts by which the habit of virtuous action was formed would be from non-moral motive. How the repetition of a series of acts influenced by *wholly* non-moral motives would result in a habit of acting from moral motives . . . is never satisfactorily explained; that is the great hiatus of Aristotle's ethical system.

Undoubtedly, if Aristotle assumed that a habit of morality was formed by repeated performance of non-moral actions, there is a remarkable break in the continuity of his ethical theory. As, however, Aristotle did not assume this, but on the contrary disclaimed it, the "great hiatus" must be credited to his interpreters.

Professor Dewey's[21] use of Aristotle's text is preposterous. He cites it in proof of his opinion that habit is a prerequisite of all voluntary activity, whether moral or immoral, yet he holds at the same time the "conflict theory" of morality, which we shall examine presently. Clearly the two positions are incompatible. It suffices to note, first, that Dewey wholly misunderstood the nature of the Aristotelian habit (ἕξις) which he confuses with disposition (διάθεσις), and secondly, that Aristotle is not discussing the voluntary in the passage cited. It is only in the following book [22] that he examines the generic concept of the voluntary. This he does with a view to defining one of its species, the volitional. Of the three elements involved in a habit of virtue, namely knowledge, choice, and a formed stability of inclination, only the first two are requisites of a volitional act, and only the first of a merely voluntary act. Aristotle therefore asserts the direct contrary of what Dewey attributes to him: voluntary actions produce habit; habit is not an antecedent condiiton of an act being voluntary.

MODERN THEORIES. We have already disposed of theories which confine morality to other-regarding acts, or at least to acts the consequences of which affect others, and which consequently look on acts having an exclusively personal bearing as morally indifferent. There remains for examination a class of theories advocated by modern writers on Ethics, which make conflict and struggle an essential element of a morally good act. Simmel proposes an extreme form. [23] There is no moral goodness, he holds, unless the virtuous inclination comes in conflict with an evil inclination, and has had to struggle in order to prevail, and the goodness of the act is proportioned to the amount of effort used in overcoming the evil inclination. Martineau [24] in defining the "mode of moral judgment" requires as a condition of moral self-consciousness that there should appear in us "two incompatible impulses at once or the interruption of one by the invasion of another," and that the difference between them should amount to strife. Quoting the proposition of Heraclitus that "strife is the father of all things," he says, "the maxim has a just application to the phenomena of our moral life."

The estimates of morality set up by theories of this sort are not uncommon. Philosophically, they are allied to Stoicism, especially to Kantian Stoicism, which refuses to acknowledge any action to be good that is done for the sake of pleasure. But they compromise with common sense by admitting that many actions are indifferent; or as Kant admits in a momentary "love of humanity," they are "correct," but not worthy of moral esteem. Popularly, a puritanic conception of goodness, which would hardly consider an action virtuous if done with pleasure or delight or without inner wrestling of the spirit, pervades much of our literature and our essays at righteousness.

An element of truth in these erroneous views of moral conduct gives them plausibility. Conflict with ill-regulated impulses does occupy a large and notable place in the experiences of our moral life. It would be however a narrow exaggeration to say that outside of such conflict there is no moral life. Virtue undoubtedly is attained by struggle. This Aristotle, who makes the perfection of virtue consist in the joyous doing of virtuous acts, not only admits but maintains. "Power is made perfect in infirmity," says St. Paul.[25] The practice of resisting and overcoming temptation strengthens the will. That men who have conquered great passions have been men of great virtues no one will gainsay. Furthermore, we concede that morally "the life of man upon earth is a warfare"[26] and that every grade of self-mastery obtained reveals and fixes attention on subtler disorders of the spirit. It is not necessary to hold that the best of men will ever attain in this life the Aristotelian perfection of virtue in every line of conduct. The exercise of self-denial, or asceticism, in the proper significance of the term, will always be needed by one whose aim it is to preserve the even measure of reason in all his conduct.

But we hold it an extravagance to say: (a) that the successful exercise of self-restraint in presence of irregular movements of the appetencies must always "amount to strife" before it can be moral, or that it must be even a struggle or a painful effort; (b) that one who by past resistance to passions and repeated self-conquest has formed habits of virtue and finds the effort to overcome increasingly easier and pleasant should be in a less favorable condition to put moral acts, than when he could win mastery only through painful struggle amid the strife engendered by warring impulses.

(a) Martineau's contention that advertence to alternatives of conduct is not aroused until there arises "a breach of the peace within our nature, and the clamour of impatient propensities disputing for simultaneous admission, or prematurely cutting short the career of the principle in possession," covers only a part—it may be a prominent part in the moral experience of the average man—of the phenomena of moral consciousness. All that is requisite for volition is that alternative modes of action should be compared and that one should be preferred to the other. Between them, it is true, there may be objective "strife," but this need not necessarily rouse what Martineau would call "idiopsychological" strife. Without ceasing to be moral, a man may fight and conquer a temptation, preserving an inner calm and peace during the whole time. Antecedently to every preferential judgment there is, of course, incompatability in the objects of choice, but this incompatability is not necessarily moral, for the objects themselves may be indifferent and the morality of the action be derived from the motive of the agent.[27]

(b) The contention that our activities cease to be moral, so far forth as we have brought our evil inclination into subjection, turns our moral life topsy-turvy. The paramount worth of life is moral. If by continuous victory over inordinate impulses it becomes neutral, it loses its paramount worth, through the activities that give it that worth. Yet such is the logical consequence of a theory which teaches that every virtue gained would restrict the field of moral endeavor, and that the facility, promptitude, and peace of soul, which are the fruits of virtue, would render actions indifferent, which if performed amid internal strife, conflict and struggle would be moral.[28]

NOTES

1. *S. T.*, 1, 2, qu. 18, aa. 8, 9, and *De Malo*, qu. 2, a. 5.
2. *De Bon. et Mal. Act. Hum.*, Disp. IX, Sect. 1.
3. *De Bon. Act. Hum.*, Disp. VII.
4. *2 Dist.* 7, qu. 1, a. 1 and *2 Dist.* 41.
5. *S. T.*, 1, 2, qu. 18, a. 9.   6. *De Malo*, qu. 2, a. 5.
7. *Ibid.*, qu. 2, a. 5, ad. 11.   8. *Ibid.*, qu. 9, a. 2.
9. *1 Cor.* 10:31.   10. *De Malo*, qu. 2, a. 5.
11. *2 Dist.* 26, a. 5; *S. T.*, Suppl. qu. 49, a. 2, ad 6.
12. *S. T.*, 2, 2, qu. 168, a. 2; 2, 2, qu. 141, a. 6, ad 2; *2 Dist.* 40, qu. 1, a. 5.
13. *S. T.*, 2, 2, qu. 141, a. 6, ad 2.
14. *S. T.*, 2, 2, qu. 168, a. 2.
15. *De Malo*, qu. 2, a. 5.
16. *Eth. Nic.*, Lib. II, Ch. IV, and St. Thomas Comm. in h. l.; also *S. T.*, 2, 2, qu. 168, a. 2, ad 3.
17. *S. T.*, 1, 2, qu. 100, a. 9; *De Malo*, qu. 1, a. 4, ad 7.
18. Cf. Com. of St. Thomas in *loc. cit.*, Lect. 4.
19. *Ethics of Arist.*, 4th Ed., pp. 429, 495.
20. *The Theory of Good and Evil*, Bk. II, Ch. III, §3.
21. *Ethics* (American Science Series, 1908), p. 202.

22. Bk. III, Chs. 1-3.
23. *Einleitung in die Moralwissenschaft,* Bd. I, p. 264.
24. *Types of Ethical Theories,* Vol. II, Ch. I.
25. 2 *Cor.* 12:9.   26. *Job* 7:1.
27. Martineau's position is connected with his theory of a moral faculty, which he calls conscience, and defines as a sensibility of the mind to the relative moral worth or excellence of ordered and graduated springs of action. He is an Affective Intuitionist. "To ask after the *quality* of an object," he says, "is to ask about the way it affects us, i.e., about a feeling of our own in its presence or idea. *The springs of action* are here our object." It is the function of conscience to decide intuitively that this spring of action is worthier than that.
28. The "Conflict Theory" of morality is generally, though not exclusively, held by Emotive Determinists.

CHAPTER XIV

Imputability

Morality is formal and imputable only insofar as it is volitional. The evil consequences of a volitional act which are foreseen by the agent are or are not imputable to him according as they objectively fall within or without the intention of the agent.

FORMAL MORALITY. Every act of the will is an integral of an elicit and an imperate or series of imperate acts, having a twofold relation, one objective, a relation of accord or disaccord with a norm of goodness, the other subjective, a relation of dependence on the principle by which it is elicited. Now the eliciting principle, which is the will, is brought into act by an *emotive* principle, namely, the intellect which presents an object as vested with qualities that make it desirable or undesirable. Evidently then the act of the will is limited in range by the intellectual presentation; nothing is willed except as known and only so far as it is known.

The moral quality, therefore, of the elicit act depends first on the completeness with which the object of conation is presented by the intellect. Again, on presentation of the object there arises in the will an impulsive response or initial movement (*motus primus*) towards or away from it, which though it falls short of actual desire or aversion is nevertheless an affection to the object. Thereupon, as we have seen, the will elicits one of two acts: either it yields (*actus secundo—primus*) without deliberation to the initial movements; or after deliberation it accepts the initial movement as its own, or rejects it in favor of an opposite movement with which it was compared in deliberation (*actus secundus*). The moral quality, therefore, of the elicit act depends secondly on that specific perfection of the will through which the agent has mastery over his action and can claim it as being preeminently his own. Now between the response of the will to the attractive qualities of an object as presented by the intellect, and the preferential act by which it was accepted or

217

rejected in favor of a competing will-movement, there exists a relation that is loosely analogous to that which obtains between the constituents of a composite body, one of which, the matter, is ultimately determined in its kind by another called the form. The indeliberate act, therefore, whether in its first or second stage, has the moral quality of the object of conation which is psychically presented, but it has not the final perfection which an act of the will is capable of having, and is consequently *materially* good or bad. The act, however, which the agent after deliberation freely chooses to perform, has the final form which it is fitted to receive. Morality is formal, therefore, only insofar as it is volitional.

IMPUTABILITY. An act is imputable to an agent when its excellence or fault can be accounted to him personally and when as a consequence he deserves praise or blame. (Imputation is often used in a derogatory sense, as when one is said to impute motives to another, or in a certain theological sense to dignify the act of ascribing merit to one on account of another. In our sense of the word, either good or evil is imputable, and the imputation arises from moral qualities pertaining to the person himself.) The conditions of imputability are, therefore, that the act be attributable to the agent as to its cause, and that the agent be personally responsible for it as for an effect.

The first condition is verified in every voluntary act, even in those that antecede deliberation. A man is as truly the cause of his impulsive and unconsidered acts as he is of acts of reflective choice; but he does not acknowledge responsibility for the former, except, as we shall see later, insofar as they are traceable to habits for which he is inwardly accountable. The second and essential condition is found only in acts over which the agent has preferential power, and which, if performed, he is conscious are creditable or discreditable to him. These are acts the eliciting principle of which is necessitated neither by the inner exigencies of a psychic state, nor by the preponderating weight of the motive intellectually present in consciousness. Now only acts which are volitional have these characteristics; only when a man knows that the choice of one course of conduct rather than another depended on himself, and that the motives which induced him to choose it did not compel consent, will he acknowledge that he is a responsible agent.

In two respects moral responsibility differs from amenability to sanctions which impel to or restrain from action. It regards in the first place the inner and formal goodness or badness of the act rather than its merely outward and material consequences, and secondly, it imports a sentence pronounced on the present or past act rather than a constraining judgment affecting the future. We can submit brute animals to disagreeable or pleasurable experiences when they do certain actions, in order to induce them to abstain from doing those that are displeasing to us, or to perform those which we like. Through the discipline of sensory experience we create in them states of memory in which pleasure or pain is associated respectively with the desired or undesired actions. Now if we look on men as being governed in their actions solely by similar associations, even though these be of a higher and more complex kind, we might indeed explain how they are amenable to personal interests or utilitarian sentiments, or how they might be made manageable for the future, but we should totally ignore the fundamental fact of Ethics, namely, that men are conscious of inner responsibility for what they have done, and in the moment preceding consent for what they are about to do.

DETERMINISM. Running counter to our conclusion are those theories according to which choice between alternatives of conduct is in every case finally and fully determined by conditions that immediately precede volition. The schools of Determinism are as many as are the philosophies on which they are based. For our present purpose they may be divided into Physiological Determinism, which holds our action to be the mechanical resultants of compounded and interacting modifications of the nervous system; and Psychological Determinism, which finds the necessitating antecedents of volition in a sheaf of psychic states, which is made up by heredity, temperament, the discipline of personal experience, and the education of social influences.

We need not delay over the first class of Determinists. One who would maintain that our conduct is the inevitable resultant of nervous phenomena, and at the same time hold us responsible for it, is beyond the reach of argumentation. We can say of him what Hume said of those who refused to admit the reality of moral distinctions —he is to "be ranked among the disingenuous disputants."

The second kind of Determinism is the prevailing one today among those who admit the fact of moral responsibility and deny that freedom of choice is an indispensable condition of it. According to this theory actions are the necessary outcome of a man's existing temperamental constitution as derived from nature, and as modified by the influences which have serially acted on him from the moment of birth to the moment of volition. The aggregate of inherited and subsequently formed active tendencies, convictions and interests with which the Self is at a given moment invested, is called "character."[1] Now character so understood, or those facets of it which react to an objective attraction, determine necessarily one's mode of conduct; and we inevitably will at a given moment what the strongest of our psychic states dictates. As J. S. Mill puts it: "The conflict is between me and myself; between (for instance) me desiring a pleasure and me dreading self-reproach."[2] The stronger state necessarily prevails. If, he says in illustration, his aversion to murder and his dread of its consequences had been weaker than the temptation to commit it, he could not have abstained from committing it. The psychological disturbance preceding the ultimate act of decision may be brief or prolonged but the balance comes to rest at last solely because one phase of character outweighs the other.

In estimating the bearing of Determinism on moral responsibility, we should in fairness note that more recent Determinists acknowledge that emotive causality differs in essential respects from physical causality. Even in the brute creation we can distinguish between causes that attract and induce an animal to action and causes that drive or compel it, whether these be applied from without or be dynamic impulses imbedded in the animal nature. The former work through cognition presenting an object that appeals to appetite; the latter, even when accompanied *by* cognition do not work *through* cognition. They repudiate, therefore, as readily as we do, the notion that the reaction of character to the stimulation of an objective motive is of a mechanical kind, and recognize that such theories, stripped of irrelevancies and evasions, leave man as irresponsible for his actions, as is a magnetic needle, when disturbed by a paramagnetic substance, for the position which after some oscillations it finally and inevitably assumes.

They maintain, on the contrary, that the will is determined by emotive causality, which, because it is causality, works inevitably, and, because it is emotive, does not work by inner constraint of a physical sort. The agent consciously, willingly, and necessarily submits to the influence of an objective attraction presented through its idea, whenever it is in keeping with the stronger phase of character affected. Now we need not deny that character has an influence on choice. It cannot, in fact, be controverted that certain motives are more congruous to one character than to another, that to men of certain temperaments, casts of thought, and associated interests, some motives make a stronger appeal than they do to a man whose psychic states are different. Furthermore it may be admitted that this congruity might become so complete as emotively to necessitate. But the very conception of choice in the theory of these Determinists is that competing motives solicit to action, that each is congruous to one and incongruous to the other side of character, and that complete congruity is out of the question. Conflict there may have been for a time, and consequent indecision of will, but the weaker phase of character is finally and irresistibly overborne. An elicit act of the will emerges which is free in the sense that the agent posits it consciously and voluntarily. This sense of unvexed complacency, with which the will finally acts after its experience of inner struggle, produces, they say, the delusion that we are immune from the necessitating determination of character and influence of motive which is congruous to it.

Emotive Determinism mistakes the nature of will, which like intellect, the other spiritual faculty of the soul, is necessarily determined to action only when its appropriate object is presented without adverse qualifications. If consent of will is necessitated by the surplusage of attraction over attraction, then also the stronger of two probabilities must necessitate the intellect to assent. But if intellectual assent is not compelled unless the object is apprehended to exhibit the ground of cognoscibility (*ratio veri*) without qualification, then neither should volitional consent be necessitated unless the ground of appetibility (*ratio boni*) is presented without qualification. The indetermination is as natural a consequence of the spiritual character of the faculties in one case as in the other. Between a theory which holds that this indetermination can be removed by the stronger of two competing causes, and one which holds that it can be removed only by a personal spiritual self which controls choice and gives the final decision (*finalis sententia de agendis*) there seems no alternative. But the first ultimately involves a mechanical conception of volition, which is incompatible with responsibility. Emotive Determinism is, it is true, an advance beyond the crude mechanism of Physiological Determinism. It takes cognizance of the facts of consciousness, yet in analyzing these facts it reverts to a mechanism of its own. The qualitative superiority of one side of character over the other is looked at quantitatively. It is the excess that determines to action. That this excess is emotive rather than physical changes the region of its application, but not the conception of its quantitative causality. The will is moved irresistibly by the weightier attraction or by the side of character that overbalances the other. "So turns the needle to the pole it loves with final librations quivering as it moves."[3]

REFUTATION. Emotive Determinism is, therefore, a denial of personal responsibility for the moral quality of our acts. If choice is necessitated by character, and character at a given moment is necessarily what it is through previous workings of objects of choice upon it, it is impossible to see in the serial interaction of character and choice, however indefinitely prolonged, where the personal causality of self enters.

For first, if character in its changing modes is conceived of as an intermediary between a permanent self and action, and to it is attributed the total causation of choice, then the permanent self in isolation has no other office than the passive one of receiving the modifications produced by character. The moral responsibility of one who has no personal causality outside of character and no personal causality in the formation of character is merely an ethical fiction. The assertion of Emotive Determinists that the personal self is responsible for his actions, since he can act rightly or wrongly if he chooses, is verbal trifling if his choice is necessarily determined by his character.

Or secondly, if we thoroughly identify character with Self, we lapse into the theory of a fluid self, which the Associationists, William James and others, have invented. And in this case, since Self never is what it was, its responsibility is transient and evanescent. The Self of today cannot be held responsible for what was done by the Self of yesterday. This Self is gone, never to return, and consequently our belief that we are morally responsible for what it has done is a delusion.

The only doctrine, therefore, that is reconcilable with the twofold aspect of the ethical fact, namely, that our volitional acts are directed and motived by intellect, and that we are intimately conscious of moral responsibility, is the doctrine of free-will as previously exposed from the teaching of St. Thomas.

IMPUTABILITY OF CONSEQUENCES. One's volitional acts may have results which are beyond or beside the intent of the agent, and which are foreseen by him before the imperate acts which lead to the realization of his intention are posited. Thus, one could use an alcoholic beverage solely for the purpose of producing exhilaration, knowing at the time, however, that inebriation and other undesirable toxic effects would eventually follow. Or again, one might advocate a governmental measure with the intention of promoting the best interests of the community, though fully aware that it would afford opportunity and be an occasion to some individuals of leading immoral lives. Whether these consequences follow by a causality that is physical and therefore necessary, or by one that is emotive and therefore not inevitable even when unfailing, they are impertinent to the purpose of the agent. They do not further nor complete it, but like shadows follow beside or upon it. They differ from consequences which fall within the scope of the agent's integral intent, either as means for fulfilling his purpose or as constituting partially or wholly the purpose itself. A schoolboy who feigns sickness in order that he may be excused from attending class, and so have leisure to finish the novel in which he is interested, intends all the consequences of his imperate act, the deception of his mother, the exemption from class work, and the reading of the novel. The consequences of a volitional act, therefore, may be willed either directly or in themselves, or indirectly or in their cause. The former are evidently imputable, since they merge into the integral object of volitional intention. The latter, we assert in the proposition, are imputable only when they are necessarily included within the intent of the agent.

INCLUSION OF CONSEQUENCES IN INTENT. We can put the problem more clearly thus. A volitional act may have consequences of two kinds, one of which is good and the other evil. The cause of the evil consequence being in this supposition imputable, the question arises as to the imputability of the evil consequence itself. To solve the question it does not suffice to show that the evil consequence is or is not comprised in what the agent proposes to himself as the purpose and scope of his action. For the case we are discussing assumes that it does not subtend, metaphorically speaking, the agent's purpose at all. He neither uses it as a means, nor desires it as an adjunct of the end he seeks. The question is not one of purpose, therefore, but of intent, understanding by intent the total object towards which the will's conscious endeavor tends. The question of course concerns good and evil consequences equally, but is usually discussed in its application to evil consequences, the principles established in one case being valid in the other. The problem then may be proposed as follows: When are the evil consequences of a volitional act so connected with the total object to which the imperate acts are directed that the good consequences cannot be directly intended without at the same time indirectly intending the evil consequences?

Now it is clear that these evil consequences are, in the precise sense in which we have defined the term, circumstances of the imperate acts. In the first place they do not pertain to the *end of the agent,* since the supposition is that, though foreseen, they do not fall within the scope of his purpose, but on the contrary are disagreeable and unwelcome appendages of it. Nor, secondly, do they pertain to the *end of the action,* that is to say, they do not constitute a necessary element of that to which the successive imperate acts are immediately directed, since they are adscititious, and in other circumstances could be absent, the ends of the agent and action remaining the same. To take a well-worn illustration: the commander of a besieging army shells a city or fortress in order to compel surrender, foreseeing and deploring the death of many innocent noncombatants. Clearly these consequences do not form a part of his purpose, which is the capitulation of the beleaguered enemy, nor are they the immediate object of the military operations which he employs. Precisely as physical effects of his bombardments they are to be judged as circumstances. Or to take the case as an illustration of emotive causality, the attacking commander may know that the defenders will be moved to a more speedy surrender by the mental distress experienced at the sight of sufferings and deaths among the children and women. In this supposition we have true emotive causality, namely, the fear of further impending calamities which induces the besieged city to yield. But this emotive causality is only as imputable to the besieger as are the physical effects by which it was brought into play. If the latter are not imputable, then neither is the former. Assuming, then, (a) that the evil consequence is foreseen; (b) that it is in nowise comprised in the purpose of the agent; (c) that it forms no part of the object to which the imperate acts are directed; (d) that it is, nevertheless, connected with them by a causality that is physical or emotive, the question then presents itself, whether this evil consequence can be unintentional, or in other words, whether the agent seeking the good effect may suffer the circumstantial evil effect to happen without at least indirectly intending it.

Psychologically the answer is not difficult. Everyone can verify from his own experience that he has sought a good, foreseeing the occurrence of concomitant or subsequent evil effects. Towards these his will may have no leaning, they may in fact be detestable to him; or he may in spite of his repugnance accept them as inevitable in view of the good that he is resolved on obtaining. Now comparing the good and evil effects in their relation to the norm of morality two suppositions arise. Either the attaining of the good effect is of greater moral importance than the avoiding of the evil effect; and consequently to abstain from seeking the good effect solely for the sake of warding off the evil effect would be to subordinate the lesser to the greater good. I say, *solely for the sake of warding off the evil effect,* because undoubtedly a person's action may be in accord with the norm of morality, when for personal motives that are sufficient he sacrifices his own good to save another from harm, or refrains from seeking it rather than risk the danger of incurring evil. But the principle that an action, one of whose effects is good, should always be omitted, if at the same time or thereupon an evil effect also follows, could not be accepted as an objective and universal canon of volitional activity without introducing disproportion into the moral order. Inversely, to preclude the evil effect through inaction may be of greater moral worth than to procure the good effect through action, and consequently to seek the latter at the expense of the former is to subordinate the greater to the lesser good.

In the first supposition the evil effect falls objectively without the intention of the agent. The intent of volition, or that to which the will tends, is the good effect insofar as it excels in worth the avoidance of the evil effect that besets it. The will's attitude towards the evil effect is said to be *permissive,* using the word in its older English sense to signify[4]—bearing involuntarily with what cannot be eliminated. In the second supposition the evil effect cannot fall objectively without the intention of the agent. Whatever be the psychological repugnance to the evil effect, as a matter of fact that to which the action of the will is directed is the good precisely as it is inferior in moral worth to the avoidance of the evil that overshadows it. We do not, of course, maintain that the lesser of two objective goods may not morally be chosen, but that such choice cannot be moral when the rejection of the higher entails the admission of an evil exceeding that which would be incurred by not seeking the lesser.

Theoretically these objective principles seem clear: (a) Evil is to be avoided, but not when such avoidance subordinates a higher good; (b) Evil is to be avoided unconditionally, when its avoidance surpasses a lesser good. Nor does the psychological phase of the problem raise a difficulty; for in the first case the attitude of the will may be *permissive,* while in the second case it is necessarily *admissive.* The detailed application of the principles, however, involves questions to which answers will be given hereafter, questions namely of the prevalence of one right or duty over others.

NOTES

1. The Associationists identify character with self, and deny permanency to both. Hume declares that the idea of a permanent self is a fiction. Spencer assures us that his ego is nothing more than the aggregate of feelings and ideas, actual or nascent, momentarily existing in him, and that he is his own phenomena. The matter is not rendered more intelligible by saying that self is a *series* of mental states or a *"stream* of consciousness." If the I or self is the passing psychic state of the moment, it assuredly cannot have imputed to it the deeds of a self that is gone. The present cross-section of the "stream of consciousness" or link in a series of mental states cannot be held responsible for what has been done by a past cross-section or link unless there is a real proprietor who owns both. For a criticism of these theories the student is referred to Maher's *Psychology,* Bk. II, Ch. XXII. Apropos of them, it is interesting to recall a remark of St. Thomas, noting that one of the remarkable characteristics of his style was continence of language in dealing with an opponent. He says: "Quidquid dicatur de potentiis animae, tamen nullus unquam opinatur, nisi insanus, quod habitus et actus animae sunt ipsa ejus essentia." *De Spir. Creat.,* a. 11, ad. 1.

2. *Exam. of Sir W. Hamilton's Philosophy,* 5th Ed., p. 585.

3. Erasmus Darwin, *Botanic Garden,* II, 26.

4. *Permittere* from which the word is formed, in its primary signification simply intensifies *mittere.* In this sense the will is said to permit what is sent away completely from its intention. Later meanings of the word, namely, to leave unhindered or to grant leave, imply a positive attitude of will.

CHAPTER XV

MODIFICATIONS OF THE VOLITIONAL

The volitional is modified by lack of knowledge and by the working of passions.

MODIFICATIONS OF THE VOLITIONAL. Volition, as we have seen, is an act of the will motivated and directed by deliberate reason. It is affected therefore by the measure of knowledge which was had before deliberation was instituted, by the degree of deliberation employed before decision was reached, and by the kind of decision on which consent followed. Evidently, then, when knowledge of the action in prospect has been full, when deliberation has been regular, and consent eventuates, the volitional is *perfect;* and, on the contrary, defects of knowledge, deliberation, and consent render the volitional proportionately *imperfect.*

IGNORANCE. Nescience, ignorance and error have this in common that they are each an absence of knowledge. They differ, however, in respect of the subjective condition they indicate. *Nescience* is the mere absence of knowledge in a subject having a capacity for knowledge,[1] as for instance, a schoolboy who does not know the effects of an electric current. It becomes ignorance, when it is a privation of knowledge, or a lack of it in one who should fittingly have it, as for instance, in a medical man who does not know the functions of the liver. *Error* adds to ignorance a positive assent of the intellect to what is false. Although it is only through ignorance that we err, says Augustine,[2] error is not always a consequence of ignorance, but only in him who thinks he knows what he is ignorant of.

DIVISION AS TO SUBJECT. Ignorance is divided in respect of its *subject* into invincible and vincible. The agent is *invincibly* ignorant: (a) if he has no suspicion of his mental condition, or of his need of knowledge; or (b), if he have a doubt on either head, cannot after due diligence resolve it and remove the ignorance. Invincible ignorance in the first sense is not imputable, since it is

227

not wilful, nor in its effects since these cannot be foreseen even conjecturally. Neither in the second sense is it imputable in itself, though action posited with such ignorance may be imputable, when, namely, the rules which we shall establish later for the guidance of an uncertain conscience are not observed.

The agent is *vincibly* ignorant, when, a doubt having arisen touching the moral quality of the action he is about to perform, he neglects to use due diligence in resolving it. By due diligence is not understood the greatest possible diligence of which one is physically capable, but a diligence which the importance of the issues at stake in the alternatives of choice, the circumstances in which action is to be taken, and the mental capacity of the agent, reasonably demand. A juryman may be called on to cast his vote on a case in which the life or acquittal of a defendant is at stake, or one in which an action in tort has been brought. Evidently a more thorough investigation is to be made and more exacting diligence to be used when the death penalty is in question than is prudentially required when a decision is to be reached in an action for libel or trespass. Again, a medical man may confront an emergency in which decision, to be of any worth, must be practically instantaneous; the necessity of acting may be so urgent that little or no time can reasonably be employed in deliberation. Lastly, the agent may be a person of untrained mind, who in order to act reasonably need not often do more than take counsel of those who are wiser.

Vincible ignorance is not imputable in itself, until the agent, becoming conscious of it and of its bearing on conduct, neglects to use suitable means of knowing. The volitional character and consequently imputability of vincible ignorance is increased when the agent through wilful indolence neglects to make any investigation on the validity of his doubt. This ignorance is said to be *crass*. It becomes *supine* when it grows into a wonted attitude of will. One may, for instance, be aware of the important bearing of the truths of religion on one's moral life, and yet, without precisely declining knowledge, not trouble himself about acquiring it; or again, one may drift heedlessly into practical unconcern regarding these truths, though in a vaguely speculative way cognizant of their significance. Finally, one may designedly shun knowledge for the purpose of more freely evading duties which it is suspected knowledge might have revealed. Ignorance of this sort is called studied or *affected.*[3] Studied ignorance is clearly volitional in itself and consequently imputable.

DIVISION AS TO OBJECT. Ignorance is divided in respect of its *object* into ignorance of *the right,* that is, as to whether actions of a given kind are right or wrong, and ignorance of *the fact,* that is, as to whether or no the circumstances that put an individual action in a category of right or wrong are present in the contemplated action. Ignorance of the first kind may obtain among all classes of men, the learned as well as the unlearned, with regard to certain kinds of right and wrong, the evidence for which is gotten only by processes of reasoning. Thus dueling was once widely considered a reasonable mode of vindicating honor, and larval species of it are still in esteem among some peoples. Some medical men do not consider the operation called craniotomy to be murder, when they deem it necessary for preserving the life of the mother. Many do not know in what precisely the evil of lying, stealing, or suicide consists. Now, notwithstanding the inconclusive grounds on which these or other false principles of right and wrong are held, men may as a matter of fact be in invincible ignorance regarding them.

Ignorance of the second kind may similarly be invincible. A number of circumstances must often concur to integrate an individual action and include it under a moral principle. One or more of these may not be known at the time the action was put. The person who jokingly fires a gun at another not knowing that is was loaded, and the person who fires at what he fancies is a deer and kills a man, are still existent. Apart, however, from extreme cases, it happens in the moral affairs of life that some of the elements of a particular action escape notice, and consequently are not comprehended in the will's intent.

St. Thomas's rule is clear.[4] An action is volitional only inasmuch as it is known. If therefore of the same action something is unknown, the action is volitional with regard to what is known, and non-volitional with regard to what is unknown. And this holds true, whether the thing unknown was the moral principle that covered the action, or a circumstance of it that was required to bring it within the scope of the principle.

DIVISION AS TO VOLITIONAL ACT. Ignorance is divided lastly in respect of *the volitional act* into antecedent, concomitant and consequent ignorance. When the agent deliberately posits an imperate act the nature or result of which is unknown to him, and would not have posited it had he known its nature or foreseen the result, his ignorance is a cause of the elicit volitional act and is said to be *antecedent*. The causality of this ignorance is not of course positive but privative, that is to say, it does not positively induce to action, but, by depriving the object as presented to the will of an element which would have destroyed its motive power, it gives it a causality which knowledge would have annulled. Thus a temperate man might drink a wine or other alcoholic beverage, unaware of its insidious strength, and thereby get drunk, lose discretion, and commit actions of a morally degrading character. Being temperate by habit he would, had he foreknown the effect and consequences of his act, have abstained from drinking the wine. In this case, though the act of drinking is volitional, the outcome of it is *non-voluntary* because not an object of the will, and *involuntary,* because it is opposed to the actual inclination of the will.

Ignorance is said to be *concomitant,* when the agent posits an imperate act, the results of which are not known or not anticipated, which nevertheless he would have posited in any case, even had they been known. Thus to adapt the example given, if the man had taken the wine for the sake of the exhilaration it would afford, not foreseeing drunkenness or its consequences, yet so intemperately disposed that he would have taken it whether or no, his ignorance does not even privatively affect his motive for drinking. It neither adds to the volitional character of his act, nor detracts from it. His drunkenness and the evil consequences that may ensue, though not involuntary, are simply non-voluntary.

Ignorance is *consequent* to the volitional act in two ways: either *directly,* as when, in studied ignorance, knowledge of the right or the fact is wilfully declined, or lack of knowledge wilfully fostered, in order that one may do evil with less annoyance of conscience; or *indirectly,* as when it is the effect, surmised or through negligence not foreseen, of an act or habitual state that is volitional. Ignorance of this sort is volitional in itself or in its cause.

SOLUTION OF DIFFICULTIES. Suarez discusses the logical validity of this threefold division.[5] The difficulty arises regarding the act of the will with regard to which the ignorance is said to be antecedent, concomitant or consequent. Briefly the solution is: (a) that the terms do not indicate a temporal relation, but one of causality; (b) that they relate to an elicit act of which the ignorance is either cause or effect, or to which it has neither relation. In other words,

ignorance is either the cause of an elicit act, in the sense that privation of knowledge gives the motive for acting an influence it would
otherwise not have; or it simply accompanies the elicit act, and as
usually happens precedes it in time, without, however, in anywise
affecting the motive for acting; or it is the effect of the elicit act in
the sense that, preceding it in time, its continuance is either directly
or indirectly willed, with the consequence that it colors the motive
for putting subsequent acts.

How and to what extent ignorance modifies the volitional character of these subsequent acts is easily determined so far as antecedent and concomitant ignorance is concerned. The results attributable to the agent because of ignorance cannot be more volitional than the ignorance itself. But antecedent and concomitant
ignorance being invincible, are not at all volitional, and therefore
no actions done in ignorance of their moral quality are volitional.
Consequent ignorance on the other hand is vincible, and therefore
in varying degrees volitional. Yet it is clear that no sort of ignorance
can increase the will's free movement towards the object precisely
as it is unknown. Hence no other causality can be assigned to consequent ignorance with respect to further consequences than such
as has already been assigned to antecedent ignorance. There is a
difference however; antecedent ignorance being wholly involuntary, the agent is in no wise responsible for the attraction exercised
by the motive which induced to action; whereas since consequent
ignorance is more or less volitional, he is proportionately responsible,
since he could by acquiring knowledge have counteracted or co-
hibited the attractive power of motive.

Consequent ignorance is then a sign of the will's attachment
to an object, certain knowledge of which is either negligently
shirked, because of the inconvenience its pursuit would cause, or
studiously evaded for the purpose of escaping its effects. Now ignorance due to negligence and indirectly willed diminishes the volitional character of consequences that ensue upon it. These do indeed fall within the intent of the will, but they are incidental to its
purpose. Though surmised or anticipated, they do not exercise a
motive power on the will. On the contrary, the will, moved by the
direct object which it has chosen, chooses at the same time, because
of the strength of its desire, to hazard or admit the consequences of
its choice. Studied ignorance is directly willed and therefore chosen
as a means. There is an apparent disparity of opinion regarding the

effect of this ignorance on volition. St. Bonaventure[6] teaches that it diminishes volition of the consequences on the general ground that it diminishes knowledge of them. A person, he says, who studiously abstains from acquiring knowledge of a law, hoping thereby to follow with impunity the course of conduct that pleases him, does not as fully will the violation of the law as he who, clearly knowing the law, directly elects to violate it. St. Thomas[7] seems to hold the contrary. But the reason he assigns explains his meaning. In studied ignorance, he says, the bent of the will towards evil is such that one foregoes an intellectual good like knowledge rather than submit to what he anticipates would be its restraint. The studied disregard for knowledge, therefore, indicates the intensity of the will's desire for evil, but cannot properly be said to increase it.

The division and principles just exposed are, it is important to note, applicable to inattention, forgetfulness, inadvertence and error.

NOTES

1. The term is sometimes applied to philosophic theories which teach that certain forms of reality are unknowable, as for instance, God, the soul, matter, and in general the thing-in-itself; and that, if from the exigencies of practical thought we accept their existence at all, it must be unverifiable belief. In this sense the term denies not only knowledge, but the subject's capacity for acquiring it.

2. *Enchiridion,* C. XVII.

3. Not used in the sense that it is an outward assumption or pretence, for the ignorance is actual; but in an older sense of the word, to signify that one has a liking or an affection for the ignorance.

4. *De Malo,* III, a. 8.

5. *De Vol. et Invol.,* Disp. IV, Sect. 1, nn. 1-10.

6. 2 *Dist.* 22, 2 pars, a. 1, qu. 3.

7. *S. T.,* 1, 2, qu. 76, a. 4.

CHAPTER XVI

THE PASSIONS
(EXCURSUS TO CHAPTER XV)

THE PASSIONS. In modern psychological usage, the term "passion" generally signifies a strong uncontrolled emotion. By emotion is understood complex feeling of a vivid kind following upon sensation or perception in which appetitive consciousness predominates. An emotion is called passion, when it becomes so strong that other appetitive movements are rendered passive by it, or when from habitual indulgence, it has produced a deep-seated inclination, or when it is the expression of a vehement tendency of temperament combined with a defective power of self-control. Understood in any of these senses its common characteristic is that in its presence the reflective and deliberative use of reason is practically arrested, or impeded.

The scholastic sense of the term—not unfamiliar to older English philosophers—keeps closer to the original meaning of the word. In a generic sense passion is a condition of being acted on by something distinct from the faculty or nature affected. More precisely it applies to faculties receptive of physiological change, and consequently is peculiar to faculties of our animal nature, which as they are localized in corporeal organs are susceptible of qualifications. In a still more refined sense it is attributed to organic faculties so far as they are principles of action. These are the sensuous faculties, which are moved by mental pictures of the agreeable or disagreeable. Passion, therefore, as we use the term, is defined by St. John Damascene, whom St. Thomas follows, as a movement of a sensuous appetite attended by an organic excitation, and arising from an imaged or re-imaged object presented as sensuously good or bad.[1] The characteristic commonly assigned it of intensity or dominance is not distinctive in the scholastic conception. Passions may be feeble as well as strong, controlled as well as controlling. They are to be distinguished on the one hand from original instinctive propensions

233

to sensuous good or aversions from sensuous evil. These are subjective appetencies that go before any presentation by sense or imagination, whereas passions are the movements that follow. And on the other hand they are distinct from purely intellectual emotions, since these may be experienced without organic agitation. One may be truly penitent for one's sins without sensible sorrow, or one may hate evil on rational grounds without any stirring of the irrational appetencies.[2] Nevertheless, owing to the oneness of the human soul and its substantial union with the body, all our appetencies are radicated in the same ultimate principle of action. Hence the passions of our organic nature are not strongly felt without usually moving the will to some initial response at least; nor does the will elicit with any intensity a volitional act without a concurrent action of the corresponding sensuous appetite setting in.[3]

MORALITY OF THE PASSIONS. Aristotle, whom the Schoolmen follow, holds that there are three principles of action in our nature: faculties, passions, and habits, none of which are evil in themselves.[4] The Stoics on the contrary seemed to have maintained that all passion was inherently evil, and that the truly good man was immune from the movements of the sensuous appetites, or, if he experienced them, was wholly unaffected by them. The essential characteristic of their ideal wise man was impassive equanimity.[5]

The modern philosophic exponent of Stoicism is Kant. His distinction between the autonomous man, who unmoved by any emotion is governed solely by the principles of pure aprioristic reason, and the heteronomous man, whose elective will is affected by emotion, is parallel to, though not identical with, the distinction of the ancient Stoics between the wise man and the fool. An affinity with the morality of the Stoics may be discovered in the Puritan ideal of goodness and in the works of many writers who have been influenced by Calvinism, though it lacks the moderation of the ancient school.

FORMAL AND MATERIAL ELEMENT. In solving the question, St. Thomas[6] analyzes passion into two elements, a formal element, which is the movement of the sensuous appetite itself, and a material element which is the accompanying organic excitation. Now the *formal* element may be considered in itself or in its relation to reason and will. Under the first aspect it is merely an action of the sensuous appetite, which is common to all animal nature. The craving for instance for food or drink, for repose or muscular activity, so far as they arise from sensuous appetite (*motus primus*) are simply movements of our animal nature. They call attention to an uneasiness of the organic system and are provisions of nature having in view the preservation or physical well-being of the individual or species. Merely as such they are neither good nor bad morally. Under the second aspect they take on a moral quality, when subject to the direction of reason and the control of will, and approved or disapproved of for the circumstances in which they are felt.

This control, unlike that exercised over the outward members of our bodily members, is indirect. We cannot manage our sensuous appetites as we manage our muscular and locomotive powers. The latter are brought into action by a direct impulsion from the will, the former move necessarily in response to a presentation of sense or imagination. The will's ascendency over irrational appetites, therefore, is only such as it can acquire over the presentation of their objects. This it gets through reason, which because of the interactions and concurrent operations of sense and intellect, can present conflicting or competing attractions, and thus inhibit sensuous movements of an ineligible kind or initiate those that are admissible or expedient.

Consequently, passion formally considered is morally either good or evil according as it is indirectly controllable by will, and is in or out of accord with the purpose which the sensuous appetite is designed to serve in the economy of nature. The indirect control of the will over the sensuous appetite may be exercised in three increasingly perfect degrees. (a) When the will is drawn prior to deliberation into an impulsive movement corresponding objectively to a sensuous movement (*actus primo-secundus*), reason can on advertence intervene and forestall further action of the will, or, in other words, induce it to abstain from volition (*actus secundus*). (b) Through formed habits of vigilance and self-control the attention of reason can be roused at the first suggestion of the sensuous appetite and thus ward off even the indeliberate reaction of the will. (c) In certain extraordinary states of virtue reason may have, through reflection or insight produced by meditation, denuded some objects at least of their sensuously attractive or repulsive quality so that the sensuous appetite no longer responds to them.

The whole controversy concerns the *material* element of passion. The organic disturbance accompanying the activity of the sensuous appetite is pleasureable or painful. Its insurgence therefore, the Stoics contended, always impeded to greater or less extent that calm and unperturbed use of reason which is proper to the performance of a virtuous act. We shall see that this is true in many cases that, when passions are aroused independently of reason, they may indeed darken understanding; but we cannot admit that it is universally true that the impulse of passion is always toward evil, that it never cooperates with reason, or that the truly virtuous man is not one who merely resists passion when it is opposed to reason, but only one who finally extinguishes it. In the first place a passionless man is an impossible man, and in effect would be a disembodied spirit. Secondly, as an ideal he is abhorrent to the highest calls of our nature. He would never feel the joy of friendship, the emotions of pure love, the noble sorrow of one bereaved, the righteous indignation of one fighting against an unjust cause. Thirdly, an extreme dualism in the conception of composite nature which denies the substantial unity of its parts, pervades ancient and modern Stoicism, and a psychological dogma that bodily nature is radically diseased is its essential implication. Lastly, Stoicism is morally pernicious. To assign man a goal of virtue which the analytic powers of his reason finally discover to be unattainable, results sooner or later, but inevitably, in the decay of moral energies.[7]

ERRORS OF STOICISM. St. Thomas, in the article to which reference has just been made, finds three errors underlying the Stoic tenets. First, the Stoics failed to distinguish between what is absolutely and what is relatively best. It happens that what is best in itself or absolutely may not be best for a given kind of being. To use a modern example: a grade of intellectual being in which an agent never acted from a motive, that is to say, was so self-sufficient that it could not without contradiction be moved by a cause extrinsic to itself, would be a higher perfection than one in which the agent was moved to act by the desire of an end distinct from itself. In fact, a being of this kind is the highest conceivable, and peculiar to Infinite Actuality.

Now Kant sets this grade of being before us as the aim of our moral endeavor, unmindful of the fact that it is wholly incongruous with any grade of finite being. "I will ascend above the height of the clouds, I will become like the most High"[8] is the utterance of one whom neither religion nor philosophy can regard as a consummate type of moral character. A philosopher can by abstraction attain a conception of intellectual being from which limitation is excluded, since intellect as such does not involve limitation. And because such a concept can be formed, some have inferred that an intellectual nature of the kind must exist; but they cannot conclude that human nature is such, without closing their minds to the most obvious facts of man's personal existence and experience. As, therefore, the nature of man is a composite of soul and body, and as his rational activities are conditioned by his sensuous activities, whatever perfection he can reach must be consistent with his unitary nature, which is at once spiritual and corporeal. Both body and soul must consequently serve in the performance of virtuous acts, not as parts alien to one another, one of which is constantly to be repressed, but as cooperating causes the inferior of which contributes to the efficiency of the superior. Thus in the virtue that impels us to the vindication of wrongs the movement of the sensitive appetite reinforces the energy of the will.

Secondly, the Stoics overlooked the psychological fact that passions arise subsequently to the exercise of reason as well as antecedently. When aroused by the senses or imagination previous to the advertence of reason, their tendency, it is true, is to cloud the judgment, and when they have made some headway in strength it becomes difficult for reason to act judiciously. But when passions are subsequent to reason's approval of a mode of conduct they stimulate the will to prompt and resolute action. The test of a formed habit of virtue, Aristotle shows, is the pleasure or pain one finds in performing its acts. One has not acquired in its fulness the virtue of temperance, he says, who does not abstain from bodily indulgence with joy, nor is he rightly called an habitually just man whose acts of justice are painful to him.[9] Peripatetics, therefore, held a middle position between the Epicureans who made pleasure the end and be-all of virtue and the Stoics who taught that its presence as a motive power spoiled the act morally. Looking at human nature as an harmonious whole, they and their followers, the Schoolmen, recognized the functions of the passions in man's active life, and the naturalness of pleasure in the energizing of his faculties.

Thirdly, the Stoics erred in confusing passions with other appetitive movements. As they made no distinction between intellect and sense, neither did they discriminate between emotions of our rational and irrational nature. Emotions of wonder, humor, self-esteem or reverence, equally with those of anger, desire or sexuality, were reckoned diseases of the soul which disturb the serenity and

independence of reason; and emotionless life is the ideal of reason.
They made it a duty to seek "apathy" which was not, as Kant
insists, subjective indifference or insensibility to the objects of the
elective will, but rather an immunity of reason from the influence
of emotion. Like the Stoics, Kant maintained that "emotion always
belongs to the sensibility no matter by what sort of object it may
be excited." Enthusiasm he compares to the apparent strength of
fever patients that makes even the lively sympathy for good degenerate into an emotion. "Emotion, even when excited by the idea of
good, is a momentary glitter which leaves exhaustion after it";
though in itself unmoral, it cannot enter as an element of motive
or a spring of conduct without undoing the autonomy of reason and
rendering the action of the elective will immoral.[10]

EPICURISM. Stoicism was, as we have said, a protest against
Epicurism. The norm of goodness of the Epicureans was the natural
impulses as expressed in sensuous feeling and desires, and accordingly they gave authoritative precedence to the emotional side of
human nature. The Stoics on the contrary held that man's emotional nature should be absolutely divorced from reason, and that
the rational side of his nature should be wholly independent of
emotion. To the Epicureans reason was the mere servant of emotion; to the Stoic emotion was a rebel against reason. An antithesis
of this kind necessarily resulted in exaggeration, for it denied by
implication the synthesis of Aristotle, who viewed the rational and
emotional sides of human nature as correlative and implicated
phases of the same unitary being. The Stoics therefore came finally
to put all emotions in the same category with the sensuous feelings
and desires of the Epicureans. They outlawed all of them from the
moral life, refusing them any legitimate function in the impulsion,
direction, or control of conduct.

Now there are emotions, like self-respect, compassion, wonder,
reverence, which never arise prior to an intellectual cognition. They
always presuppose reflection and comparison. It is not, indeed, denied that they affect the body in a sensible manner; but it is evident
that they originate from intellectual processes and appertain to our
rational nature. Their morality, therefore, is that of their origin. If
the thoughts, judgments, and convictions from which they spring
are befitting a rational nature, they are morally good; if unbefitting,
they are morally bad. Thus self-respect may be laudable or repre-
hensible, compassion may be ennobling or degrading, wonder may

be rational or irrational, and reverence may be virtuous or vicious. It is admitted, of course, that intellectual emotions, once they have arisen lawfully, may subsequently become excessive. Thus, respect for self, which is becoming to one possessing the dignity of a rational nature, may degenerate into an unbecoming self-esteem. But just so far are they morally worthy or unworthy at any stage, as they depend on the formed judgments of that moment.

CLASSIFICATION OF PASSIONS. Many classifications of passions have been proposed.[11] We adopt the classification of St. Thomas[12] because it takes more clearly into account than other classifications the nature of the passions properly so called, and explains more satisfactorily their relations to human activity. Passions properly so called are movements of the sensuous appetite, which are attended by a bodily uneasiness and feeling that there is need of something adapted to restore the organic balance. Now the object presented by imagination is sensible good as such, which either brings pleasure or relieves pain, when the absence of the former or the presence of the latter is a discomfort to the animal nature; or it is a sensible good the attaining of which is beset with difficulties and calls for spirited effort. Briefly the sensible good presented by the imagination is either good simply as such, or good that is hard to attain. Hence, St. Thomas infers:[13]

In the sensitive part of man there must be two appetitive faculties: one whereby the soul is simply inclined to take what sensuously suits it and to shun what similarly hurts it—and this is called the *concupiscible* appetite; another whereby the animal nature resists the onset of what strikes at its good or brings harm to it—and this is called the *irascible* appetite.

In classifying the passions three observations are to be made. First, the same appetite that is attracted by an imagined good is repelled by the imagined contrary evil. The faculty, for instance, that likes some foods, dislikes others; that finds some odors agreeable, finds others disagreeable; or, in general, that desires the pleasant, abhors the painful. Secondly, the irascible appetite arises out of the concupiscible. Before one can make a spirited effort to reach a good or avoid an evil, the good must be desired and the evil hated. Thirdly, to the note of agreeable or disagreeable in the object of the concupiscible appetite, the object of the irascible faculty adds the note of a difficulty to be overcome which the imagination presents as superable or insuperable.

The passions, therefore, or movements of the *concupiscible* appetite, are classified first according to the contrariety of their objects, namely, of good and evil, and secondly according to the stages in movement towards the good or away from the evil. These are three: (a) an initial responsive stage by which the appetite has simply a feeling of liking or dislike for the object; (b) a progressive stage, by which it reaches out for the object or shrinks away from it; and (c) a quiescent stage in which it possesses the good it reached out for, or endures the evil it could not shun. Hence we have three passions in the movement of the concupiscible appetite toward good: *love, desire, joy;* and three in the movement of the same away from evil: *hate, aversion, sadness.*

In classifying the *irascible* passions we must bear in mind that their object is not good or evil as such, but good that it is hard to get and evil that it is hard to shun. The irascible appetite, therefore, confronts a twofold contrariety in its object, namely, that between good and evil, and that between the superable and insuperable difficulty of obtaining one or avoiding the other; and as a consequence the movements of this appetite, unlike those of the concupiscible appetite, may be a tendency towards or a recession from the same object, according as imagination exhibits in higher lights the good that appeals or the difficulty that dissuades. First, then, with regard to the good, if the difficulty seems surmountable, the passion aroused is a sanguine expectation of getting the good, or *hope;* but if it is imagined to be unsurmountable, there arises a despondent feeling of the uselessness of effort, or the passion of *despair.* Secondly with regard to the evil, this may be either anticipated and threatening, or instant and experienced. If the evil, that seems to threaten one, seems at the same time to be hardly avoidable, the passion stirred is *fear;* if on the contrary it is presented by imagination as a danger that can be vanquished, the passion of *daring* is excited. Finally, if the evil is a present affliction, there arises the passion of *anger.* This, although it is immediately a movement of the irascible appetite to expel the existing evil or to redress it, is not, as St. Thomas shows, a simple passion but springs from the concurrence of many.[14] It presupposes hate of the harm inflicted, desire and hope of reparation or of reprisal on the cause of it. Anger, therefore, may present a twofold aspect: when governed by reason it is vindicative; when it escapes the control of reason it is vindictive.

The distinctive passion of the concupiscible appetite is that which is conative or impelling to action. This is desire, aversion being its obverse. Hence the name of the appetite from *concupiscere,* to wish for eagerly, to endeavor after. The term desire, so far as usage goes, seems to be applied more appropriately to the conation of the rational than to that of the sensuous appetite, and in this sense it is not a passion. The earlier psychologists, as Locke for instance, apply the word to all conative movements whether aroused by imagination or intellect. There is a tendency among more recent psychologists to confine its use to the designation of intellectual conation. They do not, however, so far as the author is aware, supply a generic term for the various sorts of sensuous conations, which would be the English equivalent of the Schoolmen's word *concupiscentia.*[15] We shall call the distinctive passion of the concupiscible appetite *sensuous desire.* The distinctive passion of the irascible appetite is that which arises from the imagined difficulty of obtaining or retaining a good. This is *fear.* Its object is an evil imagined to be impending and superable only with difficulty. Its effect is to weaken or hinder outward action. St. Thomas[16] gives an apt illustration: it is more difficult because of fear to walk on a beam placed high in the air, than on the same beam laid on the ground. Both sensuous desire therefore which impels to action and fear which tends to hinder it, though primarily affecting the bodily organs and their functions, may exert an influence over reason and so modify the volitional character of conduct.

SENSUOUS DESIRE AND VOLITION. Sensuous desire may stand in one of two relations to the deliberate decisions of reason (*finalis sententia de agendis*). It may arise previously to deliberation, and therefore to the volitional act. So viewed it is called *antecedent* sensuous desire. Or it may be looked at precisely as it follows on a deliberate decision of reason, and as consequent, therefore, on the volitional act. The passion of sensuous desire, in other words, is either a potential cause of a volitional act, or its effect.

Consequent sensuous desire has no causal influence on the volitional act, though it is an indication of intensity in the will-movement. This happens in one of two ways. Either the strength of volition is such that, owing to the natural interaction of the higher and lower appetites, a cognate passion is aroused, or the will deliberately chooses to be affected by a passion in order to work more effectively. Thus one's rational love of God or hatred of sin may be such that it overflows, as it were, to the sensible faculties. Or one may desire an evil object, and studiously excite passion for the purpose of more promptly executing, or more fully enjoying the evil actions intended. The morality and imputability of consequent passion is that of the volitional act of which it is an effect and indication.

Antecedent sensuous desire, though its tendency is to intensify the movement of the will, diminishes its volitional quality. Freedom of consent, by which a voluntary act is volitional, is had in its fulness when reason in making its decision is not acted on by heterogeneous causes that tend to disturb the balance of deliberation. Whatever impedes, hampers, or clouds deliberation diminishes to a proportionate degree the freedom of the volitional act. Now antecedent passion, because of the individual unity of our composite nature, and the interaction of its faculties, may in varying degrees interfere with the equable use of reason.

St. Thomas explains the modes of this interference in three ways.[17] First, since all the faculties of the soul are radicated in the same nature, the energy with which one works draws off a certain energy from another. Hence the keenness with which an inferior appetite acts slackens, or may even override the movement of the rational appetite. In extreme cases the organic disturbance which accompanies passion may become so vehement that reason for the time is paralyzed; as might happen in the case of excessive anger, vindictiveness or lust. Secondly, when the mind's attention is drawn to an object, it is partially or wholly distracted from other objects. If therefore passion is aroused by the suddenness or vividness with which perception is stimulated, then prior to deliberation reflex or voluntary attention to the interesting object preoccupies the mental field, and may hamper or hinder volitional intention. Thirdly, as only knowledge of the concrete induces to action, antecedent passion may, by coloring the psychic representation of an action, cause it to appear desirable. Thus for instance revenge, though on general principles known to be wrong, may through the influence of passion on the primary movement of the will, be made to seem tolerable or justifiable in certain concrete circumstances.

Antecedent sensuous desire therefore is not imputable in itself, since it precedes volition. With regard to action done under its influence, it bars imputability, if so intense as to preclude the use of reason; and diminishes it, if it disturbs without incapacitating reason. As long, however, as the agent is capable of deliberation, his action is to some degree imputable, since reason can suppress passion, especially in its initial stages, or divert it through imagination, or at least control the outer action to which it impels.

FEAR AND VOLITION. The passional disturbance of mind caused by the imminence of an evil probably unavoidable is, broadly speaking, either grave or light. It is *great* if the evil threatening is of serious or momentous import, as for instance the loss of life, of fortune, or of social estate; and *light,* if it seems of small account, of less moment, tolerable, or incidental to daily life, or if, though appearing to be serious, is nevertheless thought to be of unlikely occurrence. Fear may have its source in the objective character of the impending evil or in the subjective conditions of the one who is apprehensive of it. In both cases fear may be grave. The dangers, misfortune, or hostile agencies that threaten may be such as to justify grave fear in one of adult courage; or, though not objectively a reason for grave fear, may as a matter of fact excite it in one who because of age, sex, temperament, bodily or mental infirmity is unduly susceptible to fear. Notably this may obtain in the reverential fear one feels of offending another of superior power and worth, or the other-regarding fear of parent, guardian, or friend, regarding danger to those in whom they are interested.

Now the effects of fear on the deliberate use of reason are similar to those produced by sensuous desire; the energy of the mind is diverted, its attention is held, and the difficulty is depicted in higher lights. Hence (a) when grave fear rises to extreme fright or a certain pitch of terror, it temporarily overwhelms reason, and consequently extinguishes imputability. (b) Apart from this case, actions done through fear are volitional. Of the alternatives present in consciousness during a state of fear, namely, the evil to be avoided or the good to be sacrificed, the will actually chooses the former, while the latter remains at most an object of inefficacious wish or mere velleity. The elective act expresses the decision of deliberative reason that one good is in the circumstances definitely eligible and to be retained or compassed, and the other definitely ineligible, and to be abandoned or rejected. The essential conditions therefore of volition, namely intention, deliberation, and choice, are present. Imputability however is diminished, since the use of deliberation is disturbed by the persistence of a velleity for what has been set aside. (c) Actions done through fear may be wholly uninfected by any admixture of a contrary velleity. In the first place an act may be agreeable of itself, which nevertheless would not be done except under the influence of some fear. Thus a lad may through fear of contracting an illness or incurring a danger absent himself from school, and find the holiday wholly welcome. Or again an act which in the absence of fear would be desired, on the arising of fear may be entirely in disaccord with the inclination of the will. Thus one who from fear of death, bodily sufferings, or torments of mind renounces a life of sensuous excesses, may through fear of their inevitable consequences find the excesses themselves hateful.

NOTES

1. *S. T.,* 1, 2, qu. 22.

2. Martineau's use of the word is peculiar. In *Types of Ethical Theories,* Pt. II, Bk. I, Ch. 5, he describes the passions as impelling tendencies, which urge us, in the way of unreflecting instincts, to "repulsions," that is to feelings of *antipathy* towards an object of natural aversion, of anger towards that which has just hurt us, and of *fear* towards that which menaces us. Besides confusing impelling tendencies, instincts, or appetites with the passions, which, following on sense perception, modify their activities, he excludes from the category of passions many of which the common speech and judgment of men include.

3. The nature of the passions is fully explained by St. Thomas, *S. T.,* 1, 2, qq. 22-26; see also *De Ver.,* 25, a. 3, and 26, a. 3.

4. *Ethics,* Bk. II, Chs. III, V. See *Com.* of St. Thomas in loc., Lects. III, V.

5. Only fragmentary portions of the writings of the Stoics have come down to us. What information we have regarding their teaching is supplied mainly by Cicero, Plutarch, Sextus Empiricus, Diogenes Laertes, and Strobaeus. Their doctrine appears to be Semitic rather than Greek in origin. It spread rapidly through the intellectual centers of the East, and finally got a foothold in Rome. Seneca, Epictetus, and Marcus Aurelius are representatives of Roman Stoicism. See Zeller's *The Stoics, Epicureans, and Sceptics.*

6. *De Ver.,* qu. 26, a. 7.

7. St. Augustine, *City of God,* Bk. XIV, Ch. IX.

8. *Isaiah* 14:14.

9. St. Thomas in *Eth. Nic.,* Lib. II, passim.

10. Kant's *Ethics,* Abbott's transl., pp. 319sqq.

11. See Suarez, *De Act. Hum.* Tract IV, Disp. I; Descartes, *Traité des Passions,* Art. 51 et sqq., whom Spinoza in his *Ethics* practically

follows; Martineau, *Types of Ethical Theories*, Part II, Bk. I, Chs. V, VI, and VII; Maher's *Psychology*, Ch. XX. Any standard scholastic work as the psychology of Urraburu or Pesch, treats of the nature, classification and functions of the passions.

12. *De Ver.*, qu. 26, and *S. T.*, 1, 2, qq. 22-25.

13. *S. T.*, 1, qu. 81, a. 2.

14. *S. T.*, 1, 2, qu. 46, aa. 1, 2, 3.

15. The English word *concupiscence,* which one finds in some text-books has become narrowed in signification and is misleading. Jowett's translation of τὸ ἐπιθυμητικόν (Plato's *Republic,* 439, E.) by "the concupiscent part" of the soul is merely an acknowledgment that he could find no more precise word in English.

16. *S. T.*, 1, 2, qu. 44, a. 4.

17. *S. T.*, 1, 2, qu. 77, aa. 1, 2; *De Malo*, qu. 3, a. 9.

CHAPTER XVII

RIGHT OBJECTIVELY CONSIDERED

The right objectively considered is an ideal norm of conduct obligatory in character.

RIGHT. The term is derived from a root, *rego,* meaning that which is kept straight. It applies primarily to the movement or path of a material body towards a point or mark without deviations in lateral directions; then by a natural extension of sense to actions or processes in conformity with a standard of aim or purpose. We say for instance that a medical man's method of treating a disease is right, or that a plant is subjected to right conditions for proper development. Finally, by an elevation of meaning, it designates movements of a supersensible or higher kind which are in accord with the type of excellence befitting the faculty that originates them. Thus we speak of right reasoning or right conduct, implying a norm which sets the specific aim of the movement, and keeps it within its proper boundaries. The term *wrong* affords us the same evidence. Allied by etymology to the participle "wrung," it signifies primarily that which is wrung aside or twisted from its direction, scope, or type; and then in its application to movements of intellect or will, that which is in discord with the norm of excellence peculiar to these faculties.

Now the adjective sense of the term by which reasoning and conduct are qualified presupposes a substantive sense. The activities of our higher faculties are said to be right when they conform to their appropriate regulative principles. The regulative principle is the nature of the faculty itself which defines its specific tendency, and is therefore not only directive but also impulsive. It not only guides the faculty to seek by its action that only which is informed with the attribute of its proper object, but by its innate tendency impels it also to action in presence of an object so informed. It exhibits therefore an ideal norm of action inwrought in the constitution of such a faculty and manifesting its connatural purpose. Now the impulsive necessity imposed by the ideal norm is congruous with the nature of the faculty and varies accordingly with its peculiar excellence or perfection. It is of one kind for intellect and of another for will. We have seen that the only necessity to which will in its volitional activity is subject is moral necessity, or a necessity arising from the presentation by reason of an object which is perceived to be essentially and imperatively connected with the ideal norm, but which leaves the will physically free to embrace or reject it. This necessity is called obligation, and expressed in the ethical word "ought."

OBJECTIVE RIGHT. From the exposition given, Objective Right may be defined as an ideal norm of conduct, imposing on the will a necessity, which is (a) *objective,* i.e., perceived by the intellect to have validity independently of and prior to desire, persuasion, education, custom or legality; (b) *absolute,* i.e., unconditioned by further purposes of the agent, or by the personal or social difficulties that may be met with in its actuation; (c) *moral,* i.e., presented by reason as a good imperatively to be desired. A phrase in Lincoln's Second Inaugural Address, "with firmness in *the right,* as God gives us to see *the right,*" illustrates the primary use of the term.

The notion of Objective Right superadds to that of Good a distinctive note. It is true that good—as predicated of conduct—is always in accord with Objective Right, and that Objective Right prescribes only what is good; and that therefore we may in the concrete infer one from the other. But conceptually they differ in comprehension. Hooker's assertion, for instance,[1] that "goodness in action is like unto straightness; wherefore, that which is well done we term right," is as a concrete inference valid; as a philosophic inference it misses the full import of the concept behind the word *right.* The good signifies that which because of intrinsic worth is perfective of the nature of which rational will is the appetitive faculty; the right designates an authorative norm by which the pursuit of perfective good is binding on the will. Defective analysis of these two terms is responsible for the confusion and inexactness that obtain in many theories regarding the ultimate categories of Ethics.

A necessary derivative of Objective Right is moral power, inviolable by reason of the objective right which man has over his actions in the pursuit or protection of the essential, social, or material goods of life. This we call Subjective Right; it will be discussed in a future proposition.[2]* In an allied sense the term is applied to matter over which Subjective Right may be exercised. Life, liberty of conscience, good repute, for instance, are rights which one may defend and vindicate in virtue of his having a subjective right over them. The treatment of these and similar rights belong to special Ethics.

OBLIGATION. The authoritative character perceived to inhere in Objective Right, or the sense of obligation expressed by the word "ought" is the *pons asinorum* of moral theorists. To the questions, what precisely does obligation mean, and what is the source of its validity? the answers are as varied as are the attempts to construct a philosophy of conduct. The questions are essentially related. We cannot give an intelligible meaning to obedience, even though it be analogous or merely metaphorical, without implying a power that claims compliance with its dictates on grounds which are rational and emotive.

The concept of obligation involves a threefold relation: an authority that obliges, a subject who is obliged, and that to which the subject is obliged. The subject obliged must be one with whom the personal decision of obeying or disobeying ultimately resides, who is therefore capable of respecting or condemning the mandates of reason; otherwise obligation is indistinguishable from the emotive coercion used in disciplining the brutes, and the sense of personal responsibility is a delusion. That to which the subject is obliged is that which furthers or frustrates the realization of the ultimate end and the supreme good of life. We have no consciousness of obligation in matter that does not involve the final purpose and perfection of our rational life. Formally, then, *obligation* is a moral necessity imposed on the will by a power having authority, known by reason, and impelling to the positing or omitting an act which has an intrinsic connection with or opposition to an ultimate end and supreme good.

SOURCE OF OBLIGATION. The question, whence comes the binding force of the moral imperatives of reason and what is the ground of their validity? has received three main answers. The interpreta-

---

*EDITOR'S NOTE: For this *primary* meaning of the word "right," cf. *A New English Dictionary* (Oxford), *sub voce,* I, 1, where it is defined: "The standard of permitted and forbidden action within a certain sphere; law; a rule or canon." Also Salmond *Jurisprudence,* 9th Edit. (1937), by J. L. Parker, Bk. I, Ch. I, §8, p. 30, and Black *Law Dictionary,* 3rd ed. (1933), *sub voce* "Right," p. 1558.

tions of what obligation is, are based ultimately: (a) on the different conceptions of the supreme good of life; and (b) on the nature of the faculty which reveals the quality of actions that leads to or turns away from the supreme good. The position held regarding what befits volitional activity necessarily prefigures the theory held regarding the right that binds it; and the kind of bond to which will is subjected can be such only as is made known by the faculty that perceives it.

Now three supreme goods have been proposed by three different schools or classes of schools as the end of human endeavor, namely, the Hedonistic, Stoic, and Eudaemonistic. And as a matter of fact there are but three ultimate conceptions of the supreme good, i.e., perfective good, delectable good, and the complex of both. The common tenet of the hedonistic schools is that pleasure or happiness is the only ideal goal of man's activity. The Stoics set up an excellence of character defined by abstract reason, as being not only wholly apart from, but exclusive of, the emotional side of human nature. The Eudaemonists placed the supreme good of man in the final perfection of his rational nature adequately considered, comprising therefore not only the fulness of rational life and activity for which he has a capacity, but also the complementary delight that crowns such a life.

Now the faculty by which the supreme good is made known to us is either an emotional faculty or a rational faculty, that is to say, either a faculty by which we feel the moral charm, harmony or attraction of certain modes of actions, and the moral ugliness, discord, or repulsiveness of others; or a faculty by which we perceive that the former are imperatively prescribed and the latter in like manner forbidden. An emotional faculty can reveal only pleasure or happiness as the supreme good and the authoritative character of objective right does not rise above a psychological impulse which is indistinguishable from a similar impulse in brutes except in range. The aspects of an action that fall under the observation or within the experience of this faculty is more ample than in brutes but its impulse to action does not in its mode of working differ in the dog which wavers between the pleasure of seizing an agreeable morsel, and the fear of detection and punishment, and in the man who balances the relative quantity of pleasure or pain likely to ensue from his action. "Vice may be defined," Bentham tells us,[3] "to be a miscalculation of chances, a mistake in estimating the value of pleasures or pains. It is a false moral arithmetic."[3] Ought, obligation, duty, and allied terms of the same vocabulary have therefore no ethical meaning, no meaning, that is to say, which is distinctively moral. "Ought," at best is but a weakened form of a psychological "must."

* * *

[Thus, unfinished, stands Fr. Brosnahan's *opus magnum*. It does not seem unfitting to quote the note in the Parma edition of St. Thomas' *Compendium Theologiae ad Fratrem Reginaldum* (Tom. xvi, p. 85): "Hucusque compilavit S. Thomas de Aquino brevem compilationem Theologiae; sed, proh dolor! morte praeventus, eam sic incompletam dimisit."]

Notes

1. *Eccl. Polity*, I, 18.
2. This promise was left unfulfilled. But the present editor adds, as Appendix B, a brief analysis of right and duty which he found in Fr. Brosnahan's writings.
3. *Deontology*, Vol. I, p. 131.
4. Gassendi in his *Philosophiae Epicuri Syntagma*, Pars I, c. 4, generalizes the rules for the application of this moral arithmetic: 1. that pleasure with which no pain is connected should be chosen; 2. that pain with which no pleasure is connected should be shunned; 3. that pleasure which either hinders a greater pleasure or gives rise to a greater pain should be shunned; 4. that pain which either wards off a greater pain, or is the cause of a richer pleasure should be chosen.

Part II

A DIGEST OF ETHICS

PART II

A Digest of Lectures on Ethics

I. PROVINCE

Ethics is a normative science, based on reason, which interprets a specific and paramount fact, the elements of which are conduct and oughtness. Its province is to determine the principles by which conduct ought to be regulated, and in accord with which character ought to be formed.

1. FACT. Every department of thought presupposes some distinctive fact or aggregate of facts, which it reduces to a common category, and undertakes to explain. Ethics presupposes a fact of consciousness, viz., that by an intellectual impulse we are prompted to approve and commend, as having a specific and paramount worth, certain actions of our own or of other men, and to disapprove and blame others as wanting it. We are conscious that we judge some actions to be good and right and some to be evil and wrong, and that we ought to do the right and avoid the wrong. The peculiarity of this estimate is, that it is: (a) *universal,* applicable, and in fact applied, however erroneously at times, to all actions for which we feel we are responsible; (b) *supreme,* i.e., regulative of all other estimates; (c) *general,* i.e., characteristic of the race, and hence called by a name that signifies *customary,* i.e., ethical. We cannot deny these facts of moral consciousness without logically gainsaying every deliverance of reason.

2. THE ELEMENTS OF THE FACT. These elements are (a) actions which we are conscious are under our control, and for which we are responsible, i.e., conduct; and (b) a necessity, which though peremptory is not compelling, of putting our conduct into accord with a standard of right, i.e., oughtness. *Conduct* is an attribute of man alone. Not all actions performed by man, even when peculiar to him, are conduct; for instance, assent to a self-evident truth.

253

Only actions which spring from motive, and are consciously directed
to the attainment of a purpose, are conduct. Conduct when it becomes uniform and continuous is *custom*. The determinants of
conduct, then, are the determinants of custom. But determinants of
actions which uniformly, constantly, and generally affect men necessarily respond to an inner and essential demand of their nature, and
conduct resulting therefrom exhibits the activity of that nature in its
specific and paramount aspect. Hence customary conduct, which
arises from an innate tendency of reason to discriminate between
right and wrong, receives by historical usage the name Ethical
(from the Greek ἔθος—a customary or characteristic way of acting), in order to distinguish it from customs of an inferior kind,
and to designate it as preeminently the distinctive custom of mankind. *Oughtness* expresses a necessity which is less than the necessity
that arises from expediency or propriety. It is revealed by reason as
an authoritative and absolute dictate. Its necessity leaves man a
responsible agent, and, therefore, physically free to respect or condemn the imperative of reason, but volitionally bound to obey it.

   3. CHARACTER. Conduct uniformly in accord with the dictates
of reason results in the formation of habits of conduct. A habit is
a quality superinduced in a faculty by repeated performance of its
functions, giving an impulse to, and a facility in the exercise of its
proper activity. Habits are of two kinds—habits of thought and
habits of conduct. Both are acquired: the former determines intellectual dispositions in a particular direction, and is the product of
disposition and training—(apperception); the latter confers ease
and inclination in the active determination of the will to certain
ends. Both may be good or bad. Character is the integration of
habits of conduct which individuate moral personality. The scope of
Ethics is to determine, therefore, the principles by which *conduct
ought* to be regulated in order that finally *character* may be rightly
formed.

   4. NORMATIVE SCIENCE. Any body of truths, whether phenomenal or rational, coordinated under principles by which they are
explained and methodically formulated into a system is a *science*.
Every science deals with a generic subject-matter common to it and
other sciences. For Ethics this is conduct. This it views under a
specific aspect and in the light of principles peculiar to itself. For
Ethics this is oughtness and its principles. Sciences either investigate
the nature of things primarily for the sake of knowing, or estimate

the meaning and value of things in their bearings on action. The first are *speculative,* the second practical. Practical sciences either establish principles for the direction of human activities to the achieving of an outer end in material extrinsic to man, or establish norms by which human activities are regulated and directed to the realization of an end proper to, and perfective of the nature of the faculty that originates them. The latter are called *normative* sciences. If the faculty regulated is reason in its pursuits of *truth,* the science is Logic; if it is will in its tendency to *good,* the science is ETHICS.

5.   BASED ON REASON. The principles on which a science is based may be either immediately known or inductively inferred. In the case of a science of Conduct the induction would be from psychological experience or from the facts of history and ethnography. The first method is *intuitional,* the second *empirical.* There is no logical device by which the validity and authority of the principle: "One ought to do right" can be induced from experience. The imperatives of empirical sciences of conduct are at best optatives, conditional, and contingent.

There are three classes of theories regarding the nature of the faculty by which ethical principles are immediately known: the *Affective Intuitionists,* who assert that we have a special moral faculty for feeling the difference between right and wrong— Shaftsbury, Hutcheson, Hume, and in general the hedonistic and esthetic schools; the *Moral Reason Intuitionists,* who require "a faculty in kind and in nature supreme over all others, and which bears its own authority for being so,"—Butler; the *Rational Intuitionists,* who hold that one or more of the primary principles of morality are immediately known to reason, which when it perceives emotive truths is called *Practical Reason.*

We reject *Affective Intuitionism,* because (a) feeling is a merely passive experience, "subjectively subjective," as Hamilton notes; (b) it is not a special faculty, but a consciousness accompanying the energizing of every faculty; (c) it varies with the individual, the country or the age, and deprives all moral truths of validity or fixity independently of the feeling mind. We reject Butler's theory, because (a) a special faculty is superfluous, since the same intellect can perceive speculative and practical truth; (b) it is founded on a defective and superficial psychological analysis.

References: Martineau's *Ethical Theories*, Vol. II, Bk. I, Ch. I, Sect. I; Ladd's *Philosophy of Conduct*, Ch. I; Maher's *Psychology*, Introd., Ch. III. See also Hamilton's *Metaphysics*, Lect. XLII.

II. POSTULATES

The fundamental postulates of Ethics are: (a) that God exists who made all things according to archetypal ideas, and for His external glory; (b) that man, His only visible rational creature, has a free will and an immortal soul; (c) that man is endowed with certain primitive impulses to individual and social well-being by which his nature is adjusted to the purposes of his creation.

1. Postulate. A postulate is a premise which a given science claims as valid without demonstrating it; not because it cannot be demonstrated, but because the demonstration of it belongs to a science other than that which uses it. A postulate differs from an hypothesis. Confusion in the modern acceptation of the term "postulate" is due to prevalent theories of knowledge. Every science has need of the external assistance of other sciences and is their debtor for postulates. Ethics, which is concerned with the highest and most far-reaching activity of man, must impetrate largely from other sciences of which man is the subject.

2. The Cosmological Postulate. Any ultimate explanation of the cosmos must start either from sheer nothing or from sheer actuality, i.e., the universe either sprang from nothing and became what it is through some process of creative evolution, or it was produced by a being of sheer actuality. The first is untenable initially and progressively; the second demands a being of sheer actuality from the fact that there is any being at all. The existence of the universe, therefore, postulates: (a) a *necessary self-existing* Being, possessing the plenitude of being, and specifically, in a transcendent degree, the intellectual attributes of mind and the moral attributes of will; (b) this Being is the efficient, archetypal and final Cause of all other beings, which are consequently analogues of sheer actuality; (c) such beings are *contingent,* i.e., owe nature and existence, endurance in existence, and activity of nature to the Self-existing Being; and are necessarily images of the Creator's archetypal ideas; (d) the Self-existing Being bestowed existence on contingent being

freely and for a purpose, though not from a motive; (e) the only conceivable purpose of a Self-existing Creator is to communicate being in such a way as to manifest His own perfections. The ethical import of these truths.

3. THE PSYCHOLOGICAL POSTULATES. These are: *freedom*, a logically necessary and immediate antecedent of the moral act; and *immortality*, a necessary though remote consequence.

4. FREEDOM. Variety of meanings. Generically it means immunity from *necessity*. Necessity may arise from causes *extrinsic* to the agent: (a) *physical*, when the agent is constrained by force to an action that is incongruous to native appetency, or restrained from an action that is congruous thereto—*necessity of coaction;* (b) *emotive*, when an end is absolutely wished, for whatever reason, the will, of necessity, wishes the *means* to the end; or when an end is authoritatively assigned by a superior, the will is subject to the necessity of conforming its action to the command of the superior—*emotive* or *moral necessity*. The will cannot be subject to the first necessity in its elicit acts; it may be subject to the second necessity.

5. NECESSITY. Necessity may arise from causes *intrinsic* to the agent. Inherent in every nature there is a tendency or motive power that specifies it. It is as much an attribute of intellect as it is of matter, as distinctive of will as of a magnet. This necessity is called by the Schoolmen the *necessity of specification*. It does not drive the faculty to action, but when tendency is actuated, it determines its specific functions and defines its range of operations. In cognitive beings the appetitive tendency is actuated by sensuous and intellectual apprehension. The *necessity of actuation* is had when a faculty, in the presence of its proper object duly and rightly proposed, cannot withhold action. The will is always subject to the necessity of specification; and to the necessity of actuation, when the object presented to it is absolute good, or good without qualification.

The cases in which freedom is claimed for the will are when the object either has not and is seen not to have a necessary connection with the specific satisfaction of the will's inherent tendency to good as such; or, if it have such a connection, is presented through false apprehension as not having it. The attitude of the will towards qualified good is similar to the attitude of the intellect towards probable truth.

The theory of free-will is not a theory of pure Indeterminism. The will, even when freely acting, acts from a motive and for a purpose. The causality of motive is not reducible to the attractive power of a physical force; it is peculiar to the faculty that is moved by cognition. The will, as every faculty, needs the stimulation of some cause distinct from itself before it can act. This cause, an object present in consciousness, and known to be desirable, arouses a will-movement towards the object. This *first act* is necessary. If other and undesirable aspects of the known object come into consciousness (as normally happens, unless the will is hurried into action either by the suddenness with which the object is presented or the intensity with which it attracts) a conflicting will-movement away from the object is aroused. The will concurs or refuses concurrence with one or other of these movements. In this *second act* the will is not necessitated. Though it could not consent to either will-movement but for a motive, its consent is not compelled by either motive.

6. IMMORTALITY. The individual soul, or the spiritual principle in man by which he is a rational and a moral being, will survive the dissolution of the body, and continue endlessly to lead a life of intellectual and moral activity. But the soul is *not immortal of its essence,* as is the Creator; it never ceases to be a contingent being. It is *naturally immortal,* in the sense that the purpose for which it was created, stamped on its highest faculties and tendencies, demands its conservation in endless existence.

7. THE ANTHROPOLOGICAL POSTULATE. Every created being has its own mode of operation, and an innate inclination to perform those operations that agree with its nature and fix its place in the scheme of the universe. As we ascend in the grade of being these modes of operation become many and complex; are performed by different faculties each having its own natural inclination. All the faculties of a being are radicated in the same nature; their inclinations are coordinated with one another, and subordinated to a dominant inclination, which manifests the inclination of the unitary nature. This inclination of the unitary nature we call *natural appetency.* Man is a composite being in whom are found appetencies analogous to those characterizing inferior creatures; he is a microcosm. These are subordinated to the good of his unitary nature through mind, i.e., intellect and will. As each separate faculty has its appetency for what is connatural to it, so his nature has its natural appetency for its good.

This latter appetency manifests itself in four fundamental directions: (a) in common with all creatures, he has an inclination to resist dissolution, i.e., to self-preservation; (b) in common with all animals, he has an inclination to perpetuate his species, to care for and educate progeny; (c) as an intellectual being, he has an inclination to know the source and purpose of his existence; (d) as a social being he has an inclination to live in the communion of thought and endeavor with his fellow man. This latter inclination has universally actuated itself in three distinct natural societies: domestic, civil, and religious, through which the objects of the three first inclinations are more securely and adequately realized.

Other inclinations of our nature are extensions, derivations, or complexes of these.

III. MATERIAL AND FORMAL OBJECTS

Conduct, which is the material object of Ethics, is volitional action, elicit or imperate, self-regarding or other-regarding. It differs from behavior, or purely voluntary action. Oughtness, which is the formal element of Ethics, involves an ultimate end, a supreme good, and an absolute right.

1. ELEMENTS OF CONDUCT. Action springing from motive and consciously adjusted to an end is the outcome of various acts of intellect and will, some of which are concerned with the end, and some with the means conducive to the attainment of the end. As the intellect progressively apprehends an object as good in itself, as good relatively, i.e., to the agent, as not impossible of attainment, there responsively arises in the will the acts of *liking, wish,* and *intention.* These concern *the end.* Note the distinction between *intention* and *intent,* confounded by Bentham, Mill and their followers. *Intention* is a movement of the will to gain a particular object (*in-tendere*) in virtue of which it desires in an undefined way the means that lead to the realization of the end. Upon the formation of intention, there follows a series of acts which concern *the means.* The intellect investigates, compares, and weighs the disparate procedures by which the intention may be executed, with a view to deciding the means suitable to the end and to the agent. This act is called *deliberation.* It may be a prolonged or a practically

instantaneous act. Through it intention is known to be definitely practical; and responsive to it there arises an act of the will called *consent,* which is an acquiesence in the deliberative judgment of reason; regarded as the preference of one out of many examined ways of proceeding it is called *choice.* Consent and choice may be identical but are not necessarily so. Conduct, therefore, is defined as a free conative act towards a determined end, through chosen means. Hence, all acts of this kind, whether internal or external, whether self-regarding or other-regarding, are conduct. The measure of volition is the knowledge of the end and means, and advertence to indeliberate will-movements of liking and wish. Any given end was a means in a prior state of appetition, chosen for the realization of a further end; every good except goodness itself can come into deliberation and be a matter of choice.

2. BEHAVIOR. Actions done from a sense of propriety or honor bear a resemblance to actions done from a sense of oughtness; and as man is a social being, social sanctions act as a direct incitement to moral conduct that comes or may come within the purview of others. But behavior is (a) judged by its outward conformity with certain canons of propriety; (b) conditioned on the approbation or disapprobation of others, and the advantages or disadvantages thence accruing; (c) varies with social environment and standards.

3. OUGHT. The word is employed in other than its ethical sense: (a) loosely, to express a conjectured necessity, the frustration of which is not deemed impossible; (b) in an appropriated sense, to denote a necessity of action conditioned on expediency, propriety, or the end of a profession or social state of life; (c) analogously, instead of "should," to signify a logical necessity, or the ultimate reasonableness of a mode of acting.

The *ought* of Ethics is different from any of these three. It is (a) *certain,* not conjectural, and *objective,* i.e., valid independently of the individual or social mind, not a subjective persuasion of a person or a community; (b) *absolute,* its cogency is not conditioned on any further purpose that we may have resolved on, nor contingent on inclination or adopted ideals—its incidence is ultimate and comprehensive of cognate and implied conditions; (c) *emotive,* in the sense that its cogency directly affects the will, though it is first perceived by the intellect. Thus the intellect, which is the faculty determined by truth, first perceives *ought,* and thereafter *ought* affects the will which is the first efficient principle in man of all rational action for which he is responsible. Briefly, the binding power of *ought* is not merely logical, i.e., on the intellect; it is also moral, i.e., on the will. *Ought* in this sense is the either expressed or implied "copula" of every ethical judgment. Ethics, then, does not investigate what actually is in the past, present or future, but what ideally *is*, and actually *ought to be,* i.e., an objectively valid ideal, which ought to be actualized in conduct.

4. ANALYSIS OF OUGHT. The objective, absolute, and emotive necessity imposed on the will presupposes a logical necessity imposed on the intellect. In every ethical judgment, therefore, is involved the idea of something that it is ultimately reasonable to aim at doing, of something that appeals to will as being intrinsically and unconditionally good to do, and of something which practical reason cannot help recognizing as right to do. In the ethical judgment, then, three judgments are contained: (a) that there is an objective and absolute *end* which is proper to action controlled by will; (b) that this end is an unconditioned object of will, i.e., *good,* or perfective of the nature of which will is the appetitive faculty; (c) that the necessity of attaining the end and realizing the good through the free actuation of will exhibits an ideal obligatory in character, i.e., *right*. These three conceptions, the *end,* the *good,* and the *right,* constitute the formal principle of Ethics or the specific aspect under which it views conduct and character.

5. CONTENT OF OUGHT. *Ought,* therefore, implies a twofold canon of morality: one *incomplete,* which furnishes a *rule* by which the worth of conduct—i.e., its conformity with the end and the good—is discerned; and another *complete,* comprising the first, and adding the idea of *law* prescribing right and proscribing wrong conduct. A rule is practical in respect of matter and speculative in mode; a law is practical in respect of matter and in mode. The notion of *ought* contains the idea both of rule and law. Any system of Ethics that ignores the latter element in its content is not competent to explain the Ethical Fact.

6. SUMMARY. We have seen: (a) That "ethical" means what is *customary to the race;* (b) that the customary is uniformly recurrent *conduct;* (c) that conduct uniformly recurrent conforms to some *norm;* (d) that this norm exhibits a universally perceived and accepted *rule* and *law;* (e) that "ought" is the expression of this norm; (f) that conduct habitually conformed to this norm produces a type of moral personality, called *character*. The subjects of

General Ethics are, therefore, Conduct, the End, the Good, the Right, and Character.

REFERENCES: Rickaby's *Aquinas Ethicus,* Vol. I, pp. 40-46, 52-54; Ladd's *Philosophy of Conduct,* Chs. 4 and 5.

IV. THE END

The absolutely ultimate intrinsic end of man's volitional activity is blessedness, or the final perfection of his rational nature with the happiness consequent thereupon. Through no finite object or combination of finite objects is blessedness obtainable, but only by the perfect knowledge and perfect love of God.

1. THE END. In its primary meaning end signifies the *terminal part* of a material object; thence, by analogy, (a) the *close* and *outcome* of a continued operation; (b) the *result* of conative activities foreseen before achievement; (c) the mental representation of this result as desirable and as inducing to action. In the last sense, end is a *final cause,* i.e., that for the sake of which and on account of which anything is done. Looked at as that which induces to action it is *motive;* as the object or state which the action is intended to attain it is *purpose.* Motive and purpose are correlative for created wills. The Uncreated Will acts for a purpose, but not from a motive. An end is, therefore, that which is desirable *in itself*; or that on account of which or for the sake of which anything is done.

2. DIVISION OF ENDS. An end is desirable in itself, but at the same time may be a means to a more desirable object; hence, we distinguish *immediate, intermediate,* and *ultimate* ends. An ultimate end may be *relatively* so, i.e., within a certain sphere of activity; or *absolutely* so, i.e., for the whole unconditional range of volitional activity. Again we distinguish between *the end of the action,* or the result in which the action of its nature terminates; and *the end of the agent,* or the purpose which the action is made to subserve by the free will of the agent. These may be identified; but for finite intellects and defectible wills they may be distinct and incongruous. Furthermore, we distinguish between the *intrinsic* end of nature, i.e., an end realized within the nature itself through the attainment of the fullest development and perfection of which it is capable;

and the *extrinsic* end, i.e., an end outside of the nature, to which its final state of perfection is ordained by the Author of Nature. The two ends are essentially related. The extrinsic end of man, we learn from the Cosmological Postulate, is the extrinsic glory of God.

3. NATURE AND END. The intrinsic end of a nature is known from its appetencies; either by finding a resultant tendency or a dominant tendency, which exhibits the final tendency; the first impossible, since man's nature is composite and of heterogeneous parts, i.e., matter and spirit; the second alone possible. Man's tendencies may be classed under two heads: the *apprehensive* or cognitive tendencies, and the *appetitive* or conative tendencies. The object of a faculty rightly presented rouses the mind to some sort of activity; its tendency, before potential, becomes actuated. In every mental act a relation between the mind acting and the object of the act is established. This relation is either receptive, bringing the object vicariously into consciousness, or is subsequent to the physical presence of the object in consciousness, and is active in its attitude to the object. By the first the object is known, by the second it is sought. Now the first is the condition and measure of the second; the second is the completion and *ratio essendi* of the first. By the first we know, by the second we do. The final tendency of man's nature, therefore, is found in his appetitive tendency, and in the object of this is discerned his end. But this is the higher or rational appetency, i.e., will, to which his lower or sensuous appetency is of its nature subordinated.

The adequate and appropriate object of will is goodness—this by the necessity of specification. In every elicit act while freely moved by the desirability of a particular object, it is necessarily moved by a common and comprehensive ground of appetibility, i.e., goodness.

Blessedness on its *subjective* side is the complete satisfaction of the rational desire that expresses the final tendency of human nature. The *objective* ground of this satisfaction includes (a) perfect well-being of life and activity; and (b) the full and unalloyed happiness that arises from perfect well-being. Neither can be had apart from the other. The dissensions among schools of Ethics regard the logical or ontological priority of one or the other. Blessedness then is a state of existence in which (a) man possesses the full measure of well-being for which he has a capacity, or, in other words, the final perfection of his rational nature; (b) and enjoys an abiding pleasurable consciousness arising from the fact that supreme tendencies energize in the full possession of their object, or in other words, final happiness. A corollary of blessedness is that it should be *stable* and *unending*. It could be subject to change only in the supposition that the capacity of human nature for blessedness (a) could be continuously and progressively enlarged; or (b) could be finally diminished. Both suppositions untenable. If terminable, the blessed (a) either know it; (b) are in doubt regarding it; or (c) are ignorant of it. Any of these suppositions vitiates blessedness.

4. Proof. The absolutely last end of man's volitional activity is known, first, from the innate tendency of the will to its adequate and appropriate object, since this is, as it were, the essential gravitation of the faculty towards that for which it has capacity and need, and which, reciprocally, adequately responds to the one and fully satisfies the other. But the state that responds to the innate appetence of will must be one in which the full ground of appetibility is realized, or all goodness that responds to the rational desire of will. Now, this is complete well-being or final perfection, and the final happiness consequent thereupon.

It is known, secondly, from the elicit appetence or the innate appetence actuated in regard to a particular object. The formal element in desire, *qua* desire, is the natural inclination of the will towards an object that shall be repletive of its innate tendency. Therefore, in every actual volition the fullness of well-being is either explicitly or implicitly sought. This is confirmed by the experience of our inner life. We pursue objects of desire, but possession does not bring surcease of desire; we are occupied with some interest, but no measure of success brings permanent content. Rational desire can never be sated except in the attaining of a state of existence coextensive with the good for which the will has capacity and need; but its capacity and need are measured by the range of the intellect's power of conceiving.

This state is *attainable,* i.e., happiness cannot be an infinite progress to a state of existence or of perfection eternally in advance of any given grade of atainment. 1. The divine *Wisdom* would be in contradiction with itself, if it implanted in our nature a tendency to a goal that could never be reached. 2. The divine *Veracity* would belie itself, if the promises which the tendency reveals were false; a mere lure to lead us on. 3. The divine *Goodness* would defeat its own purpose, if man, through the faculties by which he excels the brutes, were rendered more wretched than they.

5. THE OBJECT. Since the adequate object of the intellect is truth as such, and the object of the will is good as such, the final perfection and happiness of man's nature will consist in a knowledge and love, commensurate with his capacity, of an object, which is supreme truth and supreme goodness. This is God and God only.

Finite objects are: (a) *Goods of fortune*—but these are extrinsic and instrumental; are acquired or lost independently of merit; are of an inferior kind. (b) *Goods of the body*—but these are common to us and the brutes; are unsatisfying, in the absence of goods of fortune; like these are possessed or lost without relation to moral life. (c) *Goods of the soul,* as knowledge, love, and virtue—but these are formal, not objective goods; their capacity for rendering blessed depends on the capacity of the objects with which they are concerned for adequately satisfying man's final tendency. Nor can they satisfy in combination, first, because some of them are incompatible, and secondly, because each is insufficient, not quantitatively only, but qualitatively also.

REFERENCES: Rickaby's *Aquinas Ethicus,* Vol. I, pp. 1-39.

V. THE GOOD

Good is perfective, delectable, and useful. Man's supreme good is EUDAIMONIA, *or the attainment of his absolutely ultimate intrinsic end. The proximate norm of goodness is rational nature looked at in itself and in all its essential relations; the ultimate norm is the Divine Nature as known to the Divine Practical Reason. The determinants of goodness are the end of the action, the end of the agent, and modifications intrinsically affecting either.*

1. GOOD. The notion of good presented *a posteriori* is that which satisfies appetence. Rational appetence (with which we deal), involves a relation of the faculty to an object, the ground of which is want on the part of the faculty and on the part of the object fitness to appease want. The latter ground constitutes the *goodness* of the object. An object is good, not because it is likable or desirable, but inversely. Good, therefore, is an attribute intrinsic

to an object by which it is fitted to satisfy appetence. A volitional act is good when it is fitting to the rational agent.

2. CLASSIFICATIONS. (a) Want arises from the absence of a perfection which the agent needs, from the presence of an imperfection which is discordant to the agent, or from the absence of a perfection to which the agent aspires. Want comprehends more than need. The good that satisfies this want is *perfective* good. Concomitant with and arising from the absence of desired perfection or the presence of undesired imperfection there is a consciousness of dissatisfaction ranging from mere discontent to pain. This want is a psychological symptom of the primary want. The relief of it becomes an object of appetence. The good that brings this relief is *delectable* good. Like the affective state that it replaces it may vary from mere assuagement of unpleasant feeling to the glow of delight, depending on the energizing of the faculty through which perfective good is obtained. Lastly, an object is good when it is a pure means to the attainment of perfective and delectable good, i.e., when the ground of its desirability is wholly extrinsic to it, and outside of its usefulness it is not desirable. This is *useful* good. Perfective good is good *in itself* and *of itself;* delectable good is good *in itself* but *not of itself;* useful good is good neither in itself, not of itself, but as a *means* to perfective or delectable good. Everything that is desired is desirable on one or more of these three grounds. (b) There are as many sorts of goods as there are specific wants to be satisfied. Man's wants are as numerous as are the contacts of his many-sided nature with reality. His primary want is for that which sets desire at rest; this is perfective good. But perfective good may befit the unitary nature as such, or some faculty in subordination to it; or it may befit a faculty out of subordination to the nature. The former is *real good,* which, when it superadds a relation to the norm of volitional activity, is called *moral* good. The latter is apparent good. Distinguish two meanings of "desirable." *Eudaemonism.* The word happiness is usually accepted as the English equivalent of the Aristotelian term; but erroneously, since this would confound it with Hedonism. The supreme good of man is: (a) a well-being of life and its activities; (b) which is desirable in itself always, and never on account of anything else; (c) which suffices man in all his essential relations and is outside of comparison with other goods; (d) which is to be found in his distinctive and specific functions, i.e., in the activity of his rational life. This is Eudaemonia, i.e., the highest

energizing of his rational life in conformity with the laws of its excellence, and the essential delight following thereon.

3. THE PROXIMATE NORM. The *norm* is that by conformity with which an action or object of volition takes on the attribute of goodness; it is distinguished from a *criterion* of goodness by which conformity to norm is known and tested. The difference between good and evil is *objective,* i.e., independent of the moral agent; and *intrinsic,* i.e., the concept of good essentially excludes the concept of evil. The distinction does not arise from custom or education, nor from the free will of God. But an objective and intrinsic difference between good and evil necessarily involves a norm by which these generic types are essentially fixed.

The fitting perfection of an agent is its good. The norm of its perfection, therefore, is the norm of its goodness. But the proximate norm of man's perfection is his rational nature insofar as it is the primary principle by which his actions are produced, and the immediate subject modified by them. This principle and subject adequately considered is: (a) a composite nature, in which faculties and functions are mutually adjusted and subordinated to rational will—*an individual order;* (b) a social nature, allied by innate impulse, needs and destiny with other social natures—an *order of rights and duties;* (c) a contingent nature, owing origin and continued existence to the Creator, and its meaning and value to his design— an *universal order.*

4. THE ULTIMATE NORM. The objective, intrinsic, and absolute difference between good and evil necessarily involves a norm of morality, which is original and ultimate. The only norm of this kind is the Supreme Nature, which is at once the source of his nature, and archetypal of it. Now this is the Divine Nature, first as the efficient cause of all contingent natures, and secondly as the archetypal cause of all grades of analogous being, which are related to It as an exemplar, and have reality insofar as they represent in diverse stages of finite being, in resemblances or traces, the Infinite Being. (See Digest II, the Cosmological Postulate.)

5. THE DETERMINANTS OF MORALITY. Good as well as evil actions differ in kind. Good actions are different in their special relations of conformity to the norm of morality, and endue the will with distinctive perfections; and inversely evil actions. They are differentiated, first, by the end or result in which the volitional act whether elicit or imperate normally issues. The end of the action

may be in conformity with the natural purpose of the faculty from which it proceeds, either positively or negatively: *positively,* when it is so in accord with the nature of the agent, that its alternative is in discordance—the action is good; *negatively,* when neither the end of the action nor its alternative is out of accord with the nature of the agent—the action is *indifferent.* Difformity with the natural purpose of the faculty or nature of the agent makes the action *bad.* But every will-movement is objectively specified by the result in which it normally issues. They are differentiated, secondly, by the end of the agent when distinct from the end of the action, which, though extrinsic to the end of the action, falls within the compass of the integral volitional act. The reason is the same; the end of the agent is the purpose of the elicit will-movement. Circumstances, lastly, which intrinsically modify either the end of the action or the end of the agent, and have moral bearings, also specify the morality of the action. An action is good when the three causes to which it owes its specific morality are good, evil if one of these is evil. Material and Formal Morality.

REFERENCES: *Aquinas Ethicus,* Vol. I, pp. 55-80; Cronin, *Science of Ethics,* Vol. I, Ch. III.

VI. OBJECTIVE RIGHT

The right, objectively considered, is an ideal of conduct obligatory in character. Obligation arises from moral law. Moral law is imposed on us by the Divine Will, and promulgated by the light of reason; and, presupposing the decree of creation, the act of the Divine Will imposing the moral law is necessary, universal and immutable.

1. RIGHT. The term is derived from a root (*rego*) meaning that which is kept straight. It applies primarily to the movement of a material body towards a goal without deflections in lateral directions. By natural extension of meaning it applies to movements of a higher kind, viz., of intellect and will, e.g., right reasoning, right conduct. It connotes an ideal norm, which determines the aim of the movement and keeps it within its proper boundaries. Wrong (*wrung=twisted*) gives the same evidence. The necessity imposed by the norm is appropriate to the nature of the faculty. For free-will

it is moral necessity or obligation. The term "right," therefore, may be used in three senses: (a) an ideal of conduct obligatory in character, i.e., *objective* right; (b) that which conforms to the ideal; (c) a moral faculty inviolable by force of the ideal, i.e., *subjective* right.

2. OBLIGATION. The concept of obligation involves three relations: one who obliges, a subject obliged, and that to which the subject is obliged. Formally, then, obligation is a necessity, known by reason, of positing or omitting an act, which has an intrinsic connection or opposition with an ultimate end and an absolute good, imposed by one having authority.

3. LAW. Law *primarily* signifies a rule of action, mandatory in form, established and promulgated by a competent authority for the common good; *derivatively,* an intrinsic necessity physically compelling to uniform action; and *loosely* the observed uniform sequence of phenomena, or the formal statement of such uniformity in a given class of cases. In the first sense law imposes a bond on the will in keeping with the nature of the will; in the second it is a physical necessity inherent in the nature of things; and in the third a formulated necessity of uniformity in phenomenal sequence. Law is *ethical, physical,* or *theoretical.* Ethical law must be promulgated to be obligatory. It is promulgated orally or by writing if *positive,* e.g., civil and ecclesiastical law; or it is revealed by reason if *moral* law.

4. MORAL LAW. The moral necessity inherent in law is imposed by self, by one's equal, or by one's superior. The first empties the concept of obligation of all content; one cannot have authority over oneself and be subject to oneself in the same respect. The control of reason, and of will over lower faculties is not authoritative. Kant's distinction between the noumenal and phenomenal man, and the subjection of one to the other, is futile. The second is untenable; as moral beings, all men are equal, and no man or body of men has original jurisdiction over another man or can bind him in conscience. Such jurisdiction as they have must be derived from an authority that is superior to them and their subjects.

5. MORAL LAW EXISTS. Reason makes known to us a moral law: (a) that between good and evil actions there is a difference which is intrinsic to the nature of things, which is founded in the three essential relations of man, i.e., to self, to others, and to the Creator, which consequently arises from a necessary connection or

opposition to man's ultimate end and absolute good; (b) that the former are unconditionally prescribed and the latter in like manner prohibited. These imperatives of reason have the attributes of law; they are *universal,* i.e., experienced by all men; *objective,* i.e., not produced, but perceived by reason; *constant,* i.e., independent of the variations of times, places and persons. Therefore there is a moral law. But it must exist somewhere. It cannot exist in material things; it can exist nohow or nowhere but in a mind. An absolute and objective moral law must exist in a mind which is the source and archetype of whatever is true in our moral judgments. The true in our moral judgments is the expression of our essential relations to reality. Therefore, the absolute moral ideal of right exists in a mind that is the source of all reality, other than itself.

6. THE SOURCE OF MORAL LAW. Though in *form* law is an ordination of superior reason directing subject reason, it is *in effect* a necessity put by a superior will on a subject will to follow the direction of the ordinating reason. An act of legislation, therefore, is from reason, presupposing an act of will in virtue of which it *directs* and *moves* through reason. The source of moral law, therefore, is the will of a being which is the source of all reality, and which has supreme authority over every created will—the *Divine Will.*

7. THE DIVINE WILL IMPOSED MORAL LAW NECESSARILY. All law supposes subjects or a community. Logically prior to the decree of creation, there could be no subjects of moral law. The Divine Will imposing moral law presupposes, therefore, the decree of creation. Now God was free to create or not create, but having decreed to create He must necessarily create beings, which in varying degrees of perfection were analogues of His Divine Essence and Nature. But such beings must be in nature vestigial or imitative manifestations of the Divine activity, and have modes of operations which are to be conformed to the archetypal ideas of God. Therefore the Divine Will, supposing the decree of creation, necessarily willed that all creatures should act in accord with their natures, necessarily if they are irrational, freely if they are rational. The moral law, or the decree of the Divine Will obliging all free agents to act in a defined way, is *necessary, universal,* and *immutable,* since it is on God's part the expression of the Divine Practical Reason, and on man's part written in his reason insofar as that reason is an analogue of Divine Reason.

REFERENCES: Rickaby's *God and His Creatures,* Bk. II, Chs. XLI-XLVI; Cronin's *Science of Ethics,* Vol. II, Ch. XIX, pp. 597-612; Newman's *Grammar of Assent,* Ch. V, Sect. I; Kant's *Ethics,* Abbott's Translation, p. 321; Rashdall's *Theory of Good and Evil,* Vol. II, pp. 206-216.

VII. MORAL LAW AND CONSCIENCE

So far as its first principles are concerned, the moral law is knowable to all whose reason is developed. Conscience, or reason, when it applies the principles of the moral law to individual acts, is to be obeyed when it is prudentially certain; and when it is in doubt, recourse must be had to reflex principles affording certainty before action becomes lawful.

1. FIRST PRINCIPLES. Principles of the moral law are practical truths, i.e., they affirm an ideal of conduct, and an obligation of acting in accord with it. So far as the ideal of conduct is affirmed they are of the same character as speculative truths; as an affirmation of obligation they have motive power on the will. A truth is immediately evident when it can be known without the medium of reasoning. Such a truth is necessarily knowable to all who apprehend the meaning of the terms. Truths of conduct are of three kinds: (a) those universal and ultimate truths, which neither need, nor are capable of, demonstration; (b) truths which by an easy and obvious inference are deduced by the application of ultimate truths to specific cases of right and wrong; (c) truths inferred by more or less difficult processes of reasoning.

2. KNOWABLE. Reason is as subject to limitations in regard to practical as to speculative truths. It may receive different degrees of development, and may be perverted. Moral education is as necessary for moral development of reason as are other kinds of education for the development of reason in other departments of thought. *Primary* principles of conduct cannot be unknown, nor is the intellect subject to error in their regard. *Secondary* principles may be obscured in their particular application by defective or perverted moral education, or by apparent conflict between them. *Tertiary* principles may themselves be unknown in various degrees, and by particular persons, even in a developed moral environment.

3. DIFFICULTIES. These may be solved: (a) by distinguishing between the extension of a command and prohibition of the moral law; (b) by distinguishing between the law, which is unchangeable, and the matter of the law, which may vary. Difficulties from ethnography may be solved: (a) by showing that facts were observed in the light of preconceived theories, or by disproving through later research the narratives of earlier travellers; (b) by showing that barbarian people have erred through defective or perverted moral education with regard to remote and difficult inferences from primary and secondary principles, or in the application of the latter to particular cases; (c) by not reading into their actions the viewpoint of civilized people. Inferences, sometimes made, that our morality in its higher aspect is conventional, because lower or degraded races do not know it, are invalid. Error is subjective, and even when general does not invalidate objective truth.

4. CONSCIENCE. Conscience is spoken of as a *witness,* a *judge,* a *monitor.* In its basic meaning it is the faculty which, by applying the principles of morality to particular cases, gives individual promulgation to the moral law. This faculty is reason. The reasoning by which the individual dictates of morality are reached may be *correct* or *erroneous, certain* or *doubtful.* The doubt may regard the *law* or the *fact;* it may be *rational* or *emotional.* When doubt is rational, the probability of reason's conclusions may be *slight* or *solid.* If solid enough to justify a normally prudent man in action, it is said to be *prudentially* certain.

5. CONSCIENCE AS A GUIDE. (a) To act, when conscience is doubtful regarding the morality of an act or its omission, is to act with a prudent fear that the act or its omission is immoral, and to deliberately expose oneself to the danger of doing what is objectively wrong. This is to incur moral guilt. (b) Conscience is the subjective norm of individual morality, since it is the promulgation of the moral law for individual action. When certain, therefore, whether it be correct or erroneous, it must be obeyed. (c) Prudential certainty suffices for action, since in the individual affairs of practical life it is generally the only certainty that can be had, and since it is prudential. (d) Before action, one must be prudentially certain that the moral law concretely applies to the individual act; otherwise one acts with a doubtful conscience.

6. CERTAINTY THROUGH REFLEXIVE PRINCIPLES. If doubt persists after investigation, two cases may occur. (a) The doubt

regards the existence of the law or the comprehension of the individual case under the law, and neither alternative of conduct imperils the certain rights of others. (b) Or the doubt regards the means necessary for fulfilling the law or for safeguarding the rights of others. In the first case, the law, whether as self-regarding or other-regarding, is doubtful. And as we may not posit an action or omit it, when conscience is doubtful, so we are not bound when moral obligation is doubtful. Prudential certitude therefore regarding the lawfulness of an act or its omission may be had by appealing to the principle: *A doubtful law does not oblige.* In the second case, as the law is certain, of alternative means, that is to be chosen which will more probably secure the observance of the law. Prudential certainty may be had by invoking the principle: *In doubt, the safer part is to be chosen.*

Morbid conditions of conscience are *laxity, scrupulousness,* and *perplexity.* Their cure varies with their causes which may be intellectual, emotional, or physiological. No general rules can be safely prescribed for the self-guidance of such consciences.

References: Rickaby's *Aquinas Ethicus,* Vol. I, pp. 281-285, 303-307; Cronin's *Science of Ethics,* Chs. XIV and XVI; Rashdall's *Theory of Good and Evil,* Vol. II, Ch. IV, p. 356, and Ch. V, p. 414. What is said on pp. 430, 431 and 432 may be discounted until further investigation. Lea who is quoted is utterly unreliable; Pascal is a partisan of the Port-Royalists.

VIII. MERIT

Man may truly merit with God, though the merit that obtains from man to God is not of the same kind as that which obtains between man and man.

1. MERIT. In common usage the word is applied to actions deserving reward, and the word demerit to those deserving punishment. Absolutely taken, it simply means desert either in a favorable or an unfavorable sense. It may be defined as the quality of a volitional act having a beneficial or detrimental bearing on another person by reason of which the agent deserves recompense or requital. An act may deserve reward or punishment on two grounds: (a) because it is entitled to a reward, or punishment is in justice

due to it; or (b) because it is appropriate that it should be rewarded or punished. The first is *condign* merit by right ("condign" in present usage is generally confined to punishment); the second is *congruous merit,* or merit by worth.

2. MERIT BETWEEN MEN. Confining the term, for the sake of brevity, to its favorable sense, merit by right, as it obtains between man and man, requires the verification of these conditions: (a) the one meriting should have conferred a benefit on the one with whom he merits; (b) there must have been a pact or formal agreement between the two regarding the benefit to be conferred and the reward to be given; otherwise only merit of worth is had; (c) there must be a proportion of equality between the action and its reward; (d) prior to the payment of the reward there must exist a disproportion in the order of justice between the person meriting and the person benefited by reason of which the latter is a debtor and the former is a creditor, and which can be removed only by giving the reward due; (e) the person rewarding is deprived of that by which he pays the reward. It is to be noted that the presence of merit by right is not prevented by the fact that the action is already due on other grounds than those of an onerous condition fixed by pact and fulfilled. The action may be due on grounds of benevolence, filial piety, equity, and yet be meritorious because of the conditions fixed by agreement.

Imperfections or limitations are implied in all these conditions of merit as it obtains between man and man, and, therefore, this merit cannot be of the same kind as that which obtains from man to God. (a) To receive a benefit implies a want; there can be no want in God. (b) To enter into a formal agreement implies that both parties may be subject to obligation, and, therefore, to a law superior to them. But God is not subject to obligation and is not bound by law. (c) That there should be a proportion of equality between the action and its rewards implies that there is no intrinsic dependence of the one meriting on the one with whom he merits. But man can in no wise be independent of God. (d) The state of being a debtor to another entails limitations in the creditor. But God cannot be limited by any action of His creature. Logically prior to any promise of reward our actions are due to God, either because they fall under the commandments or under the counsels, either in justice or in *pietate*. (e) It would be an imperfection in God, if by giving the reward His possessions were diminished.

3. MERIT WITH GOD. There is true merit in both cases, but in an intrinsically analogous sense. Hence the conditions can be analogously verified. (a) It is within the power of our free-will to give God formal extrinsic glory. (b) There is implanted in our soul a natural promise that ultimate well-being and happiness will be the reward of a moral life. Hence the Creator is *necessitated* by His *own attributes* of sanctity, wisdom, and justice, to give us the eudaemonistic completion of our nature, when in its activity it has been in conformity with the archetypal ideals and norms of nature. (c) There is a proportion, not of equality, but of teleology between our actions and their eternal reward, i.e., the proportion that exists between a nature and the final state in which its activities naturally issue. (d) Our reward is not due until the end of probation. Hence payment is not deferred, but awaits ultimate fitness for its reception. (e) By giving the reward God does not diminish his own possessions, since the reward is union with Himself; a friend loses nothing by bestowing friendship on one meriting it.

Now, man can put many actions which (a) are volitional, imputable, and give formal glory to God; (b) being in conformity with the archetypal norms of conduct, of their nature require the ultimate perfection of a rational being—which is its reward; (c) by the natural promise impressed on the faculties of the soul are necessarily accepted by God as being meritorious. But in actions of this kind the essential conditions of merit are verified. Man can, therefore, truly merit with God.

REFERENCES: Rickaby, *God and His Creatures*, Bk. II, Ch. XXIX; *S. T.*, 1, 2, qu. 114, a. 1.

IX. SANCTION

The perfect sanction appertaining to the moral law, which is the realization or frustration of the final perfection of man's rational nature, is obtainable only in a future life.

1. SANCTION. The term is used either to designate the decree of the lawgiver by which rewards or penalties are apportioned for the observance or violations of the law, or to designate these rewards or penalties themselves. The *primary intrinsic* purpose of sanction is to induce to the observance of law or to dissuade from the violation of

it. The *secondary intrinsic* purpose is the readjustment through reward or punishment of the objective order of justice. The first purpose is emotive, i.e., moves the will to observe the law or avoid the violation of it; the second is effective subsequently to the observance or violation of the law, and independently of volition on the part of the subject to the law. With regard to premial sanction there is no controversy; penal sanction has been challenged by Atheistic Rationalism. Its vindicative character is regarded as vindictive. But primarily it is preservative, secondarily, i.e., subsequent to the volitional act, it is vindicative. The lawgiver does not will punishment as an evil to the subject, but as a reparation of order; nor can the preservative character of sanction be retained, if its vindicative character is denied.

2. CLASSIFICATION OF SANCTIONS. Sanctions are either *natural* or *positive,* arising, namely, as the natural outcome of actions or imposed by the free-will of the legislator; *adequate* or *inadequate,* according as they are or are not of themselves sufficient to move a rational will to observe the law; *proportioned* or *unproportioned,* according as they are fully or are only partially adjusted to the merit of observing the law or the demerit of violating it.

A *perfect* sanction is one that is adequate and proportioned.

3. ORDER OF SANCTIONS. Natural sanctions are found in three orders. In the *individual* order, which consists in the subordination of the lower appetites to the dictates of right reason, the sanctions are approval or remorse of conscience, the enjoyment or loss of mental or bodily health. In the *social* order, which consists in the essential relations of man to his fellow man, the sanctions are the social good or evil that follow upon the attention to or disregard of these relations. In the *universal* order, which consists in the relation of man to his Creator and his last end, the sanctions are final union with, or separation from God, and attainment or loss of man's last end.

4. SANCTION AND MORAL LAW. No *righteous* legislator can be indifferent as to whether his law be observed or violated; and will, therefore, safeguard its observance by sanctions. A *wise* legislator will necessarily assign an adequate sanction. A *just* legislator will proportion the sanctions of his law to the merit of observing it or the demerit of violating it. But the Supreme Legislator is righteous, wise and just. Moreover, the very concept of law founded in the nature and essential relations of things involves, as a complement

of its observance or violation, a good or evil justly proportioned thereto. A law, the observance of which would ultimately result in harm to the subject, and the violation of which would redound to his ultimate benefit, would be irrational.

5. THE SANCTIONS OF THIS LIFE. In order that the sanctions of this life be perfect: (a) the benefits must outweigh the disadvantages of observing the law, and the goods that are found in violating the law must be less than the evils that likewise follow, and (b) the rewards for observing and the pains for violating must be proportioned respectively to observance or violation. But these conditions are not universally verified in this life, as is evident from an examination of the natural sanctions of the individual or social order, and from the fact that the need of positive sanctions is recognized to supplement the efficacy of natural sanctions. Furthermore, it may happen that life itself should be sacrificed for the observance of the moral law.

6. SANCTIONS IN A FUTURE LIFE. Perfect sanction of the moral law can be had only in a state of existence which is the fulfilment and completion of this probationary existence. But this state consists in the realization or frustration of the ultimate perfection of man's rational nature. Natural sanction, as has been said, is the agreeable or disagreeable state that follows naturally upon the right or wrong use of one's faculties; care of one's health brings as its reward, for instance, the enjoyment of life, abuse of one's eyes brings finally as its punishment loss of vision. Now our moral life when rightly used tends increasingly to the perfection of our rational nature, and when abused to its increasing degradation. The limits of one is the realization, and of the other the frustration of our last end.

X. SUBJECTIVE RIGHT

Right, subjectively considered, is an inviolable moral faculty to do, to hold, or to exact; and is derived from man's moral responsibility. The correlative of right is duty, i.e., the moral obligation either of not impeding the exercise of another's right or of cooperating with it.

1. DEFINITION. The notion involves: (a) moral power or liberty in the subject to do, to hold, or to exact; (b) and a moral restraint on others not to interfere, or constraint to cooperate with the exer-

cise of this liberty. Hence, the want of physical power does not invalidate right, nor the exercise of superior might destroy its moral inviolability.

2. THE ORIGIN. To have a right it is necessary to have, (a) appetencies which indicate to us the proximate *end* of our faculties and the ultimate end of our nature; (b) the power of directing our appetencies, as we judge best, to the attaining of our good, i.e., not license to do as we please, but liberty to choose as we please what is for our good; (c) the *moral obligation* of directing appetitive tendency to the end and the good; a creature morally free to abuse or use his function could not have a moral power that others are bound to respect. Every right, therefore, is in its last analysis the morally inviolable liberty of doing, holding, or exacting something which is mediately or immediately for the rational well-being of the subject; hence, it is derived from man's moral responsibility to use appetencies implanted in his nature, insofar as their use is directly or indirectly under his control, for the purpose of realizing his proximate ends and the ultimate end of his creation. An infant has rights in the same sense that it has intellect and free-will.

Hence right is not derived: (a) from the mere possession of superior physical power—Hobbes; (b) from personal liberty considered in itself—Neo-Kantianism; (c) from primary sensuous appetencies through evolution; and is not resolvable into two elements, one *positive,* by which man recognizes his claim to the unimpeded satisfaction of his appetencies, the other *negative* by which he is conscious of limitations imposed on him by the like claims of others—Spencer.

Hence, prior to every right is duty, general or special; and prior to every duty is God's right to the ultimate purpose of creation.

3. CORRELATIVES OF RIGHT. (a) *Subject-party,* an existing person, whether physical or moral; (b) *ground,* the law from which the right is derived; (c) *title,* the fact by which the right is actuated; (d) *matter,* what one may by right do, hold, or exact; (e) *object-party,* the person, present or future, on whom the duty of respecting the right devolves.

Duty is the moral obligation of doing or omitting an action in favor of another. To every right in one there is at least a *negative* duty in another of not hindering the exercise of the right. *The positive* duty of cooperating is *merely ethical,* when the obligation arises from a virtue other than justice; it is *juridical* when the obligation arises from justice. Every duty carries with it the right of freedom in the exercise of it. To *every juridical* duty of one person, there responds a *perfect right* in another person, and the latter is the immediate ground of the former. Every right is limited by the duty, general or special, from which it springs and in case of apparent conflict of one right with another, the prevailing right is that which is founded in a higher duty.

4. PERFECT RIGHT. A perfect right includes, as a property of it, the *right to the use of coaction* in its defense or vindication. It is *inviolable,* not only in the sense that it puts a bond on the will of another, but also in the sense that it gives the right to the use of force in order to compel physical inviolability. *Coactive rights* spring either from *commutative justice* or from *social justice.* The former differs from the latter, first in respect of *matter;* in that matter of the former regards the good of the individual, of the latter the good of the community. They differ secondly in respect of *reparation.* The violation of commutative justice demands reparation of the injury inflicted; the violation of social justice cannot be repaired, since nothing can be done but what would have been obligatory, if there had been no violation. The penalty imposed for violating social justice belongs to *distributive justice.* The obligation of undergoing it does not exist antecedently to the sentence of the judge.

5. DIVISION OF RIGHTS. In respect of *law* from which they are derived: *natural* and *positive.* In respect of *titles: connatural,* if possessed by the very fact of existence; *acquired,* if possessed because of a fact supervening on existence. In respect of *correlative duty* in the subject of right: *inalienable,* if they cannot be ceded or renounced, because they are a necessary means of fulfilling an unconditional duty; *alienable,* if they can be ceded or renounced without contempt of duty.

6. EXERCISE OF RIGHT. The exercise of even an inalienable right may be delegated; not so the right itself. The exercise may in certain circumstances be restrained by law, though the right retains its vigor.

The right to the use of coaction in matter of commutative justice belongs primarily to the subject of the perfect right, secondarily and vicariously to the person (moral or physical) who has authority in the community of which the subject of the perfect right is a member. But the *actual exercise* of the coactive right belongs primarily to the head of the community, and secondarily, when the community fails to protect, and invasion of right is imminent, to the subject of the coactive right. The *right* to use coaction in matters of social justice belongs *exclusively* to the community, and its *actual exercise* to the representative of the community.

REFERENCES: Rickaby's *Aquinas Ethicus,* Vol. II, pp. 11-17, 22-23; Cronin's *Science of Ethics,* Vol. II, Ch. XX; Rickaby's *Moral Philosophy* (Stonyhurst Series), Pt. II, Ch. V, Sects. 1 and 2; Ming's *Data of Modern Ethics Examined,* Ch. XIV.

XI. CHARACTER

Character is an integration of habits of conduct superimposed on temperament. It is morally perfect when it results from the combined and harmonized virtues which determine our ethical and judicial duties to God, and our neighbor, and in respect of self.

1. THE NOTION. Etymologically character means a significant mark stamped or cut on a hard material. Thence it was applied to a combination of qualities distinguishing one individual or group of individuals from others. The notion, therefore, varies with the science that employs it. Ethically it means the sum of moral traits or qualities which distinguish a person or class of persons from others, and by reason of which they receive a special moral designation.

The qualities which individuate personality coalesce in two syntheses: *temperament,* due to *nature;* and *character,* due to *nurture.*

2. TEMPERAMENT is the fusion of the various dispositions of our composite nature into a resultant disposition of the whole man. *Disposition* is a native bent towards action of a certain kind, and capacity for a certain form of development. In a secondary sense it is a tendency that has been awakened by previous workings of bent, without, however, giving formed capacity; so understood it is the initial factor of habit in formation.

Habit is a quality superinduced in a faculty by repeated performance of its functions, giving an *impulse* to and an *ease* in the exercise of these functions. Dispositions are congenital and plastic, i.e., receptive of form through use, and liable to degeneracy from disuse; habits are acquired and stable, i.e., once fixed can be thrown off only by the continued exercise of contrary acts. Habits of our rational nature are of two kinds: *habits of thought,* i.e., of intellect, and *habits of conduct,* i.e., of will. The latter may be either good or bad. We are concerned with habits of good conduct. Habits of thought invigorate intellectual dispositions and determine them in a particular direction, and are the products of disposition and training. Habits of conduct confer impulse and ease in the active determination of the will to appropriate ends, and are the product of will freely exercised on disposition, thought, emotion, and action.

3. CHARACTER. What dispositions are to temperament, habits of conduct are to character. As the mental constitution due to the fusion of the former is temperament, so the blending of the latter into a unitary principle is character. Character, therefore, is an integration of habits of conduct superimposed on temperament.

4. DUTIES. The term "duty" is used in two senses: (1) In a comprehensive sense to signify moral obligation of any kind, and in this sense it is the immediate effect of *objective* right; (2) in a restricted sense to signify the moral obligation of doing something in favor of another, and in this sense it is the immediate effect of a *subjective* right. All duty in its last analysis is the duty of obeying the Supreme Legislator. But duties regard different object-parties. The object-party of all duties is a person, namely, an intelligent being. We have duties *concerning* inanimate or animate beings; and as they rise in the grade of being towards us, our duties *concerning* them become more intensive, but we have no duties *to* them. Now, intellectual beings are in two categories, created and increated beings; and created beings are either self or others. The object-parties of duties, therefore, are God, self and our neighbor. Duties are *natural or positive;* are *affirmative or negative;* are *merely ethical, or juridical also.* The former in the last division is based on charity and the allied virtues, and the latter on justice.

5. JUSTICE. The notion of justice is founded in the objective order of rights and duties. Parallel between physical order preserved by the balance of physical forces, and moral order preserved by the "ad-justment" of moral powers. As the equilibrium of the forces of nature is essential to the physical stability of the universe, so the equilibrium of the juridical order through proximate or final "adjustment" is essential to justice. The equilibrium of rights that justice aims to preserve or restore entails an equality between men that is *real* and *personal;* but not quantitative. As in the physical order

equilibrium is preserved not by each body having mathematically equal powers, but by each having its own; so in the juridical order, equilibrium is preserved not by all persons having the same rights, but by each having its own inviolate. *Real* equality in justice does not require that each should possess the same goods, but that they should be secure in the possession or use of those to which they have a right. *Personal* equality does not consist in the possession of equal mental or bodily qualities, but in a juridical independence with regard to rights conferred by nature.

6. VIRTUES are habits of conduct prompting to the performance of duties. In relation to God virtues determine the attitude of intellect and will, which man should hold to Him both inwardly and outwardly. The virtues which fundamentally secure this are those by which he is prompted to seek knowledge of God and give Him intellectual submission, to love Him above all things, and to desire final union with Him, i.e., wisdom, faith, charity, hope; and to give the worship and honor due Him, because of His infinite excellence, absolute dominion, and supreme good, i.e., religion. In relation to self, virtues give a readiness and ease in the right use of practical reason, i.e., prudence; moderate the passions that allure to sensuous delights, i.e., temperance; control the passions that arouse fear or impel to rashness in the presence of impending loss or threatening danger, i.e., fortitude. In relation to the neighbor, individually or collectively, the virtues which regulate conduct are benevolence and justice. These virtues and those that are intrinsically allied to them, combined and harmonized, produce a character which is conformed to rational nature in all its essential relations, and is, therefore, *perfect.*

REFERENCES: A treatment of the virtues is given in Rickaby's *Aquinas Ethicus,* passim in both volumes, but especially Vol. I, pp. 155-195; Cronin's *Ethics,* Vol. I, Ch. XXIII.

XII. DUTIES TO GOD

By the moral law man is obliged to render to God, both privately and publicly, interior and exterior worship; and to believe in a divine revelation when it is made known to him.

1. RELIGION. With the babelizing of language describing our moral and religious experience, the term "religion" has taken on a subjective and emotional meaning in modern philosophy. In this sense it can be defined as a *feeling* of self-abasement in the presence of an idealized object apprehended to be forever above us, and a simultaneous *feeling* of personal exaltation and participation in the perfection of the ideal. In the union of these contradictory forms of emotion the essence of religion consists, independently of its object. Historically, religion means the conscious apprehension through intellect of a bond between beings possessing a spiritual nature and a Supreme Being of transcendent excellence, on whom they know or believe they depend. Following on this intellectual apprehension an emotional consciousness ensues. Religion, therefore, is a moral bond supervening on the physical bond of dependence in existence. A moral bond presupposes certain truths to which intellectual assent is given, entails certain duties arising from these truths. *Theoretic* religion is the sum of truths defining our relation to the Supreme Being; *practical* religion the sum of duties inferred from these relations and prescribed by the moral law. Considered, therefore, in itself, or *objectively,* it is a complex of these beliefs and duties; considered in him who practices it, or the subject of religion, it is a virtue, the seat of which is the will, and which inclines us to render to the Supreme Being, because of His excellence, the worship that is due Him. It is, therefore, a virtue allied to justice.

2. THE RELATIONS OF MAN TO GOD. These may be reduced to two; to Him we should cling as to the *first cause,* and toward Him we should tend as to our *last end.* The duties of intellect are, therefore, to acknowledge: (a) His infinite excellence; (b) that He is the origin and Lord of all things; (c) that He is the Last End of all things. The duties of will are to show Him: (a) special reverence because of His infinite excellence; (b) special service because of His supreme lordship; (c) special love because He is the Last End. These duties of religion are expressed by the words *divine worship,* or *latria.*

3. DIVINE WORSHIP. Worship—worthship—admits of various degrees, according to the worth or excellence of him to whom it is given. The solemn act of worship distinctive of religion is called *adoration,* (*ad-oro; os, oris*) and is payable only to the Deity because of infinite worth and absolute lordship. By it we acknowledge the dependence of our intellect on His infinite intellect, of our will on His infinite will, of our nature and its faculty on His infinite nature. This is done either *interiorly* by mental acts, or *exteriorly* by bodily acts. That worship is due to God is clear from the truths demonstrated in natural theology: that God is the Creator of all, the absolute Lord, Supreme Ruler, a Being of infinite excellence, and the last end of man; and that from these relations follow moral relations by which is acknowledged man's manifold dependence.

4. EXTERIOR WORSHIP. 1. Man, being a composite of body and spirit, is so constituted that (a) he naturally gives exterior expression to interior affections; (b) his interior affection is strengthened by exterior expression and decays in default of it. 2. Man owes to God a worship commensurate with his dependence. But man is not spirit merely, but a spirit in substantial union with a body and using the created goods of time.

5. REVELATION. Revelation, which is the unveiling of truths hitherto hidden, is either *natural,* when the unveiling is done by human reason, or *divine,* when done through the formal communication of thought by God. Divine revelation is *not impossible* (a) on the part of God—if man can communicate thought, his Creator can; (b) on the part of man—if man can receive a revelation from his fellow man auricularly, he can receive one from God through intellectual illumination; (c) on the part of the truth revealed— for these are truths the existence of which could not be known by unaided reason, and which when revealed to an intelligence of finite compass may be relatively unintelligible; (d) on the part of its purpose—for obedience of intellect is as essential in a creature as other obedience.

6. PROOF. The moral law obliges us to believe one, (a) who can neither deceive nor be deceived, (b) who speaks, in order to be believed, (c) who has the right of speaking and of requiring intellectual assent to what he says. But when God reveals anything to man, and the fact of such revelation is known, these three conditions are present.

7. OBJECTIONS. It might be admitted that a divine revelation of some truths not essentially beyond human ken would be advantageous, in order that *all men* might *easily and in due time* and *without admixture of doubt or error* know what is necessary for their moral life, i.e., God, immortality and freedom. But a knowledge of mysteries is useless—to believe them is unworthy of a reasoning being—such belief enslaves the intellect and begets intolerance. These difficulties miss the point at issue or exaggerate the truth.

REFERENCES: Rickaby's *God and His Creatures,* Bk. I, Chs. III-VIII; Newman's *Grammar of Assent,* Ch. X; Gerard's *The Wayfarer's Vision.*

XIII. DUTIES IN RESPECT OF SELF

The moral law obliges man to acquire the knowledge essential to his eternal welfare, and to the performance of the duties of life; to govern his volitional activity by this knowledge, to have a rational care of health and life, to seek the external goods of life insofar as they are necessary and useful for fulfilling the duties of his state in life.

1. LOVE OF SELF. Every one, by a primary impulse of nature, wishes and does well to self. This impulse indicates a precept of the moral law, rationally confirmed by the fact that we are essentially servants of the Creator, and ought to use the faculties He gave, and the means at our disposal for procuring our well-being. Love of self is, therefore, a duty. Like every impulse indicative of the purpose of life, it may be irregular. It must conform to the supreme purpose of creation and the essential relations of man. It becomes excessive or defective if it goes beyond, or falls below, the measure and mode presented by reason. Its excess is Egotism, or the placing of man's supreme good in the happiness of self; its defect is Altruism, or the making the happiness of others the supreme norm of conduct—Comte. A sane reconciliation of self-love and benevolence is had in the precept of Christ: "Thou shalt love thy neighbor as thyself."

The duties of man in respect of self regard: (a) the soul, i.e., the due development of intellect and will; (b) the body, i.e., rational care of life and health; (c) the outer goods of life, i.e., such personal goods as wealth, and social goods as good name and honor.

2. SOUL. The essential duties of man with regard to his soul are: (a) to perfect his intellect by acquiring the knowledge necessary for attaining the ultimate purpose of life, for filling the obligations of his social nature in the family and in civil society, and for performing the offices belonging to his occupations in life; (b) to perfect his will by self-mastery and self-reverence, and by acquiring the virtues that befit it.

Defects of intellect arise from: (a) unreasonable attachment to previously formed opinion; (b) disregard for the value of objective truth; (c) the exaltation of imagination above reason. *Defects of will* arise from: (a) want of will-power; (b) predominance of passionate will over reason; (c) arbitrariness in forming views.

3. BODY. Life, health and bodily faculties are given by nature for instrumental purposes defined by the ends to which of their nature they are directed. Their use for other purposes is abuse. Their worth is subordinate to the higher purposes of the soul. We are not absolute masters to dispose of them wilfully, but stewards to use them in accord with reason. *Mens sana in corpore sano* does not emphasize *corpus* but *mens*. Hence (a) to imperil life or health from rashness, vanity, or inordinate love of pleasures, is a violation of duty; (b) to sacrifice the higher good of the soul for the preservation of life or health is equally a violation of duty; (c) to indulge in mental or bodily satisfactions, or in experiments which perturb reason or weaken will-power, is also a violation of duty.

4. OUTER GOODS. These outer goods of life are a *good name, freedom of action,* and *wealth*. These it is our duty to retain or procure insofar as they are *necessary* for fulfilling the obligations of our personal, social, professional or business life. They, too, are instrumental goods, and may be sought only within the bounds of reason; insofar as they are *useful* to our state of life, the rational pursuit of them is lawful.

Good name is either good *repute* or the esteem in which we are held by others, or *honor,* i.e., the manifestation through outward signs of that esteem. Esteem is *general,* viz., that which is due to us as *persons,* by reason of which we have a right to be treated in accord with the dignity of rational beings; that which is due to us as moral beings by reason of which evil is not to be imputed to us unjustly; that which is due to us as *composite beings,* by reason of which disgraceful defects or conditions of mind or body are not to be attributed to us groundlessly. Esteem is *special,* when arising from personally special virtues of mind or heart, or from social or civic dignity.

Freedom of Action is immunity from the coaction of force in the performance of our duties or the exercise of our rights.

Wealth is the possession of a sufficiency of material goods, i.e., of material goods required for satisfactorily fulfilling duties incumbent on us personally, or because of our state in life. Wealth is distinguished from *riches,* which is a superabundance of such goods. There is no duty of becoming rich, but it is lawful to acquire riches, provided the moderation of reason, benevolence, and justice, is preserved. The rich have a duty of beneficence, the object and mode of which is left to their own determination of using for the advance of industry and social prosperity what is superfluous in their riches, i.e., what is above the demands of personal well-being and their state of life. They may also be obliged by the virtue of munificence. All men have the duty of helping their neighbor individually who is in the extremity of need, from their personal resources which are above their personal needs.

REFERENCES: Rickaby's *Aquinas Ethicus,* Vol. I, pp. 93-100, 375-389.

XIV. DUTIES REGARDING LIFE

The direct mutilation or killing of oneself of one's own motion is prohibited by the moral law.

1. SUICIDE. The killing of self may be *direct* and *indirect.* It is direct when the agent's action is of its nature destructive of life, and when the agent intends such destruction as the result of his action. What is true of action destructive of life is true also of omission of actions preservative of life. We assert the duty not only of not destroying, but also of preserving life. It is indirect when the agent's action has two effects, one of which is destructive of life and the other productive of a good effect. The indirect killing of self is not suicide, when (a) the action from which the two effects issue is in itself good or indifferent; (b) the good effect is not obtained through the intermediation of the bad effect; (c) the agent in-

tends only the good effect; (d) the motives for obtaining the good effect are comparatively of equal gravity. Neither is it suicide to omit actions for the preservation of life, when the enumerated conditions obtain.

The killing of self of *one's own motion*, i.e., when the volitional action is within one's power both physically and morally. Hence it is suicide to kill one's self at the command of an authority whose jurisdiction does not extend to proprietorship over human life.

2. MALICE OF SUICIDE. The question is whether suicide is intrinsically evil, and hence, whether in given circumstances it can ever be right. Many writers assign reasons for the malice of suicide which are extrinsic, not universally valid, or beg the question. Arguments from rational love of self as usually presented beg the question; arguments deduced from our duty to human society, to the state, to relatives and friends, are not universally valid, and are extrinsic, i.e., derived from consequences of the suicide's act; arguments from God's supreme dominion over us do not prove, since God's dominion over all things is supreme. A valid argument must prove that God's dominion over man's life is not only supreme, but *exclusive*.

3. PROOFS.

(1) By suicide one exercises an act of ownership (a) over his personality as existing in his composite nature; (b) over the moral fruit of his personal existence; (c) over the providential ends of his Creator.

But (a) God has *exclusive* dominion over man's personality as existing in his composite nature, for man is *essentially not merely a creature, but a servant of God*. (b) God has *exclusive* dominion over the moral fruits of man's personal existence, for He alone has the right to determine the *measure of glory* to be given by man. (c) God has *exclusive* dominion over the providential ends for which He created man, for He alone can foresee those ends and has a right to determine the length of life for their realization.

(2) Hence the rational love man owes himself prohibits self-destruction, since he cannot destroy his life without withdrawing himself from the field of moral and meritorious service to which he has been assigned by his Creator, and consequently unfitting himself for his final perfection. Hence, the instinct of self-preservation is indicative of a fundamental and prohibitive precept of morality.

(3) Hence, a social being, bound to other men by the "solidar-

ity" of social nature, he cannot withdraw from life, without breaking the social bonds of charity and justice by which he has to further the providential ends of his Creator, with regard to self and others.

4. DIFFICULTIES.

(1) A gift may be returned to the donor when found to be intolerable. Life is a gift.

(2) When a man becomes useless, burdensome, or harmful to others, he may be compared to a diseased member of the body, which may be lawfully cut off to save the whole body.

(3) It cannot be wrong for a son to return to his father from a distant country. God is our father, we are His sons, separated afar from Him.

(4) At least it is right to kill one's self in order to escape from a life of turpitude, which one cannot avoid. From *Hume.*—If it is wrong to kill one's self, because one thereby invades the dominion of God, it is wrong for the same reason to fly from impending physical dangers to life, since these dangers arise from necessary causes of which God is the author.

5. INJURIES TO HEALTH. The arguments already given apply with due proportion to all actions or omissions by which bodily or mental integrity and health, are *directly* affected. Hence, to mutilate one's body, to expose one's self rashly to danger of death or disease, to indulge in vices by which the faculties of soul or body are debilitated, are invasions of God's rights, who gave body and soul to be used for the purposes, proximate or ultimate, of creation. Questions regarding indirect killing of self or self-injury are settled on the principles determining the moral lawfulness of an action having a good and bad effect.

REFERENCES: Rickaby's *Aquinas Ethicus,* Vol. II, pp. 39-52.

XV. DUTIES REGARDING VERACITY

The deliberate utterance of what one thinks to be false is prohibited by the moral law; but to conceal the truth in certain cases may not only be lawful but obligatory.

1. VERACITY. Speech may be false, either because it is out of accord with the fact, or because it is out of accord with the mind's judgment of the fact. Both are deviations from the truth; the first

may be unintentional, the second is deliberate and intentional. We are concerned with the deliberate utterance of what the speaker thinks to be false, whether as a matter of fact it be so or not. A lie has been variously defined. 1. It is usually defined as the utterance of what one thinks to be false *with the intention of deceiving*. But (a) one can deceive by telling the truth, and tell the truth with the intention of deceiving; (b) one can deliberately utter what one thinks to be false, without hope or intention of deceiving, e.g., to avoid self-conviction. In this notion of a lie, therefore, there are two distinct and separable, though generally concomitant elements, each having a malice of its own. 2. It is often defined as the deliberate utterance of an untruth to one who has a *right* to know the truth. But (a) in this definition also there are two distinct and separable elements; (b) the term "right" is used in a vague and scarcely definable sense; (c) the malice of a lie becomes relative. 3. It is defined as in the proposition. The definition is justified by the common conception of men, who regard lying and truthfulness as contraries. But one is truthful when one's utterance is in accord with one's mental judgment. Accessory phases of lying may modify its intrinsic malice. Besides its own, it may have the added malice of injustice or malevolence.

2. The Intrinsic Malice of Lying. A lie is primarily a degradation of the intellectual nature of the speaker, since (a) it puts discord between the judgment of his mind and its natural complement, speech; (b) between the intellect whose good is truth and the will intending falsity in speech; (c) in general between the inner conviction and the connatural outer expression of it. Secondarily, its natural tendency is to weaken the social bonds of mutual trust and intercourse, and consequently it is a deformity of man's social nature.

3. Concealing the Truth. A truth which one is under obligation not to reveal, or which one has a right to conceal, is a secret. A *natural* secret is one which is such from the nature of the thing known: one's own or one's neighbor's private affairs, which cannot be revealed without giving reasonable offense or doing an injury. A secret *of promise* is one which, on discovering the fact by one's own lawful observation, one promises not to reveal, whether such fact be a natural secret or not. A secret of *trust* is knowledge received on the express or tacit agreement that having been communicated for a serious purpose it be held in trust, e.g., knowledge

communicated to a lawyer, physician, confidential agent, or even in circumstances to a friend. A *sacramental* secret, the secret received by a priest in confession. This secret is absolutely privileged under all circumstances, and against all inquirers since it is a secret communicated to a priest, not as a fellow-man, but *precisely as a minister of God.* A secret *of trust* is privileged over the first two, and against all inquirers, except when the good of the community is gravely imperiled. The other two secrets are not privileged against an authority empowered to inquire in the department in which the secret lies. The precept of veracity is not only *negative,* forbidding lies, but *affirmative.* commanding speech when competent authority asks.

4. KEEPING SECRETS. The social bonds of mutual trust, intercourse and security depend as much on the keeping of lawful secrets, as it does on veracity. One who attempts to discover unlawfully another's secrets is an unjust aggressor. To keep a secret it is never allowed to lie. It may be kept by reticence, or by deceiving one against whom the secret is privileged, i.e., by inducing him into error. Deception as such is a wrong done to another's intellect, and never lawful except in blameless and legitimate self-defense against an unjust aggressor.

5. SPEECH AND LANGUAGE. Speech is natural, language is conventional. Speech takes its meaning not only from the grammatical signification of the words used, but also from the circumstances of time and place in which, and the person to whom they are uttered. Speech may be verbally false, yet by the usage of society either true or a form of reticence. The use of speech verbally false, but having an established meaning by convention, is lawful when required for the lawful retention of a secret.

REFERENCES: Slater's *Manual of Moral Theology,* Vol. I, Bk. VI, Pt. VIII, Chs. IV, V; Rickaby's *Political and Moral Essays,* IV; Rickaby's *Aquinas Ethicus,* Vol. II, pp. 213-222. For discussion of the subject without analysis of the thing discussed see Paulsen's *System of Ethics,* Bk. III, Ch. XI; Sidgwick's *Method of Ethics,* Bk. III, Ch VII.

XVI. DUTIES TO OTHERS

The moral law obliges man to respect the rights of others to moral and intellectual integrity, to health and life, to good name and property. The rights enumerated are co-active rights; and may be protected from unjust aggression, provided the moderation of blameless defense is used, by the use of force suited to secure them and proportioned to the loss threatened.

1. DUTIES IN GENERAL. Our duties to others are comprised under charity and justice. Charity or love of others is based on the facts: (a) that all men have the same essential dignity of rational nature; (b) the same social nature; (c) the same ultimate destiny. The obligation varies with closeness under these heads. The rule: "Love thy neighbor as thyself" does not mean that the neighbor is to be loved with the *same measure* of love as self, but, that love of self should be the exemplar of love of others. But love of self should be (a) in respect of its *end,* rational; (b) of its *form,* benevolent; (c) of its *effect,* beneficent. Many duties of love involve analogues of justice, as gratitude, veracity. Justice is based on the right of each to have and to hold what is his own in peace and security. The duties are enumerated in the proposition.

2. MORAL INTEGRITY. The neighbor has the right: (a) that no unbecoming word or deed of ours be to him an occasion of moral corruption; (b) that by no action of ours is he deprived of necessary or salutary means of preserving or promoting his moral integrity. The first violation is called *scandal.* Scandal may be *given* without being *taken,* or taken without being given. Scandal, when taken, though not given is: (a) scandal of the little ones, i.e., a word or deed, which harmless in itself, is, when uttered or done in presence of the young, an occasion to them of moral injury. *Maxima reverentia debetur pueris*; (b) pharisaical scandal, i.e., when through malice what is harmless is taken as an occasion of evil. Scandal, properly so called, i.e., when given and taken is: (a) *indirect,* when the offensive word is uttered or deed done primarily for one's own pleasure with disregard of its effect on others; (b) *direct diabolical* when the direct purpose is to lead others astray either as a means or as an end. Moral injury is done to the neighbor: (a) by depriving him of the means of leading his spiritual life —children, orphans, prisoners; (b) by failing to give him the

example due him: parents, teachers, persons of exemplary prominence; (c) by putting one's employees in circumstances in which the employer's interests are furthered by frauds or dishonesty.

3. INTELLECTUAL INTEGRITY. Sufficiently treated already. Truth, leading into error. Infidelity to promises.

4. BODILY INTEGRITY. The violations arise from unjust aggression, culpable negligence, greed of material goods.

5. GOOD NAME, AND HONOR. Everyone has a right to acquire by his legitimate industry a good repute among his fellow men, and having acquired it to retain it. This right is violated (a) by *calumny,* i.e., by falsely imputing to another moral defects, or physical defects of a dishonoring nature; (b) by *detraction,* i.e., by revealing the hidden defects, moral or physical, of another. Causes justifying such revealing are: (a) the common good, which is imperiled by keeping the secret; (b) necessary and blameless self-defense.

6. DEFENSE AND VINDICATION. Coactive rights may be defended if attacked, or vindicated if violated. But (a) recourse must be had to civil authority; (b) if this is not available, the means used must be suited to secure the rights and proportioned to the loss threatened; (c) they must be used only against unjust aggression; (d) though used in vindication, they must not be used vindictively; (e) the means least harmful to the neighbor must be used.

Hence (a) to preserve one's honor or fame, or to exact its restoration by inflicting death or grave bodily injury on one's detractor or calumniator is not lawful, because first, there is no proportion between the two goods at stake, and secondly, the means is not suited for the purpose intended. Hence (b) a woman may defend her honor by the death of the unjust aggressor, but not by self-destruction, since her honor is appreciatively as valuable as life. Hence (c) a man may inflict death on an unjust aggressor of life, since the loss threatened is irreparable, and in the conflict of rights, the prevailing right is that of the innocent party. Hence (d) the mutilation of another *with his consent* is lawful when a necessary means of securing a higher good, but the mutilation of another *without his consent* is never lawful to a private individual, and is lawful to civil authority only when it is punitive in character, i.e., inflicted for a crime committed, and proportioned to it. The state has no more right to multilate in order to prevent prospective crime, than it has to put to death in order to prevent prospective murder.

REFERENCES: Rickaby's *Aquinas Ethicus,* Vol. I, pp. 365-373; 413-419; Vol. II, pp. 39-51, 60-90.
Violations of property rights will be treated later.

XVII. RIGHT TO MATERIAL THINGS

Everyone has a connatural right to the material things by which life is sustained. The right of ownership, though conditioned on a contingent and universal fact, is, when actuated by a legitimate title, based on moral law. In case of extreme need the connatural right prevails over the right of ownership.

1. MATERIAL GOODS. Some material goods are of such a nature that they are not consumed by use, and that their supply is inexhaustible, as light, air. These are by nature *positively common* to all men in the sense that they neither are nor can become the property of either an individual or a community. Others are limited in supply, or are consumed by use, or have no utility unless appropriated, as the contents of the earth and sea, fruits, animals. These are by nature *negatively common,* i.e., nature does not assign them to individuals or communities as property, which must be held by one party, whether individual or communal, to the exclusion of the other, but leaves their appropriation to be determined by the exigencies of life, the nature of the goods, and the dictates of reason. The utility of some demands their possession by the community, either as common property, a roadway; or as things in common, a fountain to drink from; the utility of others demand their possession by an individual, as food, clothing.

2. RIGHT TO MATERIAL GOODS. By the fact that one has come into existence one has a *connatural* right to live, to the means of existence and self-development, and to the exercise of his activity therefor. This right is *absolute,* i.e., it does not depend on a fact supervening on existence, but it is as unconditional as is the right to life itself. It is *indefeasible;* it cannot be set aside or made void by other rights which are acquired. It is *regulative* of other rights to material goods, i.e., it indicates the ideal end of material goods, to which any form of acquired tenure must be conformed, and by which it is limited.

Hence (a) economic conditions that frustrate this ideal end of material things, by congesting these goods in the hands of the few, by making it unreasonably difficult for the many to obtain them, are by the very fact against the moral law; (b) personal ownership is justifiable insofar as it safeguards for men generally the equable, effective, and peaceful realization of the ideal end of material goods; (c) no acquired ownership is so absolute that it overrides the connatural rights of the community; (d) the end of individual ownership, though primarily personal is secondarily social.

3. THE RIGHT OF OWNERSHIP. By ownership we understand the stable right of disposing of the substance, utility, and fruits of a thing as one's own, for any purpose not incompatible with a higher right. It includes proprietorship and usufruct, undefined as to duration. The institution of personal property is based on the application of moral principles to the facts of human nature as manifested in history. Its origin is historical and juridical. Neglect of either aspect leads to error—extreme individualism, or socialism. The *juridical* principles are: (a) every man, as a person, has a connatural right to means of providing for himself and those depending on him; (b) as a social being he has the duty of so exercising this right as to respect the equipollent rights of others. The *historical* facts are that: (a) man is by the laws of psychology more solicitous of what concerns himself, than of what concerns others; (b) human affairs are conducted more orderly when each has charge of what concerns himself; (c) social peace is better preserved and social prosperity better promoted when each can normally satisfy his instinct of possession. This fact is *universal,* in the sense that it is and has been true of man generally; it is *contingent* in the sense that it does not impose a necessity on all men. Now, an institution that is necessary in order that men, as they historically are, may exercise effectively, orderly, and peacefully their connatural rights and social duties, is based on the moral law. But stable and exclusive proprietary rights over some of the material goods of life is necessary for this purpose. The personal right of providing for his present and future sustenance, protection, and development, and his social duties towards the family and toward his fellow men, are better secured by the right of ownership. Civilization has advanced with the evolution of the institution of property. The abuses that exist are diseases of civilization, not due to the right of ownership itself, but

to the contempt of connatural rights, juridical principles, and historical facts by the morally depraved or undeveloped.

4. THE TITLES. The titles by which the right to property is actuated, are original and derivative. Two *original* titles are natural and therefore juridical by the moral law: occupancy and labor. *Occupancy* is the effective taking of a thing that is nobody's (*res nullius,* or *res derelicta*) with the intention of holding it as one's own. The moral validity of this title was first denied by Ferguson, and subsequently by Legalists who derive the right of ownership from civil authority, and by Socialists who say that it is the source of all economic evils. Its moral validity is proved: (a) because it is an invasion of nobody's right; (b) because it is presupposed to all original ownership, and the rejection of it would destroy any ownership whatsoever even of a temporary character. *Labor* is productive activity by which a material thing is specifically changed for a useful purpose, or by which ideas are combined for the communication of ordered thought or the devising of practical methods. Labor is manual or mental. The title of labor is universally conceded to be a valid title, except by some extreme Socialists in the case of mental labor. *Derivative titles* are two: exchange and hereditary succession. No difficulty exists regarding the moral validity of *exchange.* The civil law may, for the protection of rights, put conditions for its legitimate exercise. *Hereditary succession* is the acquiring by one's heirs of the goods and rights one was possessed of at death. Its moral validity is denied by Legalists, its legitimacy by Socialists. It can be proved, so far at least as immediate linear heirs are concerned. For the right of the parent to acquire and hold property has not merely a personal but a family purpose. But these ends cannot be securely guaranteed without the right of hereditary succession. The denial of this right involves social evils. The alternatives would be, that the goods of the defunct would become *res nullius,* subject to first occupancy, or would be escheated to the state. The evils arising from these would be manifold.

REFERENCES: Rickaby's *Aquinas Ethicus,* Vol. I, p. 284, Sect. 3; Vol. II, pp. 53-57.

XVIII. SOCIALISM

Socialism as an economic theory, or Collectivism, is, in view of the above mentioned fact, adverse to the material prosperity of the race; as a philosophic theory it entails a crude materialistic interpretation of history; as a political theory it leads to democratic Absolutism.

1. COLLECTIVISM. Collectivism is Socialism looked on economically. It holds that economic justice can be secured only by the institution of a social system in which (a) all productive goods, i.e., the resources, materials, and instruments of production will be owned by the community; (b) all labor and service will be collectively organized; (c) products personally needed will be distributed according to the productive value of the individual's labor. It repudiates reform of the existing system of holding property, and advocates revolution which will wholly abolish it.

2. MARXIAN BASIS. All wealth is the *product of labor;* the *value* (i.e., in exchange) is fixed by the amount of labor employed in its production. Labor is *measured* by the length "of time required to produce an article under normal conditions of production, and with the average degree of skill and intensity prevalent at the time." We hold (a) that wealth is the product of nature, intelligence, and labor; (b) that its value is determined by the element common to all commodities, namely, capacity to satisfy human *wants,* or desire of them *affected* by difficulty of getting them; (c) that this value is not measured in a mechanical way, i.e., quantitatively, but *appreciated* relatively. The social appreciation, when not interfered with by industrial conspiracies, is expressed by the *market-price.* The *determinants* of the market-price are: (a) the qualitative excellence of the raw material; (b) the qualitative form given to it by the workmen; (c) the capacity of the finished product to satisfy human wants; (d) the greater or less abundance of the things wanted; (e) the cost of production. The error of Marx is twofold. 1. A defect—he does not credit labor with its full causation. The workman not only consumes so many hours of labor-time: he creates, in accord with his ability and industry, *utilities.* 2. An excess—he minimizes the productiveness of intelligent direction, supervision, and invention; and, therefore, cheats some and overpays others, in order to reduce all to economic equality.

3. PROOF. The material prosperity of a people in view of the historical facts mentioned in the last lecture, depends on four principles: (a) that men should have a personal *motive* for laboring; (b) that men should have personal *freedom* in their modes of labor; (c) that men should be personally *responsible* for the outcome of their activities; (d) that men should *compete,* with the moderation of justice. Now Collectivism (a) would paralyze the personal impulse to acquire wealth for the sake of personal culture, family improvement, or social advance through literary or inventive talent; (b) all persons being servants of the state, it would crush freedom, independence, personal dignity, and initiative; (c) it would extinguish personal responsibility by doing away with providence, personal, domestic, or civic; (d) it would close opportunity for healthy emulation.

4. SYNDICALISM. This is a form of revolution advocated by the I. W. W. Its aim is not community ownership, but sectional ownership, i.e., the workers of each trade or business own their respective instruments and materials of production, fix wages and prices. It is a revolt against Socialism, has not been elaborated into an intellectual system, and in practice would set the various trade-unions at war with one another and with the community.

5. SINGLE TAX SOCIALISM. This is a theory which holds (a) that the site value of land is a creation of the community; (b) that this site value should be taxed and other taxes abolished; (c) that this system would abolish "privilege." But (a) "site value of land" is not more a social product than are business values; (b) it is frequently due to industrial causes; (c) a single tax would sin against distributive justice, by ignoring the incidence of fair taxation; (d) it would lead to proprietorship becoming a perpetual lease, and hence to land nationalization; (e) it could not be gradually introduced without gradual denial of equitable compensation to existing owners.

6. SCIENTIFIC SOCIALISM. Every social movement is based on some theory regarding the forces that gave being to social institutions, their proximate purposes, and the ultimate goal of the human race. Philosophic Socialism holds the theory of *Economic Determinism,* i.e., all human progress arises from and is determined solely by economic motive forces. It holds that the supreme purpose to which man ought to subordinate every other purpose and institution is material well-being and comfort. It holds that the ultimate

goal of human life is to attain this universally; that morality, either personal, domestic, or civil, is meaningless out of relation to this.

This philosophy is *materialistic,* since it lowers man to the level of a high-grade animal, for whom there is no after life, and whose only purpose in this life is to survive in the struggle for life. It is *crude,* since it contradicts what we know of human nature; material well-being does not bring happiness, nor does it make men virtuous. It is a *falsehood,* since it promises what it cannot fulfil, and what, so far as we know human nature, cannot be attained in this world.

7. POLITICAL SOCIALISM. The institution of Socialism involves some form of the State. It would be some form of representative democracy in which every office was elective, and subject to the immediate control of the people. On the other hand it would necessitate the thorough organization of government throughout the whole range of production and social service. The government would have *monopolistic* powers over all the materials and instruments of production, *supreme control* of all the supplies of life, *authority* as far as its power and control extended over every citizen. It would be a system of democratic absolutism. The majority would have tyrannical power over the minority with regard to the means of subsistence, intellectual life, the worship of God, and the constitution of the family. Within the majority a ruling power would arise —whether an individual or a body of individuals—who would rule the state. Anarchy would be the alternative. Over this power the checks that can be used today, through the independence of the individual from the State in numberless relations, would be abolished. In effect we should all become serfs of an "inner circle" which could work unseen to keep us in intellectual, civil, and political subservience. Such a government would be omnipotent—the realization of Hegel's State.

REFERENCES: Schaeffle's *The Quintessence of Socialism,* and *The Impossibility of Democratic Socialism;* Ely's *Socialism,* and *The Labor Movement in America;* Ming's *The Morality of Modern Socialism,* and *The Characteristics and the Religion of Socialism; The Common Cause,* a magazine (no longer published), exposes the movement and theories of the Socialism of the present day; De Tunzelman's *The Superstition Called Socialism;* Goldstein's *Socialism.*

XIX. MONOPOLY

Monopoly exists by favor or tolerance of the civic community, and is lawful only when it subserves the common welfare. It may become a social evil, economically, politically, and ethically.

1. MONOPOLY. Monopoly (μόνος, πολεῖν) is such a control of commodities, business, or powers of nature, as enables the person or persons exercising it to fix prices. Whatever is marketable, as material goods, labor, natural resources, or money, may be the subject-matter of monopoly. The essence of monopoly does not consist in exclusive ownership, but in exclusive or dominating power to regulate the market in regard to things which are not of their nature the exclusive possession of an individual or body of individuals, and which, therefore, are subject to competition.

2. KINDS. Monopolies are either *social,* i.e., owing their existence to social causes; or *natural,* i.e., owing their existence to the nature or condition of the marketable thing.

3. SOCIAL MONOPOLIES. These exist: (a) because they are instituted by civil authority, e.g., the postal service; (b) because, though established by private individuals, they owe their existence either directly, as patent rights, or indirectly, as monopolies springing from an unnecessary protective tariff, to laws enacted by civil authority; (c) because they owe their existence to favors or concessions granted to powerful associations of capital, such as railroads or banks. Now, in all three cases they exist either because the civil authority legalized them, or because it favors them by legal concessions or by legal toleration.

4. NATURAL MONOPOLIES. These owe their origin to the fact (a) that the commodity is limited in quantity or confined in place, e.g., anthracite coal, platinum; (b) that the business is of such a sort that it cannot be effectively administered unless controlled by one person, private or corporate, e.g., a telephone system; (c) that the business is of such a sort that it cannot be established and conducted except by a combination of capital, e.g., a railroad system; (d) that its production is by processes known only to one or a few. Now these monopolies exist either because the civil community considers it for the common good that they should so exist, or because it neglects to appropriate them, when it is contrary to the public good that they should be in private hands.

5. WHEN LAWFUL. Monopolies are lawful when they subserve the common welfare: (a) when legalized, they protect the rights of individuals and secure them the fruits of their industry, e.g., copyrights; (b) when established in order to restrain the production and sale of an article, the immoderate use of which is prevalent, and seriously harmful to the community, e.g., the opium monopoly in Japan; (c) when established in order to encourage an industry of the community, which cannot be brought into existence except by monopoly; (d) when necessary to produce fiscal revenue. These cases are to be taken strictly, because once established for the reasons given they are liable to abuse.

6. WHEN UNLAWFUL. Monopolies may become social evils economically, politically, or ethically. Monopoly is an evil *economically* (a) when it raises prices beyond and lowers wages below what they would be under competition; (b) when it does not equitably share with producers of raw material, employees, and consumers, the economies effected by monopoly; (c) when it exacts dividends beyond what a fair return for investment justifies. It is an evil *politically* (a) when it uses its power to corrupt the legislature or judiciary; (b) when it interferes with the exercise of the right of suffrage, or the selection of candidates for political offices; (c) when it refuses to recognize lawful labor unions. It is an evil *ethically* (a) when it compels railroad favoritism or special privileges from any common carrier, practises discriminative underselling, or employs factory agreements; (b) when it does not promote material prosperity equitably and distributively; (c) when it induces the decay of individual initiative and independence, lessens business opportunity, concentrates wealth in the hands of the few, fosters the abuse of industrial power, and tends to the production of a proletariat.

REFERENCES: *Aquinas Ethicus,* Vol. II, pp. 90-98; Ely, *Monopolies and Trusts; The Irish Theological Quarterly,* July, 1908: "The Moral Aspect of Monopoly," by Dr. Ryan.

XX. SOCIETY

Society is a stable union of two or more for a common purpose attainable by cooperative activity. Its material element is the constituent members; its formal element, the bond which obliges them to social cooperation. Society is factitious when its nature, purpose and bond are fixed by man; it is natural, when these are fixed by the moral law or the Author of Nature. The three natural societies are domestic, civil, and religious; the two latter are supreme in their respective spheres, the primary range of which is fixed by the nature and purpose of the society.

1. SOCIETY. The term is used in a conventional sense to signify a more favored or fashionable class of the community which pays particular attention to the forms of social intercourse; or in a natural sense to signify a collective body of persons forming a community or association. We use the word in the latter sense. It is the stable union of two or more *socii*, the union arising not merely from coexistence in the same place, nor from mere identity of purpose, whether such identity be known to the person prosecuting the purpose or not, but by pursuit of a purpose which is *common* to all taken *collectively*, not merely distributively, which is consequently attainable by the cooperative activity of those who conjointly will it and work for it. The purpose is the common good as defined by the specific end of the particular society, and thereby the good of the individuals who compose the society. The common good varies in comprehension with the kind of society. The material element is the subjects who, precisely as persons, are not determined to one rather than another society. The formal element is the bond that unites them in a determined kind of society, and obliges them to the social cooperation peculiar to the society.

2. KINDS OF SOCIETY. Society is *factitious* when its nature, i.e., its purpose, the means it uses, and its bonds are fixed by the agreement, either contractual or promissory, of the persons who instituted it, or by legislative statute. It is *natural* when its nature is fixed by the moral law or the Author of Nature. The end of the first is a subsidiary and incidental good of life. The end of the second is an essential good of the race. The appeal of the first is to some men or classes of men; of the second to men generally. The former *imperfectly* actuates a social instinct; the latter *perfectly*. The *perfect*

actuation may be *inadequate* when the society, though the appeal of its end is to men generally, has not within itself all the resources to realize the end; it is adequate, when such resources are possessed.

3. NATURAL SOCIETIES. Natural societies are those which respond perfectly, either adequately or inadequately, to the inborn aptitudes, inclinations, and needs of the human race. These are three, domestic, civil, religious. *Domestic* society starts from conjugal society, naturally evolves into parental society, and is completed usually by a society between the heads of parental society and servants. These three, or at least the first two combined, form domestic society (*domus,* the home). *Civil* society is composed of domestic society as its immediate material element, and provides for temporal well-being by protecting rights, and insuring the means socially necessary for common prosperity. *Religious* society provides for the spiritual well-being of man. Now, the worthy propagation of the race, its temporal and spiritual well-being, are goods which respond to the natural aptitudes, impulses, and needs of the human race. Both civil and religious society afford means which domestic society lacks for its well-being, and are themselves in their respective spheres self-competent. The ultimate and proper purpose of each is distinct from that of the other. Though these purposes are interlinked (*colligantur*) they can never be identical, nor from their union can a third unitary society be formed.

4. AUTHORITY. Authority is the *right* of the community to direct and compel the individual members to live in accord with the specific purpose of the society of which it is a prerogative. It is derived from the *duty* of the community, as such, to seek its specific purpose, and this in turn arises from the bond by which a number of persons are formally constituted a society. The very concept of society in which it is the *duty* of the community as such, and, therefore, of its members individually, to further its specific good, involves the right in the community, as a primary property of the community, to enforce this duty. The *subject* of authority is an individual person, a body of persons, or the whole community, depending on the nature and constitution of the society. There is an analogy between society and a human being. Both are composed of a material and a formal element; both have a directing and controlling faculty which resides in a special organ; both have rights and duties, and are, therefore, (in appropriate senses) persons. But this analogy cannot be pushed to parallelism, otherwise we fall into the materialistic extravagancies

of Comte, Schoeffle, Spencer (*The Study of Sociology,* Chs. 14 and 15) and Bluntschli.

5. THE RANGE OF AUTHORITY. The range of the right to compel obedience cannot be more or less extensive, in the matter or over the persons with which it deals, than the duty from which it springs. But this duty arises from the bond that unites men in a specific society seeking a specific purpose, by means which are suited to the purpose, and in character subordinate to it. Authority, therefore, is limited by the nature and constitution of the society in which it is exercised.

XXI. CONJUGAL SOCIETY

Conjugal society is a contract properly so called, but differs from other contracts in that its nature, purpose, and bond are determined by the Author of Nature. Its primary intrinsic purpose is the procreation of rational beings, and its secondary purpose is the mutual love and aid of the contracting parties. Its essential properties are unity and indissolubility.

1. CONJUGAL SOCIETY. This is the stable union of a man and woman in community of life for the fitting procreation of children, and for mutual love and aid. It is a *natural* society, as is evidenced by the physiological and psychological faculties, tendencies, and temperaments by which they are fitted and impelled to enter matrimony, and thus mutually complement one another in the constitution of a unitary principle of procreation and a social unit of love. It is a *primary* society, because it is primordial, historically and conceptually, and because, naturally evolving into parental society, it is primarily essential to the well-being of the race.

2. CONTRACT. A contract is a formal agreement between two (or more) persons in which each binds himself or herself to do or forebear in favor of the other, and each acquires the right to what the other promises. But a conjugal society owes its *existence* to an agreement by which both parties freely, mutually, and expressly promise to enter into a union, the purposes of which are defined by nature. It *differs* from other contracts in that its nature, purpose, or bond is not determined by the contracting parties, who are free to make the contract or to abstain from making it, but cannot

change its essential conditions. These are, that it should be in accord with the animal and rational nature of man. Any animal function of man that is performed in a manner unbefitting the dignity of a rational being becomes bestial.

3. PURPOSE AND END. Matrimony may be regarded as an *institution of nature,* or as an intimate *association* of two in *community of life.* Under the first aspect its *extrinsic* and regulative purpose is the well-being—not mere increase—of the race, and its *intrinsic* purpose is the procreation of children, in a manner befitting rational nature and promoting the extrinsic purpose. Under the second aspect its purpose is the enduring attainment of what was the natural impulsive motive of its formation, i.e., mutual love of head, heart, and hand. Both are essential purposes; the first is primary in the sense that the second is intended by nature for the promotion and becoming realization of the first. Both being social, neither can be subordinated to the personal gratifications of one or other of the contracting parties. The secondary purpose affecting the mutual right of individuals should always be sought; the primary purpose, being the befitting growth of the race, and therefore, not obligatory on individuals singly, but on the collective body, need not always be sought by each and every conjugal society; but it can never be frustrated by positive acts without contravening the laws of nature.

The end of the conjugal society is that in which it naturally issues. But this is a rational being, who (a) possessing an immortal soul is destined for eternal blessedness, and possessing a rational spirit exists for the glory of his Creator; (b) possessing a social nature is destined for cooperative life among his fellow men. Hence (a) conjugal society by its end is endowed with a natural sanctity and sacredness which connects it with religion; (b) it has a human consecration higher and wider than any given civil society, which it subserves only insofar as that civil society itself promotes the advance of the race.

4. UNITY. The conjugal union of one man with one woman is a precept of the natural law, though not immediately evident. The reasons are: 1. From its secondary purpose it is a society of equals. The contracting parties contribute equally to the purposes of conjugal and parental society and have equal rights. In other forms of union the love given is not the love received. 2. The primary purpose of parental society is difficult of attainment in other forms of marital unions. 3. The extrinsic purpose, as history witnesses, is best

obtained in monogamous unions, and is hampered and retarded where polygamous unions prevail.

5. INDISSOLUBILITY. The conjugal union is permanent during the life of the contracting parties. It can be dissolved neither by the contracting parties nor by any human authority, civil or ecclesiastic. Being a contract, conditions for its validity in accord with the good of the race may be put by the society to which it is subject. If these are not observed, the society can declare it null *ab initio*. Indissolubility is a prescription of the moral law, though not immediately evident, but more evident probably than the prescription of unity. The reasons are: 1. From the intrinsic purpose, that dissolubility of a valid union by either of the contracting parties or by a human authority would be adverse to the good of the race, as it destroys the fundamental unit of the civil society, lowers the moral standards of the community, and leads logically to free love, and thence to animal promiscuity. 2. It entirely frustrates the primary intrinsic purpose of parental society, and is, therefore, a grave injury to the child. 3. It would normally put the woman in an injurious position. 4. The reasons usually advanced for it are based on abnormal egotism or animal passion.

REFERENCES: Rickaby's *God and His Creatures*, Bk. III, Chs. CXXIII-CXXIV.

XXII. PARENTAL SOCIETY

The primary intrinsic purpose of parental society is the education of the children who are members of it. To parents alone belongs the inherent right of educating their children. The duty from which this right springs may be enforced, should need arise, by civil and religious society.

1. PARENTAL SOCIETY. This is the natural outgrowth of conjugal society. Its *extrinsic* purpose is the well-being of the race to be obtained by realizing its *intrinsic* purpose, which is to fit children for their mission in life. Its *bonds* are parental love for those who are, as it were, their other selves; and filial reverence towards those who are the authors of their being. Parental society owes neither its origin nor its continuance to a pact, as Rousseau and others held, nor to proprietary rights, as Kant seems to have held, but is derived from

the natural relations between the child and its parents, whose authority is defined by its intrinsic purpose.

2. EDUCATION. In its proper sense the word signifies a process (or the result of a process) of instruction, training, and discipline, by which the physical, mental, and moral powers are suitably developed and rendered efficient for the duties of life. On the one side it is determined by the capacity for development of the individual, and on the other by the duties of life for which he is destined. The capacity for development may regard either the *formative* period of life or the *evolved* period. The duties of life are either *common* to all human beings, and are consequently fixed by the social environment in which they live, or are *peculiar* to particular individuals and to specialized social functions. Our question concerns the formative period and the common duties of life. Every child that is brought into the world has a right to this.

3. THE RIGHT OF EDUCATION. Education comprises the giving of information and formation, and for the sake of brevity we confine the discussion to formation of intellect and will. Everyone who is able has the right to give information, i.e., to impart knowledge, but this right implies no correlative duty on the part of the pupil, and, consequently, no authority *ad hoc* on the part of the teacher. The right and authority to educate is founded on the duty of educating, and this, in turn, on the right of the child to education. Primarily, the child has a right to formative and common education, and this right involves the duty and authority on the part of another.

4. THE AUTHORITY TO EDUCATE. The inherent right to educate belongs (a) to those on whom the child has, by nature, the first claim; (b) on whom nature has imposed the duty, and, therefore, the authority to educate; (c) between whom and the child nature has put the closest bonds of mutual love and understanding. These are the parents alone.

5. PROOF. (a) By the action of the parents, the child is brought into the world in a condition of extreme physical, intellectual and moral want. (b) The parents are the authors of the child's existence, which is, as it were, a part of their own substance, and to whom, therefore, the child belongs, to be fashioned to manhood or womanhood. (c) Between the parents and the child whom they procreated there is the closest natural bond; hence in the parents the strongest other-regarding love, and in the child the strongest responsive love. Love of this kind necessarily implies a mutual prac-

tical understanding. Note: (a) that the authority of the parents over the child must be in accord with the personal dignity of the child, and the peculiar bond of love that unites them; (b) that the parents in educating the child should supplement their limitations by external aids; (c) that the two natural and supreme societies, of which both parents and child are members, have authority in their respective spheres to protect the natural rights of the child, but not to invade the sphere of parental authority; (d) that the duty of supervising the scholastic companionship and instruments of formation is incumbent primarily on the parents.

6. THE DUTIES OF THE STATE. (a) The State has the duty of prohibiting teaching subversive of public morality and social order. It has not the right to determine in detail the curricula of studies, except insofar as it is necessary in order to safeguard the natural rights of the child to a common and formative education. (b) It has the duty of providing schools and other accessories for formative and common education, when these cannot be otherwise provided; it has not the duty of supplying the means for advanced education beyond the formative period. It has no direct, and much less exclusive, authority over formative and common education.

REFERENCES: Conway's *The Respective Rights and Duties of the Church, Family, and State Regarding Education.*

XXIII. INDUSTRIAL SOCIETY

The proximate and individual norm of wages, due on grounds of commutative justice, is the net value of the work that the laborer produces; the supreme and general norm of wages, due on grounds of social justice, is the common welfare of the laboring class.

1. INDUSTRIAL SOCIETY. It is for the best interest of the civil community that between employers and employees there should exist concord; that by their mutual cooperation the material prosperity of each should be promoted; and that their relation should be governed by benevolence and justice. The causes that introduce discord between them, setting class against class, ultimately redound to the injury of the whole community. These are radically ill-feeling and distrust, or injustice in the relation between wages paid and work done.

2. LABOR. Labor, in a comprehensive sense, is an exertion of mind or body undergone wholly or mainly with a view to acquiring an outer good of life. It is *industrial,* either skilled or unskilled; *ministrative,* giving personal, domestic, business, or professional service; or *governmental,* pertaining to the public service. Our question is about industrial labor, which is the intelligent expenditure of muscular power on the matter and energies of nature, contributing directly or indirectly to the production of specific utilities. *Work* is what is done by labor; its purpose is to procure the necessities, comforts, or luxuries of life.

3. WAGES. Wages, as distinguished from salary, stipend, or fee, is the payment under contract for industrial work done for another. It differs from *price* paid for a commodity, because the laborer is a living being whose wages are necessary for the conservation of existence and efficiency, and whose work is primarily directed to this purpose. Labor is not, therefore, a mere market commodity. It differs from the *hire* of an animal, because the laborer is a person with the rights and duties, individual and social, of a person; his labor is his own, and of its nature destined for his own utility and the utility of those dependent on him. The *iron law of wages* regards him as a hired animal. The distinctive notes of wages, therefore, arise from the *necessity* and *personality* of the laborer.

4. THE NORM. The contractual relation between laborer and employer is proximately individual and based on commutative justice: *do ut des.* It is ultimately social, affecting the welfare of the community, and subject to the regulative preeminence of social justice. As a relation of commutative justice the *objective norm* of it cannot be determined by mere contract, since this may fall below or rise above the demands of commutative justice; nor by the market value of labor, since this may be depressed or raised by artificial causes; nor by personal or family needs, since these may exceed or be less than is due by commutative justice. In its relation, its supreme norm is determined by the welfare of the working class in frugal and becoming comfort.

5. THE INDIVIDUAL NORM. Commutative justice is kept when equality is preserved between what is given and what is received. The thing contracted for is work insofar as it is directly or indirectly productive of utilities. This the laborer sells and the employer purchases, because thereby both obtain a benefit not otherwise obtainable. "Capital cannot do without Labor; nor Labor without Capi-

tal." The product of labor is gross or net, i.e., the sum total of what he produced, deducting the expenses of production. Therefore, deducting the cost of material, instruments of production and taxes, of recompense due to the employer for his labor and expense in directing production and marketing the output, and of interest due for money invested, what remains belongs to the workman. This, however, cannot be equitably fixed from day to day, but by the average value of products during periods varying from business depression to business prosperity, or obtaining in normal economic conditions.

6. THE SOCIAL NORM. Social justice regulates the outward actions of men in their bearing on the common welfare. As a *supreme* norm it is directive of outward conduct in which equity between man and man is to be preserved; as a *general* norm it is determinative of the relations that individuals or parts of the community should bear to the organized whole. But equity requires that the connatural right of living in accord with dignity of his personal nature, of enjoying, namely, the opportunity of subsisting in becoming comfort, of raising a family, of attending to his mental, moral, and religious perfection, should have fair play. If the economic order denies this, it is out of accord with moral law. Again, the welfare of the community as a whole requires that the largest component of it should enjoy its equitable rights. If this is denied, social discontent and disunion, class hostility and conflicts arise, i.e., unarmed civil war.

REFERENCES: Leo XIII's *The Condition of the Working Classes;* Ryan's *A Living Wage.*

XXIV. CIVIL SOCIETY

The genetic origin of civil society is to be found in the inclination, aptitudes, and needs of man; its historical origin, in the various facts that caused the aggregation of many men in the same territory; its juridical origin, in the consent either tacit or expressed, of those who instituted it. The distinction between people, nation and State.

1. EXISTENCE. The existence of some form of civil society is a universal and uninterrupted fact of history. The *homo solivagus* is a figment or hypothetical assumption. A universal and constant fact

is due to a universal cause. The *Contractualists* attribute it to the educational efficiency of experience. The *Evolutionists* to natural impulse physically necessitating. The *Schoolmen* to natural impulse emotively necessitating. 1. The *genetic* origin is due to emotive causes operating on all men at all times, and impelling indeterminately to civil unions. Man has a natural fitness for civil society, evidenced by his social faculties; a natural inclination to it, evidenced by his social inclinations; and a natural need of it, evidenced by his physical, intellectual, and moral wants, which cannot find relief outside of civil society. The genetic impulse is ultimately reducible neither to fear, as Hobbes held, nor to self-love, as Rousseau held; but to a rational love of self and others. It is neither purely altruistic nor purely egoistic. 2. The genetic impulse has been *historically* actuated along different lines, and has produced different forms of civil society. The primary historical causes of these developments are four: unity of race; the common need of many unrelated families gathered, from whatever cause, in the same territory; the social or military prepotency of one or more families, compelling political subjection of others; the special influence of religion, resulting in theocracy. Usually in the primary formation of civil society these causes intermingled, though one or other was predominant. 3. Whatever the form of society, man recognizes that it is his duty to live and act in conformity with the dictates of social justice. The *juridical* origin of civil society explains the existence—not the source—of this obligation. The material element of civil society is a multitude of persons living in the same place. The formal element is the bond that obliges them to live in accord with the purpose of civil society.

2. THE ORIGIN OF CIVIL OBLIGATION. The material element of civil society may be considered: (a) as a multitude of persons coexisting in the same territory; (b) as bound by mutual obligations of benevolence, commutative or contractual justice, filial piety, and other virtues defining the moral relations between man and man or parents and children; (c) as bound by the common obligations of an organized political body. Historical causes gradually dispose and induce the multitude to assume the bond of social justice, they do not give it existence. Reasons: 1. Descent from a common father obliges the descendant only to filial piety and family love. 2. Territorial coexistence obliges only to the mutual social duties comprised under benevolence and justice. 3. Tenancy under a territorial lord obliges only to respect for his right. 4. Military or other prepotence

imposes no obligation on the weaker; might does not originate right. Historical causes show the emotive and moral necessity of forming a civil society. But the moral necessity of entering a natural society does not constitute one a member of it.

The efficient cause which originally gives existence to the bond of social justice is the consent of the multitude or its *natural* representatives, given either expressly, or implicitly, by actions freely posited and implying assent. This consent may be given by the practical acceptance of life in a growing community that finally and gradually becomes a civil community, or by formal agreement to a form of government. Social circumstances may be such that the multitude is morally obliged to give such consent, and human nature is such that it inevitably will; but until it is given, the bond of social justice does not exist.

3. Proof. The genetic impulse to civil society must be actuated by some fact; men are not by nature members of a concrete civil society. By nature, therefore, each man is politically equal and independent of others. Hence, the stable union of many seeking by their cooperative activity a common civil good must, in the case of adults having the use of reason and free-will, arise from their perception of its objective moral necessity and their fixed intention of realizing it. Such an intention is an act of the will, or an explicit or implicit consent.

4. Contractualism. This doctrine differs from that of the Contractualists, (a) in asserting that man is by nature a social being, and that civil society is a natural society; (b) in asserting that the bond of civil society, i.e., the obligation to social justice, though it owes its existence in one or other form of political body to the consent of the constituting multitude, does not derive its obligatory nature from that consent; (c) in asserting that the genetic impulse is not accidental to human nature, arising from the education of experience and directed merely to self-protection or self-betterment, but essential to human nature, and ultimately directed to the temporal welfare of the race, to be obtained by the temporal welfare of the individuals constituting the race.

5. Political Designations. *People,* an aggregate actually existing in an organized political community, and constituting its material element; sometimes applied to an aggregate that once had political existence and yet retains territorial unity. *Nation,* a people precisely as organized in a political unity, bound by civil obligation,

and endowed with at least the internal rights of sovereignty, but considered in abstraction from its government. *State,* the body politic in its entirety comprising the material element, i.e., the people; the formal element, i.e., their union by the bond of social justice; and a distinctive form of government.

XXV. THE END OF THE STATE

The State is not an end to itself, but exists for the temporal well-being of the community. Its primary purpose is to secure the rights and liberty of its members, and its secondary purpose is to afford equitably the opportunities socially necessary for temporal prosperity.

1. AN END IN ITSELF. A person, either physical or moral, is said to be an end in itself: (a) *negatively,* in the sense that being *sui juris* it cannot be regarded as directly subordinated in worth to another person; (b) *positively,* in the sense that its own preservation and growth is the ultimate purpose of its existence, to which its constituent elements are subordinate and referable. The State is an end to itself in the first sense, because it is a supreme natural society. It is not an end to itself in the second sense, because the citizens are not for the sake of the State, but the State for the sake of the social purpose of the citizens, as manifested by the genetic impulses that impelled men to form society; because the State is not an entity abstracted and distinct from, and superior to the people that compose it. We reject, therefore, Hegelian theories of the State. The same principles apply to other abstractions like Society, Humanity, The Race. A comparison between the relations of citizens and State, and of soldiers and army.

2. THE END OF THE STATE. The proper purpose of the State is to realize in the temporal order that which the social impulses and needs of man demand, and which outside of the State cannot be permanently and efficiently obtained. But this is temporal welfare, (a) by security in their rights to life, liberty, and the pursuit of temporal well-being; (b) by opportunity to acquire a stable sufficiency of the goods of this life. Both are essential purposes. The theory of Kant, Spencer, and others, who confine the purpose of the State to securing rights is—except as a protest against State Paternalism—untenable. It ignores the natural sociability of human

nature, the fact that men live in community of life, because it satisfies their inclinations, gives play to their aptitudes, and enables them to satisfy needs which can be satisfied only in society. This theory which makes the purpose of State simply the protection of men from one another is appropriately called by the Germans *Polizeistaattheorie*.

3. THE PRIMARY PURPOSE. The primary purpose is one which immediately concerns the preservation of the social bond, without which other purposes cannot be obtained, and which it is the direct duty of the state to secure. This is social peace and tranquillity, i.e., protection against external foes and immunity from internal discord. The primary purpose is not the *paramount* purpose, i.e., that which is ultimately intended, but that which is primarily necessary in order that through the prevention or removal of social disorder the community may seek in harmony advance in temporal prosperity.

4. THE SECONDARY PURPOSE. This completes the primary purpose. By *temporal prosperity* is understood not only material prosperity, but also intellectual, artistic, and moral perfection, insofar as these add to the temporal well-being and happiness of the community. It is *socially necessary*, (a) in the sense that it regards general necessity or supreme utility; (b) in the sense that it can be obtained by the State alone, or by the State in a way far superior to that of private effort or cooperation. It *affords opportunity*, i.e., it does not provide individual citizens, or classes of citizens, with the means of procuring temporal prosperity, but offers to all such social conditions as give free play to personal initiative and enterprise.

5. THEORIES OF THE STATE'S PURPOSE. Apart from the Hegelian theory that subordinates the individual citizens to the existence and evolution of an abstract entity personified as the State, there are three theories of the State's purpose. The Kantian theory that tends to the development of excessive police power; the Paternal theory that tends to the increasing dependence of citizens on the State for individual prosperity; the theory of the Schoolmen that limits the powers of the State to the protection of natural rights, the providing and regulating of public utilities, and the supervision and fostering of social conditions affording equitable and potentially universal opportunity for its citizens. It acts *ultra vires*, i.e., beyond the charter given by nature when on the plea of the "common good" it invades individual, family, or class rights, or takes upon

itself the care of private morality or health *as such,* or opposes the exercise of religious belief not out of accord with moral law. It has no jurisdiction over the acts of the citizens, except insofar as these are socially externalized, and become injurious to the life, liberty, or property of others; or to the efficiency or permanence of the State; or seriously and detrimentally affect the conditions of social prosperity.

XXVI. THE NATURE OF CIVIL AUTHORITY

Civil authority, the organ of which is the government, is an essential property of the State. It can oblige in conscience only so far as it is ultimately derived from the Supreme Legislator.

1. AUTHORITY. There are two meanings of the word: the superior *knowledge* conjoined with veracity of one, which is the ground of another's intellectual submission; the superior *moral power* or the right of one, which is the ground of another's volitional submission. We use it in the latter sense. It may be defined: the right of effectively directing the members of a community to its proper and specific end. It is parental, civil, ecclesiastical. It must reside in a subject. The subject, whether the members of society taken collectively, a selected body, or an individual person, is the government. The government has therefore two rights: the right of authority, and the right of exclusive possession and exercise of authority. Hence two questions: *Whence comes authority as such?* and, *Whence comes the right of the subject to possess and exercise it?*

2. THE RIGHT OF AUTHORITY. There are four theories: The *Anarchists,* whether philosophical, as Proudhon, or revolutionary, as Bakunin, deny the right of authority; the *Contractualists* regard it as the summation or resultant of individual rights arising from a primitive contract, either actual or constructive; the *Evolutionists* hold it to be a social power produced by superorganic evolution, much as biological powers are produced by organic evolution; the *Schoolmen* hold it to be a property of civil society, which, being a natural society, receives its nature and attributes from the Author of Nature.

3. PROOF. The right of effectively directing others to a specific end necessarily presupposes the duty of those others to cooperate to the attainment of the end. Civil authority, therefore, presupposes in

the members of a civil society the duty of social justice, and is derived from and measured by that duty. But this duty, assuming the existence of civil society, has its source in the right of the Supreme Legislator of obliging those who are members of a natural society to work for the purposes of that society. Therefore, the right of authority is ultimately derived from the Supreme Legislator. Hence government can oblige in conscience only insofar as the members of civil society are antecedently bound by the moral law, and consequently bound by an authority that has the right to declare and define the conditions of social justice.

4. The Other Theories. Anarchism by denying the right of authority, denies social justice and the social nature of man; the Contractualists deny any motive for obedience to law except fear or self-interest, and consequently the social nature of man. The evolutionists admit the social nature of man, but cannot raise the duty of obedience above the instinct of the herd.

5. The Right of Government. There are three theories. (a) The right of government is immediately from God by divine but positive designation, as in the case of Saul in the theocracy of Israel, the divine rights of kings. (b) The right of government is immediately from God by natural designation, as in the case of parental authority, a milder form of the "divine rights" theory. (c) Authority itself is from God, but its inhesion in one or other subject, i.e., the right of government, is from the people, who are and always remain the radical depository of it; and from whom it passes to a determined form of government, which thereby secures an inviolable right to the possession and use of authority in keeping with the constitution that determines its tenure and extent.

6. Proof. The right of civil authority is of its nature radically in that subject to whom belongs the right of attaining the end of civil society and of providing the means thereto. But this is the people. The people, however, are incapable of direct and effective exercises of it, except in communities in which the members are comparatively few in number, and upright in regard for social justice; otherwise "the will of the people" may be adverse to the ends of social justice. To attain the end of civil society, the people should therefore pass the right of authority to a form of government best fitted to attain the ends of social justice. This government, therefore, exists by the express or tacit consent of the people.

7. CONSENT OF THE GOVERNED. The formula: "Governments are instituted among men, deriving their just power from the consent of the governed," may have two senses: (a) the Contractualists sense, that "the will of the people" is the original source of authority; (b) the Scholastic sense that the powers of government are only just when derived, by the expressed or tacit consent of the people, from the duty of social justice incumbent on the people itself. The first sense leads to tyranny, the second to right government.

XXVII. THE FUNCTIONS AND FORM OF GOVERNMENT

The functions of government are legislative, judicial, and executive. The purposes of government are best obtained when these functions are distributed in different depositories, in such a way as to preserve the organic unity of the State. No form of government is without defects. The best form is that which is suited to the political capacity and character of the people, as determined by historical causes. Generally speaking, for the political temperament of modern peoples, this is best effected in a constitutional and representative government.

1. THE FUNCTIONS. The functions of government regard the future, past, or present conditions of social order and temporal prosperity. In view of the primary purpose of the State they are: (a) to define and prescribe the internal and external conditions necessary for the security of social order; (b) to decide controversies arising from these prescriptions, and determine their violations and vindicate them; (c) to manage the affairs of the State in keeping with these prescriptions and the decisions that determine their concrete applications. In view of the secondary purpose they are: (a) to define and prescribe the conditions of temporal prosperity; (b) to decide controversies regarding the applications of these prescriptions; (c) to put these prescriptions into effect.

The first function under both heads is, philosophically speaking, *legislative*, i.e., general and prospective. Legislative functions are, therefore: to make civil and criminal laws; to assign sanctions for laws; to give interpretations of laws; to make treaties and declare war; to make fiscal and economic laws; to impose tribute or taxes;

to define the uses of State monies; to provide public utilities socially necessary; to grant charters. The second function under both heads is, philosophically speaking, *judicial,* and is, in general, to decide in the concrete all controversies regarding violations of legislative prescriptions, and to impose penalties according to the sanctions fixed by the legislative power. The third function under both heads is, philosophically speaking, *executive,* i.e., to give execution to legislative enactments and judicial decisions, and to administer the affairs of government in accordance with laws, their interpretation, or the decision of the judicial power.

2. LAWS. Civil laws when rightly promulgated bind in conscience either to the positing or the omitting of the actions prescribed or proscribed; or, if they are *purely* penal laws, to paying the penalty after sentence of the judiciary. For they are: (a) either declarations of a moral obligation already existing, or determinations of conditions fitted for the protection of social order; (b) necessary for attaining the purposes of civil society; (c) made by an authority ultimately derived from the Supreme Legislator. Civil laws not conforming to these canons do not bind in conscience. The *subject matter* of civil law is not the common good without qualification, but the common good as defined by the primary and secondary purposes of civil society, namely, actions socially externalized, which gravely affect the rights and liberties of others, or the State's functions of furthering temporal prosperity. With the private morality or well-being, *as such,* of the citizen the State has no concern; its laws should be accommodated to the natural conditions and the moral development of the community.

3. THE FORMS OF GOVERNMENT. The *simple* forms of government are democracy, aristocracy and monarchy. The mixed forms are those in which one of the simple forms is modified and tempered by the others. Modern representative government is a mixed form in which at least the members of the lower legislative house are directly chosen by the people. In our federal government, the House of Representatives is directly chosen by the people, its functions are mainly legislative, the exceptions being the judicial function of impeaching civil officers of the United States, but it does not possess the fulness of legislative power; the Senate is directly* chosen by the people, its functions are legislative, executive, and judicial in cases of impeachment; the President is indirectly chosen by the people,
*By the Seventeenth Amendment to the Constitution, proclaimed May 31, 1913.

his functions are executive, legislative through his veto powers and through the power of making treaties with the advice and consent of the Senate, and judicial through his power of granting reprieve and pardon. The Constitution of the United States, unlike the constitution of a State, is a grant of power. A State possesses all powers inherent to civil authority, unless it is deprived of some by restrictions in the fundamental law or constitution.

4. ALL FORMS DEFECTIVE. No form of government is without defects. The best form of government is that which is suited to the political capacity and character of the people, as determined by historical causes, and in which authority is so exercised, and liberty so secured as to inspire citizens with loyalty. For the political temperament of modern people at least, this is best effected in a constitutional and representative government, in which the functions of government are distributed in different departments, but in such a way as to preserve organic unity. (a) Loyalty is greater when the citizens have political power. (b) Freedom is safer where government is limited by a constitution. (c) Effectiveness in government is better secured when functions calling for different habits of mind are appropriately distributed; and rights are better safeguarded when two or more of these functions are not in the hands of one man or body of men. (d) Organic unity is preserved when these functions in all their exercises are not separated in different depositories, but interlinked in such a way as mutually to restrain one another.

5. DISTRIBUTION OF FUNCTIONS IN THE UNITED STATES. The functions of the House of Representatives are, with one exception, legislative, but it does not possess the fulness of the legislative power; of the Senate legislative, judicial, and executive; of the judiciary, judicial, and legislative by interpreting laws; of the President, executive, legislative by the power of veto, and judicial by granting pardon and reprieve.

REFERENCES: Willoughby's *The Government and Administration of the United States;* Rickaby's *Aquinas Ethicus,* Vol. I, pp. 286-301; Woodrow Wilson, *The State,* Ch. XI; St. Thomas, *S.T.,* 1, 2, qu. 105, a. 1.

XXVIII. THE CHURCH AND THE STATE

Though Church and State are in their respective spheres perfect and independent societies, the absolute irrelation of both is impossible, and attempts to effect it are against the moral law.

1. CHURCH AND STATE. Assuming that religion is not a mere emotional product, but a habit of will based on intellectual assent to certain truths which define our dependence on and our duties to our Creator, we understand by the *Church* a body of believers cooperatively professing these truths, symbolically expressing them by a ritual, and practising the duties they inculcate. In view of the unitary character of religious truth and purpose there can be but one Church, though, apart from a divine revelation, there might be many rituals, and one section of believers might more thoroughly grasp and ritually more perfectly express the truths of religion than another. Complete spiritual well-being and happiness of its members is the ultimate and specific purpose of the Church, which has within itself the means of realizing its purpose. The Church is, therefore, a perfect society, supreme in its own order. Societies are said to be *independent,* (a) when the end of one is not *per se* a means to the end of the other; and (b) when the activity of one is not directly subject to the jurisdiction of the other. But the Church and the State, which, as we have seen, is also a perfect society and supreme in its own order, are in this sense independent of one another.

2. THE RELATIONS OF CHURCH AND STATE. The subjects of both Church and State are the same, i.e., the same persons are subject to the jurisdiction of each, and destined by nature to the purpose of each. But the absolute irrelation of two supreme societies having jurisdiction over the same subjects is impossible, and the absolute irrelation of two supreme societies, the members of which are destined by nature to attain the purpose of each, cannot be attempted without impugning a law founded in nature. Moreover, the purpose of each is more fully realized by mutual aid; temporal prosperity is more secure when right is reinforced by religion, and religious welfare is promoted by temporal means. Attempts to divorce absolutely the interests of Church and State are, therefore, against the moral law.

3. THEORETIC RELATIONS. There are three thories: (1) *Extreme European Liberalism,* which holds that the State, as such, ignores God, and seeks its end irrespective of religion. Pushed to its logical conclusions this means: (a) that civil society does not derive its authority from the Supreme Legislator; (b) that the State is the ultimate fount of all rights; (c) that the Church is not a supreme society and has no rights beyond those conceded or permitted to it by the State; (d) that when "public policy" requires, the spiritual should be sacrificed to State welfare. (2) *Moderate Europeon Liberalism,* which admits that Church and State are each a supreme society, but holds that each should pursue its purpose unconcerned with or unhindered by the other. But this supposes the absolute irrelation of both to be practicable. (3) *Catholic Doctrine,* namely, that Church and State are independent, yet their interests are interlinked because of the identity of membership and the unity of human life.

4. SUBORDINATION. This is the relation of one order to another which is higher than it in some attribute. The attribute determines the kind of subordination. It is *direct,* when the purpose of the lower order is a means partially conducting to the realization of that of the higher order. Such subordination, when existing between social bodies, entails jurisdiction of the higher over the lower, whether the higher derives its existence from the lower or not. It is *indirect* when the purpose of one order is lower in grade and worth than that of another, but the orders themselves are independent of one another in nature and rights. Indirect subordination is either positive or negative: *positive,* when the lower order, though independent, is such by nature that its purpose, when rightly sought, aids the purpose of the higher, and it is so correlated with the higher, because of the reciprocal bearing of the well-being of one on the other, that it must, for its own highest welfare, promote the interest of the higher; *negative,* when the purpose of one has no immediate relation to the purpose of the other. Now, (a) neither Church nor State is directly subordinate to the other; this would imply dependence of one on the other, would negate the supremacy, in their respective spheres, of one or the other. (b) The purpose of the Church is of a higher order than the purpose of the State. The State should so order the exercise of its activities as not to antagonize the spiritual welfare of its subjects, and so as to render the practice of religion

safe and easy. Much misapprehension has arisen from the use of the ambiguous phrases "union" or "separation" of Church and State.

5. ACTUAL RELATION. The theoretic relations, are under modern conditions, unrealizable, because of the diversity of religions. Hence, we hold (a) that a State may not by force destroy the unity of religion already prevailing, nor by force compel its citizens to profess one religion; (b) that where religious tolerance or equality is established by fundamental law, it must be respected by citizens and government. The State's tolerance or neutrality does not extend to cults in which the well-being of the people is evidently and seriously threatened, whether that well-being be material, intellectual, or moral.

REFERENCES: Leo XIII's *The Christian Constitution of States;* Devas' *Key to the World's Progress,* Pt. II, Ch. IV; Rickaby's *Aquinas Ethicus,* Vol. I, pp. 328-332.

XXIX. THE STATE AND CONSCIENCE

Liberty of conscience, properly understood, is a connatural and inalienable right of man. In the external exercise of his right the citizen may not be constrained by the civil authority, though he may be restrained by this authority whenever such exercise is seriously harmful to the general welfare.

1. LIBERTY OF CONSCIENCE. By conscience is understood the reasoning faculty insofar as it distinguishes between right and wrong, reveals obligation, and dictates to will. Liberty of conscience is immunity of this faculty from necessity. Much ambiguity attends the phrase. It may refer to the inner acts of reason or volition, or to the outer acts of conduct. Regarding the inner acts it may mean: (a) that reason in making a moral judgment is free to reach any conclusion that pleases; (b) that the will is free from any necessity compelling volition. The first is freedom of thought; is destructive of all certainty, makes reason the slave of emotion, and is irrational. The second is a psychological fact already proved and admitted. Regarding outer acts it may mean: (a) immunity from obligation or from any moral or legal bond by which one is prevented from speaking or acting in accordance with one's arbitrary and personal

judgments; (b) immunity from external compulsion in following outwardly the reasoned dictates of conscience. The first is moral lawlessness, and has never been maintained unconditionally by any one possessing the use of reason. The latter is the proper sense of the phrase. In this sense conscience has two aspects. It dictates the *omission* of an act which is judged to be evil, or the *positing* of an act which is judged to be good. We maintain that no one can be *constrained* to posit an act which his reasoned conscience judges to be evil, even when his conscience is erroneous, provided it is invincibly so; but that he may be *restrained* from positing an act which he judges to be good, whenever the positing of such an act would be gravely injurious to the social welfare, or when it would be a direct violation of another's equipollent right.

2. THE RIGHT. Liberty of conscience, as explained, is an absolute, inalienable, and indefeasible right. Blackstone recognized three absolute rights: to life or personal security; to freedom of going or coming, or of employing oneself as one pleases; to the pursuit of temporal well-being. Modern jurisprudence recognizes the right to liberty of conscience, though it was denied in 1854 by the Supreme Court of Maine (*Donohue v. Richards,* 38 Maine), and by some other State Courts it has been treated in effect as a relative right, the exercise of which may be conditioned by statutory enactments.

3. PROOF. An *absolute* right is one which is not conditioned on any civil enactments, or on any fact supervening on existence, and which in the present case is essential to the moral well-being and moral dignity of a person. But the right of abstaining from outward acts which one honestly judges to be evil, or of performing acts which one honestly judges to be good, when these are not injurious to the community or others, has these attributes. An *inalienable* right is one which, arising from an unconditional duty, a person cannot dispossess himself of. But the right to liberty of conscience is such, since it is essential to the attainment of one's final destiny, namely, the promotion of God's glory through the attainment of the ultimate perfection of one's rational nature. An *indefeasible* right is one which cannot be set aside or made void by any authority. But no authority can dispossess a moral being of the right of following the dictates of conscience.

4. CONSTRAINT AND RESTRAINT. Conscience either prohibits a mode of conduct or prescribes it. A *prohibition* is of its nature unconditioned and obliges always and in every circumstances; a *pre-*

scription is necessarily conditioned by other prescriptions, and obliges when circumstances demand and permit. Two prohibitions mutually conflicting cannot come from the same law; two prescriptions may apparently conflict, because of the superior good that one or the other prescribes. Now constraint by which a person is compelled to posit an act which his reasoned judgment declares to be wrong, is clearly a violation of liberty of conscience. But when there is a conflict between his judgment that an act should be posited, and the reasoned judgment of upright men that such an action is injurious to the good of the community or a direct violation of another's equipollent right, public authority may proscribe those acts, since they are dictated by an erroneous and unreasonable conscience. The case of the Quakers, whom conscience forbids to take part in war, and of the Mormons, whose conscience approves the practice of polygamy, illustrates the two principles. Perpetual and complete sacrifice of individual good, prescribed by right conscience, could not be prescribed by authority without entailing inherent contradiction in law, either moral, civil, or ecclesiastical.

XXX. INTERNATIONAL RIGHT

Nations as well as individuals are subject to moral law, and have certain ethical and juridical duties, with corresponding rights. International law governs the relations existing between independent nations; and comprises both the principles, which right reason perceives to be consonant with humanity and justice, and such definitions and determination of these as may be established by general consent.

1. THE PERSONALITY OF THE STATE. Two extreme opinions have been advanced to explain the nature of the State: A *mechanical* theory, which likens it to an elaborate piece of mechanism, of which the individuals form parts and their summed rights the motive power. These, mutually adjusted and modifying one another, give a resultant which is the authority of the State—Rousseau, and contracturalists generally. A *biological* theory, which asserts a "fundamental parallelism and kinship" between the biological structure of an animal organism and the sociological structure of the State—Comte, Spencer in his earliest works, and the older Evolutionists generally. The *Scholastic* theory compares the State to a

living organism between which and it there exists a figurative analogy. The State is a natural society, though it receives its concrete form from the volitional activities of those who compose it. As a natural entity, it is composed of parts bound together by the obligation of social justice, each of which retains its personal liberty of action, but cooperates to the purpose of that of which it is a part. Like a physical person, it has duties determined by its purpose, and rights to secure and safeguard its well-being and the means thereto. In an appropriated sense it is, therefore, a "person."

2. SOVEREIGNTY. It belongs to the essential dignity of personality that a person (a) should for the purposes of his existence have supreme control over his members and faculties; (b) should be *sui juris,* i.e., not a means to any other person; independent, within the rights of personality, of other persons; and, within the same range, not subject to their authority; (c) should be treated with the respect due to one having a destiny of his own, and being *sui juris* in the prosecution of that destiny. Analogously, therefore, the sovereignty of the States involves authority, within its sphere and as defined by its end, over its citizens and resources; the fulness of civil power inherent in the concept of state; independence of political subjection to other States; and a public majesty by reason of which a reverence is to be shown it, commensurate with its dignity as a political personality. The fundamental subject of sovereignty is the organized political community; its proximate subject varies with the form of government. There is a special difficulty with regard to the proximate subject of sovereignty in a federated State strictly so called. There is a difference between an alliance of States leagued for mutual interests, each of which retains its full sovereignty, though delegating the exercise of it in matters defined by the terms of the league to a general government, and a union of States by which is constituted a federal government itself sovereign within the powers granted it by the act of union. The former is usually designated a confederation, a *Staatenbund;* the latter a federation, *Bundesstaat* —though English usage in the use of the terms is not wholly fixed. The question of sovereignty causes no difficulty in a confederation, since the general government is only the agent of the leagued States. In a federation, however, there is a division of sovereign powers, while sovereignty is theoretically indivisible. There is a distinction between sovereignty itself and its various functions. The former is indivisible, and has one common subject; the latter may be dis-

tributed in many. So far as international relations are concerned, a federal government is sovereign and supreme over the constituent States.

3. STATES AND MORAL LAW. The claims of a State are based either on force, expediency, or reason. The claims of expediency can be sustained only by force or reason. The alternative bases, therefore, of the rights of a State, are either force or reason. But the first identifies might with right, and renders rights unstable and varying. The second is only the expression of moral law. The rights of a State, therefore, are based on reason, and ultimately derived from the moral law, revealed by reason and applied by it to the contingencies of life. The subject of rights is a person, physical or social. Rights have their source in moral responsibility. Moral responsibilities suppose duties. Duties are either those of benevolence or justice. A State, therefore, as a natural society and a social person, has towards other States the duties of benevolence and justice.

4. INTERNATIONAL LAW. This is a body of duties and rights by which nations are mutually and morally bound. It must be distinguished from the *jus gentium* of the Schoolmen. It is either natural or positive. *Positive* international law, like positive civil law, is either a more definite declaration of an already existing natural or moral law recognized by reason, or a determination of conditions required for the uniform and general practice of international intercourse and the practical safeguarding of international duties and rights. It comprises, therefore, principles which right reason perceives to be consonant with humanity and justice, and such definitions and determination of these as are established by general consent.

The primary duty of a nation towards other nations is to treat them with the benevolence, respect, and justice due to an equal sovereign personality. Its primary rights are the rights of self-preservation, of self-development, of independence and self-control, of territorial dominion, and of a voice in matters affecting the community of nations.

REFERENCES: Merriam's *History of the Theory of Sovereignty Since Rousseau;* Bluntschli, *Theory of the State,* Bk. VI, Ch. XXIV, and Bk. VII, Chs. I-III; Taparelli, *Droit Naturel,* LIV. b.

Part III

APPENDICES

PART III

Appendices

APPENDIX A

THE KANTIAN OUGHT

Within the last twenty-five years* ethical controversies—so far at least as they are confined to the English language—have come to range more and more around the meaning and the nature of the idea expressed by the word *ought*. English Ethics since the times of Hobbes, that is to say, since the time that the England of the Reformation began to form for itself a systematized philosophy of conduct, has been distinctively hedonistic and utilitarian. It constituted pleasure and pain the ultimate norms of morality toward which man must of psychological necessity tend, "quite apart from any sense of *duty*," as Spencer says;[1] and made good and evil consist in the external consequences of his actions. The few examples of intuitional Ethics that appeared as protests, like one or two bright colored flowers in a monochrome field of green, only served to bring into greater prominence the hedonistic character of English Ethics. Now Utilitarianism, when egoistic, must repudiate the word "ought" and the underlying idea. It is unmeaning—if it is not absurd—to say that *I ought* to seek pleasure in all my actions, if psychologically I can do nothing else, and if no motive of mine to act is or can be otherwise than good. In fact, Bentham, the most straightforward and logical of English hedonists tells us in a spurt of hedonistic fury that "the talisman of arrogancy, indolence and ignorance, is to be found in a single word, an authoritative imposter. . . . It is the word 'ought'—'ought' or 'ought not,' as circumstances may be. . . . If the

---

*This paper was read at the Seventh Annual Meeting of the Catholic Educational Association, Philosophy Section of College Department, at 4:00 P. M. on Tuesday, July 5, 1910, at Detroit College (now Detroit University), Detroit, Michigan. Reprinted, with permission, from the *Proceedings* for that year.

use of the word be admissable at all, it *ought* to be banished from the vocabulary of morals." [2] Nor does the concept of ought find any legitimate place in Altruistic Utilitarianism. If it is not always repudiated, it is so emptied of content as to be a merely larval symbol of itself. All such theories trace the origin of the idea to the individual's experience of pleasure and pain, and attempt to account for its non-hedonistic manifestations either by association of ideas or by the theory of evolution; and assume that in accounting for the genesis of the idea they have assigned the reasons why it has moral force. "There is no distinction which has to be kept more steadily in view," says Sir Arthur Balfour, "than this between the causes or antecedents which produce a belief, and the grounds or reasons which justify one." [3] But there is no distinction which is more steadily ignored by altruistic utilitarians. The fact, for instance, that certain emotions responding to right conduct have, as Spencer informs us,[4] arisen from ancestral experiences of pleasure and pain transmitted through cerebral modifications and accumulating through successive generations, would, if it were a fact, simply assign the psychological cause of those emotions, but would not tell me why I *ought* to obey them.

Today, however, Bentham's wild diatribe against the word "ought," would create either amusement or amazement, or raise the suspicion that he was suffering from an utilitarian brainstorm. Spencer's manufactured moral emotions are, like clothing that has gone out of fashion, now offered in the markets of thought only to inexperienced college or university students by secondhand professors. Huxley's taste for good conduct belonging to the same category as an ear for music now serves no other purpose than to give a spice of intellectual deviltry to ethical discussions. English moralists have been going to school—mostly in Germany. They have learned from Kant, or from his disciples or from the systems derived from his, that the idea behind the word "ought" cannot be eliminated from the human mind. It may be obscured, misinterpreted, assigned this or that origin. It may, as Bentham says, have "in it something disagreeable and repulsive"; nevertheless, we cannot get rid of the consciousness that there are some actions that we *ought* to do, and some others that we *ought* not to do; and there resides within our breasts an authoritative law that prescribes or proscribes certain forms of conduct; that there is indwelling in our minds an internal monitor who has an exclusive right to the verb "ought."

Whatever bones of contention there are between us and Kant—and they are neither few nor unimportant—we are indebted to him for the reinstatement of the verb of conscience in the English ethical thought of today. Even Utilitarianism has felt his influence. Sidgwick, who began by being an out-and-out follower of John Stuart Mill, finally, as he acknowledges in the preface of the last edition of his *Method of Ethics,* written shortly before his death, admitted the intuitional character of the concept of *ought;* though with that curious weakness of the English mind for compromise in principles which affect conduct, he tried to eat his bread and have it, and accordingly enriched the catalogue of ethical systems, which vex professors of Ethics, with Rationalistic Utilitarianism.

But if the concept of *ought* is again accepted with practical unanimity by those who philosophize on morals—it was never absent from the minds of those unsophisticated by theories—the source of the idea and the ground of the obligation which it signifies, are matters on which conflicting schools will widely differ.

There are in fact but two possible theories: that of the Schoolmen who find the origin of the moral law in the archetypal ideas of God and the ground of obligation in the necessary will of God; and that of German Rationalism which makes reason the origin and ground of obligation, whether that supreme law-giving reason be our individual reason as Kant taught, or in a *quasi* pantheistical sense the reason of the universal ethical substance, as Hegel taught and as derivative Hegelian schools teach with various modifications.

Now, I propose to confine myself during the time at my disposal to an examination of Kant's theory. I do this for two reasons. First, he is the father of modern rationalists. They have lighted their tapers at his torch and have not illumined what he left obscure. And secondly, because I think Paulsen[5] has put his finger on the intellectual pulse of the times when he declared that there are no philosophic alternatives between Neo-Scholasticism and Kantianism, and that as the Ethics of Catholicism is based on Thomism, so the Ethics of Protestantism is based on Kantianism. The conflict is between authority and private judgment pushed to their legitimate conclusions.

We are all acquainted with the formulas in which Kant's theory is succinctly presented, namely, that practical reason gives laws *a priori* to man as a rational being, or in other words, that man as a rational being is autonomous or a law unto himself. There is, of course, a sense in which we may affirm that man is a law unto himself. St. Paul, for instance, tells us[6] that "when the Gentiles who have not the law, do by nature those things that are of the law; these not having the law are a law unto themselves." It is a psychological fact that man finds within him a faculty by which he is self-compelled to recognize that certain modes of action are good and others evil, and to acknowledge that he ought to do the one and to avoid the other. We can no more deny that reason declares to us a moral law than we can deny that our senses declare to us the existence of an external world. "To deny the deliverances of our own reason," says Rashdall,[7] "is to deprive ourselves of any ground for believing anything whatsoever. To admit that our reason assures us that there are some things which we ought to do, and yet to ask why we should believe that those things ought to be done, is to ask why we should believe what we see to be true." Assuredly, we cannot ask why we should believe what we see to be true; but we can ask why we ought to do what we believe ought to be done. We need not in other words confound the psychological or the logical question with the ethical one. Psychologically I cannot help believing, that is to say, I *must* believe that I ought not to do evil; logically, or in order that my conduct be rational, I *should* do what I believe ought to be done; but ethically why *ought* I, or what binds my will to act in accordance with the deliverances of my reason? Man is, therefore, a law unto himself, first in the sense that his reason is so framed that he perceives of necessity certain truths of conduct; secondly, in the sense that he is conscious of the obligation of conforming his conduct to the dictates of his reason; but he is not a law to himself in the sense that his reason is the supreme lawgiver and the ultimate source of obligation. It is in this last sense that Kant and those who confound *ought* with an ultimate *should* of reason, or a psychological *must* declare that man is a law unto himself, and as a consequence, denude *ought* of any ethical authoritativeness.

The word "ought" is the *copula* of every ethical judgment either directly or indirectly. It is for a practical proposition regarding conduct what the substantive verb "is," is for a speculative proposition. It may not be without significance that it is timeless and moodless. The word is sometimes, it is true, used in other than its ethical sense. By a loose and inexact usage it expresses a reasonable anticipation of what should take place, or a conjectured necessity the frustration of which is not deemed impossible; as when a weather-wise farmer gazing on the sky, says: *It ought to rain tomorrow.* Again it is used in an appropriated sense to denote a necessity of acting conditioned on expediency, propriety, or an end conceived to be the ideal of an enterprise, profession or state of life. In this derivative sense we say that a politician ought to be a "good mixer," that a gentleman ought to yield his seat in a trolley-car to a lady, or that all of us after our years of study ought to know more than we do. Furthermore, it is used analogously instead of "should" to signify the ultimate reasonableness of a mode of acting. I may say, for instance, that a scientific mind ought not to give unwavering assent to a mere theory, meaning that such assent is in opposition to the unconditioned laws of reason. But the *Ought* of Ethics has a meaning different from any of these three.

It is in the first place, *objective;* it declares a truth that has validity independently of the perceiving mind. Human reason, individual or universal, is not the source from which truths of conduct spring as Minervas from the mind of Jove, nor the matrix into which the data of experience is cast, and out of which they are moulded, nor the alembic from which they are distilled as pragmatic values out of the raw material of thought. They do not become true, because reason is so constituted that under given conditions it pronounces them to be true; but because they are true, reason, which has been fitted for their perception by Him who framed it, inevitably assents to them. They would still be true if all the university professors and intellectualists of the country became paranoiacs and denied them. They do not become true because they are the expression of the *Ethos* of the race produced by a traditional or hereditary way of looking at conduct; but because they are true, and because human reason is framed to recognize them and the human will by an innate tendency feels their appeal, they have formed the moral customs of civilization, which, when embodied into a system, have received by historical usage a name that distinguishes it from customs of an inferior kind and designates it as pre-eminently the Ethics or distinctive custom of mankind. They do not become true because they have a utilitarian or pragmatic value, or because by assenting to them we avoid the indignity of intellectual contradiction, but because they are true, they subserve our highest utility, give the finest practical meaning to life and action, and save us from intellectual suicide.

In a word, they are objective in the sense that they are neither mere subjective convictions, nor objective projection on a background of nothingness of the individual, collective, or if such a thing were given, the universal human reason.

In the second place, the *Ought* of Ethics is *absolute* in the sense that its cogency is not conditioned on any further purpose on which one may have resolved, or by any rational ideal at which one may aim. When I affirm that a politician ought to be a good "mixer," my meaning is that a man who has chosen a political career should, if he would succeed, be approachable by all, and able to adapt himself to the views and moods of others; but I do not assert that he ought to be a successful politician. When, however, I affirm that a reasonable man ought to worship his Creator, I assert not only the duty of worship, but also of the condition being fulfilled on which the duty is predicated. The incidence of oughtness is ultimate, and comprehensive of cognate and implied conditions.

In the third place the *Ought* of Ethics is *final;* its bond is ultimately on the will not on the reason; it directly affects the faculty that is moved by good, not the faculty that is determined by truth. It is not the cognoscitive faculty that ought or ought not to do, but the faculty which is the first and efficient principle of all rational movement and action for which man is responsible. A false psychology of this faculty will necessarily involve a false conception of ought. If "will is nothing but practical reason," then it is not an appetitive but at most a conative faculty.[8] An appetitive faculty is drawn to an object, a conative faculty makes a *conatus* or effort to do something. Conation denotes the efficient causality of the will; appetence its response to an object external and congruous to it, and perfective of the being of which it is a faculty. If we ignore the appetitive side of will, as is widely done—not so much in expression as in thought—by modern ethicians who have been influenced by Kant, *ought* no longer expresses final causality; and in spite of verbal protestations we are committed either to Determinism and the destruction of morality, or to sheer Indeterminism and its meaninglessness.

Lastly the *Ought* of Ethics regards an ideal that is *realizable.* I can be morally bound to do only that which it is possible for me to do. The end itself of conduct cannot be obligatory, if it be an ideal term of perfection towards which we can tend, but which we can never attain, though we may continuously approach it. There may be an obligation to tend towards such an end, but there cannot be an obligation to attempt the end itself. The ethical *Ought* therefore, declares an obligation which can be fulfilled, not as the poet says,[9] a golden lure

> "to sway
> The heart of man: and teach him to attain
> By shadowing forth the Unattainable."

What, then, is the nature and source of the objective, absolute and final realizable reality which *ought* signifies to us? We are told today with some insistence and iteration that *ought* is "an ultimate category" of Ethics, and that the notion itself is unanalyzable. The inferential suggestion being that we should be content to accept *ought* as an averment of reason and should not too curiously attempt to seek its origin. Minds which have hitherto done their thinking in terms of Hedonism and Empiricism, cannot wholly cast off their positivist caution, even after they have made profession of Intuitionism. The timidity of the novice yet clings to them. They seem to fear that if they are not on their guard against the leadings of thought they might actually discover that there is a God behind all morality and that without Him its binding force is a delusion or a convention. Some of them who do admit God as a *ratio essendi* of morality, do so with a chariness that is apologetic, as though they wished to escape, as far as may be, the censure of being metaphysical or theological. But after all, ought simply signifies obligation, or the necessity imposed on will by a superior; and undoubtedly we can analyze obligation. We have only to invoke the four causes so familiar to the Schoolmen, and we shall have an efficient cause of obligation, or one who obliges, a material cause or the subject obliged, a final cause or that to which the subject of obligation is obliged, and a formal cause, or the moral necessity actually and intrinsically affecting the subject of obligation.

In the first place, then, who is it that imposes obligation on us? It must necessarily be one who is superior to us. Kant, in a well known passage,[10] puts the problem with sufficient clearness:

Every man has a conscience, finds himself observed by an inward judge which threatens and keeps him in awe. . . . Now this original intellectual and moral capacity, called *Conscience,* has this peculiarity in it, that although its business is a business of man with himself, yet he finds himself compelled by his reason to transact it, as if at the command of *another person.* For the transaction here is the conduct of a *trial* before a tribunal. But that he who is accused by his conscience should be *one* and the *same person* with the judge is an absurd conception of a judicial court. . . . Therefore, in all duties the conscience must regard *another* than himself as the judge, if it is to avoid self-contradiction. Now this other may be an actual or merely an ideal person which reason frames to itself. Such an idealized person must be one who knows the heart; . . . at the same time he must also be *all-obliging,* that is, must be or be conceived to be a person in respect of whom all duties are to be regarded as commands. Now, since such a moral being must at the same time possess all power (in heaven and earth) . . . since such a moral being possessing power over all is called *God,* hence conscience must be conceived as the subjective principle of responsibility for one's deeds before God.

An incautious reader might be led to conclude from this passage that the Kantian and Scholastic systems were one on the ultimate source of obligation. But he would in the first place overlook a fundamental tenet of Kant's philosophy, namely, that we can have no theoretical knowledge of God, that even for practical reason He is an assumption, a necessary one, it is true, but not a condition of morality. And in the second place he would fail to notice that in the passage cited it is "merely an ideal person which reason frames to itself," which "is called God," in fact not objectively different from Hobbes "power invisible framed by the mind." The actual person who dictates to us regarding conduct and hales us before a tribunal is the noumenal man, or man as he is in himself, the object of pure intellect and not at all cognizable through experience. The difficulty that arises from the twofold aspect of conscience Kant solved by conferring on man a twofold personality. In each of us there is the noumenal man, and, what is specifically distinct from it, the rationally endowed *homo sensibilis,* or the phenomenal man. The noumenal man is the author of obligation, and the rationally endowed phenomenal man is the subject thereof. The former is the sovereign judge, the latter is the accused. Presumably, too, the noumenal man possesses all power in heaven and earth over the phenomenal man, and knows the secrets of his heart. It is by recourse to some such arbitrary Dualism of human personality that Kant avoids the contradiction that is not very far below the surface of every ethical system except that of the Scholastics, and which gives them their provokingly shallow and turbid character.

If Kant would adhere to this theory of a dual personality in man, we might acquit him of the contradiction involved in the idea of the same individual being at the same time sovereign over himself and a liegeman under himself; a supreme lawgiver imposing laws on himself and a subject who finds that he is bound in conscience by his own laws; a judge who presides in a tribunal of last resort, and a culprit who stands in awe of his *alter ego*. On psychological grounds we might find such a theory untenable. We have no consciousness from which we could infer that there were two persons in our unitary nature. If a case of duplicity could be made out against us at all, some disagreeable moral experiences might lead us to think that we had two clashing natures wedded to one person. Medical men, it may be suggested, tell us that those who suffer from some functional nervous diseases, and a consequent disorganization of memory, manifest a double personality. But in these cases the personalities alternate, and the conditions that induce the manifestations are pathological. To save Kant's ethical theory from contradiction, our two selves, that is, our over-self and our under-self, should be simultaneous and our personal duplicity should be normal—unless, of course, we are willing to concede that the sense of moral obligation is due to a nervously diseased condition of the race engendered by some obliquity of evolutionary processes. Moreover, there are jural difficulties, besides the psychological ones. If the rationally endowed phenomenal man should challenge the authority of the noumenal man, the latter would have no way of enforcing his authority except to threaten himself with the loss of his own dignity. The sovereign would incur the penalty of being immoral when the subject disobeys. There is a sense, as we know, familiar to asceticism, in which the higher man is said to exercise rule over the lower man, and in default of which a rational nature does suffer personal degradation. But this sense does not regard our lower nature as the personal subject of moral law. The rule of the higher faculties over the lower is psychological control, not moral supremacy. Morality enters only insofar as man, through his higher faculties of reason and will, is commanded by an authority other than himself, to govern himself in the use of his lower faculties in accordance with a moral law of which he is not the independent and original source. But this is not Kant's sense. His theory, if it has any moral significance, necessarily entails in man the existence of a supreme lawgiving power specifically distinct from the rationally endowed sensitive nature on which it imposes moral obligation. His *ought,* if it is not purely psychological in meaning, necessarily implies the contrast between sovereign and subject which the mandates of conscience disclose.

Although the passage regarding conscience which I have just quoted appears in one of the last works of Kant, published nine years after the *Critique of Practical Reason,* it does not seem to convey his true meaning on the source of moral obligation, if it is understood literally to assert a real personal distinction between the noumenal man and the phenomenal man. Both in *Fundamental Principles of the Metaphysics of Morality* and the *Critique of Pure Reason* he repeatedly, and in different formulas, declares that the laws to which a rational being is subject are only those of his own giving; that his will, or what is the same thing, his practical reason, is morally good only when it is autonomous. In the former work he presents us with an argument to prove this which is characteristic, inasmuch as from premises luminously clear, we have suddenly flashed upon us a conclusion that seems not only not to follow, but even to contradict the premises themselves. "Everyone must admit," he says, "that if a law is to have moral force, i.e., to be the basis of obligation, it must carry with it absolute necessity; that for example, the precept, *Thou shalt not lie,* is not valid for men alone, as if other rational beings had no need to observe it; . . . that therefore, the basis of obligation must not be sought in the nature of man or in the circumstances in which he is placed." [11]

We may indulgently ignore the example by which Kant seeks to conciliate assent to a principle, which he says, every one must admit, for though the precept, *Thou shalt not lie,* is valid for every being that has an intellect and can communicate thought, that is not the reason but the consequence of its absolute necessity. A precept of the moral law may have absolute necessity, even though it were valid for man alone, as for instance, *Thou shalt not commit suicide.* Its absolute character is not determined *a posteriori* by its extension, and its extension may vary with the nature of the beings for whom it is absolute. Apart from the illustration then, which only obscures what it was meant to illumine, every one must admit, who admits any real morality at all, that a law to have moral force must carry with it absolute necessity; it cannot be conditioned by any wish, desire or inclination of the being whom it obliges. Admitting this premise, we should naturally conclude that the basis of morality is to be found only in a being who transcends all rational beings that are themselves subject to law. A moral ideal of goodness and duty can exist only in a mind, as Rashdall truly observes, and an absolute ideal can exist primordially only in an absolute mind, one namely, that is the origin of all reality subject to law. Our moral ideal, therefore, can claim absolute validity only insofar as it is the impression on our minds of a conception eternally existing in the Divine Mind—*"participatio legis aeternae in rationali creatura,"* says St. Thomas. This, however, is not Kant's conclusion. The basis of obligation, he immediately infers, is to be sought *"a priori"* in the conception of pure reason. But we ask, in the conception of whose pure reason or what pure reason? If in that pure reason which is superior to all limitations and conceptually excludes all imperfections, we again revert to the doctrine of the Schoolmen. But Kant clearly and expressly denies that God is a condition or *ratio essendi* of morality, and puts between himself and Scholasticism a chasm which it is impossible to bridge. If in a pure reason that is neither God's nor creature's we have as a basis of moral obligation a chimerical and nondescript being, which like the *intellectus agens* of Avicenna or the ethical substance of Hegel is a cross between a figmental abstraction and a supposititious reality.

But Kant was never quite so absurd as those who improved on his theory. The pure reason in whose *a priori* conception he finds the basis of obligation is a faculty with which each individual rational being is endowed. Yet it may furthermore be asked: Does not the pure reason that is an endowment of a rational being belong to his nature, and if in this pure reason is found the ultimate source of morality, why may not the basis of morality be sought in the nature of man? The only answer that can be given is, that Kant arbitrarily restricts the meaning of nature to the physical or phenomenal nature. His argument simply concludes that man's phenomenal nature is not the basis of obligation—a rather ridiculous bantling to be the issue of such ostentatious intellectual gestation. Straightway and by immediate inference he adopts the only alternative that his theory of cognition permits him to entertain. If the origin of morality is not the phenomenal man there is no other origin left for it in Kant's universe but the noumenal man.

In the *Analytic of Pure Practical Reason* he indulges in a loose, rambling rhapsody on Duty:

"Thou sublime and mighty name," he exclaims, and with much propriety, since in his system it is nothing but a name. "Thou sublime and mighty name, that dost embrace nothing charming or insinuating, but requirest submission, and yet seekest not to move the will by threatening aught that would arouse natural aversion or terror, but merely holdest forth a law which of itself finds entrance into the mind, and yet gains reluctant reverence (though not always obedience), a law before which all inclinations are dumb, even though they secretly counterwork it; what origin is there worthy of thee, and where is to be found the root of thy noble descent which proudly rejects all kindred with the inclinations; a root to be deprived from which is the indispensable condition of the only worth which men can give themselves?"[12]

Answering his question, he continues:

It can be nothing else but a power which elevates man above himself (as a part of the world of sense), a power which connects him with an order of things that only the understanding can conceive, with a world which at the same time commands the whole sensible world, and with it the empirically determined existence of man in time, as well as the sum total of all ends. . . . This power is nothing but personality, that is, freedom and independence of the mechanism of nature, yet regarded also as a faculty of a being which is subject to special laws, namely, pure practical laws given by his own reason, so that the person as belonging to the sensible world is subject to his own personality as belonging to the intelligible world.

The origin, therefore, of the sublime and mighty thing named duty to which man pays reluctant reverence, before which his inclinations are dumb, is man himself. He is the root of its noble descent. This peculiar posture of man standing in dumb reluctant reverence before himself, seems the very sublimity of bathos. As a philosophic concept it seems akin to the viewpoint of a Bowery metaphysician who expresses his moral disgust at another's presence in the curt advice: Go chase yourself. The feat of chasing one's self does not seem more unthinkable than the maneuver of standing in reluctant reverence in one's own presence. I venture to say that there are but two conceivable interpretations of this ethical posture. Either we must frankly admit that there are two distinct personalities in man, one of which reluctantly reverences the other as his sovereign lawgiver; or that there is but one and that this one reluctantly reverences himself as a sovereign lawgiver to himself, somewhat, I presume, after the fashion of the character who loved nobody but himself, and loved himself with regret. Which of these interpretations gives Kant's meaning let Paulsen or other loyal commentator decide.

Perhaps the well known passage on "the Kingdom of Ends"[13] will throw some additional obscurity on the subject. Kant writes:

By a kingdom I understand the union of different rational beings in a system of laws. Now since it is by laws that ends are determined as regards their universal validity, hence, if we abstract from the personal differences of rational beings, and likewise from all the content of their private ends, we shall be able to conceive all ends combined in a systematic whole . . . that is to say, we can conceive a kingdom of ends. . . .

Thereafter he continues:

A rational being belongs *as a member* to the kingdom of ends, when although giving universal laws in it, he is himself subject to those laws. He belongs to it as a *sovereign,* when, while giving laws he is not subject to the will of any other. A rational being must always regard himself as giving universal laws either as a member or as a sovereign in a Kingdom of Ends. This sovereign man Kant furthermore tells us, is a completely independent being, without wants and with unrestricted power adequate to his will.[14]

Now, the main thing that concerns us all in this intellectual prestidigitation is that man in the world of morality is a completely independent being; that he is not bound by the will of any other being in the universe; that he is subject only to the laws of his own giving; that the sovereign obliging and the subject obliged are one and the same.

If this is the last word on the source of obligation of that system of Ethics which is to supersede Scholasticism, what, we may ask, is the meaning of "ought," what is obligation or the moral necessity actually and intrinsically affecting the subjection of obligation?

Obligation, as defined by Kant, is "the dependence of a will, not absolutely good, on the principle of autonomy."[15] An absolutely good will is one whose maxims or subjective reasons for acting always and inherently coincide with the laws of autonomy; such a will is not subject to obligation. But the human will is not inherently good, is not in itself in accord with reason; it becomes so when it is autonomous. Autonomy of the will is that property of the will by which it becomes a law unto itself, or acts independently of any property in the objects of volition.[16] A law should of its nature be universal, applicable namely to every member of the Kingdom of Ends, and it should also be absolute, binding unconditionally and without exceptions. The will is autonomous therefore, when it is determined by imperatives of conduct that are universal and absolute, and that are of its own giving.

Kant maintains then that every rational being gives laws that are universal, to which as a member of the Kingdom of Ends he himself is subject, while as a sovereign in the same kingdom he is not subject to any other will. This may sound like a contradiction. For if each rational being who is not subject to any other will could give laws that are universal, it would seem to follow that each will is at the same time autonomous and heteronomous—autonomous, insofar as it would be subject only to the laws of its own giving; heteronomous, insofar as it would be subject to a universal law given by every other will. The contradiction, however, is only apparent, and arises from the fact that Kant uses the phrase, "to give universal laws" or "to legislate universally" in a sense that is his own and that is sophistical. No will in Kant's theory legislates in any proper sense of the word for any other will, nor could it do so without that other will becoming thereby heteronomous.

The universality of the Kantian law as proceeding from the will of a rational being does not regard its imposition, but the form that a personal reason for acting must take in the mind before it can become a law. It does not put an obligation on any will but the will from which it proceeds, and it is universal only in the sense that it can be conceived to be a principle of acting for every other rational being without thereupon contradicting or destroying itself. When it can be so conceived it is said by Kant to be objective. Its objectivity, therefore, like its universality, is conceptual, not ontological. An illustration of Kant may make his meaning clearer than his explanations do. Let the question be, for example: May I when in a difficulty make a promise with the intention of not keeping it? The answer is determined by my answer to a universal question: May every one make a deceitful promise when he finds himself in a difficulty from which he cannot otherwise extricate himself? "Then I presently become aware that while I can will the lie," says the sage of Königsberg, "I can by no means will that lying should be a universal law. For with such a law there would be no promises at all. . . . Hence my maxim, as soon as it should be made an universal law, would necessarily destroy itself."[17]

Bearing in mind, therefore, that Kant makes no distinction what-soever between will and practical reason, moral law is an *a priori* conception of consistency in action universally considered; and an obligation, the constraint put on the will by the rational necessity of avoiding contradiction in practical reason, or in other words, it is the ultimate reasonableness of action determined negatively by the conceptual application of the principle of contradiction to universal volitional activity. Shakespeare discovered that consistency was a jewel, it was not till towards the end of the eighteenth century that it was proclaimed the only hall mark of absolute goodness.

The absoluteness that the Moralist of Pure Reason demands for his moral law is as characteristically his own as is its universality. It consists in this: *first,* that the law be given a rational being who is an end to himself, whose existence has in itself a worth irrespective of its dependence on any other being, and unconditioned by any relation of whatever kind to any other being; and *secondly,* that it be given thorough *a priori* conception out of all relation to and independent of any inclination, desire, purpose or authority distinct from pure practical reason itself. Scholastic Ethics admits, of course, and maintains that every rational being is *sui juris,* that is to say, not subordinated in worth to any other rational creature, but denies that his existence does not subserve the end and purposes of his Creator. Again it admits that the obligation of the moral law is absolute in the sense that it is not contingent on our inclinations and desires, but it denies that it is out of all relation to our natural in-clinations, to the primary impulses of our being, or the disinterested purposes of our existence. But Kant would have us admit more and deny less. The absoluteness which he claims for reason as a law-giving faculty is an absoluteness which we can concede only to the infinite source and term of being, truth and goodness. Though pro-testing often and fervently against the inroads of self on our morality, and exacting its entire and positive exclusion from every moral mo-tive, he bases his morality finally on the apotheosis of human per-sonality.

But while thus exalting the noumenal self until it becomes like unto the Most High, the absoluteness that he prescribes as an essen-tial condition of formal obligation would compel us to regard our phenomenal self or our rationally endowed sensitive nature, as poisoned in root and branch by a more than Calvinistic depravity. There is no action of ours, the spring of which is any inclination however noble, but is immoral on the principles of this magniloquent and denaturalized morality. When the Psalmist prayed, "Incline my heart unto thy testimonies" (*Ps. 118:36*), he asked for a grace, which, if granted, would have made his will heteronomous, and a life lived in accord with those testimonies devoid of moral worth; and his later acknowledgment: "I have inclined my heart for a reward to do thy justification forever,"[18] proclaimed him no saint but an exceedingly heteronomous man. He subjected himself to the will of another, he did so from inclination, and worst of all, he did so for the hope of reward. Poor David, had he aimed at being an autonomous man, should have lived in accord with God's testimonies and done his justifications moved thereto by no command of God, impelled by no love of Him or His rewards, prompted by no response of his nature to the attraction of any good distinct from himself, but solely by respect for the principle of contradiction as applicable to the world of volitional activity, or as Kant sophistically calls it the Kingdom of Ends. Instead of the saint and sinner of Christian morality, we have the autonomous man and the heteronomous man—the autonomous man who gives laws to himself by *a priori* conceptions of reason which are absolutely devoid of any relation, and the heteronomous man who obeys the will of another or acts according to the impulses of his rationally endowed nature.

This is the system of Ethics between which and that of St. Thomas the professor of Berlin invites the world of thought to choose, warning it that if it wishes to preserve unblemished its intellectual freedom, the sacrosanct purity of "ought," the fundamental principles of Protestantism, its choice must be made in favor of Kantianism. The specific grievance against the Ethics of St. Thomas is that he makes God the supreme authoritative lawgiver of the universe, and reason, on which the light of the eternal ideal has been impressed, only His herald. The specific fascination of Kant's system is that it emancipates man from any supreme authority, and confers the supreme power of legislation on a *Deus ex machina* whom he has labeled Pure Practical Reason, and who utters its hollow mandates in categorical imperatives which conveniently have no more binding force than the commands of Alice's Queen in Wonderland, and which, as Kant himself concedes, no rational being so far as we can possibly discover ever did obey.[19]

NOTES

1. *Principles of Ethics,* Vol. II, App. C.
2. *Deontology,* Vol. I, p. 31.
3. *Philosophic Doubt,* Ch. I, p. 3.
4. Spencer's Letter in *Appendix* to Bain's *Mental and Moral Sciences.*
5. *Kantstudien,* May, 1899.
6. *Rom.* 2:14.
7. *The Theory of Good and Evil,* Vol. I, p. 103.
8. P. 29 of Abbott's *Kant's Theory of Ethics,* 5th Ed., for this and subsequent page references.
9. Tennyson's *Timbuctoo.*
10. P. 321. All italics in citations from Kant are his own.
11. Pp. 3, 4.
12. P. 180.
13. *The Fundamental Principles of the Metaphysics of Morals,* p. 51.
14. *Op. cit.,* p. 52.   15. *Op. cit.,* p. 58.
16. *Op. cit.,* p. 59.   17. *Op. cit.,* p. 19.
18. *Ps.* 118: 112.   19. *Op. cit.,* p. 23.

APPENDIX B

RIGHTS AND DUTIES

I. *Right and Duty*—which is prior ontologically?

(a) *God's right* to formal extrinsic glory through the free activity of man, in whom he has implanted appetencies indicating the right direction of his activities *is first;* and arises from his supreme and absolute dominion.

(b) *Man's duty* to use and direct his appetencies to their proper ends *is second.*

(c) *Man's right is third,* i.e., man has a right (a) to use and satisfy the appetencies of his nature, (b) freely without hindrance from others, (c) for the advancement of God's glory.

In order to have a right, it is necessary: (a) to have appetencies by which we have indicated to us the proximate ends of our faculties, and ultimately the end of our nature (all creatures have these); (b) to have the power of exercising or not exercising these as we please, i.e., free will (only intelligent creatures have this); (c) to have the duty of exercising them aright, i.e., for the end for which they are given (only creatures *obliged by law* have this).

These three elements are to be taken collectively, so that the first is *generic,* the second a *remote differentia,* the third an *ultimate differentia.* So that (1) if you could conceive a creature with no appetencies to indicate the purpose of its functions and the end of its nature, you would conceive a creature having no source of information regarding its duty, and therefore wanting in the generic element in the source of right. (2) If you conceive a creature having appetencies but no free will, but compelled by the necessity of its nature to act always in one way, such a creature would not have a duty and consequently no right. It is necessary that there be a field for intellectual choice and the play of free will. The appetencies must be morally indifferent in the sense, that though they are each indicative of the purpose of a faculty—and in this sense good—this or that function may not be universally necessary under all conditions for the end of creation, and may in comparison with a

346

higher function become an excess or defect. (3) If a man had appetencies and free will, and could use or abuse his faculties or their functions unrestrained by the law of his creation, there would be no duties and hence no right.

It follows: (1) That man alone has rights, because he alone has appetencies which he is free to use according to the law of his creation to attain the proximate and ultimate ends of his creation.

(2) That right is not derivable from personal freedom considered in itself. (The opinion of Kant.)

(3) That right is not derivable from superior physical power. (The opinion of Hobbes.)

(4) That right is not derivable through evolution from the primary appetencies; and is not resolved into a *positive* element by which each man recognizes his claim to the benefits of his unimpeded activities, and a *negative* element by which he is conscious of the limitations imposed on him by the like claims in other men. (The opinion of Spencer.)

II. *Right and Duty*—which is prior *relatively?*

Relatively, or between man and man, right is prior to duty, whether it be a merely ethical duty or a juridical duty—with some qualifications, however.

(1) The fact that one has an *imperfect right* is the immediate reason why another has the *negative juridical duty* of not impeding him in its exercise. The ground for the positive ethical duty is found in the other's duty (ontologically considered) of using his faculties in accord with the end of his social nature; for instance, if one has the right of not being deceived, it follows that there is in the other the correlative duty of not deceiving, but this duty is not founded in the prior right but in the duty of the other of using the faculty of speech in accord with his social nature.

(2) The fact that one has a *perfect right* (the designation is comparatively modern), arising either from the fact of existence (connatural) or from some title supervening on existence (acquired), is the reason why another has the *juridical duty* not only in respect of its exercise, i.e., by not impeding its exercise, but also in respect of its matter, i.e., by cooperating in the retaining or obtaining of the matter.

A *perfect right* is one that includes the right of coaction to secure its exercise, or it is inviolable in the sense that it not only puts a bond on the will of another but also has power over the organism subject to that will. The right to coaction inheres in rights that are perfect from *commutative justice* and from *social (legal) justice.* They do not differ so far as the inviolable moral power is concerned, which in both cases is perfect, i.e., over will and organism subject to will. They differ (i.e., a right perfect from commutative justice and a right perfect from social (legal) justice) in respect of their *matter.* The matter of one is the good of the individual, of the other the good of the community. Hence the necessity of reparation or restoration in the first case, and the impossibility of it in the other. In the case of a *right from commutative justice,* the violation of it entails the obligation of restoring what was taken. In the case of positing an action against the common good, we can do nothing but what would be obligatory even if there were no violation. Penalty imposed for violating the common good belongs to *distributive justice,* the obligation of paying which does not exist antecedently to the sentence of the judge.

Divisions of Right.

I. In respect of *meaning*:

(a) *objective,* i.e., law, whether natural or positive.

(b) *subjective,* i.e., the moral power derived from law.

(c) *terminative,* i.e., the thing over which we have moral power.

II. In respect of *law* from which derived:

(a) *natural,* if derived from natural law.

(b) *positive,* if derived from positive law.

III. In respect of *title*:

(a) *connatural,* if possessed by the very fact of existence.

(b) *acquired,* if possessed because of a fact supervening on existence.

N.B. All *connatural* rights are at the same time natural; but some natural rights are *acquired.* All positive rights are acquired, but all acquired rights are not positive.

IV. In respect of *correlative duty in others*:

(a) *perfect,* if it connotes a juridical duty in others, namely, a duty arising from virtues other than those of formal justice.

(b) *imperfect,* if it connotes only an ethical duty in others, namely, a duty arising from virtues other than those of formal justice.

V. In respect of *correlative duty in subject of right*:

(a) *inalienable,* if it cannot be ceded or renounced because a necessary means to fulfil an unconditionally obligatory duty.

(b) *alienable,* if it can be ceded or renounced, without contempt of duty.

Notanda:

I. The *exercise of a right* is to be distinguished from the *right itself.* The former may for a time be by law restrained, though the later retains its vigor. Again, the exercise of even an inalienable right may be delegated, not so the right in itself.

II. A perfect right carries with the right to use physical force in its vindication or defense, that is to compel respect of it. A perfect right is therefore a coactive right, i.e., a right to a thing and a right to coaction to retain or obtain the thing.

III. The right to coaction belongs *primarily* to the subject of the perfect right; and *secondarily* and *vicariously* to the person who has natural authority over the subject of the perfect right, whenever there is question of a perfect right arising from commutative justice, i.e., the father for the son, the civil power for the citizens.

But the *actual exercises* of the right of coaction belongs *primarily* to the person having charge of the juridical order; and *secondarily* to the subject of the coactive right, when the juridical power perchance fails in affording protection.